SOLDIERS FROM EXPERIENCE

CONFLICTING WORLDS

New Dimensions of the American Civil War

T. Michael Parrish, Series Editor

SOLDIERS
FROM
EXPERIENCE

**THE FORGING OF SHERMAN'S
FIFTEENTH ARMY CORPS
1862–1863**

ERIC MICHAEL BURKE

LOUISIANA STATE UNIVERSITY PRESS

BATON ROUGE

Published by Louisiana State University Press
lsupress.org

Designer: Barbara Neely Bourgoyne
Typeface: Ingeborg

Maps created by Eric Michael Burke.

Cover illustration: *Sherman's March Through South Carolina—Burning of McPhersonville, February 1, 1865,* by William Waud. Morgan Collection of Civil War Drawings, Library of Congress Prints and Photographs Division.

Library of Congress Cataloging-in-Publication Data
Names: Burke, Eric Michael, 1987– author.
Title: Soldiers from experience : the forging of Sherman's Fifteenth
    Army Corps, 1862–1863 / Eric Michael Burke.
Other titles: Forging of Sherman's Fifteenth Army Corps, 1862–1863
Description: Baton Rouge : Louisiana State University Press, [2022] |
    Series: Conflicting worlds: new dimensions of the American Civil War |
    Includes bibliographical references and index.
Identifiers: LCCN 2022007941 (print) | LCCN 2022007942 (ebook) |
    ISBN 978-0-8071-7809-6 (cloth) | ISBN 978-0-8071-7876-8 (pdf) |
    ISBN 978-0-8071-7875-1 (epub)
Subjects: LCSH: United States. Army. Corps, 15th (1862–1865) | United
    States—History—Civil War, 1861–1865—Regimental histories. | United
    States—History—Civil War, 1861–1865—Campaigns. | Sherman, William T.
    (William Tecumseh), 1820–1891—Military leadership. | United States.
    Army. Infantry—Drill and tactics—History—19th century.
Classification: LCC E493.1 15th .B87 2022 (print) | LCC E493.1 15th (ebook) |
    DDC 973.7/41—dc23/eng/20220406
LC record available at https://lccn.loc.gov/2022007941
LC ebook record available at https://lccn.loc.gov/2022007942

For

CHELSEA ANN BUNCH BURKE

and

WINSLOW CHANDLER BURKE

with all of my heart

CONTENTS

MAPS

ACKNOWLEDGMENTS

No feeble attempt of mine could ever hope to enumerate all of those to whom I am deeply indebted for insight, support, and guidance throughout this long project. Any such list, however, would have to begin by acknowledging the endless love, support, and encouragement of my parents, Donald and Cindy Burke; my sister, Nicole Parigo; and above all, my dearly beloved late wife, loving companion, and lifetime partner, Chelsea. Absent the bulwark of emotional sustenance they continue to provide on a daily basis, any laborious project like this would be utterly impossible.

I have grown incalculably as a thinker and historian due primarily to the patience, diligent efforts, and invaluable guidance of an unmatched roster of mentors: Drs. William Barney, W. Fitzhugh Brundage, Joseph Caddell, Kathleen DuVal, Joseph T. Glatthaar, Wayne Lee, and Harry Watson. Each of these scholars has materially improved my capacity to do deep historical research and explore the frontiers of historiography. My advisor, Dr. Glatthaar, has left nothing wanting in his tireless efforts to assist me in shaping my inchoate ideas into a manageable and coherent (I hope) expression of the conclusions arising from my research. His support and patience throughout this project, but most especially during particularly trying personal challenges, has extended well above and beyond the role of an advisor.

My colleagues in North Carolina have turned into my best friends. The patience with which Joshua Akers, Robert Colby, Brian Fennessy, and Joseph Stieb have received countless late-night text messages filled with nothing but my ranting about the Vicksburg campaign can never be fully acknowledged. Their friendship, support, and always fruitful feedback has kept me going at several critical junctures of this journey.

Beyond Hamilton Hall, my friends and colleagues in the wider world of Civil War history have also contributed signally to the completion of this lengthy project. Drs. Wayne Hsieh, Christopher Rein, and Brian Schoen have each been central to my intellectual and professional development. Historians David Powell, Christopher Barr, Lee White, Adam Toering, and Robert Williams have likewise proven both invaluable resources and wonderful friends who have entertained no shortage of often late-night rambling conversations about any number of topics concerning military operations during the war. Far more than thanks are due one particular historian, Rabea Rittgerodt, whose strength, courage, support, and love I am grateful for each and every day.

The many archivists and staff at the following repositories, listed in no particular order, have been every historian's dream. Their efforts to assist me at every step in identifying the most fruitful and relevant collections for this project always extended well beyond the call of duty: National Archives and Records Administration (Washington, DC); Missouri State Archives; Iowa State Archives; Ohio History Center; Southern Historical Collection (Wilson Library, University of North Carolina); David M. Rubenstein Rare Book & Manuscript Library (Duke University); Stuart A. Rose Manuscript, Archives, and Rare Book Library (Emory University); State Historical Society of Missouri; Missouri History Museum; State Historical Society of Iowa–Des Moines; State Historical Society of Iowa–Iowa City; the Abraham Lincoln Presidential Library; Filson Historical Society; and Bentley Historical Library (University of Michigan).

My sincerest thanks also to the wonderful editors at Louisiana State University Press, most especially T. Michael Parrish and Rand Dotson, who helped guide me through the publishing process for the first time during the most trying period of my life.

Last, but certainly not least, no other individuals have patiently listened to each and every one of these chapters read aloud quite as many times as my dog, Bell, and cats, Lana and Poppy. Their capacity to quietly wait long and boring hours for my completion of each chapter draft was central to my ability to complete the project, and their unconditional love is both invaluable and mutual.

Finally, any and all errors and shortcomings contained within the pages that follow remain the sole responsibility of the author. It is my sincere hope that I have produced something that the aforementioned can be proud of after having played such a vital and pivotal role in enabling it.

SOLDIERS FROM EXPERIENCE

INTRODUCTION

They spoke of other corps . . . "The Ninth"—"The First"—
"The Fifth"—"The Sixth"—"The Third"—the simple numerals rang
with eloquence, each having a meaning which was to float through
many years as no intangible arithmetical mist, but as pregnant
with individuality as the names of cities.
—STEPHEN CRANE, *The Little Regiment*, 1896

This feeling that grows up between regiments, brigades,
divisions and corps is very strong and as strange.
—CHARLES WILLS, 103RD ILLINOIS

On a frigid December 11, 1871, in Washington, DC, Lt. Gen. William Tecumseh Sherman, then commanding general of the Army of the United States, took the stand after a lengthy adjournment to finally answer for crimes allegedly committed by soldiers under his command six years prior in the city of Columbia, South Carolina, partially destroyed in a violent blaze in February 1865 while occupied by his troops plodding northward through the state. Considerable amounts of private property and cotton—much of it foreign-owned—had been incinerated along with a significant portion of the city, and the responsibility for its near-total destruction needed to be ascertained. Most Northerners remained convinced that either the retreating remnants of the Rebel army, drunken slaves, the wind, or some combination of the three was to blame. Many Southerners, on the other hand, maintained that Sherman's "devils" had deliberately fired the town with the same vindictive spirit they were sure had motivated all of the general's fiery campaigns across Georgia and the Carolinas.[1]

Cross-examining attorney George R. Walker thought he knew precisely how to illustrate that Sherman had taken deliberate steps to reduce the city to ashes from the moment he selected which of the four *corps d'armée* comprising his army group would enter Columbia first. After meandering through a long series of questions related to prior testimony, Walker came abruptly to the point. "Can you tell me anything about the 15th corps?" he asked directly. The corps had been the first to enter the city that day, and many of its inhabitants still invoked the particular temperament of the "diabolical 15th," as one of them called it, as an explanation for the ruinous conflagration's origins. Sherman's erstwhile somewhat defensive demeanor shifted immediately at mention of the command. "Yes, indeed I can," he quickly replied, beaming with pride. "I know all about it; they were as fine a body of men as ever trod shoe-leather." Walker took this in stride. "They had the reputation of doing their work well?" he asked, pointedly. "Yes, sir; thoroughly," Sherman replied, adding that when it came to "going into a fight and going through a fight, they were the men they are described to be." Indeed, the Fifteenth Corps had earned quite the name for itself in the victorious United States as among the hardest fighting and furthest marching contingents of "Sherman's veterans." But the corps's combat exploits were not what Walker was after. "Hadn't they a reputation in Mississippi?" he inquired. "They had a very high reputation," Sherman agreed, referencing the corps's famed service among Grant's "Vicksburg rats," prying open the Mississippi River in the summer of 1863.[2]

Recognizing a need for more direct questioning, Walker cut to the chase. "Had they not a reputation there [Mississippi] for leaving their mark upon the country?" he asked. "Yes, sir, they left their marks wherever they went," Sherman said. With this, Walker could almost smell victory, or so he thought. "You were aware of this?" "Perfectly." "When you reached Savannah?" "Indeed, I was; I knew every officer and every private in that corps." Likely sporting a sly grin and intensely satisfied with his imminent coup, Walker did his best to rub it in. "They were a wild set, were they not?" he asked loadedly, only to receive an unsuspected rebuttal. "No, sir; they were composed of first rate men—farmers and mechanics, and men who are to-day as good citizens as we have in our country, but who went to war in earnest." This caught Walker off guard. Certainly, Sherman had meant what he had said before, he insisted: "They were good men for destroying property?" The aging general again concurred: "Yes, sir; when told to do so, they destroyed it very quickly." But what about when "they thought they might do it and it not be objectionable to their officers," Walker prodded. Sherman tellingly evaded. "They could do their work very thoroughly when they undertook it." Growing frustrated, Walker began to show his anger: "Do you mean to say that you were not aware . . . before you reached Columbia, that the 15th corps were a corps distinguished for the marks they left upon the country through which they passed?" Still calm, Sherman replied, curtly: "I may have known it, and very likely I did; I knew generally what was going on." His avoidance further irritated Walker. "I asked you did you know it; I should like you to answer that question," he demanded, "were you not aware that the 15th corps were remarkable for the manner in which they left their mark upon the country through which they passed?" "Explain what you mean by mark," Sherman asked. "Devastation," Walker replied. "They killed every rebel within range of their guns and left their dead bodies to mark the ground," Sherman smiled. "Devastation of property, I mean," Walker clarified. "No more than the rest of the troops," the general finally answered.[3]

Sherman's answer was disingenuous. Just as divulged within one of his most famous dicta: "There is a soul to an army as well as to the individual man," the Fifteenth Corps, and indeed every corps of Sherman's army, had a soul all its own—a soul that, by the spring of 1865, Sherman knew better than all the rest.[4] Writing to Major General Henry Halleck less than two months prior to reaching Columbia, Sherman had laid out his plans for his army's fiery forthcoming entry into the first state of the so-called Confederacy. "When I move, the Fifteenth Corps will be on the right of the right wing," he explained. Though later altered, his original plans for the Carolinas campaign would have naturally carried the corps into the streets of the rebellion's first capital: Charleston. Contemplating the likely results of their arrival, along with Halleck's implication that South Carolina ought rightfully to pay heavily for its sins, Sherman did "not think 'salt' will be necessary." After all, "if you have watched the history of that corps, you will have remarked that they generally do their work pretty well." He had full confidence that the port city "deserves all that seems in store for her." He also added, after a brief glance at his map, that he "look[ed] upon Columbia as quite as bad as Charleston."[5]

Sherman had every reason to know the "soul" and "the history" of the Fifteenth Corps better than any other of the four which then comprised his army group. He had taken command of the veteran nucleus of the formation during the late winter of 1862, and it had represented his first independent corps command in then Maj. Gen. Ulysses S. Grant's Army of the Tennessee. Much time had passed between those days and the moment at which he opted to send his beloved original corps into the streets of Columbia, and the mountain of intervening experience which he and the corps had mutually accrued had molded both of them into distinctive instruments of warfare. While historians have traditionally made much of the impress of "Uncle Billy" upon the character of his army, in truth the army, and even more especially the "diabolical 15th," also played a powerful role in shaping the character of "Uncle Billy" as a tactician and strategist. Although no longer commanding the corps directly since his promotion to field army command in the winter of 1863, even by the spring of 1865 Sherman knew just what he could dependably expect from the command, as well as what he could not. He was well acquainted with the "soul" of the Fifteenth Corps, in large part because he and the command had forged it together across a tempestuous year of bloody and trying campaigns by which both the corps and Sherman were mutually forged into, to use his own phrase, "soldiers from experience."[6]

Originally devised by Napoleon I to improve operational flexibility and ease the management of titanic nineteenth-century field armies, *corps d'armée* (in English, army corps), subdivisions of an army ranging in size from around twelve thousand to thirty-five thousand men, often operated as self-contained miniature armies unto themselves. Their two to five constituent divisions, the two to five brigades of those divisions, and ultimately the three to seven regiments and batteries assigned to those brigades all prosecuted the orders of a single general whose objectives were assigned by the army commander himself. Designed for independent operations remote from the direct oversight of army headquarters, the component units of every corps naturally underwent particular experiences on and off the battlefield more or less distinct from those experienced by soldiers serving in other corps of even the same field army. While, during the American Civil War, most soldiers identified first and foremost with their close-knit company and regiment, the commonality of experiences they shared with members of other regiments serving in the same corps bred a familiarity and *esprit de corps* that was often defined by corps membership.[7]

Although it took the better part of a year serving together for its members to begin to think of their corps designation as much more than an extra line in their postal address, by the winter of 1863–64, after the corps's first turbulent year in service, a palpable pride borne of accomplishments in and out of combat suffused the organization. That pride extended to a close affiliation with Sherman, their original commander, having by that time risen meteorically to command of the entire Military Division of the Mississippi, in which the corps served. Along with the confidence with which the corps carried itself in the camps of northern Alabama prior to its stepping off on the decisive Atlanta Campaign in the spring and summer of 1864, however, was a distinct set of assumptions, predispositions, and beliefs about the manner in which operations ought to be conducted, which tactics were most appropriate for particular situations, and even how the war itself ought to be prosecuted. These ideas, shared broadly across the command, all came from the specific experiences which had forged the Fifteenth Corps.

VETERAN CHARACTER

In his landmark 1985 study of Sherman's army group during its famed late war campaigns for Savannah and the Carolinas, Joseph T. Glatthaar highlighted the importance of what he called the western army's "veteran character" in enabling its success during those legendary operations. "At the expense of rigid discipline, precision drills, and tidy appearance, all trademarks of the Army of the Potomac," Glatthaar explained, "Sherman's command [had] developed a sense of self-reliance and self-confidence based upon the lessons of several years of active campaigning." The western veterans "had learned the best ways to perform certain duties and how to handle themselves in all sorts of situations." The resultant "veteran character . . . utterly dominated Sherman's army," enabling operations that "required company-level officers and enlisted men to bear a much greater burden and shoulder a much larger share of the responsibility for success" than in most other campaigns of the Civil War.[8]

Glatthaar never explicitly outlined the individual components of this "veteran character," though he did allude to many. Above all else, the western army was one filled with experienced soldiers "who knew what to do and how to care for themselves."[9] They had, as two of them put it, already "learned nearly all that was worth knowing" and, by the latter campaigns of the war, understood "just what to do and what not to do" in and out of battle.[10] Across a lengthy tenure in uniform, they "had learned to perform those small yet critical tasks that often decided engagements," even if such mastery occasionally "undercut strong discipline by fostering a sense of independence and self-reliance."[11] Sherman, Glatthaar argues, had himself learned to masterfully realize the natural advantages accruing to such an army of veterans by allowing the men and officers of his army "enough freedom to put their experience to work."[12]

To be sure, Sherman's learned legions were by no means confident in all things. "Experience had taught Sherman's men the foolhardiness of frontal assaults," Glatthaar observed, "particularly against earthworks held by nearly equal numbers." Instead, they much preferred flanking maneuvers, which usually "conserved lives and were much more successful." The same lessons which had impressed upon them the "foolhardiness of frontal assaults" had likewise taught them the immense advantages accruing to fortified defensive positions as well as the accompanying "importance of pure firepower" when delivered from their protection.[13] They had also learned to pay relatively little attention to Army-prescribed drill manuals when it came to tactical maneuvering under fire. After all, "marching in step elbow to elbow, [was] a physical impossibility in the heavily wooded South." These rigid tactics were replaced by predominately open-order skirmishing in battle and an experienced soldier's innate understanding of "the underlying principles that troops act as a coherent unit and remain manageable under all circumstances," even when outside of tight formations.[14]

The process by which the conversion of green citizen-soldier recruits into Sherman's battle-wise veterans took place, the manner in which his corps and army gained its "soul," has never been systematically unpacked by historians. In fact, the process of what might be called "veteranization" or even the expression "veteran troops" has been employed colloquially by both military practitioners and historians in the West since at least the Roman era but has rarely enjoyed a clear and unambiguous definition. "Veteran," "crack," "elite," or "experienced" units are still today somehow known primarily when they are seen. One of the many problems with such vague employment of the terms "veteran" or "experienced" in reference to any individual or group, past or present, is that all experiences have specific content. Each of us accrues experience from the day we are born, but the differences in our experiences, and the different ways in which we make sense of them, play a powerful role in molding us into the particular individuals we become.[15] While merely being human beings means that all of us share a number of experiences that are remarkably similar, even those experiences that are most similar to those of another individual still contain distinctive and unique aspects that may become more or less important over the course of our lives. The very same applies to groups—most especially groups that maintain a lengthy tenure of stable membership, and which are called upon to engage in the most traumatic of human activities: warfare. Soldiers living and serving alongside one another naturally accrue shared experience that, just as with individuals, tends to produce a distinctive group "personality" or "character." Perhaps the most salient and distinguishable characteristics of a military organization's "character" that an outside observer could discern represent artifacts of the unit's "tactical culture": the body of shared normative ideas, beliefs, assumptions, and habitual behaviors that shape the command's manner of prosecuting its assigned objectives.

Also like the individual volunteers that comprised them, the "character" and tactical culture of Civil War commands, like Sherman's Fifteenth Corps, was forged by an interrelated combination of factors borne of both "nature" and "nurture." Instead of genetic code, the organizational structure and doctrine to which a regiment trained and drilled, both of which its volunteers inherited from the antebellum US Army, represented certain imperatives that substantively shaped and limited the ways in which it could behave in and out of combat. Whether or not a regiment was an infantry or artillery command, how many regiments a given brigade contained and at what strengths, and the specific maneuvers Casey's or Hardee's *Infantry Tactics* or the *Revised United States Army Regulations* prescribed for deployment and movement on the battlefield were all structures which operated in a manner similar to that of genetic code, or "nature," in shaping how Civil War units behaved.

Just as the behavior of individuals is not exclusively determined by genetic destiny, neither were all the volunteer units serving in the US Army during the American Civil War confined to, or even capable of, responding to any particular tactical situation in exactly the same manner as any other. Despite subscribing to the same linear maneuver doctrine and maintaining more or less the same force structure, due to the lack of any standardized initial entry training in tactical operations, Civil War military organizations frequently differed markedly from one another in the manner in which they approached the missions and objectives assigned to them. Although all US volunteers drilled in maneuvers drawn from identical Army-prescribed drill manuals, as late as the 1880s these works remained exclusively focused on the efficient maneuvering of formations of men to, about, and from the battlefield. In the words of Bvt. Maj. Gen. Emory Upton, they were "simply a collection of rules for passing from one formation to another," but provided no practical instruction in "how to fight"—a topic which was habitually "left to actual experience in war."[16] Tactics, first concretely defined by the Army in 1891 as the "art of handling troops in the presence of the enemy, *i.e.*, applying on the battlefield the movements learned at drill," were during the Civil War left entirely to practitioners to learn from experience. As a result, as historian Paddy Griffith has observed, officers at every echelon within the armies of both sides developed their own personal styles of tactical command, their own "set of reflexes when faced by the great questions of attack or defence, advance or retreat," derived from a mixture of personality, education, and accrued experience. At the same time, the tactical habits of each and every regiment (and thus also those of the brigades, divisions, corps, and armies they comprised) developed along their own distinctive evolutionary path, "according to the specific circumstances" their members collectively endured, including each regiment's "combats, its leaders, its marches and its losses." In fact, due to the intersection of diverse officer and unit "learning curves" at particular moments on and off the battlefield, "it was impossible for a higher commander to make confident generalisations about the likely efficacy of any particular system of tactics."[17] Thus, to explain the differences in the ways in which specific commands and commanders conducted themselves under fire, the historian must historicize their behavior by analyzing how their collective past experiences as individuals or units played a role in informing and shaping future decisions or actions under fire.[18]

The emergent tactical culture of the Fifteenth Corps, borne of its specific experiences, was in many ways similar to, but also distinct from, that which an observer might have encountered within any other of the wartime US Army's twenty-five army corps by the close of the rebellion. Indeed, the corps was by no means unique in the fact that a distinctive tactical culture informed its behavior. All organizations develop a culture of their own over time. Even so, despite major similarities, the tactical cultures organic to each corps were likewise the direct by-products of the specific experiences each formation underwent while in service. Such evolutionary processes shaped the emergent tactical culture of Sherman's Fifteenth Corps during its powerfully impressionable first year serving together across the long Vicksburg and Chattanooga campaigns of 1862–63. While all cultures remain perpetually in a state of flux, ever updated based upon the experiences of those who are informed by them, social scientists believe the initial phase of any team or organization's life span to be crucial to cultural formation. Early periods marked by particularly jarring novelty, like a fighting force's first combat experiences, often result in shared beliefs, norms, habits, and values within an organization that prove especially long-lasting even in dramatically different future circumstances.[19] It was for this very reason that the Fifteenth Corps's first year was so influential in shaping the manner in which it conducted operations during the remainder of its time under arms.

The apparent penchant of the "diabolical 15th" for the destruction of Rebel property and what historians now call "war in earnest" and "hard war" arose from the specific historical experiences of its component regiments. Its specific experiences likewise shaped the manner in which the corps behaved on the battlefield, how its members organically developed an informal doctrine which anticipated most all of the postwar Army's tactical doctrine of predominately open-order light infantry tactics, a preference for the use of field fortifications to defend against Rebel counterattacks even while plunging ever deeper into the so-called Confederacy, and a powerful bias toward the seizure or destruction of Rebel means to prolong the war in lieu of direct confrontation with usually entrenched enemies on the battlefield.[20] Finally, this view of tactical culture offers a new window into Sherman's own development as a military leader, showing how the experience of commanding the corps gradually transformed the much derided "Sherman the Stormer" into the famed "Sherman the Flanker."

TACTICAL CULTURE

The study of the complex interactions between culture and human behavior by scholars across many disciplines has evolved significantly over the past half-century. Most now agree that, while culture provides a repertoire or "tool-kit" of shared values, norms, and standards of behavior within a society or group, it does not dictate human behavior. Rather, it functions in a way that brackets and directs individual vision, delimiting perceptions of what is possible, acceptable, or correct behavior in a given context, circumstance, or environment.[21] Military historians have begun to examine closely the structure and function of "military culture," its relationship to prevailing cultural norms in a parent society, as well as its historical role in influencing the behavior of soldiers. Historian Isabel Hull has defined the concept of "military culture" as "habitual practices, default programs, hidden assumptions, and unreflected cognitive frames" embraced by the members of a nation's military.[22] While usually conceived of as informing the entirety of a nation's military in a relatively homogeneous manner resulting from uniform training and indoctrination, like all forms of culture, military culture exists simultaneously on many different (and often conflicting) levels. Historians are only beginning to understand this multilevel structure and its historical influence on military behavior.[23]

The complicated and confusing multilevel structure of military culture was prominently on display within both US and Rebel armies throughout the Civil War. Only five days after formally taking command of his newly formed Fifteenth Army Corps, Sherman was already complaining to his brother, Senator John Sherman, about the perplexing challenges of bringing order to a polyglot collection of volunteer regiments. "Human power is limited and you cannot appreciate the difficulty of moulding into an homogeneous machine, the discordant elements which go to make up our armies," he wrote. The vast majority were "new & strange to me," making it especially difficult to anticipate their likely future behavior under fire.[24] Still, professional soldiers like Sherman maintained an assumption prevalent within the antebellum Army, that sufficient amounts of standardized drill and discipline could eventually produce a kind of cultural homogenization among volunteers that would mold their regiments into more or less functionally interchangeable units. Alas, these prevailing assumptions about the power of indoctrination through training ignored the natural tendencies of all human groups to forge their own distinct way of doing things based on shared experiences and learned behaviors, even if such habits ultimately represented mere "variations on a theme."

The idea that individual military units naturally evolve their own cultures and "ways of doing things" over time has a deep past. Military commanders and theorists across the globe have long wrestled with ways of either mitigating these differences and culturally homogenizing their commands through uniform training and indoctrination or, alternatively, leveraging the distinctive capabilities of idiosyncratic subordinate units when preparing their campaign and battle plans. Ancient Greek commanders put considerable thought into the assignment of particular phalanges to certain particular portions of their battle formations, placing those particular units with a reputation for high performance, endurance, or raw strength in positions of greatest advantage.[25] Despite Roman efforts to standardize the training and organization of the post-Marian legions, martial reformer Vegetius, in his classic *De re militari* (ca. fourth century CE), observed how each and every legion and auxiliary command inevitably developed its own distinctive *consuetudinem*—habits, manners, culture—which commanders ignored at their own peril.[26] Even the French theorist Maurice Count de Saxe, in his widely influential *Reveries* (1759), lamented the "variety and . . . difference in their methods of performing the service" between even regiments of a single brigade. "The same words [often] do not signify the same things among them," he observed. As a result, brigadiers all too often were forced to look upon their subordinate commands, just as Sherman initially did, "as strangers to him."[27] Because of this stubborn heterogeneity, as Paddy Griffith observes, Civil War commanders ultimately realized "that each regiment had to be allowed to operate in the way to which it had become accustomed, in the hope that it would encounter the type of enemy it could 'whip.'"[28]

Today, social scientists who study the emergence of such cultural "variations on a theme," which organically arise within all wider cultures, refer to such phenomena as "subcultures." According to sociologist Edgar Schein, subcultures "form around the functional units of [an] organization" that include most of the cultural values and artifacts of a larger organization, but also additional assumptions, beliefs, and habitual behaviors derived from their fundamentally unique responsibilities, tasks, experiences, and shared histories.[29] Insofar as such subcultures inform the manner in which any specific "functional unit" of a particular military command (corps, division, brigade, regiment, battalion, and so forth) prosecutes its assigned tactical objectives on and off the battlefield, they constitute unit-level tactical subcultures. In an effort to simplify language, throughout this work they will simply be referred to as "tactical cultures."

For the purposes of this book, a military command's tactical culture is formally defined as the web of beliefs broadly shared between its members concerning the relative efficacy of applying certain learned tactical methods in particular situational contexts (as well as those concerning when and how such methods ought to be employed) that informed, but did not necessarily determine, patterns of habitual decision-making and collective action on and off the battlefield. Like all other forms of the phenomenon, tactical culture was malleable, emerging as a direct result of meaning-making processes engaged in by the officers and soldiers of a particular command, and constantly evolving in response to their subsequent shared experiences. Due to the outsized influence of commissioned officers on unit behavior in and out of combat, the tactical beliefs of some members were especially salient. At the same time, sufficiently widespread beliefs within the ranks of a given command concerning the relative efficacy of a particular maneuver in certain circumstances could and often did overwhelm even the most strident efforts of those charged with formal authority. While operating as subordinates in subordinate units, officers and soldiers had no control over the orders issued to them, but they always remained the ultimate arbiters of the particular manner in which they prosecuted such orders.

Though boasting an authorized strength of eight hundred, each of the forty regiments that formed the nucleus of Sherman's corps averaged only about three hundred men during its first year together under arms. This extreme deficit was not so much due to an inability of the government to procure recruits, but rather a combination of constant attrition and the Lincoln administration's politically motivated policy of organizing fresh recruits into brand new regiments instead of assigning them to existing commands. This policy severely limited the Army's ability to replace its losses during the war, and Sherman, for one, regarded its reform as "more important, than any other [matter] that could possibly arrest the attention of President Lincoln"—even more important, in fact, "than the conquest of Vicksburg, and Richmond together."[30] But the policy also had another overlooked influence. While most regiments did eventually receive a handful of re-placements late in the war, most remained, despite many years in service, predominately single-generation organizations. That is, the majority of those in their ranks at the end of the war had been with their respective regiments from the date of their original formation. Volunteer regiments functioned as veritable silos of particular shared experience and institutional memory to an extent almost singular in American military history.

The subcultures within these commands, shared among all of their veteran members, rarely required transmission to newcomers because newcomers were rare. Moreover, due in large part to the relatively close physical proximity in which a regiment's members usually conducted operations, and to the limitations of what historian John Keegan termed their "personal angle of vision," which could make their experience of an action so different from that of even an immediately adjacent command, the regimental tactical cultures contained within a single brigade could be remarkably diverse.[31] The diversity of tactical cultures within a command as large as a corps was entirely contingent upon the diversity of experience between the "personal angles of vision" of its subordinate officers and units over time.

Like all forms of culture, tactical cultures were the organic by-product of cycles of perception, action, reflection, and adaptation within each regiment. Colonel James Powell, in his study of the 112th Cavalry Regiment in World War II, has offered an excellent model for analyzing such change over time within the context of military commands. Most subordinate military commands do not experience war as it exists in the minds of general officers. Instead, they simply find themselves "plugged into" an operational-level stream, mostly aloof of the specifics of larger plans, performing some small part in the greater whole, and then reflecting on their limited experiences while awaiting reinsertion into the next operation. Lacking any formal "Lessons Learned" initiative as exists in today's US. Army, Union volunteers could only reflect upon the particular tactical circumstances they had encountered, and thus developed highly specific assumptions, skills, mental models, and habits of thinking and acting derived only from the particular situations they had confronted together in the past. Any given unit, Powell explains, "could only interpret the knowledge it acquired," and thus each tended to develop highly specific tactical "toolkits" and skills most immediately relevant to the particular battlefield problems they had previously come up against. Specific combat experiences imparted "the context that allowed leaders [and the men] to reflect on the strengths and weaknesses of their outfit," generating varying levels of collective confidence and efficacy when confronting particular tactical assignments in the future. All of this became a part of the unit's tactical culture, a finite body of assumptions, skills, mental models, and habitual behaviors that could either prove useful in future operations, or conversely, depending upon the particular character and exigencies of future assignments, prove disastrous. When fate, or insensitivity to a unit's tactical culture by commanding generals, thrust a command into a mission for which its tactical culture was fundamentally incompatible, either because it had not yet had a chance to learn and develop adequate skills, had evolved maladaptive habits of thought or action, or lacked crucial confidence relevant to a specific task, disaster could strike.[32]

Although several historians and sociologists have explored the evolution of military culture at the national and branch levels, few have examined its impact on tactical-level unit behavior, and none has yet analyzed military culture within the highly focused context of a particular military command smaller than an entire field army. *Soldiers from Experience* provides a model for probing the lowest levels of military culture through an investigation into the ways in which unit-level tactical cultures, in the form of shared beliefs, ideas, norms, and varying levels of confidence emerged and played a powerful role in informing the tactical behavior of a specific collection of US regiments during the Civil War.

The Fifteenth Army Corps was born in the late winter of 1862, as Sherman hurriedly gathered together all the troops he could find scattered across the vast Western Theater in preparation for an amphibious expedition to capture Rebel Vicksburg. Formally taking command of the embryonic formation, and the expeditionary force of which it was a part, on December 22, he drew its raw material from three primary sources, each embodying an already distinctive if nascent tactical culture borne of specific past experiences and the impress of particular officers. The first chapter analyzes each of these streams of past experience which coalesced to forge the tactical predispositions of the new corps. It also explains the risks Sherman took by ignoring the many qualitative differences that existed between the regiments, brigades, and divisions of his new patchwork command.

The brutal baptism by fire the corps experienced at the Battle of Chickasaw Bayou made clear the severe coordinative handicaps organic to a corps containing such high levels of diversity in the tactical cultures of its subordinate units. As explained in the second chapter, these handicaps were exacerbated by the nightmarish terrain of the Yazoo bottoms, army-wide breakdowns in command and control, and an uneven adherence to prevailing maneuver doctrine by Sherman's lieutenants. In the aftermath of multiple bloody repulses, the dejected members of the new corps forged the foundations of a revised tactical culture based primarily upon a toxic lack of trust in Sherman's headquarters and an intense wariness of frontal assaults. At the same time, a very different retrospective narrative took shape within corps headquarters, threatening a dangerous cultural discontinuity within the command.

While historians have traditionally portrayed the Battle of Arkansas Post as a resounding success for Federal arms, banishing the despondency of the Chickasaw Bayou defeat, the third chapter paints a much more complicated picture. A combination of smoke and difficult terrain across a broad front mixed with Rebel "shock volleys" prevented Sherman's corps from successfully prosecuting a frontal assault against the rudest of entrenchments containing a mere a fraction of their number. Though the Rebel garrison did eventually surrender, almost by accident, the bittersweet experience reified the rank and file's conviction that frontal assaults were all but impossible. The experience likewise caused Sherman to double down on his own convictions that the corps simply lacked the spirit and will to overcome enemy works from the front. This interpretation, a product of his imbibing of the antebellum Army's tactical culture at West Point, proved increasingly out of step with the tactical realities on the ground as experienced by those in the ranks of his corps. Even as Sherman remained fixated on employing massed close-order assault columns to achieve a tactically decisive, if perpetually elusive, physical penetration of the enemy line at the point of the bayonet, the men and junior officers of the Fifteenth Corps instead habitually found their tight formations broken up by terrain and deadly fire from enemy entrenchments. In response, they began to forge their own informal tactical doctrine that looked at least as much to survival as to victory. This new "way of war," emerging first in the ranks of Second Division, emphasized the employment of open-order "clouds" of light infantry skirmishers deployed well to the front of advancing assault columns and charged with gaining fire superiority while the massed formations to the rear advanced by a series of rushes. Once near enough to the enemy works to add the weight of their own fire to the active suppression of the enemy, the massed formations likewise dispersed behind cover after laying down. These new tactics were in many ways in diametric opposition to Sherman's plans, but they also allowed the rank and file to preserve the honor of themselves and their regiments while simultaneously avoiding what they almost universally deemed a suicidal physical penetration of the enemy line.

Despite this lingering discontinuity between the prevailing tactical cultures within the ranks of the corps's regiments and that embraced at headquarters, Sherman took no substantive action to alleviate the command's glaring tactical weaknesses across subsequent months. The fourth chapter examines this period, during the late winter and early spring of 1863, when Maj. Gen. Ulysses S. Grant assigned Sherman's Fifteenth Corps to a variety of noncombat missions designed to support his efforts to capture Vicksburg without the necessity of any more Chickasaw Bayou–style assaults. These missions required adaptive organizational and cultural responses within all of the corps's subordinate units. The challenges of conducting ad-hoc engineering projects and aggressive area denial raids into the Mississippi hinterland promoted the development of a panoply of new tactical skills and widespread beliefs within the ranks of the corps which were added to those accumulated under fire at Chickasaw Bayou and Arkansas Post. As the Lincoln administration's Emancipation Proclamation began to take effect on the ground, the men and officers of Sherman's corps quickly recognized the strategic efficacy of "war in earnest" as they operated deep within the bowels of the so-called Southern Confederacy. As intense trials of disease and hardship took a heavy toll on the strength of every regiment in the corps, the command's successes at levying "hard war" on the hamlets north of Vicksburg offered a glimpse of a possible alternative recipe for victory to those in the ranks hoping to both win the war and survive it. Witnessing firsthand the psychological impact of the seizure or destruction of cotton and foodstuffs on secessionist planters along with the crucial and eager assistance of emancipated slaves, many members of the corps began to feel that, in the words of one Hawkeye, "with the policy now being carried [out] . . . we are crushing the rebellion and will continue to crush it though we be repulsed from every stronghold for months to come."[33]

The particular assignments Grant handed down to the corps during the subsequent legendary campaign for Vicksburg during the late spring and early summer of 1863 were heavily influenced by his abiding confidence in and friendship with Sherman, its commander. The fifth chapter chronicles the corps's participation in the army's long circuitous march from its camps at Young's Point, Louisiana, across the river, and east to Jackson,

Mississippi. As the Fifteenth Corps trailed the remainder of Grant's army during the daring maneuver, it suffered significant hardships along the way due to a severe lack of available forage not already consumed by the remainder of the massive Federal host. These trials forged an impressive capacity for endurance within the ranks, even as the cathartic culmination of the movement at Jackson offered the corps a chance to apply its recently fine-tuned capacity for destruction of Rebel property in the state capital. Intensely proud of their accomplishments on the march despite constant hardship, the men began to grow more confident in the capacity of "our Generals" to outsmart the Rebels. Unfortunately, after being launched by Grant and Sherman into a series of horrific and utterly futile frontal assaults immediately upon their arrival at the well-fortified gates of Vicksburg, this budding confidence was severely challenged, and the corps once again sunk into a pit of despondency only slightly less traumatic than that which had followed in the wake of Chickasaw Bayou. Still, the army had made it to its long sought-after objective, even if it had suffered grievously trying to pry open the front door. While the men rightfully prided themselves on their accomplishments in maneuver warfare, their now deeply rooted conviction that frontal assaults against enemy works were suicidal affairs had been reified once again.

Opting to avoid any further frontal assaults against the Vicksburg works, Grant turned instead to siegecraft. The sixth chapter examines the long Vicksburg siege, and another at Jackson following it, through the lens of the many lessons it taught the men of the Fifteenth Corps. Many weeks spent in the trenches sharpshooting at the enemy works allowed for nearly every member of the command to practice his marksmanship to an extent unexampled throughout the rest of the wartime volunteer Army. Even more importantly, it offered similar opportunities to the gun crews of the corps's batteries, molding the rifled gun teams into an almost surgical long-range tactical tool which would be used to deadly effect on future fields. In all, the veterans of the Fifteenth Corps found the Vicksburg siege "one of the best training schools" they could have ever hoped for. By the fall of 1863, the particular experiences endured and specific tactical situations confronted by its component regiments had forged the command into a particular weapon of warfare with distinctive strengths and weaknesses. Unfortunately, when Grant called Sherman and his corps northward for participation in the effort to break out of the Rebel siege at Chattanooga, he seems to have paid little attention to these subtle realities—much as Sherman had done before him.

By the winter of 1863, the corps could reliably be expected to march great distances at impressive speed, even across the most inhospitable terrain. It could dependably sustain itself off even the most denuded of countrysides and strip even the most abundant of regions all but completely bare if ordered to do so. It could swiftly dismantle railroads and other strategic infrastructure and manage the liberation of large numbers of slaves. In combat, its extensive marksmanship experience, paired with its long tenure of operating primarily in dispersed small groups led by junior leaders, combined to make it a premiere light infantry force. Its brigades preferred to approach any and all direct combat with the enemy deployed in open-order skirmisher "clouds" instead of massed in tight vulnerable formations. In large part because of this habitual preference, nothing in the corps's operational heritage suggested that it could or should have been reliably expected to successfully carry fortified Rebel positions from the front at the point of the bayonet. Nor had the command ever been tried under fire against an enemy force in the open. These two major historical liabilities were among the gravest any mid-nineteenth-century military organization could maintain, but they had nevertheless been proven to be indisputable weaknesses of the Fifteenth Corps.

The final two chapters of the book analyze the corps's operations across the several battles for Chattanooga in the late fall and early winter of 1863, and briefly compare patterns in its habitual tactical practices with those of adjacent units outside the corps. These chapters illustrate the profound degree of self-awareness the men and officers of the command had developed about their own collective capabilities as a military organization, as well as the deep influence of their evolved tactical culture on the manner in which the corps's veteran First and Second divisions prosecuted the objectives assigned to them. Unsurprisingly, when the objectives assigned to either command were well calibrated for the corps's tactical culture, they performed admirably. When they were not, they failed miserably. These successes and failures only served to deepen the widespread beliefs and convictions of the rank and file embedded within their tactical culture. Sherman's infamous reticence and supposedly excessive caution during the battle of Missionary Ridge might instead be seen as powerful evidence of his own imbibing of his corps's tactical culture, and thus of the beginnings of his personal evolution into a legendary practitioner of maneuver warfare—a meandering journey that would see dramatic setbacks along the slopes of Kennesaw Mountain.

This study draws upon thousands of pages of rarely consulted records produced at corps, division, brigade, and regimental headquarters during the war that were never copied into the canonical *Official Records of the War of the Rebellion* but now are stored at the National Archives and Records Administration. In addition to these, it consults period newspapers, and most importantly the letters, diaries, and other writings of nearly one hundred men of all ranks who served within the corps during the first year of its service. Given the unfortunate limits of surviving extant sources, this sample represents but a small fraction of the more than fifteen thousand volunteers who served in the command's ranks during the period. To one extent or another, this problem is shared by all who attempt to deploy the surviving writings of a relatively select few to illuminate the experience of several million citizens under arms during the conflict. To account for this discrepancy, I have approached the consultation of these sources with an eye toward distinguishing patterns of thought, expression, and most significantly action correlated with the unit affiliations of authors. When little in the way of opinionated or introspective comment concerning a particular tactical maneuver survives, my analysis leans more heavily on scrutinizing consistent patterns of behavior as recorded by those present on the field—to include the corps's Rebel opponents.

Unlike within many recent works of "soldier studies," the words of soldiers within *Soldiers from Experience* are rarely employed to represent the views maintained at any given time by more than one's immediate comrades in arms in the same regiment, unless evidence exists to suggest that such ideas, tactical approaches, or opinions were held more widely across the corps. Indeed, I have striven to privilege statements composed by men explicitly referencing what "the boys" felt, thought, or said in letters home or within the confines of their diaries. To be sure, this is not to suggest that all the many thousands of volunteers who served in the corps ever completely agreed even upon the manner in which tactical operations ought to be conducted. Given the sparsity of surviving sources, such a claim could never possibly be supported. Still, as is the case in most military organizations, something bordering on consensus among those entrusted with formal responsibility and authority over tactical dispositions in and out of battle—that is to say, commissioned officers—could often prove more influential than even the combined weight of grumblings from the ranks. For that reason, the book's analysis privileges the voices of officers, most especially those company-grade captains and lieutenants directly involved in the leadership of units in close combat. Even so, my analysis illustrates a much greater extent of agreement between soldiers and officers who underwent shared experiences at the small unit level and subsequently discussed them together (or overheard them being discussed) around camp afterward in a manner that forged functional agreement when it came to matters of immediate tactical relevance. As the distinct patterns of collective behavior of particular units on and off the battlefield clearly shows, elements of "tactical culture" shared at this level did in fact play a major role in shaping the manner in which units at every echelon approached their objectives.

CHAPTER 1

SOLDIERS FROM EXPERIENCE

Christmas Day, 1862

Many are fast becoming soldiers from experience.

—MAJ. GEN. WILLIAM T. SHERMAN, DECEMBER 14, 1862

It seemed impossible, given the warmth of the air, that it could really be Christmas. It was the kind of day that one doffed his coat, rolled up his sleeves, and breathed in what fresh humid breeze was available upon the cramped hurricane decks of the forty smoke-belching steamers plowing southward through the drab Mississippi. With eyes closed, it could have been an Iowa summer or Missouri spring. Only the sight of the deserted riverbanks revealed the truth: this was Dixie. Dense groves of cypress festooned with long waving Spanish moss arose from the swamps on both flanks of the channel. Lazy alligators and monstrous snapping turtles watched as the boats crawled past.[1]

By now, the novelty of amphibious life had long worn off. A week aboard the boats with little more to do than play cards, gnaw on hardtack and raw bacon, or await evening portage at some unsuspecting planter's landing had dampened much of the initial enthusiasm of the more than thirty thousand US volunteers filling the steamer decks. Trips to the pilot house offered a quick glimpse of the impressive host of craft, half-shrouded in their own pitch-black exhaust and extending beyond sight in either direction. Occasionally, the vessels swept one-by-one past massive plantations. At other times, enraptured slaves climbed atop the levees, guarding the property of their absentee masters from the fickle "Father of Waters," and waved or shouted to the passing boats. Groups of shadowy riders occasionally meandered their mounts through the cottonwoods along the bank, casting menacing looks toward the invaders, but never dreaming of molesting the free passage of what those aboard referred to, somewhat ingloriously, as "the Castor Oil Expedition."[2]

No bystander watching the vessels float past could have guessed they were observing the passage of the Thirteenth and Fifteenth army corps. In fact, even those crammed aboard the boats were unaware of this fact. Few could keep up with the seemingly constant changes made to their official identity anyway. For the most part, each volunteer thought of himself as a member of a particular company, regiment, and occasionally brigade. His officers, he assumed, kept track of all the rest. This time, however, even the highest ranking among them, Maj. Gen. William Tecumseh Sherman, then commanding the four divisions en route to the Yazoo River and Rebel-held Vicksburg, was ignorant of the most recent changes to the army's organization. Three days prior, and nearly two hundred miles away at Holly Springs, Mississippi, Maj. Gen. Ulysses S. Grant had, on the War Department and President Lincoln's orders, formally reorganized the divisions of his Army and Department of the Tennessee into four army corps. Cut off from all communication with Grant, the flotilla had no way of knowing of General Order No. 14, which assigned half of them to the command of an officer then absent—Maj. Gen. John A. McClernand—officially designating them the Thirteenth Army Corps. The other half, embracing troops of Sherman's own original command in Grant's army, now led by Brig. Gen. Morgan Lewis Smith—along with that of Brig. Gen. Frederick Steele, which had just joined the flotilla from Helena, Arkansas—were to remain under Sherman's command and thenceforth be formally recognized in all official dispatches and reports as the Fifteenth Army Corps.[3]

Just sixteen days prior, Sherman had departed Grant's headquarters north of Grenada, Mississippi, bearing orders to return to Memphis with the 7,000 men of Smith's division. Upon arrival, he was to somehow acquire an additional 33,000 along with transportation to carry all of them 450 winding miles downriver to Vicksburg while Grant held the main body of the western Rebel army at bay in central Mississippi. If successful, they both hoped the expedition could bag the enemy garrison at Vicksburg and finally pry open the river for western commerce and the Navy after having remained shuttered by Secessionist batteries atop the bluffs for more than a year and a half. When apprised of the daring plan, Maj. Gen. Henry Halleck, then acting general-in-chief of all US armies, thought a force of about 25,000 men, along with whatever troops might be gleaned while en route downriver from the garrison at Helena, Arkansas, would be more than ample. Ever the strategic conservative, he urged Grant to avoid stripping too many troops from his army for the foray just in case the Rebels had a surprise hidden somewhere up their sleeves. Despite these concerns, both Grant and Sherman worried that any force capable of overcoming the major defensive advantages favoring the allegedly 30,000 Rebels at Vicksburg required overwhelming numerical superiority. To attempt such an operation with any force smaller than 40,000 courted disaster. But where was Sherman to find such numbers of volunteers ready for a long-distance stab deep into the bowels of the Southern Confederacy?[4]

On December 9, Sherman departed from the banks of the Tallahatchie River with Smith's division, and after a four-day forced march of over sixty miles, the 7,000-man nucleus of the forthcoming Vicksburg expedition trudged into Memphis. These men Sherman considered his "best fighting division."[5] After more than a year as their commander, Sherman was confident that their ranks were filled with "men I can depend upon."[6] An additional 14,000 of Brig. Gen. A. J. Smith's and Brig. Gen. George Morgan's divisions he found in the city. These, he thought, "seem to be good troops," but were wholly alien to him. Like Morgan Smith's division, both were a mixture of "old" veteran regiments and new regiments of recruits raised that summer. The former had arrived only recently as "mere skeletons" until being bolstered by the attachment of the new units that brought their brigades closer to, but still well short of, full authorized strength. Most of the green regiments hailed from Illinois and Indiana and had originally been ordered to Memphis in anticipation of joining an independent operation to seize Vicksburg under the command of Maj. Gen. John McClernand. McClernand had obtained presidential authority to attempt the expedition, much to the chagrin of both Halleck and Grant, who hoped Sherman might covertly co-opt McClernand's troops and thereby prevent a command crisis in the theater. It worked. Having not yet arrived in Memphis to take command of his private legions due to the combined maneuvering of Halleck and Grant to delay his orders from the War Department, McClernand was not available to guard against the scheme.[7]

Even after stealing McClernand's two divisions, Sherman was still well short of his needs. Accordingly, he took Halleck's advice and sent an aide southward to Helena with a hurriedly scrawled message for Brig. Gen.

William Gorman, commanding the garrison there, requesting "at least" an additional 10,000. He privately hoped these would be "some good men,"[8] but most importantly made a point of requesting that Gorman send Brig. Gen. Frederick Steele, with whom he was personally familiar. Beyond this, he made few other specific requests as to the character or quality of the troops he needed.[9] He apologized for the "irregularity of receiving these orders," but emphasized "the importance of dispatch" in preparations. "The enemy was in full retreat before Grant" when he had left Mississippi, "and it is all-important that we be ready by the 18th."[10] Now was "the appointed time for striking below, and all things should bend to it."[11]

Preparation for such a desperate operation required careful consideration of the mission's many special exigencies, as well as evaluation of the fitness of one's command for the task at hand. In compiling his impromptu expeditionary force, Sherman thought in almost exclusively quantitative terms, seeking raw numbers without much qualitative consideration. After all, left to beg, borrow, and literally steal any and all troops he could find, he did not have the luxury of being too picky. Even in this comparatively modest quest, however, he fell short. Gradually, it became clear that the number 40,000 was pure fantasy, and he reluctantly accepted 35,000. When ultimately all efforts to secure any more than 32,000 proved fruitless, he grew pessimistic.

The lack of available manpower for what he believed was likely to be the decisive campaign of the war in the West seemed a perfect example of flagging Northern resolve. "Like much of Our Boasts of the 'Myriads of the North West' 'sweeping a way to the Gulf' 'breaking the Backbone' &c. &c.," he griped to his wife, Ellen, "the Great Mississip[p]i Expedition will be [only] 32,000 men." While by no means a paltry command—the largest he had ever led—the force was only slightly greater than a quarter the size of the amphibious force Maj. Gen. George McClellan had taken up the James Peninsula in Virginia just six months prior in a similar bid to swiftly bag a Rebel stronghold—the so-called Secessionist capital at Richmond. McClellan had failed disastrously, in large part, the vainglorious general insisted, due to lack of sufficient numbers. If prevailing estimates were correct, Sherman's command would only enjoy a negligible advantage of about 2,000 men, just more than two full-strength regiments—hardly enough for the job. More than that would be required to merely guard supplies off-loaded from steamers before offensive maneuvers could even begin. Any remaining numerical advantage, and then some, would be neutralized by the sundry advantages accruing to a defender on any ground, let alone the twisted bayous and towering bluffs Sherman knew from personal experience dominated the lower Mississippi bottomlands. "Therefore don[']t expect me to achieve miracles," he cautioned.[12]

The idea that there were also real qualitative differences between the different regiments, brigades, and divisions, despite their reporting comparable numbers of men present for duty and equipped, was by no means alien to general officers like Sherman. Still, comparatively little attention was usually paid to the idiosyncratic differences between units on or off the battlefield by most officers when selecting particular commands for particular tasks. Though he would later boast about having personally known every soldier and officer in his corps, in private Sherman admitted that the truth of the matter was that generals paid about as much attention to the selection of particular units for specific missions as they did to the selection of horses for their daily ride. "You use those which are hardiest, and nearest," he explained. He did not "know" most of the regiments assigned to his headquarters, certainly not those beyond the confines of his beloved "old Division." All he really knew was that each "by the merest accident" had somehow come under his control.[13]

This willful ignorance of the distinctive differences between units that extended further than merely the personalities of their commanders was in part a by-product of mid-nineteenth-century American military culture. Professional soldiers believed deeply in the capacity of discipline and drill to forge erstwhile heterogenous individuals into cohesive and functionally interchangeable regiments, each of which had undergone a long process of cultural homogenization that began as soon as each recruit mustered into Federal service. Casey's and Hardee's *Infantry Tactics,* the drill manuals officially adopted by the Army, were founded upon a pedagogical philosophy of "progressive instruction," beginning with the individualized coaching of recruits, followed by that of companies, regiments, brigades, and eventually even divisions and corps. At each level of instruction in drill, emphasis was placed on developing "precision," "harmony," habituation, and "above all . . . regularity." In order to maintain cohesion and ease inter-unit coordination, the "use of the same commands, the same principles, and the same means of execution" by all the regiments of an army was deemed absolutely "indispensable." All regiments were to "conform themselves, without addition or curtailment," to the prescribed tactical doctrine. Similarly, the *Revised United States Army Regulations of 1861* provided clear and unambiguous direction on nearly every conceivable aspect of Army life. Volunteers in Federal service were "at all times" to be "governed by these rules," and were subsequently subject to trial by courts-martial for any and all deviations.[14]

The objective of such uniformity was not to create an army of veritable automatons—indeed, Northerners prided themselves on their army of "thinking bayonets," capable of adapting on the fly to whatever the Rebels might throw at them. Rather, doctrinal systems, along with the entire body of formalized military culture, was intended to impart a kind of interchangeability between regiments that would simplify the challenge of task assignment confronted by commanders in the field. Undergirding the system, though, was the central unexamined assumption that uniform drill and discipline could in fact make regiments more or less functionally identical, each similarly trained and capable of effectively conducting the same tactical tasks, with the single important exception of quantifiable differences in available manpower. Alas, this assumption was not founded in any realistic understanding of human groups or how they inevitably and organically develop, function, learn, and evolve. Nor did it contemplate the profound levels of cultural diversity that were innate to a volunteer army raised and organized as the volunteer U.S. Army had been. Though Sherman might have been mostly ambivalent about precisely which 32,000 men he commanded, or which particular regiments they happened to be organized within, in reality such specifics played a profound role in shaping the real character and capabilities of his new Fifteenth Army Corps.[15]

THE ZOUAVE

One aspect of force composition that neither Sherman nor Grant was ever ambivalent about was the selection of officers to command the divisions of the flotilla. Both Morgan Lewis Smith and Frederick Steele were handpicked by Sherman for their assignments. Nor was it any coincidence that, of the four divisions initially assigned to Sherman's expedition, it was their two that Grant ultimately chose to remain under the control of his most cherished lieutenant following the army's reorganization into corps. Grant took good care of his friends, and over the course of their now nearly yearlong service

26

together he and Sherman had already become very close companions.[16] Grant knew, unquestionably, that Smith was Sherman's favorite subordinate. Although having only known each another for fewer than eight months, Morgan Lewis Smith and Sherman had already developed much the same kind of relationship as the latter enjoyed with Grant. To "Cump," Smith was not only his most trusted lieutenant, but also his personal friend, confidant, and living proof that all so-called "citizen-soldiers" were not necessarily inherently incompetent. To be fair, Smith was nobody's stereotypical version of a volunteer officer. Having enlisted under a pseudonym into the Regular Army in the summer of 1845, he was eventually promoted to sergeant and spent five years as a drill instructor on the parade fields of Newport Barracks in Kentucky during the Mexican War.[17] His natural skill in disciplining and training recruits who arrived at the barracks en route to Mexico prompted post commander Captain Nathaniel Macrae to deny his requests for reassignment to the active Army in the field. Instead, he spent five long years developing an impressive command of tactical doctrine and drill nearly unparalleled in the Army, even among his West Pointer peers now holding commands well above his grade.[18]

After leaving the Army in 1850 and returning to civil life as a steamboat agent in Newport, Smith maintained a keen interest in contemporary trends in the military art.[19] Most compelling of all to him were the French *chasseurs-à-pied* ("hunters on foot"), then experimenting with a new form of light infantry tactics in their colonial African campaigns. Though their exact origins remain contested, the *chasseurs-à-pied* are most frequently credited to the visionary Duc d'Orléans, who raised his famed battalion of *Tirailleurs de Vincennes* in the late 1830s. D'Orléans's *Tirailleurs* broke dramatically with the tradition of linear maneuver systems which had dominated Western infantry tactics since the arrival of the firearm to Europe four centuries prior. Advances in weapons technology, most importantly the development of the rifled musket, along with careful observation of the fighting styles of indigenous African enemies, inspired an altogether fresh approach to infantry warfare. Though the *Tirailleurs* were expected to master the same system of linear maneuver officially adopted by the rest of the French army, the bulk of their training represented a major departure from the European and American norm. Beginning with a rigorous regimen of calisthenics and strenuous cardiovascular training, the men were required to perform all evolutions at the feverish pace of between 165 and

180 paces a minute—double the ordinary "quick step." Instead of aligning elbow-to-elbow and wheeling to-and-fro across the battlefield in a compact body, in combat each man was instructed to instead take advantage of all available cover, maneuvering with a spirit of individual independence, even while remaining coordinated with comrades dispersed to his right and left. The process of loading and firing was done uniformly from the prone or while kneeling, limiting the exposure of each *Tirailleur* to enemy fire. Extensive rifle marksmanship training and instruction in the "scientific" estimation of ranges completed the transformation of recruit into *Tirailleur*, and his subsequent donning of a flamboyantly colorful if somewhat gaudy uniform visually set him and his comrades apart from the line infantry. Success in Africa while commanding his *Tirailleurs* inspired D'Orléans to return to France and raise an additional ten battalions, which he dubbed the *chasseurs-à-pied*. Brigaded in Africa with rugged native Berber fighters of the "Zouave" tribe, the Arabs were so impressed with the novel tactics of the *chasseurs-à-pied* that they promptly adopted the novel fighting style themselves. Somewhere along the line, D'Orléans's command was erroneously referred to as *"Zouaves"* in the French press. The name stuck.[20]

Smith was by no means alone in his fascination with Zouaves. Indeed, the entire country was utterly "Zouave-struck" during the summer of 1860 when the famed militia colonel Elmer Ellsworth's "Chicago Zouaves" toured the major cities of the Northeast and West giving demonstrations of the avant-garde tactical maneuvers.[21] Ellsworth's Zouaves, at that time little more than a well-choreographed traveling martial exposition, responded to a friendly drill challenge from St. Louis's militia "Guards," who were soundly trounced before an immense audience. Ellsworth's "corps appeared like a perfect automatic machine, all the parts of which were responding magically to a single volition, as if every muscle belonged equally to one and the same will," the *Daily Missouri Democrat* raved. The Zouaves had mastered the intricate and highly athletic maneuvers of their French examples, moving with "rapid but mathematical precision" as their lines "broke and re-formed, now apparently confused and anon emerging in faultless order." Despite their unexampled discipline, these were not the rigid, hidebound maneuvers of massed Napoleonic battle lines. Most impressive of all was "the covert and fleet approach and firing of lines alternately prostrate and advancing over each other" in a display of coordination well beyond the skills of most militias. The Zouaves bounded past and literally over each other as they darted from cover to cover, protected by the fire of comrades in the prone. The crowd roared its approval, and even the few "'old line' tacticians" in the crowd, perhaps including Smith himself, who frequented St. Louis on business, were forced to applaud.[22]

With the outbreak of the rebellion, Smith again determined to don a uniform, but this time as a volunteer officer instead of an enlisted regular. Alongside his brother, Giles Alexander Smith, the two set out to organize the "American Zouaves," hoping to train a force of volunteers to maneuver and fight just like their Gallic counterparts.[23] Initial recruiting advertisements promised service in an exclusively native-born outfit, but ultimately more than three of every ten of the "American Zouaves" were foreign-born. Moreover, although the regiment was eventually designated the Eighth Missouri Volunteer Infantry upon muster into Federal service, the majority of those in its ranks were in fact recruited from Illinois. Their native state having far surpassed its volunteer quota during the first summer of the war, these "Suckers" crossed the Mississippi in hopes of finding an opening in the ranks of Missouri regiments.[24]

Smith instructed himself and his new cohort of eager Illinoisans filling Lafayette Park in the novel Zouave drill. Taking them step-by-step through the same exercises Ellsworth's cohort had performed the previous summer over the very same ground, the "American Zouave Corps" slowly started to live up to its name. In the beginning mistakes were commonplace, but this was to be expected given the complexity of the Zouave evolutions. Smith set each of his ten companies at competing with one another to master their maneuvers, jogging them at the double-quick around the perimeter of the park to build their stamina when they were not practicing skirmish or bayonet drill on the parade field. On top of their rigorous Zouave training like D'Orléans's *chasseurs,* Smith also required the men and junior officers to practice and master the standard tactical systems outlined within the Army's prescribed Hardee's manual. He knew that in order to coordinate with non-Zouave units, comprising most the rest of the Army, the regiment would have to know both forms of drill. As an ex-enlisted man, he also knew what tended to motivate young soldiers, and accordingly incentivized martial competition with alcohol. "The Colonel is going to give two gallons of whiskey to the best packed [k]napsack," one Zouave wrote home.[25] Any downtime during duty hours was filled with blocks of instruction on relevant topics taught by experienced junior or noncommissioned officers. The men were even required to regularly practice pitching and striking their tents, so as to increase the speed with which the regiment could be put on the march from nightly bivouac.[26]

The regiment initially cut its teeth as most volunteer Missouri regiments inevitably did: on the deadly conflict raging between neighbors in the interior of the state. After several months of hunting bushwhackers through the brush and trying to avoid ambush on patrols through Missouri towns and along the Northern Missouri Railroad, in the fall of 1861 the Zouaves were finally called east to Paducah to join forces gathering for a plunge into Kentucky. After several more months of Zouave drill, Smith's volunteers finally got their first taste of combat in February 1862, when Grant moved to seize Fort Donelson on the Cumberland River in an attempt to pry open a water route deep into the Southern Confederacy.[27]

Although still a colonel, Smith commanded what amounted to a "demi-brigade" during the campaign for Donelson, constituting a pair of Zouave regiments, his own and Brig. Gen. Lew Wallace's original Eleventh Indiana. Ordered by Wallace, commanding the division, to seize a wooded bluff from the enemy on the first day of the battle, Smith advanced coolly toward the objective with his demi-brigade while puffing a fresh cigar when suddenly a Rebel volley opened along the crest. This being their first experience of receiving concentrated enemy fire, the Zouave line initially wavered. "Try the Zouave on them, colonel!" Wallace screamed over the din.[28] Deep snow and difficult terrain likely would have undone a conventional massed bayonet charge, but Smith's attack was anything but conventional. On his order, three companies of Zouaves broke into four-man teams, each separated by twenty-yard intervals. Each of the four then spread out behind any available cover and commenced firing back, two men covering the other two as they advanced to the next available cover.[29] The two regiments of Zouaves "were nimble on their hands and knees far beyond the ordinary infantryman," Wallace later observed, "[so] that they could load on their backs and fire with precision on their bellies." Each man behaved "like any old Indian fighter," one Zouave proudly recalled, patiently holding their fire while "waiting for secession to show its head," then firing with careful aim when it did.[30] Unlike volunteers trained to obediently abide by the rigid dictates of Hardee's or Casey's tactics, the Zouaves "were instinctively observant of order in the midst of disorder," he explained. "Indeed, *purpose* with them answered all the ends of alignment elbow to elbow."[31]

Amid the pitched firefight, in the rear Wallace was terrified to glimpse Smith, the only officer still mounted, riding immediately behind the Zouaves, still puffing his cigar while urging his mount uphill through the snow and smoke.[32] Intent on making a show of his complete indefatigability, he had thrown caution, even prudence, to the wind. At one point a Rebel ball actually severed the smoldering end of his cigar, prompting him to calmly if frustratedly call out to his staff, "One of you fellows bring me a match!" This colorful display was not lost on the men, upon which "it had a very quieting effect," one later remembered.[33] It had the same effect on Wallace, who later wrote in awe how the assault "was the most extraordinary feat of arms I ever beheld."[34]

After driving the Rebels from the ridge, the dispersed Zouaves reconsolidated and awaited further orders. His blood still up, Smith lobbied Wallace for a follow-on attack on the main enemy works at Donelson but was denied.[35] When the smoke had cleared, Rebel prisoners admitted the confusion the Zouave tactics had sewn amongst them. "They thought they had killed all of our men [with] the first fire but when their guns was empty we was up and a firing," one Zouave crowed. "They said that they Could see us lying on our backs striking as though we were in great agony and all the time we was loading," he explained.[36] Another overheard prisoners talking about how "they could not understand our drill."[37]

Less than two months later, along the Tennessee River at the Battle of Shiloh, Smith's Zouaves demonstrated their acumen once again. After Wallace's brigade arrived notoriously late onto the field, missing the entire climactic first day of the fight, the command joined Grant's counteroffensive the next day. Ordered to push the exhausted Rebels toward Corinth in support of Sherman's division on their left, Wallace gave Smith's brigade the foremost position adjacent to Sherman's right flank. Impressed by the relatively minimal casualties sustained during the assault at Donelson by virtue of the men's laying prone while receiving enemy volleys, Wallace again ordered the tactic be employed liberally. Every time the division halted, each regiment was to lie down on their bellies until further orders were received.[38] Accordingly, as they advanced and eventually encountered Rebel infantry, the battle lines "lay Zouave style, and let the shot, shell, grape & shrapnel pass over us," one remembered.[39] Using the terrain to their advantage, Smith and Wallace masked their lines at each opportunity by bringing them to the prone behind undulating "frequent swells" that both hid and protected their commands from enemy fire.[40] A dense screen of skirmishers moving independently from cover to cover ahead of the division kept up a rolling firefight with the enemy while the rest of the command surged forward at moments of opportunity before again returning to the prone. As soon as the Rebels began to reload, the brigade would again stand and bound forward to the next available cover, consolidating the gains of the skirmishers.

These Zouave-style tactics, Wallace later admitted, were "the secret to my small loss" despite the ferocity and volume of Rebel fire.[41] "You better believe we learned to dodge and lay close to the ground," one Hoosier wrote.[42] Another in Wallace's division emerged convinced that "we could not possibly have escaped as well as we did" had they not been "ordered to lie down" with frequency.[43] Brig. Gen. John Thayer, then commanding another of Wallace's brigades alongside Smith, now at the helm of a brigade in Steele's division of Sherman's flotilla, likewise agreed that in "adopting this course and continuing it throughout the day I have no doubt but that the lives of hundreds of our men were saved."[44] The lessons of Donelson had been reinforced.

The efficiency and effectiveness of these tactics inspired a rather singular confidence within Smith, balanced with just the right amount of conservative caution. At one point during a lull in the fighting, Sherman later remembered, "I was sitting on my horse, when a strange Colonel joined my group, and after some time inquired of me what we were waiting for." Pointing to a regiment of Zouaves he identified as his own, the officer "said there was a force in front of him which he thought he ought to charge." Sherman "advised him to lay low, and perhaps they would feel forward for him, when he could knock them to pieces." The colonel promptly departed, "and in a short time I heard the firing of skirmishers, and very soon three or four full volleys, when silence ensued in that quarter." Shortly thereafter, the officer "reappeared, sat on his horse with his right leg across in front of the pommel of the saddle and said it had occurred just as I had said, and that he had 'knocked' them." Struck immediately with the officer's "undisturbed, so perfectly cool" disposition and his apparent capacity to "comprehend so well the whole situation," Sherman was "immediately attracted to him." Inquiring of his name, the man replied that he was "Col. Morgan L. Smith, Eighth Missouri."[45]

Despite their success in driving the Rebel line away from the first day's battlefield at Shiloh, Wallace's tardy arrival on the field led to his own lasting personal ignominy and his division's assignment to reserve during the army's subsequent slog toward Corinth. The reassignment initially promised a respite for Smith and his Zouaves until early May, when an order arrived from Sherman's division headquarters transferring both the colonel and his original regiment to Sherman's command.[46] "Cump" liked what he saw at Shiloh and had accordingly pulled the necessary strings with Grant in order to obtain the mysterious colonel and his command as a replacement for a regiment of Ohioans who had ignobly shown "the white feather" under fire.

The Zouaves joined Sherman's division on May 12, and almost immediately Smith began to make his mark. Shuffling the regiments of his division of Shiloh veterans to make room for the newcomers, Sherman gave Smith command of the new First Brigade of his Fifth Division. Smith's Zouaves, Col. David Stuart's Fifty-Fifth Illinois, Col. T. Kilby Smith's Fifty-Fourth Ohio, and Lt. Col. Americus V. Rice's Fifty-Seventh Ohio comprised the formation. Though none present could have known it, the brigade represented the future veteran nucleus of the division now churning its way southward to the Yazoo.[47]

"MY 'OLD' DIVISION"

The battered Shiloh survivors of Stuart's, Kilby Smith's, and Rice's regiments had emerged from their baptism by fire proud of their victory, but thoroughly shaken. Heavy losses, mixed with the blatantly obvious tactical inexperience of their citizen-soldier officers, had disillusioned many.[48] When Grant was superseded by Maj. Gen. Henry Halleck in command of the Army of the Tennessee after the bloodbath at Shiloh, the men enjoyed a chance to catch their breath. Though still oft criticized for the painstakingly slow "feel our way step by step" manner by which Halleck nudged the army towards Corinth, Mississippi—the army's next major objective—his strategy provided invaluable opportunities for the regiments of Sherman's division to learn and practice the art of siegecraft.[49] This particular brand of soldiering promoted skills that were erstwhile unfamiliar to even most of the Donelson and Shiloh veterans in the ranks. Having thus far always "regarded the campaign as an offensive one," Grant had never before required the army to dig in while on campaign.[50]

Still, all the requisite digging was not greeted warmly at first. According to one Illinoisan, the campaign "amounted to downright slavery."[51] Unaccustomed to the drudgery of cutting trenches following every slight advance of the line, few initially welcomed the sweat and toil even if they would ultimately benefit from the experience in the long run. As it "dug its way from Shiloh to Corinth," historian Edward Hagerman argues, Halleck's army put on "the most extraordinary display of entrenchment under offensive conditions witnessed in the entire war."[52] Laborious as it was, most volunteers, still traumatized from Shiloh, eventually warmed to Halleck's war-by-spade methodology. The respite from combat and the apparent care that Halleck took with their lives converted many in the ranks to advocates of his conservative approach. Even the Zouaves, whose own experience at Pittsburg Landing paled in comparison to the rest of the traumatized regiments of the brigade, took heart in that "Gen. Halleck says he intends to take Corinth without losing a man," as Captain David Grier, Eighth Missouri, noted. "I hope that this will be the case," he added, "as there has been enough lives sacrificed in this rebellion [already]."[53]

Smith and his Zouaves brought much more with them into the new brigade than combat experience and a winning record. They cross-pollinated the still traumatized men of Stuart's, Kilby Smith's, and Rice's commands with the Zouave-style tactical culture that had organically grown up and thrived in Wallace's now disbanded division. To be sure, just as all the regiments of Wallace's command never learned the finer intricacies of Zouave drill, those of Smith's new brigade would not either. Instead, the key elements, even the essence, of the Zouave tactical culture gradually began to transform the fighting style of the regiments assigned to Smith's brigade.

The "Suckers" of Stuart's Fifty-Fifth Illinois appreciated Smith's "incisive, clear-headed way of managing things," which "at once earned him the confidence of the men." The impressive display of expert skill in skirmish and bayonet drill on parade by his Zouaves made clear to all that the newcomers were no slouches. Perhaps most motivating to the Shiloh survivors was the new brigadier's simple tactical philosophy: "Never . . . present a line of battle to the enemy if a skirmish line would answer the purpose." This mantra had kept casualties among his Zouaves remarkably low while also maximizing the effectiveness of his deadly riflemen. He saw no reason why the same tactic could not be applied to the command of volunteers who were not trained as his Zouaves had been.[54]

Just a week after taking command, Smith had a chance to introduce the brigade to his particular brand of fighting. On May 17, Sherman ordered

First Brigade to advance in tandem with the rest of the division in an assault on a strong salient of the Rebel line at Corinth dubbed "Russell's House," which was guarded by an enemy brigade. There were many different ways by which the position could be contested, some entailing a steeper price in blood than others. In accordance with his Zouave philosophy, Smith chose the most conservative. It also proved to be the most efficient and effective. That afternoon, after the brigade sallied out from its works and moved a short distance down the main road toward the salient, Smith ordered his Zouaves to disperse into their four-man skirmish teams a considerable distance ahead of the rest of the brigade, which he halted well outside the range of the known Rebel position. The scattered Zouaves swept forward under Smith's orders to "advance briskly from tree to tree," keeping up a sporadic covering fire for each other as they advanced.[55]

As they neared the structure, Rebel resistance became more obstinate, prompting Smith to deploy multiple companies of Stuart's Illinoisans as skirmishers in support of the embattled Zouaves. The lack of a massed target confounded the Rebel officers, who were overheard shouting "not [to] run from the damned Yankees." Their defense collapsed when one of the crack-shot Zouaves deprived it of its commander, "shot just as he was emerging from the door of the house, and he fell dead upon the doorstep, with his brains scattered over it." Another Rebel lieutenant was shot "through the window of the chamber," killed by a carefully aimed shot from one of Stuart's Suckers. Most of the remaining eleven Rebel dead littering the ground around the house had succumbed to wounds in the head, neck, and chest.[56] Emphasis on the independent maneuver of skirmishers, each finding cover and taking deliberate aim before engaging his target and "making every shot tell," allowed for individual marksmanship skill to be exploited in ways that a bayonet assault would have wastefully frittered away.[57] "The Fifty-fifth for the first time saw the utility of a well-handled and rapid-moving skirmish line," one of the Illinoisans later remembered, "and felt its comparative economy of bloodshed." Still, the two-and-a-half-hour affair was by no means bloodless.[58] By the time the smoke cleared, Smith tallied a total of ten killed and thirty-one wounded in his brigade.[59] This Sherman judged "pretty heavy," but he still considered the attack "the prettiest little fight of the war" all the same.[60] It confirmed his opinion of Smith's tactical skill as he "witnessed with great satisfaction the cool and steady advance of this brigade" dispersed in skirmish teams.[61] All the while, the intrepid colonel had been among his command, "managing and urging on the skirmishers."[62]

Ten days later, the brigade repeated the performance when ordered to assault yet another portion of the Rebel line. "With skirmishers well to the front," the main brigade line advanced toward the objective without ever needing to fire a shot, serving primarily as a tactical reserve for the fierce firefight engaged in by the sprinting, crawling, dodging, leaping cloud of skirmishers to its front.[63] This time supported by the twin 20-pounder-rifled Parrotts of the First Illinois Light Artillery, the combined effects of the brigade's adept sharpshooting and judiciously placed rifled shells neutralized the Rebel defense long before the main line ever reached the objective. As far as the Shiloh veterans of Smith's division were concerned, this was the right way to fight a war.

Even as the brigade came to know Morgan Lewis Smith and his distinctive brand of warfighting, Smith himself was learning from the careful observation of his new command. Ordered by Sherman to immediately entrench in order to consolidate the fruits of the assault and defend against counterattack, Smith was pleasantly surprised at the flexibility of his old regiment as they took a cue from their comrades in the other regiments. "The alacrity with which the men relinquished the rifle for the spade" impressed Smith greatly, even more so when a sudden Rebel counterattack prompted them to drop their shovels and repel the assault from their hastily dug fighting positions. This performance, he judged, "promises well for the future."[64]

Smith was renowned across Grant's army for not only his proven tactical acumen, but also his unexampled vulgarity. Despite his middle-class roots, his tendency to fill almost every sentence with a profane expletive, and to habitually neglect any and all refined social conventions, were almost certainly a product of time spent among the lower classes who filled both the enlisted ranks of the Regular Army and the levees and riverboats of the Ohio where he made his living. When asked shortly after the war whether the rumors of his profanity were true, he quickly replied: "That's a damned lie. I swear very little," and further, that "the man who said he was a hard swearer was a damned liar."[65] The bond Smith cultivated with his Zouaves "could not be credited to any persuasive arts on his part," Lew Wallace observed, as Smith was "in speech the roughest commander I ever met."[66] In reality, however, it was precisely this unpretentious and irreverent air, along with his "compound of good sense and badinage," that endeared him to those in the ranks.[67] He was a soldier's general, a commissioned noncommissioned officer. "Under the free-and-easy and somewhat rough exterior of Morgan L. Smith, was a kind heart and a deep interest in the welfare of his men," one of Stuart's Illinoisans later observed. "He bandied jokes freely with the troops in the ranks, and was not averse to receiving as well as giving rough language." Even Wallace was struck with the natural facility Smith seemed to have with the men. "The faculty of disciplining raw soldiers had been in him at birth," he determined.[68] One Zouave put things more succinctly when he observed how Smith "makes us get up and howl I tell you."[69]

Smith also proved effective at engendering support from the junior officers of his command. Politically, he was considered "a conservative man," which put him in the good graces of the vast majority of officers in Sherman's army, to include "Cump" himself.[70] He also curried the favor of his lieutenants by pushing aggressively up the chain of command for their prompt remuneration during periods when paymasters were scarce.[71] In return, "they rendered him united support," Wallace later recalled.[72] Above all else, Smith benefited from being regularly under the eye of the army commander. Upon forwarding his recommendation for Smith's promotion following his unparalleled performance at Donelson, Grant admitted that there were almost certainly "others who also may be equally meritorious but I do not happen to no [sic] so well their services." Smith, after all, was an "old soldier," and thus was "in every way qualified for promotion."[73] After being recommended once again for a brigadier's star by Grant in July, Smith finally became a general two weeks later.[74]

In the wake of the Rebel evacuation of Corinth, Sherman's division commenced a nearly hundred-mile grueling march westward to Memphis through the intense summer heat. Charged with repairing the railroad en route, the excruciatingly slow pace and constant supply shortages bred considerable illicit foraging along the way. The independent spirit of Smith's Zouaves that served the regiment so well in combat also tended to produce indiscipline on the march. Theft of both Army and Southern private property was regularly attributed to the Zouaves, and even neighboring regiments were not safe. For the most part, Smith turned a blind eye to this behavior, even joking about it in his general orders in a manner that could only encourage more of the same. "I hear also a report concerning some members of the Eighth Missouri, which is too terrible for belief," he announced in early July, "nothing less than an attempt to tarnish the good reputation of their brothers of the Sixth Missouri by borrowing their elegant hats to steal sweet potatoes in."[75] In fact, in many cases, Smith almost seemed proud if not boastful of his original regiment's capacity for liberal foraging. If his pride remained mostly subdued, those in the ranks unabashedly embraced their reputation. Approaching one aggrieved farmer en route to Memphis, one of the Zouaves shouted from the ranks, "Have you any forage for man or beast?" The man replied that "the troops ahead have taken everything except my soul, and I reckon a whole regiment can't squeeze that out of me!" Alas, one Zouave remembered, the comment prompted another to reply: "Don't be so sure of that, this is the 8th Missouri!"[76]

By the time the division reached Memphis, they felt like not only veterans, but "ideal Western soldiers; not conspicuous for handsome uniforms or waving plumes, but the very embodiment of disciplined, self-reliant force," one of them later recalled. The men were proud of being "dirty, sunburned and ragged [and] bore the impress of their splendid brigade commander." They were "manifestly journeymen in the art of war."[77] The long march from Corinth had all but destroyed their uniforms, and the column was "all naked nearly," one Zouave observed.[78] Another merely observed, with more than a tinge of pride, "we are hard looking boys."[79]

Spending the fall in garrison at Memphis provided the regiments of Sherman's division with an invaluable opportunity to pursue a diligent program of "systematic drill" that acculturated the recently arrived "new" regiments to the division. It also provided for the consolidation of lessons learned at Shiloh and Corinth. "The men were in some sense the [product of the] survival of the fittest," one of the Fifty-Fifth Illinois later remembered, the survivors in every company fully appreciating the importance of mastering those maneuvers most relevant to survival in combat. "The rudimentary period of 'left, left, left,' 'eyes, right,' 'right dress,' had passed," he explained, replaced with an insatiable quest for mastery of multi-regiment coordinated maneuver, skirmish drill, and bayonet exercises.[80] Both Smith and Sherman monitored the progress of each regiment closely, levying "eccentric and epigrammatic criticisms" to officers of every rank whenever their performance failed to meet a lofty standard.[81] Overhearing such rebukes of superiors on dress parade was "entertaining in the extreme" to the subalterns in the ranks, but also set a tone of high expectations that pervaded the command.[82]

Smith's veterans of multiple fierce engagements fully appreciated the pains he took to maximize their effectiveness and survivability in the field. Presenting him with a new brigadier's uniform, sword, saddle, bridle, and spurs upon his promotion the previous summer as tokens of their affection and gratitude, funded by cash donations directly from the ranks, the officers of the Eighth Missouri spoke on behalf of the entire brigade when offering their thanks.[83] "You found us new levies," one of them announced, "[and] made us equal to veterans." His Zouaves were a model case for the conversion of citizens into "soldiers from experience," and they knew it.[84]

In early November, the arrival in Memphis of several new regiments of "fresh levies" raised that summer prompted a reorganization of Sherman's garrison. Among the most important of these administrative changes was Smith's ascension to command of a new division made up of a mixture of "old" veteran and "new" regiments, and his brother Giles to command of the division's First Brigade. The Second Brigade was commanded by Col. David Stuart, originally of the Fifty-Fifth Illinois, an ex-lawyer who had already proven himself as a quick study of the military art by his admirable performance under fire at Shiloh. Stuart took pains to ensure that the levies assigned to his brigade, including the Eighty-Third Indiana and the 116th and 127th Illinois, were trained to the same standards as his veteran regiments.[85] On at least one occasion in early December, he ordered each of his "old" regiments to detail eight officers and eight noncommissioned officers each "to drill the new troops in skirmishing & the Loadings & firings," these being by far the most highly valued skills in Smith's division.[86] The opportunity to learn from experienced leaders instead of merely from manuals was invaluable for the newcomers. It also lent a spur to the preservation of the division's tactical culture, as all the regiments of the new command strove to meet the same standards in Zouave-style skirmish drill, and learned lessons derived from the same set of past experiences. A brief spring campaign southward into Mississippi to the Tallahatchie River with Grant's army provided Smith's division with an opportunity to break-in the stiff brogans of its newest recruits, and by the time Sherman ordered his "best fighting division" back to Memphis for the downriver expedition, the command had made great strides in fully integrating its "fresh levies."[87]

The raw material of Smith's division was primarily a product of the "old

Northwest," and most especially its politically conservative lower belt. Of its ten infantry regiments, four were from Illinois, two from Ohio, one from Indiana, and three from a mixture of Missouri (primarily St. Louis) and Illinois. Those in the ranks averaged a little over twenty-five years of age at enlistment, those in the "old" regiments having already spent one birthday in uniform. Six of every ten men in the division identified himself as a farmer or farm laborer when prompted for his occupation. Only 9 percent considered themselves unskilled laborers, whereas more than 30 percent worked in a skilled trade prior to enlistment. In fact, the volunteers of Smith's ten infantry regiments had plied more than 140 unique occupations before taking up arms. On average, each of the regiments contained about eighty men, or nearly a full company, who might be considered to have worked in a technical trade as either blacksmiths, carpenters, engineers, machinists, or mechanics. Unsurprisingly, predominately urban regiments, like the Eighth Missouri (from St. Louis) and 127th Illinois (from Chicago), contained the greatest proportion of these men. Their skills had in many cases already proved a boon to their regiments and would continue to do so. About 70 percent of Smith's volunteers were native to the free states, and 10 percent to the slave South. Of the more than 20 percent of those born abroad, most were German or Irish. While the proportion of foreigners varied markedly between regiments, in none of the division's commands did they constitute a majority.

Despite these aggregate statistics, the regiments varied considerably in most of these measurements. Whereas the men in the ranks of the Sixth Missouri were twenty-seven years of age on average, those in the Fifty-Fourth Ohio were younger than twenty-four. More than eight of every ten recruits in the 116th Illinois came from an agricultural background. By contrast, the majority of Smith's Zouaves considered themselves skilled laborers back in Illinois. Whereas 80 percent of the Fifty-Seventh Ohio had been born in the free states, only 69 percent of the Fifty-Fifth Illinois could say the same. Nearly half of the Sixth Missouri were born abroad, more than 20 percent in Ireland alone, but only 2 percent of the Eighty-Third Indiana were Irish, and fewer than two of every ten of the Eighty-Third Indiana were foreign-born.

By most measures, the demographic character of "old" regiments and those recently arrived in Memphis did not differ significantly. Those regiments raised during the summer's call for volunteers averaged slightly more farmers, fewer unskilled laborers, and about the same proportion of skilled tradesmen if modestly higher numbers of those in technical trades. Most were still native to the free states. "New" regiments contained fewer Irishmen but more Germans on average, likely an artifact of the recent perceived shift in the war effort toward emancipation—a dark turn in the eyes of many unskilled Irish laborers concerned about future competition for jobs. On the whole, the "new" regiments of Smith's division contained only modestly higher proportions of foreign-born recruits than those that enlisted in 1861.[88]

Although each regiment hailed from a distinctive sociodemographic background and had endured a particular set of experiences while in uniform, the division as a whole had developed a coherent tactical culture based on a shared operational heritage and the careful crafting of a skilled commander. As the recently arrived "fresh levies" were indoctrinated into this culture on the parade fields at Memphis, they vicariously imbibed lessons learned the hard way by the "soldiers from experience" that filled the ranks of Smith's "old" regiments. By the winter of 1862, Sherman's beloved "old Division" had been molded into one of the most impressive combat teams in the Department of the Tennessee. Even so, its Zouave-style skirmish-centric tactical culture was not a panacea for all tactical problems. It also entailed its fair share of inherent disadvantages, most especially the kinds of individual independence that fueled illicit foraging during the march to Memphis. Smith's command was undoubtedly Sherman's "best fighting division," but it came with specific historically derived baggage, just as any collection of volunteer regiments inevitably did.

THE REGULAR

Months of commanding amphibious operations up and down the meandering stretch of the lower Mississippi between Helena and Vicksburg made Brig. Gen. Frederick Steele an invaluable asset to Sherman's expedition. "You having been so long on the Miss. river looking toward Vicksburg are possessed of much information as to the best method of attacking that point that I am not possessed of," Grant wrote him upon receiving Halleck's permission to go ahead with the expedition. He mentioned that he was inclined to send Sherman on the foray, and "would be very glad if you could accompany him." Steele needed no coaxing.[89] Having recently drawn considerable ire nationally due to his supposed backpedaling from District of Missouri commander Maj. Gen. Samuel Curtis's politically liberal confiscation policies after having briefly succeeded him in command of the Helena garrison, by the winter of 1862 "Fred" Steele was under fire from multiple directions.

In one particularly notorious instance, Steele had caused soldiers to assist the wife of a local planter in recovering several young girls, whom she claimed as her husband's property, then working in a Helena brothel. When this seemingly flagrant violation of Federal policy—which then prohibited the army's involvement in the return of fugitive slaves to their owners—was made public through a scathing exposé written by the abolitionist chaplain of the Third Missouri, J. G. Forman, to the *Daily Missouri Democrat*, it drew the attention of President Lincoln himself. As Steele was on the short list for promotion to major general, Lincoln wanted to make sure that such rumors were not true prior to acceding to his advancement. Had he in fact blithely allowed a planter's wife to wrench these young women from their newfound freedom back into the bonds of slavery? "There was no understanding that any of these girls should be delivered up to their masters," Steele explained in a reply to Washington. The brothel represented a threat to the army's health and morale, and thus he had no choice but to promptly shut it down and evict its occupants just as soon as its existence came to his attention. "If they had been white I should have given the same order," he insisted. Likely more persuasive was the name of the woman in question: Mrs. Charles Craig, whom Steele firmly alleged to be a staunch Unionist, and whom Lincoln must have remembered personally signing a pass for authorizing passage through army lines during her recent visit to the White House. In truth, Steele's consummate professionalism as a career officer likely played a more powerful role in motivating his behavior than did any proslavery proclivities he might have harbored.[90]

Although historians still routinely refer to Steele as acting in accordance with a "staunch Democratic background," in reality, most of these assertions of his supposed slaveholder sympathies are groundless.[91] His formal military education and lifelong Army service had acculturated him into a deeply conservative officer corps that prided itself first and foremost on its nonpartisan approach to carrying out public policy.[92] Like all of his colleagues, Steele certainly maintained personal opinions on slavery and emancipation, but these private convictions were not what guided his decision-making. His personal and professional constitution would never allow them to do so. Instead, Steele consistently upheld what he believed to be the narrowest possible interpretation of his government's intent on the ground. His public critique of Curtis's liberal interpretation confirmed this. Curtis "violated both law and orders, and instituted a policy entirely different from that indicated by the President in regard to slaves," he argued. It just so happened that, on the fringes of the reclaimed and rapidly transforming United States, the president's intent was perpetually in flux and often ambiguously expressed. In the divisive political climate of 1862, just as Steele accused the Republican Curtis of allowing "the interests of a political party" to motivate his actions in uniform, his own loyal conservatism was interpreted by many of a more partisan bent as rank disloyalty, or even treason. In reality, Steele's actions represented merely a course correction in policy that guided Curtis's increasingly radical approach to confiscation back toward that which governed affairs in Grant's army across the Mississippi and throughout a still very politically conservative US Army.[93]

Steele remained confident that the more politically conservative components of the garrison still thought highly of him. Many locals likewise hoped he would soon return to command of the post after his recent replacement by the Curtis lackey Gorman, but the ringing endorsements of slaveholding planters were hardly what he needed. In the meantime, under the far more liberal oversight of garrison commander Brig. Gen. Willis Gorman, US troops had "torn this country all to pieces," Steele lamented.[94] He was confident that alongside his fellow professionals and longtime friends Sherman and Grant he would be "properly dealt with," and thus was elated about the rumor of his imminent reassignment.[95] On December 14, both Steele and Sherman got their wish. Gorman ordered Steele to prepare a division to embark in four days, stripping its baggage down for combat.[96]

Approaching his twentieth year in uniform, Steele had by far the most military experience of any field officer in the flotilla. It was the content of this experience, however, that shaped his abilities and predispositions as a commander. Appointed to the US Military Academy at West Point in the spring of 1839 at the unusually advanced age of twenty, he had taken quickly to military life. Although "somewhat of a wag" and even a prankster in the right company, Steele was mostly reserved by nature, and averaged barely half the number of annual demerits as Grant and a quarter those of his friend Sherman, three years ahead of both. Entering the academy at an older age than most of his peers made him a natural mentor for younger classmates and friends like Grant.[97] A remarkable ferocity of loyalty to friends and family likewise made him a valuable companion.[98] After graduating in 1843 ranked nine places behind Grant, Steele was assigned to the infantry and garrisoned in a series of posts prior to the outbreak of the Mexican War. Serving as a breveted (due to a lack of vacancies in the Army) second lieutenant in the Second US Infantry, he was brevetted again to first lieutenant for "gallant and meritorious conduct" at the battles of Contreras and Churubusco. After volunteering to participate in the desperate "forlorn hope" assault party at the battle of Chapultepec, he earned yet another brevet to captain.

After frontier duty in California, Minnesota, the Dakota Territory, Nebraska, and finally Kansas, Steele was at his post in Fort Leavenworth in the spring of 1861 when word arrived that Fort Sumter had been attacked. Just a month later, he was promoted to a majority in the Eleventh US Infantry and assigned a battalion of Regulars attached to his longtime friend and West Point classmate Brig. Gen. Nathaniel Lyon's army, then campaigning across Missouri attempting to eradicate the secessionist Missouri State Guard. After he led his modest phalanx under fire for the first time at a minor skirmish at Dug Springs in early August, the real test of Steele's aptitude for battalion command came a week later at the Battle of Wilson's Creek. Concerned about the imminent expiration of the three-month term of service agreed to by the majority of the volunteers in his command, Lyon rushed his army into what he hoped would be the decisive engagement of the campaign south of Springfield. Though Lyon initially gained the upper hand, a Rebel counterattack up "Bloody Hill" tipped the scales and left him mortally wounded. Ordered to cover a desperate retreat with only his "gallant little battalion," Steele and his Regulars stood firm, repelling successive Rebel charges and saving the surviving remnants of the army from almost certain disaster. Steele's "gallantry . . . from the beginning to the close of the battle" caught the eye of Iowa governor Samuel Kirkwood, at that time hunting for Regular Army officers he might convince to accept volunteer colonelcies at the head of freshly raised Iowa regiments. Accordingly, he offered Steele a volunteer commission as colonel of the Eighth Iowa and sent him with the regiment to Sedalia, Missouri, where Steele summarily took command of a full brigade of volunteers. In January, having attracted the attention of not only Kirkwood but President Lincoln,

Steele was again promoted to full brigadier general of volunteers and given command of the entire Southeastern District of Missouri two months later.[99]

Beyond small patrols against Rebel partisans marauding the Missouri countryside, command of the district offered little in the way of vigorous field service for the newly minted brigadier. That changed when, on March 1, he received orders from Halleck to march his humble command into Arkansas and join Curtis's victorious army fresh from the Battle of Pea Ridge, then en route to Helena. The road from Batesville, Missouri, to Helena was long and hard—no less than 150 grueling miles. Most of the route required "living off the land" due to Curtis's decision to cut from his supply lines and make with haste for the river. Across a campaign remarkably similar to that many of its participants would endure with Sherman across Georgia in just over two years' time, the army experimented for the very first time with employing liberal foraging as a tactic for punishing Secessionists. While Curtis hoped for the men to distinguish between loyal and Rebel families when pursuing their daily meals, such distinctions quickly broke down in practice. Officers struggled to prevent stragglers from wandering away from the columns to fend for themselves. "I leave nothing for man or brute in the country passed over by my army," Curtis reported. It was an invaluable lesson for all, and a preview of much to come.[100]

By the winter of 1862, while Steele had reason to be proud of his proven skill in maneuvering a division-sized command through the manifold trials of the slog to Helena, he had yet to command any more than a battalion in combat. To be sure, his performance in Mexico left no doubt of his personal bravery. But courage was not itself sufficient for the complex exigencies of division command.

FROM THE "STATE OF MISERY" TO "HELL-IN-ARKANSAS"

Unlike Smith, Steele had thus far enjoyed little opportunity to make any meaningful impression on the seventeen infantry regiments and three batteries of his division, nor they on him. The units lacked much of a shared operational heritage, instead representing a tapestry of diverse regimental tactical cultures evolved over the course of disparate experiences across the Western and Trans-Mississippi theaters. Even his highest ranking subordinates, with the exception of Colonel Charles Hovey, were all but complete strangers to Steele and to each other. In many ways, this heterogeneity was a product of the unique exigencies of the war effort in the Trans-Mississippi theater. Fighting a seemingly intractable insurgency in Missouri while confronting multiple menacing field armies hovering around Arkansas with minimal available troops meant that the kinds of concentrated mass field armies found east of the Mississippi were comparatively rare among US forces in the "far West." The logistical nightmare that was southeastern Missouri and northern Arkansas would have mitigated against such large hosts even had the strategic situation been more amenable. To cope with the combined challenges of a vast area of operations, abysmal transportation infrastructure, and the need to keep a close eye on entire communities, Federal authorities tended to disperse their resources in manpower and materiel, reconsolidating them into impromptu commands when needed for offensive operations. This practice inadvertently encouraged the development of a highly culturally heterogeneous Trans-Mississippi US Army.

Many of Steele's "old" veteran regiments had spent at least a portion of their time in uniform serving in guerrilla-infested Missouri. The "State of Misery," as many out-of-state volunteers sarcastically referred to the state, was known among those who served there as being "the land of long-haired people and 'butternut clothes' . . . [and] long miles."[101] With a notorious lack of good roads, Missouri was universally estimated by footsore infantrymen as slightly "better than hell," but not by much.[102] Plodding across seemingly endless distances on patrol, the Suckers of the Thirteenth Illinois, the only regiment of Steele's original District of Southeast Missouri still under his command, had begun to refer to an altogether different unit of measurement: "Missouri miles," not to be confused with the much shorter and less painful "United States miles."[103] The pitched battles they read about in the papers seemed a world away as they traipsed through dense brush in all kinds of weather, hunting bushwhackers, interrogating the families of known "Secesh," and laying in ambuscades along roads in the dark of night. Guerrilla hunting amounted to "some very hard times," one observed. Still, the especial hardship also inspired a special pride within the ranks of regiments sent to Missouri. Volunteers in the major armies "don't know anything about hard times," one Missourian boasted to his parents. "Let them come to this state and they [will] find out that they can't ride in cars and steamboats everyplace," he jeered.[104]

The experience of fighting against Rebel guerrillas left an indelible mark on units assigned to such duties.[105] The men developed a deep distrust of Southern civilians, no matter how benign they might seem at first blush. In one particularly jarring instance, after a brush with bushwhackers the previous fall, one of the Thirteenth Illinois rolled over the body of a dead Rebel only to recognize the face of a man who had only recently been peddling pies in camp as cover for espionage. Such duplicity was by no means exclusively a bushwhacker tactic. Several of the regiments with a guerrilla hunting past had at one time or another dressed their scouts in civilian clothes so as to avoid detection by the enemy.[106] Fighting guerrillas frequently meant deliberately blurring the line between civilian and soldier—a tactic that came easiest to those Missouri volunteers operating within their own state or even home communities.

Steele's division also included multiple regiments which had mostly avoided assignment to counter-guerrilla duty, having instead participated in the more conventional campaign of Maj. Gen. Samuel Curtis against Sterling Price, Earl Van Dorn, and Ben McCulloch's Rebel army in Arkansas, culminating in the Battle of Pea Ridge. Most conspicuous among these were the Germans of the Twelfth and Seventeenth Missouri regiments now in Hovey's brigade and the Fourth and Ninth Iowa of Thayer's. Due to their combat experience, accrued trust in their leaders, and a familiarity with maneuver under fire, these four commands would quickly prove invaluable to Steele's division. In addition to these were two more veteran regiments dispatched to Helena upon the dissolution of Wallace's division of Grant's army—the very same administrative action that had sent Smith and his Zouaves to Sherman. While neither the Fifty-Eighth nor Seventy-Sixth Ohio regiments were Zouaves, both had imbibed the skirmisher-centric logic of the tactical culture that predominated within Wallace's division. They, along with Brig. Gen. John Thayer, now commanding Steele's Third Brigade, carried with them the indelible impress of lessons learned fighting alongside Wallace's Zouaves at Donelson and Shiloh.[107]

Despite each regiment's labyrinthine administrative path to Helena, all had in common the challenge of enduring singularly abysmal conditions upon their arrival. The flood-prone lowland campgrounds at Helena, which the men immediately took to calling "Hell-in-Arkansas," quickly transformed into a cesspool of dysentery, typhoid, and swarms of malarial mosquitoes.[108] Ignorance of how best to diagnose, let alone treat, the manifold intestinal problems arising from the consumption of contaminated water led to a staggering sixth of all reported cases of diarrhea, or "Arkansas flux," in Helena proving mortal. These were not the so-called "crowd diseases" that were the scourge of all new regiments encountering alien pathogens for the first time. The vast majority of men who fell ill at Helena were veterans. Many units became all but combat ineffective due to the sheer volume of men in their ranks physically incapacitated.[109] By December, 35 percent of the garrison was unavailable for duty due to illness. Nearly every volunteer in the garrison was stricken with some form of malaria, and 13 percent died from it. The sensation of helplessness combined with a lack of rigorous efforts by post commanders to alleviate their suffering crushed morale in the ranks. "Nobody seems to care whether we live or die," one of the Thirteenth Illinois lamented.[110]

The unspeakable conditions of the garrison cantonment area mitigated against drilling, and thus there were few opportunities for veterans in Steele's command to transmit their hard-won wisdom to the newcomers. Instead, the only escape from the horrific conditions consisted of periodic amphibious forays downriver to the plantations of the lower Mississippi in search of cotton. In an effort to encourage speculation in and ship-ment of Southern cotton to Northern and European mills still suffering from choked river commerce, the Lincoln administration ordered Federal troops to provide security for civilian speculators plying the Mississippi.[111] Perhaps unsurprisingly, given the amount of money to be made off the cherished commodity, corruption quickly became rampant. Speculators and traders cut deals with officers of security detachments to confiscate cotton even from erstwhile loyal planters, forging their signatures on bills of sale and sharing the profits quietly with detail commanders. Few were as heavily involved in such shady transactions as Col. Charles E. Hovey, now commanding a brigade of Steele's division.[112] While most volunteers in the Helena garrison applauded the vigor with which the Army engaged in the confiscation of "Secesh" cotton, they balked at the obvious corruption and profiteering engaged in by the officer corps. Moreover, the banks of the Mississippi were teeming with guerrillas who could quickly turn any benign outing into deadly combat. The loss of comrades while protecting corrupt speculators in the interest of padding the pockets of equally unscrupulous officers eroded morale in the ranks of units assigned to such duties.[113]

Returning from downriver expeditions to the abysmal living conditions at Helena, many soldiers complained about how the officers seemed more focused on making a profit than providing for the health of the men.[114] "I know that I but reflect the feeling of every comrade when I say that every life that was lost in those expeditions was a useless and wonton sacrifice," one Illinoisan wrote angrily.[115] At the same time, these brief amphibious outings offered many regiments in Steele's command, as well as Steele himself, a glimpse of the very ground over which they would soon campaign while serving in Sherman's flotilla.

Just as in Smith's command, half of Steele's division was filled with "fresh levies" raised over the past summer from loyal communities across Missouri and Iowa. The Twenty-Fifth, Twenty-Sixth, Thirtieth, and Thirty-First Iowa Infantry Regiments joined the division without much in the way of any preexisting tactical culture. While Governor Samuel Kirkwood's recruitment policies ensured that at least a fraction of the junior officers enrolled within each of these regiments came from the noncommissioned officer ranks of veteran Hawkeye formations, most were still commanded by neophyte field officers. Although most had received rudimentary instruction in the basic formations and maneuvers contained within Hardee's or Casey's *Tactics,* only through the experience of their forthcoming trials would these new regiments learn the martial trade.[116]

By far the most prominent of the "new" soldiers were Brig. Gen. (and Congressman) Francis Preston Blair Jr. and his four regiments of Missourians, who behaved much like a private armed retinue. Having recruited many of them personally from his constituency back home in St. Louis, Blair had already developed a special kind of bond with the predominately German rank and file of his Twenty-Ninth, Thirtieth, Thirty-First, and Thirty-Second Missouri infantry regiments. Especially prominent in both St. Louis and Missouri politics, Blair had long wished for an opportunity to prove his mettle in the field. Although he had played a major part in shaping the political contours of the early war in Missouri, he had yet to take up a sword in actual combat. Staunchly conservative if nominally Republican, he worried about the revolutionary direction the war seemed to be heading, but nevertheless would never accede to the Union his family had long struggled to maintain being rent in two. The son of Francis Preston Blair Sr. of Jackson administration fame, and brother of Postmaster General Montgomery Blair, Frank had long been a major figure in the national spotlight.

It remained to be seen, however, whether he could translate that notoriety into success in battle commanding equally inexperienced volunteers.[117]

On December 18, as the flotilla pushed off from Helena, a hopeful "Cump" wrote to Grant that the force was ready to "make something to yield and prepare your way."[118] Now, a week later, the column of steamers finally approached the murky waters of the Yazoo on the final leg of their passage. Ever the consummate paranoiac, Sherman had somehow, someway, managed to beat the odds and still remained as good as his word to Grant that he would be at the appointed place at the appointed time with (close to) the appointed number of men. Lacking the luxury of adequate time to deliberate over precisely which troops he ought to bring with him, he had taken "those which are hardiest, and nearest," hoping as he did that these would be "some good men," as he put it. Indeed, many of them had already proven themselves to be such, and, in his words, were "fast becoming soldiers from experience."[119] More than half of the others had yet to enjoy an opportunity to do so. For the eager, if nervous, "fresh levies" of the flotilla the forthcoming operation would prove their baptism by fire, just as it would for the two hastily assembled impromptu corps as coherent organizations. Their performance would ultimately be the product of a vast array of factors. Among the most important, however, were the capabilities, skills, predispositions, and assumptions that each regiment, brigade, and division carried within its respective tactical culture, arising from specific experiences across its distinctive operational heritage. The raw experiences of campaigns and battles past, represented by the names inscribed upon the regimental standards soon to be again unfurled on the muddy banks of the Yazoo, had been transformed by officers and men into habitual practices, ways of thinking, and webs of meaning that informed their behavior on and off the battlefield. Sherman and his lieutenants ignored this nuance at their great peril.

CHAPTER 2

DISCOURAGED BY SUCH MANAGEMENT

Chickasaw Bayou

It was complete madness of Sherman to think of such a thing.

—LIEUTENANT HENRY KIRCHER, TWELFTH MISSOURI

Daylight broke upon a shivering mass of blue-coated men huddled together for warmth amid the cotton fields hugging the banks of the Yazoo River. Throughout the past sleepless night, many who had only recently written home about the unseasonably high temperatures were drenched by a frigid downpour.[1] Sherman had too much to do in too little time to fret about the weather. He understood that, in order for the larger plan to come to fruition, his humble expeditionary force had to bag Vicksburg before Mc-Clernand could react to the theft of his command and before the contracts allowing the government's use of his steamer flotilla expired. He owed it to Grant to be ready when he arrived from the north. Unfortunately, although historians still debate whether Sherman yet knew it, Grant was not coming. Rebel cavalry raids had dismantled his line of communication from central Mississippi back to his supply bases in Tennessee and Kentucky. Another struck his supply base at Holly Springs. Cut off from his lifelines, Grant and the rest of his army were forced to retire from Mississippi, leaving "Cump" and his expeditionary force to fend for themselves.[2]

Sherman's plan to quickly seize Vicksburg envisioned a rapid sweep southeastward of multiple division columns from their landings along the Yazoo up the Rebel-controlled Walnut Hills, along which ran the main road south into the city. Commanders were to advance at a steady pace, driving all opposition before them. On the off chance they ran into more than tacit resistance, "a prompt, quick assault will be the most effective and least destructive," Sherman advised. Speed was of the utmost necessity. While he intended the advance to constitute one fluid movement, circumstances forced a series of shifts in the army's operating paradigm. On the first full day in the bottomlands, after probing cautiously ahead and meeting with little resistance, each of the divisions arrived at the murky waters of Chickasaw Bayou and encountered the main body of Rebels ensconced behind a series of levees rising above the far bank. On the left, Steele's Fourth Division column met stiff resistance behind a sharp bend in the levee, along which it marched, that guarded a narrow causeway across the bayou. In the center, a single modest bridge was discovered in Brig. Gen. George Morgan's front, too narrow to facilitate the swift crossing of a force sufficient to dislodge the Rebels dug-in to the south. Finally, along Morgan Smith's Second Division front on the right, a narrow sandbar that extended into the bayou was the only point shallow enough to permit a ford. Just as with the other two crossings, the sandbar was heavily guarded by Rebel infantry and multiple batteries.[3]

That evening, Sherman adapted his approach to these developments, ordering each division commander to begin clearing obstructions to the crossing points and forcing their commands through the contested defiles. Even before the sun had risen on the second full day of operations, each division established a base of suppressive fire with both infantry and artillery firing from the cover of thickets along the bayou, engaged in what one of the men referred to as a "sharp-shooting tournament" with Rebels behind the levee, while pioneer details armed with axes hacked away at trees and brush felled by Rebels to block access. This proved to be deadly work. After Rebel fire cut down several pioneers, Steele determined that further efforts would be more costly than they were worth. Upon request, he received permission from Sherman to redeploy his division from the left and instead support Morgan's advance in the center. Cut off from the rest of the army by a wide bayou tributary, Steele's redeployment consumed the rest of the day and part of the next.[4]

Along the Second Division front, things were just as frustrating. During a personal reconnaissance of the sandbar, Morgan Smith was shot in the hip by a Rebel sharpshooter and severely wounded. Command of the division fell to Col. David Stuart. Despite the loss of their beloved commander, the change at headquarters was not fated to have much of an impact on the character of the fight. Smith had already made an indelible impact on the division's tactical

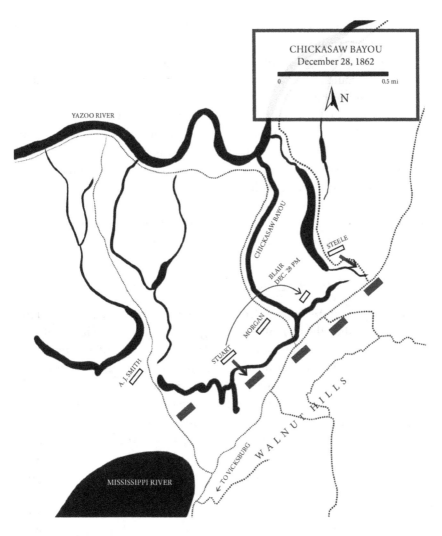

culture over the prior months, and his impress was on display in the way in which the command conducted itself under fire. Chickasaw Bayou, fortunately, was not a battle in which a division commander could have all that much influence over tactical affairs anyway.[5]

That evening, Sherman altered his plans again, personally delivering detailed orders to each division commander, providing guidance for a forthcoming attack. Though at considerable cost to the pioneers, access to two of the three crossing points had been secured, and portions of the bayou along Morgan's front were deemed fordable. The army would launch a coordinated frontal assault on the Rebels defending the Walnut Hills. The assault would unfold across the entire front, with diversionary attacks on the wings designed to draw Rebel attention and reinforcements away from the center. On the right, Stuart's division was to cross over the water and form in two lines behind cover on the opposite bank "in silence and in good order" so as to capture and hold enemy attention. On the left, Blair's brigade, detached from Steele's division, would launch its own attack in support of two of Morgan's brigades in the center, which would strike as the main effort against a hopefully weakened Rebel center. "The whole line will move as nearly east as possible as the ground will admit," Sherman instructed, "simultaneously attacking the crest of hills in their front."[6]

"IF IT BE IN THE POWER OF MEN"

Without supper and exhausted from a meandering approach march and the day's skirmishing, the men of Blair's brigade found it next to impossible to sleep during the night. Rumors passed through the ranks of a forthcoming assault, and of the treacherous ground over which it was to be made. At dawn, Blair deployed skirmishers to "feel the enemy and observe the ground over which we were directed to charge." The reconnaissance offered little encouragement. At the edge of the standing timber in which his brigade was formed, an open expanse of saplings, cut and "thrown down among the stumps so as to form a perfect net to entangle the feet of the assaulting party," stretched nearly four hundred yards to the bank of Chickasaw Bayou. At the bottom of a nearly ten-foot-high levee was a bed of mud one hundred yards across with water three feet deep and fifteen feet wide coursing through it. More felled trees overhung the southern bank, making its ascent doubly challenging for men with shoes filled with bayou water and caked with mud. Just beyond this was a line of abandoned shallow rifle pits at the edge of a stubble-filled cornfield which stretched across a wide-open incline sweeping for an additional five hundred deadly yards to the Walnut Hills, scarred only by a second line of pits filled with Rebels some two hundred yards from the crest. Altogether, the enemy positions appeared "to require almost superhuman efforts to effect their capture," Blair later professed.[7]

The ominous appearance of the Rebel works seemed even more menacing when seen through the eyes of officers and men who had never before confronted such a daunting prospect. In truth, while the expansive intervening distance and vexing terrain promised to pose significant challenges to maintaining cohesion in the assault, the works themselves were mostly unsubstantial. Lacking shovels and having abandoned the first line of works running along the bayou bank, eight guns and the roughly six hundred men of the Seventeenth and Twenty-Sixth Louisiana confronting Blair had only just scraped out a shallow indentation along the Walnut Hills using their sword bayonets the night prior. While the Seventeenth had fought at Shiloh, those in the Twenty-Sixth had only the past few days of skirmishing to their combat record. Stretching out their limited numbers single-file across the ditch and lacking any real protection from artillery, those defenders who survived a preliminary bombardment would have to rely upon destroying an onrushing enemy force with fire as it floundered across the bayou and attempted to cross the vast open expanse. If any significant number of Federals reached the shallow pits themselves, there would be no stopping them. There was no reserve available for a counterattack. Still, the Louisianans of the Twenty-Sixth Regiment were well equipped to do this, armed as they were with British-import Enfield rifle-muskets capable of delivering accurate fire across the entirety of the thousand-yard void Blair's regiments had to traverse. Firing upon massed formations advancing with glistening bayonets, "our rifles could hardly miss," one later remembered.[8]

Blair arranged his two thousand men and four regiments into two successive lines. He chose to anchor his right flank with his two eldest commands, the Thirteenth Illinois in front with the Fifty-Eighth Ohio following 150 feet to their rear. Though both were long-service commands, only the Germans of the Fifty-Eighth had ever before made an assault. The paltry numbers remaining in its battered ranks paid testament to the price of such maneuvers. Two green St. Louis regiments formed Blair's left, the Thirty-First leading the Twenty-Ninth Missouri. Both had rallied to the flag only months prior and received only rudimentary instruction in drill on the parade field.[9] Even this distinguished them from the Thirty-Second Missouri, which had yet to enjoy any drill since its muster a week before the flotilla's departure.[10] Blair mercifully assigned the regiment to guard a nearby battery during the attack. As the reality slowly began to sink in, he "whispered to one of his officers, as he explained the movement with tears in his eyes, 'Thank God the order is not mine, but we will obey if it be in the power of men.'"[11]

After a heavy artillery bombardment lifted and the guns fired an agreed-upon salvo to trigger the assault, Blair's nervous brigade leaped from the cover of a tree line and into the open. As soon as the men exited the woods, Rebel artillery and rifles opened upon them. "The hill in front of them became a volcano, which vomited fire from foot to summit," a spectator noted with horror. "Long parallel lines of flame indicated the rifle-pits; broad, heavy, concentrated flashes showed where the batteries were hurling their iron." The pace was quickened. "Guide-right, double-quick, march!" Blair screamed. Maneuvering his mount through and over the branches, he led his brigade from the front while Rebel shells, with their characteristic "sczzzz" and concussive blast, slammed into the mud nearby. Rifle fire cut through the ranks, but the formation managed to hold its shape. One Illinoisan remembered looking down the line and noticing how, "though the wings traveled a little the fastest, and the line curved a little . . . the front was bold and magnificent."[12]

Reaching and descending the steep northern bank of the bayou marked the advent of the formation's dissolution. Thousands of men sliding down the slippery embankment with fixed bayonets while under fire produced more than enough problems before the brigade reached the quicksand of the bed. "The feet of the men commenced sinking the instant they touched it," one later told a correspondent. Struggling forward through the mire and into the knee-deep water, all order was destroyed. Color-bearers stumbled and fell in the mud, handing off their staffs to any who made it to the opposite bank. Horses became lodged in the quagmire, threw their riders in the chaos, and even Blair was forced to dismount and scramble up the opposite bank on foot. Rebel gunners and riflemen plunged their fire directly into the madness. Those who managed to scale the levee found a tangled morass of disoriented, soaked, and mud-caked men. Blair and his lieutenants struggled to regain cohesion. This "took several minutes to put it in order," an observer remarked, but was eventually achieved.[13]

As the line reached the first line of empty trenches, the Illinoisans on Blair's right discovered that the pits were now occupied by troops from Morgan's brigades huddling there for cover. Although these had been assigned as the main effort, the disorganized throng of Illinoisans and

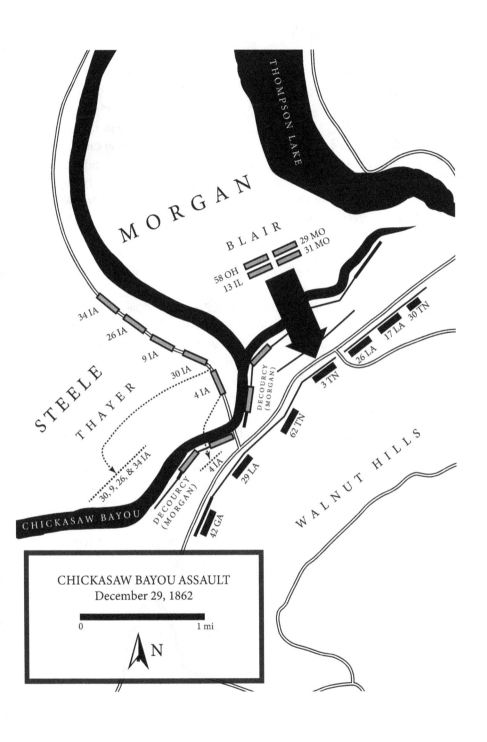

THOMPSON LAKE

MORGAN

BLAIR

58 OH
13 IL

29 MO
31 MO

34 IA

26 IA

9 IA

30 IA

4 IA

STEELE

THAYER

30, 9, 26, & 34 IA

DECOURCY
(MORGAN)

41 IA

DECOURCY
(MORGAN)

3 TN

62 TN

29 LA

42 GA

26 LA

17 LA

30 TN

WALNUT HILLS

CHICKASAW BAYOU

CHICKASAW BAYOU ASSAULT
December 29, 1862

0   1 mi

N

Germans pushed through the fugitives and over the opposite parapet. As the men spilled into the cornfield stubble, the concussion of a shell struck down the Thirteenth's color-bearer, who "dropped insensible" atop the standard, leaving "no visible rallying point," one remembered. The regiment's many months of drill came to this, a mad dash, "every man for himself," up the slope. "Men were falling on every side," Private Wilson Chapel of the Thirteenth remembered. As regimental colors disappeared amid the maelstrom, Blair himself became a final rallying point for those still struggling up the incline through the fire. "His sword waving over his head, and his hearty voice cheering us on," Chapel recalled, "we never thought of turning back."[14]

Inspiring as this might have been, by charging boldly ahead of the command, Blair was adhering to popular civilian notions of an officer's place in battle, leading men personally through the fire. In doing so, he neglected the role that drill manuals explicitly prescribed to him, the same manuals he had been so strict to emphasize to the volunteers of his brigade. Inattention to drill, Blair had reminded them while aboard the transports, was "one of the gravest offenses that can be committed." In a charge like that in which his brigade was engaged, it was the role of regimental officers and sergeants to inspire the men and drive them forward. A brigadier's was one of management and control amidst chaos. This neglect of duty could have severe consequences. Had Blair been, as his drill books dictated, "about forty paces in rear of the centre" of his command, he would have quickly realized that Morgan's brigades, the main effort, were in fact not advancing on his right. He would have immediately noticed that the fugitives cowering in the trench, passed over by his right wing, were in fact those of Morgan's lead regiments, refusing to go any further forward. Thus, with little more than a prompt bugle blast, he might have prevented the useless destruction of his brigade. From the front, he could only run, point, yell, and hope.[15]

As the muddy survivors slogged up the slope, the intensity of leaden resistance seemed to grow heavier by the step. The successive layers of natural and artificial Rebel defenses acted as a kind of sifter, each barrier excising large numbers from the ranks and scattering the remainder. All the while, enemy fire cut down men from each regiment, further eroding numbers already weakened by days of hard fighting and campaigning in the bottoms. Each regiment's capacity for resilience gave out in turn. The moment at which it did was heavily influenced by each unit's particular history.

Thus far the neophyte Missourians on Blair's left, undergoing an unforgiving baptism by fire, had managed to retain a "somewhat restored" line. Still, comparatively, "we were greatly disordered," Colonel Thomas Fletcher admitted, leading his Thirty-First Missouri through the fire at a run. As the Rebels fired a volley, one of their rounds cut Fletcher down. His second in command was struck in the head and wounded severely. His third in command was killed outright. This sudden decapitation was more than the raw recruits could take, having yet had little opportunity to forge the kinds of cohesion that could survive the sudden loss of every field officer. Although the regiment alone still likely outnumbered all the Rebels to their front, the command had sustained more than 20 percent casualties in the assault, which proved sufficient. They summarily wavered, broke, and ran through the confused ranks of the terrified Twenty-Ninth Missouri following closely behind.[16]

Reaching a shallow scar running along the slope that he took for another abandoned rifle pit, Blair and his remaining three regiments of the brigade took shelter. Turning to survey his dissolving command through the smoke, he noticed what looked to be the encouraging sight of a column of blue rushing up the slope to his right. Assuming this to be Morgan's brigades finally fulfilling their orders, he urged the survivors to abandon the scant protection of the undulation and rush forward across the final two hundred yards to the Vicksburg road. The remaining veteran Germans of the Fifty-Eighth Ohio, most especially those who had seen the carnage of Donelson and Shiloh, were wary of this. Sensing their reluctance, Colonel Peter Dister climbed atop the parapet of the works. "Vörwarts!" he screamed to little avail. Failing, he tried leading by example, starting off alone into the void. After only a dozen yards, he was cut down, his lifeless body rolling back down the slope to the ditch. His regiment became the second to reach its psychological limit of advance. Though by no means routing in confusion as had Fletcher's levies, the veterans had seen enough. Now, only the last vestiges of the Thirteenth Illinois and Twenty-Ninth Missouri comprised Blair's charging swarm of blue. Judging that these, although potentially still more than one thousand men, would not be enough to breach the Rebel line along the Vicksburg road, despite its defenders numbering less than half their number, Blair left his brigade and sprinted back through the smoke to attempt to spur Morgan's cowering men forward himself.[17]

Rushing through the corn stubble as sheets of bullets and canister tore through their battered ranks, the forward edges of what was left of

Blair's brigade eventually made it to the slight cover of a shattered copse of willows. Doing their best to keep up, a handful of surviving Missourians joined those from the Thirteenth Illinois, but not before three successive color-bearers were shot down. Finally, the Missourian flag was abandoned. "Utterly exhausted," a correspondent watching from the batteries observed, "they halted for the supporting columns. None came." When an exhausted Blair finally returned from his unsuccessful attempt to find support, he was forced to accept the fact that "there was no hope of support from any quarter," and ordered the survivors to fall back. "This we did in the same manner we advanced," one Illinoisan recalled, "every man for himself." Hoping to cover their retreat, US batteries opened in an effort to silence the Rebel guns, but several of their shells fell short. "They were thus literally hemmed in by a wall of fire, which consumed them as the flames consume the dry grass of the prairies," a horrified journalist lamented. Instead of risking the deadly passage back to the bayou, many of the survivors surrendered. Finally following appropriately behind his shattered brigade, Blair was one of the last off the field, his uniform caked from head to toe in mud with "a corn-husk clinging to his saber." Immediately calling for a horse, "with a countenance luminous with despair," he mounted and rode off to find Steele. "Who is that officer?" someone asked. "That is Blair," a reply came. "The last man to leave the hill."[18]

"WHAT A PITTY"

Sherman's original plans for the assault had not contemplated a role for any other of Steele's brigades, not knowing when or even if Thayer or Hovey might arrive on the field after their redeployment from the left.[19] When Steele himself arrived with Thayer in tow during the preliminary barrage, however, Sherman immediately directed him to assist Morgan. The latter took both Steele and Thayer aside personally to provide abbreviated instructions. "I want you to take those heights," Thayer remembered him saying, pointing southward.[20] Greatly concerned about the threat of sharpshooters, he also advised that Thayer and the rest of the officers in the column dismount and proceed on foot.[21] This would prove a fateful decision.

Thayer was by far Steele's most combat-experienced brigadier. Having, like Morgan Smith, led a brigade of Lew Wallace's division at both Donelson and Shiloh, he was the only one of Steele's lieutenants to have commanded more than a single regiment in battle. Even so, the specifics of his past experience shaped his tactical approach. The impress of Wallace and Smith's Zouave-style tactics at Shiloh was evident in his advice to the new brigade to kneel or lie down whenever possible during the assault and to take advantage of any undulating terrain. This course of action, he was convinced, had saved hundreds of lives and preserved his command through the heaviest fighting at Shiloh.[22]

As all along the line, the awkward terrain limited Thayer's deployment options. A single narrow but undefended bayou crossing necessitated launching the brigade into its assault in a column of regiments, each with four men abreast, with the intention of maneuvering into lines of battle once a wider frontage became available. In column, regulations mandated that Thayer's proper place was at the brigade's front. This negated any possibility of his influencing any but the foremost ranks of his lead regiment, the Fourth Iowa. That regiment alone, in a "column of fours," stretched rearward a distance of at least 160 yards through the trees, rendering the rest of the brigade invisible to him and he to them. Recognizing the dangers inherent in this lack of control, Thayer took two steps. First, he gave strict orders to every regimental commander to "keep close up and follow" the regiment to their front, and "to obey this order till they received further instructions."[23] Second, he dispersed his staff along the flanks of the column to provide guidance to the greener regiments that comprised half the formation.[24]

When Thayer and Colonel James Williamson's Pea Ridge veterans of the Fourth Iowa led the column over the levee on the north bank of the bayou, Rebel batteries immediately caught sight of them and opened fire. Their shells burst along the line, prompting one of Thayer's staff, having imbibed his chief's lessons learned at Shiloh, to order Colonel Charles Abbott's green Thirtieth Iowa, still north of the levee, "to lie down and make ourselves as secure as possible" until the fusillade passed. Once it did, and Abbott arose to order that bayonets be fixed and the column start forward again, he was alarmed to find that the Fourth "had got 10 or 12 rods [about sixty yards] in advance." He had wrongfully supposed that the Fourth had also gone to ground under the barrage, but in fact was already in the act of crossing the bayou. "I immediately put my regiment under a double-quick," he reported. But before he could give the command "march," Steele himself mysteriously appeared, shouting the very "further instructions" contemplated in Thayer's orders. Steele "checked us and ordered me to leave my horse, cross the next bayou in any way we could get across, and take my regiment to the right into the woods and deploy as skirmishers," Abbott later reported. An inexperienced volunteer officer, Abbott was not about to question his division commander, and immediately obeyed. The remaining regiments followed diligently, and disastrously, adhering to Thayer's orders to "keep close up and follow" verbatim.[25]

Unknowingly now at the head of only the Fourth Iowa, Thayer and Williamson sprinted across the muddy bayou, over a roadway running through the same trenches filled with Morgan's cowering troops, and over a fence skirting a cornfield, tearing it down as they advanced. It was at this moment that Blair, looking for any hope of support through the smoke, spotted the Iowans rushing forward and mistook them for Morgan's men. The Iowans kept well closed up, spilling into the field and maneuvering into line as Rebel bullets zipped through the air and shells slammed into the earth. "Bring your regiment into line!" Thayer shouted to Williamson over the din, ordering him to disperse them as skirmishers and avoid massing vulnerably in the open. Meanwhile, Thayer would "bring the whole force . . . into a parallel line," he screamed to Williamson, and turned back for the first time during the assault to check on the other regiments. "To my dismay and horror," he later wrote, "I found only the Fourth Iowa Infantry had followed me." Even through the smoke he could see the full distance back to the column's starting point on the north side of the bayou. No brigade, no regiment, no company was visible. Thinking fast, Thayer recalled Morgan's shell-shocked command the Iowans had passed over in the captured trenches during the advance and decided, like Blair, to go himself to try and move them forward. "Hold your ground, if possible!" he yelled to Williamson, and was gone.[26]

The ability of Williamson's Iowans to reply effectively to the hail of Rebel fire they encountered was extremely limited. Even though the enemy rifle pits were shallow and less than a hundred yards distant, they would have concealed most of the men fighting from them. Moreover, many of the Louisiana and Tennessee regiments manning them were armed with either Mississippi or Enfield rifle muskets. Firing individually from a supported position at close range, even a novice could hit his mark. Had they been comparably armed, the Iowans might have more effectively suppressed the Rebels to their front, potentially decreasing their casualties. Sadly, they were not. While the Harpers Ferry smoothbore muskets they responded with along the line were vast improvements over the Napoleonic "Potsdam" muskets the gun-starved Iowa state government had originally issued them, they still put the regiment at a major disadvantage. The Army's antebellum tests comparing rifles with muskets suggested that an experienced shooter with a musket could only expect to hit a six-foot square target at a hundred yards with about every other shot taken in the calm conditions of a firing range. In the chaos of battle, with the enemy shrouded by smoke and presenting no more than a square foot of himself, the Iowans were hard-pressed to hit anything at all.[27]

Very quickly Hawkeye blood began to run freely. A corporal had his overcoat "Shot from his shoulders," a ball snapped through the knee of a private, and a young lieutenant was struck by a shell fragment that sliced through his leg and severed a main artery.[28] Rebel bullets and shell fragments hit seventeen Iowans in their legs, five in their feet, six in their shoulders, and five more in the side. Two were struck in the stomach, five in the chest, and three in the hip. No less than eighteen more were hit in the hand or wrist, while fifteen suffered wounds to the head or face.[29] Sergeants along the line struggled to triage and stabilize these casualties to the best of their ability, but quickly found themselves outnumbered. When a Rebel ball careened through eighteen-year-old private William Arnett's arm and lodged in his chest, his orderly sergeant and close friend, John Miller, found he could do little for the boy under the circumstances but place a blanket under his head and make him "as comfortable as possible." As orderly, it was Miller's duty to report any losses to the company commander. "Coming up he Said that Wm Arnett was mortally wounded," Captain Randolph Sry remembered. It was the last time they spoke. Moments later Miller was struck by a Rebel shell directly "in the side of his face," killing him instantly. Knowing that the wounded private was "warm friends" with the sergeant, Sry made a point of informing Arnett of Miller's death as the boy himself lay dying. "What a pitty [sic]," he replied, "and shed tears with deep Emotion." Indeed, it was a terrible pity. With four dead and more than a hundred seriously wounded after less than twenty minutes in action, the regiment had been decimated nearly twice over. The determination of the command to hold its ground despite the obvious futility of the situation was a testament to a cohesion borne amid the bloody crucible at Pea Ridge nine months prior. Before half an hour had transpired, that cohesion began to flag, and Williamson promptly ordered the retreat. Those officers and sergeants still standing struggled to get "all the Boys started off," Sry later recalled, even as two more Iowans were hit in the back.[30] "We was in the Slaughter pen," another officer bluntly remarked.[31]

The debacle was a tragedy of doctrinal structures, erroneous suppositions, and nightmarish terrain. Thayer and Abbott both behaved as products of the rigid tactical system they had striven so ardently to master over the previous months on the parade field. To this instruction Thayer added the influence of his prior experience fighting under Wallace. Had he not been at the head of his column, as doctrine prescribed, he might have been made aware of Abbott's deviation in time to halt the advance. If Abbott had insisted upon clarification from Thayer prior to blindly following Steele's orders, the crisis might likewise have been averted. The fact that neither acted so prudently was due in large part to the doctrinal structures within which they operated. The drill manuals all made clear that the proper place of a brigadier in an advancing column was at its head. Army regulations also made equally clear, on their very first line no less, that all subordinates were "required to obey strictly, and to execute with alacrity and good faith, the lawful orders of the superiors appointed over them." No note of special clarification existed for situations like that confronted by Abbott, and thus, as Thayer himself later observed, "knowing Steele to be my superior officer, [he] obeyed the order."[32]

The problems arising from this rigid adherence to doctrine were exacerbated by a series of erroneous suppositions resulting from a total breakdown of command and control once Thayer's brigade came under fire. The first of these was the fault of Morgan. Receiving a desperate call for reinforcements from a Kentucky regiment on his far right just as the assault was underway, Morgan spent no effort investigating its legitimacy. Instead, wrongfully supposing it to be authentic, he promptly asked Steele "to turn part of the troops a little farther to the right." Instead of asking for clarification, Steele halted Abbott and ordered the Thirtieth "a little to the right, supposing the object of this was to facilitate the crossing of the troops over the bayou by preventing them from all huddling into the same place." This supposition was, of course, also incorrect. Meanwhile, Thayer urged his column on from its head until ordering Williamson to deploy the Fourth while he brought the rest of his brigade into line. Only then turning around for the first time, his heart sunk. "I had supposed that five regiments were following me," he later wrote, admitting his own disastrously mistaken supposition.[33]

Before the war, most military theorists prophesied that the increased range and accuracy of rifled muskets and artillery would render massed frontal assaults all but completely suicidal. Any mass of men boldly charging across open ground would inevitably be destroyed in detail and eroded by the long-range fire of a defender long before even approaching their objective, professionals argued. This tactic, leveraging the technological advantages of modern rifled weaponry, constituted an attritional defense.[34] If a defender could dissolve an attacking force with a combination of obstacles and fire as it approached, he could rob it of its vital mass and render it all but harmless upon its final arrival at the point of attack. The bloody failures of Blair's and Thayer's brigades seemed to bear this out.

The key to success in making an assault against an opponent relying upon an attritional defense was ensuring maximal speed of forward momentum (so as to reduce time under fire) and maintaining coordination with adjacent formations as they endured the inevitable storm of lead cutting across "no man's land." Whereas vicious terrain had robbed both Blair and Thayer of the first of these prerequisites, slowing their advance and giving Rebels more time to erode their lines, their own inexperience and individual predispositions had undermined the second. Only speed and coordination could ensure that an attacking force fell upon its objective with a force superior to that defending it.[35] Otherwise, attackers would inevitably be destroyed in detail, just as the antebellum prophesies had foretold.

"A HOT PLACE SURE"

Beyond a small working detail drawn by Stuart from the 116th Illinois to clear obstructions barring access to the sandbar on Sherman's right the night prior to the assault, Giles Smith's brigade had remained in reserve throughout the three previous days of operations. From the brigade's position in the division column behind Stuart's line, much of the battle thus far had only revealed itself to them in the form of gun teams rushing by on their way to the front and the sound of rattling musketry filtering back. Rumors came to the brigade that night, including one that startled Smith's Regulars, suggesting Rebel cavalry was crossing a bridge to their front and about to ride down upon them. Dawn, of course, would prove that there was no Rebel cavalry. It would also prove, far more vividly, that there was no bridge.[36]

By the morning of Sherman's main assault, even privates like Henry Bear, 116th Illinois, had come to the conclusion that "Gen Grant is not here yet and may not get here." The sound of artillery and rifle fire to the front had increased markedly in intensity, and his comrades felt "the time has come for a great battle" into which they "may be called in any moment."[37] When their severely wounded and deeply beloved division commander was carried past, the seriousness of the situation was underscored further. Though having known him for but a short time, the green Illinoisans sensed the passion their brother regiments maintained for Morgan Smith. His wounding "throwed a damper on the whole army," Bear noted.[38]

At some point during the division's "sharp-shooting tournament" Giles Smith, no doubt significantly shaken by his brother's plight, joined Lt. Col. James Blood of the Sixth Missouri in a personal reconnaissance of the ground he anticipated moving the brigade onto once ordered to relieve Stuart at the sandbar. What he saw was not inspiring. "I found, with the exception of some fallen timber close down to the bank, a comparatively dry and unobstructed crossing until the opposite bank was gained," he noted, "which was found to be from 20 to 25 feet high and very steep." Provided a force could make it across, they would be forced to contend with an enemy of unknown size and character, as the Rebels opposite the division were "so securely posted that their existence there in force was not known," he later reported. Although a heavy skirmish fire had been kept up over the entire course of the day, none could be certain that the force confronting them was comparable in size to their own. Regardless, as Smith noted, the sandbar itself "was from 60 to 80 yards in length and only wide enough for a regiment to march by the flank," meaning that numbers in such a scenario would be of little tactical value.[39]

Nevertheless, early on the morning of December 29, after digesting Sherman's assault orders for the entire army the previous evening, temporary acting division commander Brig. Gen. A. J. Smith ordered Giles Smith's fresh brigade forward to relieve Stuart, and prepare "to cross the bayou and gain the hills on the opposite side."[40] Accordingly, Smith deployed his brigade in line of battle from right to left: Sixth Missouri, Eighth Missouri, 116th Illinois, and Thirteenth US Regulars, and moved forward to relieve Stuart, who left the veterans of the Fifty-Seventh Ohio scattered behind cover along the bayou to continue their sharpshooting during the assault.[41] Along with these Buckeyes, Smith deployed his yet raw Regulars to add their own sharpshooting to the brigade's base of fire. Anxious to take on Rebels for the first time, the Thirteenth US rushed quickly into position, deploying "close down to the bank" behind what cover they could find, and joining the Ohioans in skimming the top of the levee whenever Rebel heads showed themselves.[42] Bear and the 116th Illinois, along with Smith's beloved Zouaves, were deployed in column down the road—Bear referred to it as "in a string"—in preparation to exploit any breach.[43]

In plotting his attack, Smith showed the unmistakable influence of his brother's conservative tactical philosophy, as well as the many lessons learned at Donelson, Shiloh, and Corinth that had engendered an especial concern for limiting the number of troops placed into harm's way. Instead of carrying the levee with massed cold steel, he opted to open the assault by sending only a single company of Blood's Missourians, along with "a working party of 20 men" to "cross and try to construct a road up the [opposite] bank." Once the men had rushed across to the relative safety of the opposite bank under the covering fire of their comrades, they would undermine the levee so as to collapse part of it into the bayou and create a crude ramp which the remainder of the regiment—and then brigade—could use to rush over the steep embankment in the way of a breach. After Blood had hurried his Missourians over the bar and through the breach, the Zouaves would follow, trailed by the green 116th Illinois and the equally green Regulars. All of this would unfold in sequence at Sherman's prescribed signal for the army's main assault: "heavy firing from General Morgan's division," Smith later reported.[44]

Unlike with Blair's and Thayer's massed assaults on Sherman's left, effecting these dispositions and setting the attack in motion marked the real limits of Smith's ability to directly impact the engagement through personal leadership. Presumably, if Blood's spearhead was successful in creating a breach, he planned to lead the brigade across the sandbar and over the levee in person, but for now all he could do was anxiously observe his lieutenants' prosecution of his plans from the bayou bank. Ordering additional weight onto the point of attack could be accomplished fairly easily, but in the absence of a breach such a deployment could be disastrous.

Even from his position, Bear could see clearly how the few obstructions still blocking the route to the sandbar extended to within sixty yards of the

Rebel riflemen, who were ensconced behind the levee along the opposite bank, and that after clearing these "there was [still] a distance of [another] Sixty yards open space before we could get to their bre[a]st works which was nothing more than the levee." The single narrow approach would mean that "their whole fire could be centered [on the attackers], and we had to file through just as if we war [sic] going through a gate." Even with most of the brigade attempting "to pick them off as they stuck their heads up to shoot," the maneuver would be "a hazardous undertaking sure."[45]

As with every regiment in Sherman's command, Blood's Sixth Missouri was markedly understrength due to the long-term attritional effects of nineteen months spent in uniform, mostly hunting guerillas, combined with the miserable conditions recently faced, first packed aboard the transports, then sopping wet and freezing in the swamps. Though unfortunately the regimental morning reports from December 29 do not survive, fragments of several company-level reports are extant, their extrapolated average suggesting that the regiment probably had a fighting strength of about five hundred men that day. This made them the largest "old" regiment in a brigade of probably somewhere near two thousand men. From front to rear, the regiment in column, if tightly dressed, would have stretched over 150 yards—exceeding the width of the bayou by more than a hundred yards. If launched splashing across the water before a clear breach was affected, the narrow band of cover provided by the levee on the south bank would force the regiment to spread out further, requiring at least 250 yards of muddy bayou silt in which to crowd for survival. Ideally, the work detail would be able to dig through the levee and effect a gap wide enough to exploit with an assault. At minimum, it needed to erode or undermine the bank, which was estimated at about twelve feet high, before there was any hope of an attacking column preventing itself from being trapped under fire at the steep levee's base like an attacking medieval army caught in the *meurtrière* of a castle gateway.[46]

When the guns first became audible on the left, the Missourian spearhead set out on its deadly mission. Regulars and Ohioans redoubled their fire as the men debouched from the cover of the trees onto the open sandbar and rushed for their lives to the cover of the opposite bank. Rebel balls immediately filled the crisp air. Despite the protective blanket of fire, several never made it. Those who did immediately began to dig away at the levee. Enemy rounds, several fired blindly over the levee, wildly overshot their mark and sped balls into the brush near Bear and the anxiously waiting 116th Illinois. "We all fell to our bellies," he remembered.[47]

Watching the working party struggle against the odds, Smith "discovered a narrow, winding path up the opposite bank about 100 yards to the left and sufficiently wide for 2 men to march abreast." This would do in a pinch. "I immediately ordered the Sixth to cross," he reported, and so they did.[48] At the head of the party, Blood led his loyal guerrilla hunters in a rush across the bayou to the relative cover of the levee embankment, halting while struggling to find the path identified by their brigadier. "The balls played fine Music around our ears," John Mains of the regiment later wrote. "They Had breastworks and we Had none [but] we gave them the Best we know how."[49] As Blood searched for the path, the working party continued to dig feverishly, knowing that the Rebels now knew full well what was happening. When a spent ball from a Rebel musket slapped into Blood's chest and injured him "considerably," the officer required the assistance of two others to so much as remain on his feet but refused to leave his regiment.[50] Worse yet, when word finally made it across the Rebel line that an entire Yankee regiment was trapped under the levee embankment, all hell broke loose. Mains was close enough to hear the Rebels screaming about "the damned yankee sons of bitches" as they held their rifles vertically over the top of the levee and fired blindly downward into the throng to deadly effect.[51]

Unable to respond in kind, members of the working party tried to slap at the enemy muzzles with their spades while others attempted to "shoot the end of their guns of[f]," but the slaughter continued unabated.[52] After having poured in a rapid fire of shell with uncut fuse "for fear of endangering the infantry in front" for an hour as the working party mined the levee, Captain Peter Woods's supporting Illinoisan battery silenced so as to avoid fratricide.[53] This left it to small arms alone to suppress the Rebel defenses, which very quickly brought their own erstwhile silent artillery into action. Unfortunately, attempting to skim the parapet with rifle balls without striking their cowering comrades left a narrow band of only several feet above the heads of the Missourians into which suppressive fire could safely be aimed. Inevitably, many shots fell short, wounding and even killing brothers in arms. "We could hear them exclaim for to 'shoot higher, for God's sake—shoot higher!'" one Ohioan on the north bank vividly remembered. Hearing these desperate cries, Rebel voices from behind the levee sardonically screamed to instead "Shute Low[er]!"[54] Watching the desperate episode unfold in front of them, within eighty yards but unable to fire "for fear of hitting our men," Bear could only lament that it "was hard to see the brave boys of the Sixth Missouri die," taking solace knowing that "those that are dead are out of their misery."[55]

From Giles Smith's position on the north bank, he could tell the Rebels "were now being heavily re-enforced." To send additional regiments across would have clearly only contributed to the slaughter. Thus, at that moment, his actions focused on effecting the withdrawal of Blood's embattled Missourians before they were wholly exterminated. His ability to identify the contingency and take immediate remedial action stood in sharp contrast to Blair's and Thayer's impetuosity on Sherman's left. Instead of frantically wandering the battlefield in search of support, he calmly ordered the Zouaves into the brush alongside the Regulars and Ohioans as sharpshooters to contribute further weight to the covering fire.[56] The Illinoisans he left on their bellies. "I wish you folks at home could have seen the 116th hug the ground for more than half a day," Bear later commented. "It would make you laugh sure but there was no fun in it. We did not dare stick our heads up."[57]

As the afternoon turned to evening and the sounds of battle on the left died down, it began to rain.[58] The added weight of the Zouaves to the base of fire temporarily muted much of the Rebel willingness to harass the trapped Missourians, but extraction was still out of the question even in the fading light. Sending an order across to Blood to return under cover of darkness, Smith ordered the entire line to redouble its fire again at dusk in order to enable the recrossing once the sun dipped below the trees. With the Zouaves "fireing as hard as they could," Bear wrote, the survivors eventually made their way back across the sandbar in small squads, Blood along with them supported by two of his men.[59] The regiment had lost fourteen killed and forty-three wounded, including two officers, one dead and another, Blood, wounded.[60] Providing covering fire had not been without its dangers. The Regulars sustained their first combat death along with twelve men wounded, while the Zouaves, despite their brief tenure on the line, suffered three wounds. Even Bear's 116th, though mostly superficial, sustained five men lightly wounded. In total, Smith's brigade sustained seventy-eight casualties during the assault—fifteen of whom were dead. The brigade withdrew from the woods guarding the crossing and moved back about a hundred yards through a driving rain in the dark to join the rest of the division. They were exhausted, demoralized, and soaked. "We stuck our guns, our bayonets, in the ground," Bear remembered, "and sat down against trees till morning."[61]

"HAD OUR TROOPS BEEN A LITTLE
MORE EXPERIENCED"

That evening and into the next day a cold rain pelted the survivors as they huddled around small fires authorized only if lit well to the rear of the picket lines. While individual efforts to retrieve dead or wounded comrades continued into the morning hours, mutual suspicion on both sides prevented any formal ceasefire for another two days. In the meantime, Sherman and Admiral David D. Porter crafted a daring maneuver whereby Steele's half-battered division and Giles Smith's brigade would silently disengage from the front, embark aboard transports in the darkness of New Year's Eve, and be deposited under the heavy Rebel guns a short distance up the Yazoo at Drumgould's Bluffs to seize the same at bayonet-point. If successful, the operation would have threatened Vicksburg's northern defenses and given the expedition access to the desperately sought-after Vicksburg road. Perhaps fortunately, thick fog in the early morning of New Year's Day forced a cancellation of the plan before the flotilla could even get underway. Knowing full well that the army would find itself adrift in a veritable lake instead of merely mired in muddy bottomlands if rain continued, Sherman finally conceded defeat, and the army withdrew to re-embark upon the transports.[62]

As the men hauled supplies back onto the steamers, Sherman and his staff received word from Porter that an irate Maj. Gen. John McClernand had just arrived from Memphis with a personal note from President Lincoln guaranteeing him command of the entire expedition. Though irritated, Sherman was willing to concede the point and handed authority over to the political general. The two agreed that the army should withdraw from the Yazoo and regroup nearby in preparation for and contemplation of the next move to reopen the river to Northern commerce. Clearly, continued frontal assaults against the Walnut Hills were not promising. When word arrived that the *Silver Wave*, a Federal mail packet, had been captured by Rebels up-river and hauled to Fort Hindman near Arkansas Post on the Arkansas River, both men saw an opportunity. A victory, however minor, was desperately needed following the demoralizing repulse the army had just suffered. The vast numerical advantage they would enjoy in attacking the fort's purportedly meager garrison would make such a victory quick and easy by comparison to the struggle through which the army had just passed. While the specifics of which officer hatched the plan remain contested, the flotilla departed northward en route to Fort Hindman on January 3. Now in command of all four of Sherman's divisions, but still in ignorance of Grant's recent order reorganizing the army, McClernand dubbed the force the Army of the Mississippi, and divided it into two corps of two divisions apiece. In accordance with his wishes, Sherman was given command of his "old" Second Division and Steele's Fourth, now renamed the Second and First divisions respectively of Sherman's new Second Corps. The two remaining divisions comprised the First Corps under Morgan.[63]

Sherman turned his otherwise embarrassing replacement by a rank amateur into an opportunity to lay the groundwork for a formal narrative of events even before sitting down to craft his official report of the battle for Grant. Issuing a statement through general orders, read to every exhausted company by orderly sergeants aboard the boats, he attempted to guide the rank and file in making sense of what had transpired while trying to maintain some vestige of control over the conclusions they might reach amongst themselves. "We failed in accomplishing one great purpose of our movement—the capture of Vicksburg," he explained, "but we were but a part of a whole. Ours was but one part of a combined movement, in which others were to assist." He and they had been "on time," but "unforeseen contingencies must have delayed the others."[64] One Illinoisan could not be sure "who the others were but I presume he means Grant," he correctly surmised.[65] The order explained Sherman's forceful pushing of the assault "as far as prudence would justify." Many must have scoffed aloud at this between coughing fits. Finding the Rebel defenses "too strong for our single column, we have drawn off in good order and in good spirits, ready for any new move." McClernand had been chosen by President Lincoln, Sherman announced, in an awkward bid to lend his new superior legitimacy. He felt the need to remind them, and probably himself, that the president "has the undoubted right to select his own agents," and trusted "that all good officers and soldiers will give him the same hearty support and cheerful obedience they have hitherto given me."[66]

Sherman's official explanation of events fell upon the freezing ears of soldiers who had, for the most part, already made up their minds as to what had happened and why. Even so, these conclusions and the narratives they were embedded within tended to vary dramatically between regiments based on each unit's experiences during the week—what historian John Keegan has called their "personal angle of vision." The tangled terrain of the bottomlands had not only mitigated against operational coordination, but also carved the corps's experience of the contest into several distinctive "faces of battle," each with its own emergent narrative and lessons.[67]

Dejection and defeatism, though widespread, were not the exclusive themes of these narratives. Several, most especially junior officers, were already showing signs of a veteran's aptitude for stoically absorbing reversals. Scribbling a note home as the fleet prowled northward, Colonel Kilby Smith was struck by laughter emanating from a group of officers playing cards nearby. It seemed remarkable to him that men, "whose lives, twenty-four hours ago, were not worth a rush, who have been in the imminent and deadly breach, [and] who have lost comrades and soldiers from their companies," could so soon thereafter seem "entirely oblivious of the fact."[68] Of course they were not oblivious but were learning that camaraderie could often prove a powerful salve for depression. Firm resolve could serve a similar purpose. "I would rather stay here another six months than go back without taking Vicksburg," Lieutenant Jacob Ritner, Twenty-Fifth Iowa, proudly wrote home to his wife.[69]

Despite the assertions of resilience issuing from some, many more had had their fill. "I dont want to get in any hotter [place]," Henry Bear, 116th Illinois, admitted. "At least I want if I do to have a chance to Shoot too."[70] James Maxwell of the 127th Illinois agreed. "I hope I will never see another battle for I want the war to end as quick as possible," he wrote to his sister. "I don't care how they end it, only so it ends." Both Bear and Maxwell insisted that, while civilians may have thought they had some idea of a soldier's life, they "don't know anything about soldiering until they try it."[71] For Maxwell's part, "I advise never to enlist."[72]

Unsurprisingly, the most indignant of Steele's division were the survivors of Blair's battered brigade, who wasted no time in loudly proclaiming their outrage. Even as traumatized men still limped away from the shattered cornfield immediately after the repulse, a nearby *Chicago Tribune* correspondent overheard several "giving vent to extravagant charges of treason, jealousy, madness and folly in high places." Despite the confusion of the assault, it was painfully clear to survivors that the effort had failed principally due to a gross lack of coordination. "The day was full of misfortunes," one volunteer later observed, adding plainly that "the divisions moved without concert of action." Despite grievous losses, his Thirteenth Illinois had acquitted itself well for having undergone its baptism by fire under such trying circumstances. Of the 600 in the regiment's ranks at the beginning of the assault, only 423 remained in bivouac that night. "Participants at Pea Ridge and Shiloh say that no Regiment there was exposed to such an awful fire as we here," one young Sucker proudly wrote home.[73]

The spirits of the veterans filling the ranks of the mangled Fourth Iowa were also severely dampened. "We as yet have accomplished nothing," one infuriated Hawkeye lieutenant fumed after preparing the bodies of two of his company for burial. "What makes this so deplorable is that it was a useless sacrifice of life," he added, "and to tell the truth I am mutch discouraged & disheartened [that] our Gen[era]ls do not understand their business & do not appear to care for the loss of life no more than were we so many brutes." Gazing up for a moment at the miserable sodden boys littered around him in the mud he quickly added that indeed, "that we are." The sheer scale of the tragedy weighed heavily on the Fourth Iowa. Prior to landing in the bottomlands, each company had lost an average of 32 of its original enlistees over the course of its service. Many of these had fallen in the fighting at Pea Ridge, where the regiment sustained even heavier casualties than at Chickasaw. Despite the reception of more than 100 replacements at Helena, the unit still mustered less than half of its authorized strength. Most had departed with medical discharges due to disease or disability.[74] While potentially debilitating, these administrative losses were far more palatable to leaders who cared deeply for their men. "I would rather loose [sic] five men by discharge than one by death," one wrote.[75]

Thayer, their brigade commander, blamed Steele for the disaster due to his failure to inform him of his fateful impromptu order and Morgan for failing to drive his command out of the safety of the captured rifle pits.[76] Had he been supported properly, Thayer "felt certain that he could have taken possession of the rebel batteries and held them until the other divisions of the army could come to his assistance," one correspondent wrote. Steele blamed Morgan. Morgan blamed Sherman. Sherman blamed Morgan.

Round and round the fingers were pointed for the rest of each officer's lifetime and beyond. The only command relationship that was improved by the debacle was the bond formed between Thayer and Williamson. The two were spotted commiserating with each other and "crying like children over the result of their costly efforts" immediately after the repulse. When approached by a journalist looking for an interview, Thayer was too overcome with emotion to oblige. "Tears stood in his eyes, and his mingled grief and indignation so overcame him that he found it difficult to speak," the reporter wrote. Mirroring the laments of his officers, Williamson could only report that the heavy loss in his regiment was "doubly painful, as no advantage commensurate with the loss was obtained."[77]

Outside of the Fourth Iowa, the experience of Chickasaw Bayou was dramatically different for the remaining regiments of Thayer's brigade. Though all mourned the loss of their fellow Iowans, their bloody example caused many in the remaining units to quietly celebrate their accidental salvation. "We give God the praise, for he has preserved us amidst all dangers, and I feel like trusting him more in the future," one member of the Ninth Iowa remarked, while still admitting that "the present prospects before us are not so flattering." Indeed, though spared any more than some light skirmishing during the assault following their disastrous diversion, the veterans of the regiment were not immune from the collective disparagement that infected the whole army. "The boys think there is much bad mismanagement, in the Commanding officers," the Iowan noted. The men had no choice but to "look to our superiors for examples, and in many cases, what do we see[?] . . . Drunkenness, Profanity, and evil of all sorts," he observed. Such officers were unsuited to command, and the recent disaster was but additional evidence of the fact. "It was po[o]rly planned," another Hawkeye concluded.[78]

Even those of Hovey's brigade spared from the ill-fated assault fumed with anger against Sherman. "Gen. Sherman brought this army here a healthy determined lot of men who had every confidence that they could open this river before turning their faces north again," Sewall Farwell, Thirty-First Iowa, raged. Finding "an abrupt bluff" protected by "an almost impassable slough," Sherman had foolishly opted to send "regiments there entirely unsupported by heavy guns or other regiments until the whole army became discouraged and old regiments refused to obey orders." Then, as if that were not enough, "he beat a retreat without trying any other point." Was it any surprise, Farwell wondered, that the army was now "discouraged by such management?" For his part, "if we are to meet with failure and reverses such as these given over to blind leaders and false," he would far prefer "peace upon any terms" over "utter destruction."[79]

Rumors freely circulated that the army had failed because "our Generals didn't want to take it," that particularly bad news had been received confidentially "by our Generals which is kept from the army," that the Rebels had agreed to a ninety-day armistice, or even that "we were taken from active operations so as to witness the effect of the Presidents [Emancipation] procla[ma]tion."[80] Others quickly realized the groundlessness of most news that reached the ranks. The men "have had no reliable news from the North or the East since we left Helena," one Iowan remarked. "Here rumor succeeds rumor and no man can believe anything he hears."[81]

For the most part, members of regiments had only each other to probe for anecdotes of recent events. Most steamers were only large enough to hold a single infantry regiment with its panoply of supplies; thus, individual units found themselves isolated from one another after re-embarkation. On the rare occasion that soldiers from different brigades found themselves in a position to swap stories and cross-pollinate their internal regimental sensemaking processes, powerful transformations could result. Iowan friends and family in Thayer's and Hovey's brigades, occupying proximate positions along the line the evening following the bloody repulse, wandered among one another through the frigid rain searching for missing comrades and sharing stories as sporadic Rebel shells lit up the night sky. Survivors from nearby regiments "came around and told us how near they had come to being almost annihilated during the day and had barely escaped," Farwell wrote. It was their understanding that the fortunate spared portions of Thayer's brigade were to attempt another desperate assault in the morning, with Hovey's regiments in support.[82] This prospect was made all the more gut-wrenching when fugitives from other battered commands stumbled into the Iowan bivouac looking for their regiments, "telling how dreadfully they had been cut up in the fight & pronounced it impossible to take the heights in the way that had been tried," Farwell recalled.[83]

Combined with the terrifying sights of that afternoon, these tales were altogether too much for the Hawkeyes. "We wondered why it was we were given over to such destruction as this," Farwell remembered, "Why it was that wisdom had departed from our counsels, that our Generals were only competent to lead single regiments into ambuscades and between cross fires of artillery thereby destroying the army and accomplishing nothing." Though having been miraculously spared from certain destruction, the men of Hovey's brigade were not insulated from the despondency of the rest of the army. The lessons they derived from their experience in the Yazoo bottoms were colored by those of less fortunate units whose traumatic accounts deeply influenced the way in which they made sense of the event. Chief among these lessons was that "our Generals" were tactically incompetent, and not to be trusted in the future.[84]

The effects of these lessons on the regiments of Hovey's command first became evident just prior to the aborted New Year's Eve assault on the heavily fortified Drumgould's Bluffs. Silently withdrawn from the bottoms and re-embarked upon transports without so much as an inkling as to their destination, Farwell remembered how "all felt a sense of relief when they found the point of attack was to be changed." This solace was immediately reconverted into anxiety when regimental commanders returned from a conference with Hovey and relayed his instructions that Steele's division would land and "with unloaded guns and fixed bayonets [we] were to form . . . into column of companies and as fast as formed, we were to charge at double quick upon the batteries," Farwell remembered. "If any faltered or showed signs of running, those behind were to bayonet them on the spot." Given the brigade's total lack of trust in "our Generals," these orders were interpreted as veritable death sentences. "Many officers quailed before such a prospect," Farwell wrote, "men fainted away, pilots refused to guide the boats and were placed in the pilot house under guard and orders given that they be shot if they attempted to run from the post." Privates were "instructed that the danger was as great in the rear as from the front, and that the heights must be taken if every man should fall." One Iowan remembered how "every man whose bowels did not overcome his bravery, supposed that he had said his last prayer." Even the veteran German officers of the Twelfth Missouri "brooded about what was going to become of us" while they "braced themselves up with whisky and steadied 'file closers' by the same means." Another remembered only that the "prevalent feeling was that this was a 'forlorn hope.'" While, fortunately, the desperate affair was avoided due to prohibitively dense fog, the lack of confidence in Steele's division had been put clearly on display.[85]

Just as regiments which had experienced empirically distinctive versions of the battle drew highly particular lessons from the same, Sherman and his staff came to their own conclusions, retrospectively evaluating the performance of the new corps and gauging the relative efficacy of ordering it to conduct similar maneuvers in the future. As far as Sherman was concerned the only "real fighting" had been the main assault, not the deadly "sharp-shooting tournament" which had robbed the command of so many officers and men on the first day. Still, despite their valiant efforts, the amateurish performance of Blair's and Thayer's brigades disappointed him. "I am satisfied," he confided to Porter, "had our troops been a little more experienced," the attack would have succeeded.[86] Adjutant John Henry Hammond agreed, writing that, given "experienced and ordinate officers we would have succeeded, for the troops were good."[87] Thus, even as many of those in the ranks determined that mismanagement in the upper echelons of the army, indeed by Sherman himself, was chiefly responsible for the defeat, their commander concluded that the amateur nature of his force, most especially the officers, was the real culprit.

As with his lieutenants, Sherman's own ability to influence the success of the multi-division assault was mostly limited to actions taken in the breach. Having mulled over the frustrating situation confronting his divisions the evening before, Cump had turned to Hammond and the rest of his spartan staff with instructions to prepare orders for each division. The staffers scribbled into the early hours of the morning, ensuring that every order was "unusually minute in detail" and that "no contingency was left unprovided for," as Hammond remembered. "All and everything was foreseen and given in writing," he wrote, "with personal explanations to commanders of divisions, brigades, and even commanders of regiments." It was all characteristic Sherman. "The commanding general, always careful as to detail, left nothing to chance," the adjutant reminisced after the war. Much of this penchant for detailed orders was likely inspired by the general's lingering lack of confidence in the citizen-officers commanding most of the formations operating under his headquarters.[88]

When the preliminary barrage fell silent and the assaulting brigades moved forward, Sherman placed his headquarters at "a place convenient to receive reports from all other parts of the line" and scattered aides in every direction to maintain a steady stream of information. Only Hammond and a handful of orderlies remained with him, "in a position easy of access" to the rest of the army. While Sherman could watch much of the drama of

Morgan's and Blair's attack, his attention frequently drifted to his beloved "old division" at the sandbar. Accordingly, he dispatched Hammond "to see what I could, and report if I met anything that he should know." Galloping through the woods to Second Division, the adjutant found Blood's beleaguered Missourians strung out across the sandbar but still attempting to "turn the levee against the enemy," and turned back to give his chief the hopeful news. Unfortunately, given Cump's tendency to wander, Hammond was initially unable to find him. "I was not quite sure of my way back to the general," he recalled, riding through the tangled swamps toward the loudest fighting while keeping the muddy bayou in view on his right for direction.[89]

Happening upon Morgan amidst the din, Hammond was discouraged to hear the general inquire about Steele's date of commission, hoping to declare his seniority. "Fearing want of harmony," the adjutant left to find Steele, whom he likewise "found cursing Morgan so fiercely that I could not exactly make out the source of the trouble, or reason why." Unbeknownst to Hammond, Steele had taken umbrage at Morgan's request for support, despite Sherman's instructions. "I receive that as a request, and shall comply with it, but I cannot take it as an order, as I happen to rank General Morgan," Steele had curtly replied, similarly infuriating Morgan just as the assault stepped off. The operation's two most crucial proponents were seemingly more consumed with each other than with the bloody work at hand.[90]

Now with much more of concern to share with his chief, Hammond finally found Cump and provided the now greatly outdated news from the sandbar. As to the Steele and Morgan controversy, Sherman had little trouble believing it, but "could not be made to believe that any jealousy or personal quarrel could lead to failure to support each other." Nevertheless, he dispatched Hammond to the front again to track the forward progress of the assaulting brigades. Discovering to his great alarm that Morgan was still, contrary to Sherman's orders, on the friendly side of the bayou, the adjutant remonstrated with the irate general, but to "no satisfaction," and determined to press forward across the water himself. Always eager to taste the burning edges of the fray, he moved carefully through the Rebel abatis until he had overtaken the rearmost portions of Blair's swarm sweeping up the slope. Looking to his left and right, Hammond "was astonished to find how small a force was making the attack," when a Rebel shell suddenly cracked nearby. "The concussion confused me," and by the time he had "got my wits about me again," the attack was over. Bloodied and traumatized men streamed past him "slowly and sullenly" toward the rear, "far more angry than frightened."[91]

The perspective of the most important of Sherman's staffers illustrates many of the challenges the army's command-and-control network faced in the bayous. Cump's detailed orders left little to chance, but still failed to address the inability of an extended front deployed in vexing terrain to adapt to unforeseen contingencies in a coordinated fashion. A spartan retinue of staffers struggled to navigate the swamps with sufficient speed to keep a mobile Sherman apprised of developments, robbing him of any opportunity to resolve emerging problems. Friction and lack of trust between officers at the highest echelons combined with nightmarish terrain to spoil coordination at the most imperative parts of the attack. The battle Sherman's orders had envisioned to seize the Walnut Hills devolved into a fragmented collection of smaller uncoordinated actions managed by colonels and even captains. No frontal penetration of such an imposing position could ever be achieved under such circumstances.

As the boats plowed northward toward Fort Hindman, orderly sergeants in each company took stock of their losses and obediently submitted casualty reports and strength returns up the chain of command. These eventually made their way to Sherman's headquarters aboard the *Forest Queen* in aggregated and much abbreviated form, providing him with a glance of the corps's strength as it approached its next major challenge. Of the 1,776 casualties suffered by the army, half were sustained by Steele's and Stuart's divisions. Of these, 139 were killed, 569 wounded, and 183 captured. Though present-for-duty numbers plummeted by the day as tired, exhausted, and miserable men finally succumbed to colds and more serious illnesses contracted under the cold rain, the reports suggested that Sherman still retained most of the flesh and blood he had brought with him to the banks of the Yazoo.[92]

Even so, the numbers that reached Cump's floating headquarters in the aftermath of the Chickasaw disaster failed to represent the invisible changes that the traumatic experience had wrought within his corps. Chickasaw represented the first lesson in the new corps's practical military education as a combat team. The experience of the repulse had imparted not only an abstract appreciation for the dangers of excessive hubris, but also more specific lessons to the component elements of the new corps about itself. Though most of Sherman's veteran regiments carried with them the impress of prior campaigns into the mud of the Yazoo bottoms, the battle represented the first time all the subordinate units of the corps had operated together under his direction. Both divisions had behaved in accordance with lessons they had gleaned from the past experiences of their commanding officers and regiments. Steele's only recently cobbled-together brigades suffered predictably from a grievous lack of coordination only exacerbated by the nightmarish terrain of the bottoms. Second Division, on the other hand, avoided such destruction (even if it failed in its primary objective) through its customary conservative skirmish-centric approach to combat. Even so, in the end, as Sherman succinctly put it in his somber report to Halleck, the army had "landed, assaulted, and failed."[93]

Although the tangled terrain of the bottoms was mostly to blame for the debilitating breakdowns in coordination during the corps's operations, that breakdown still produced a systemic crisis of confidence at nearly every echelon of the new corps, which carried grave implications for the future. While Sherman and his headquarters staff lacked confidence in the inexperienced officer corps of the command, his division commanders had shown a troubling lack of confidence in each other while their brigadiers now felt they had good reason to doubt promises of support from adjacent formations. Although many junior officers disheartened by the recent events still managed to maintain confidence in the inevitability of ultimate victory, their strident efforts would be required to buoy the most jaded in the ranks.

While both Sherman and McClernand intended what they considered to be the all-but-inevitable forthcoming capture of Fort Hindman to bolster the command's sagging morale and collective self-confidence, if the outnumbered Rebels chose to put up a fight instead of capitulating, their regiments would have to earn their redemption with sweat and blood. Moreover, just as past experiences and lessons learned in previous campaigns had informed the operational behavior of the veteran half of the corps at Chickasaw, so too would the command's nightmarish experiences in the bottomlands and resultant crisis of confidence inevitably inform its actions upon future fields.

CHAPTER 3

NO TROOPS THAT CAN BE MADE TO ASSAULT

Arkansas Post

I have yet seen no troops that can be made to assault.

—MAJ. GEN. WILLIAM T. SHERMAN, JANUARY 16, 1863

As each man of Steele's division blindly staggered forward at close intervals, the swamp was periodically lit up with flashes of light as the heavy guns of Porter's boats hammered away at the fort.[1] Stumbling through the chilly January darkness in a "wet, low swamp, & thick timber" was a miserable undertaking. "Every two or three minutes" the column was forced to halt while the lead elements adjusted their trajectory, with only glimpses of the North Star through the canopy to guide them.[2] "We were tired, our feet were wet, some of us hungry," Sewall Farwell remembered. The Third Missouri, leading the division, had to corduroy portions of the route for even infantry to pass. For some distance, the brigade's howitzers "had to be carried through on the shoulders of the men." At one point, part of the column became detached from the rest after mistakenly detouring to the right and had to backtrack.[3] At another, the lead elements erroneously thought they had stumbled into enemy pickets, more likely those from Second Division, countermarched back through the mud, and took a separate route further north. "So we went back & forth *all night & no rest,*" William Seaward, Ninth Iowa, remarked. "Oh! Such roads, & such a night as we spent wandering about I hope I will never see again," he added. "So tired & worn out, & many fell out & *could not* stand it."[4] For more than eight hours, Steele's division meandered through a "labyrinth of roads," all of which Major Charles Miller, Seventy-Sixth Ohio, described as narrow and pockmarked with pools of standing water. "The heavy artillery and transportation wagons made a perfect mortar bed of it," he recalled, adding that the march "will ever be remembered by the weary supperless soldier."[5] The men exhausted from carrying the guns and the regimental and battery wagons mired in the muddy darkness, both Hovey and Thayer finally opted to abandon their trains and artillery, continuing through the night with infantry only and leaving the battery commanders and teamsters to make their own inimitable way through the quagmire.[6]

Finally, at around two o'clock in the morning, Hovey's brigade emerged from the swampy woods onto comparatively dry ground filled with log cabins that marked the deserted winter quarters of Fort Hindman's Rebel garrison.[7] The men were utterly drained. "My feet were wet and I was as near given out as I ever was," Jacob Ritner, Twenty-Fifth Iowa, wrote home. "My back was so lame I could hardly walk."[8] Another Hawkeye considered the march "one of the most tiresome, and disagreeable nights that I experienced in helping to put down the rebellion."[9] A swift search of the abandoned cabins suggested that their intended occupants had only recently fled. Fresh meat, cornbread, "cooking and camp utensils of every kind were left scattered in every direction," one Iowan observed.[10] Sewall Farwell, Thirty-First Iowa, was struck by the "strange contrast" the comfortable Rebel cabins presented when compared to the living quarters his men had endured aboard the crowded transports.[11]

Steele's aides dispersed and advised each regiment "to make ourselves as comfortable as we could without fires."[12] Several Iowans of Farwell's company shared their blankets with him, allowing for a little fitful sleep in the cold.[13] Ritner, on the other hand, "got no sleep that night" as the bitter cold kept him awake despite his exhaustion. It did not help "not knowing but the rebels were in the brush close at hand," he scribbled to his wife.[14] There were only a few hours before daylight anyway "left the weary soldier to snatch a little sleep," Miller of the Seventy-Sixth Ohio recalled.[15] Much of Thayer's brigade never made it to the Rebel cabins, halting instead to collapse in brush piles on the sides of the roadway.[16]

The Rebel garrison of Fort Hindman numbered less than 5,000 men to McClernand's nearly 32,000. Anticipating swift victory, he had, upon the arrival of the flotilla some distance east of the bastion, ordered the army to disembark and move to surround the fort by way of a circuitous route known to local slaves recruited as guides. Looking at his map, he envisioned in this envelopment the means by which "the enemy will be equally cut off from re-enforcements and escape, and must, together with his works and all his munitions of war, become a capture to our arms." If worse came to worse, however, the fort would be carried by the combined brute force of Porter's gunboats and an army-wide frontal assault.[17]

After disembarking on the morning of January 10, Sherman's two divisions had begun their approach march. With Steele in the lead, the corps stepped off from the landing area shortly before noon. At a crossroads just west of the landing, Steele's column turned northward on a road presumed to meander through the swampy woods before debouching somewhere west of the enemy's first line of trenches. Stuart's division, on the other hand, maintained a northwestward bearing down the levee directly toward the Rebel works straddling the road, skirmishing with enemy pickets along the way. Giles Smith's Zouaves, leading the van as usual, swept forward in their customary manner "from tree to tree," driving Rebel pickets through the trees and beyond.[18] "Steadily up the hill, sometimes crawling, again gliding behind trees and logs, went the Zouaves," a correspondent observed.[19] The capture of these trenches was uneventful. Their Rebel occupants had long since fallen back to reinforce the fort's garrison. It did, however, eliminate any need for Steele to continue his roundabout course, which was convenient given that the guides proved not in fact to know where they were going. After countermarching back through a dense swamp to the landing, Steele's tired and annoyed troops had only just started to prepare their rations for the night when orders arrived once again from Sherman to "take a northwesterly course" through the swamp in order to reach jumping-off positions for an assault on the fort in the morning. Thus, the torture had begun.[20]

By dawn, though many in Steele's exhausted division were barely upright, McClernand's two corps and four divisions were finally in position for the assault. While Steele's command had been groping through the dark, Stuart's regiments shivered in their positions along the line while the Rebels used fence boards to cut a long trench complete with head-logs and a protective abatis extending westward from the fort to woods that skirted a creek, effectively preventing envelopment of the bastion. These new trenches would have to be taken, along with the multiple batteries arrayed in support to their rear, if the fort was to be surrounded as per McClernand's plan. As the sun began to rise on the horizon, the challenge confronting both divisions was obvious at a glance. Rebel flags studded the line, each representing one of eight regiments. Far from the bloodless coup he and McClernand had originally intended, Sherman's corps would once again have to launch a direct frontal assault in order to achieve its tactical objectives.[21]

The plan was uninspiring to say the least. Relying on sheer mass alone, McClernand intended to assault the fort and trench simultaneously with the weight of no less than thirty-three infantry regiments and all the artillery he could bring to bear, supported from the river by the guns of Porter's boats. After a punishing two-hour preliminary bombardment, the entire blue line would surge forward as one, striking the Rebel works at the same moment all along the line in order to neutralize the enemy's advantage of interior lines. While sound on paper, McClernand's plan underestimated the challenges of coordinating such a massive host and the inevitable deep contingency of battle, just as Sherman's at Chickasaw had before him.[22]

While Blair's and Thayer's brigades had confronted attritional defensive tactics at Chickasaw that leveraged the increased range and accuracy of modern rifles to erode their attacking columns long before they reached the Rebel positions, exhaustive surveys of extant field reports conducted by historians Paddy Griffith, Brent Nosworthy, and Earl Hess instead suggest that, in the vast majority of assaults made during the war, defending infantry usually held their fire until an attacking formation came within about a hundred yards. While opening an engagement at close range gave up any advantages provided by the increased range of rifles, this tactic ensured both maximum accuracy and, most importantly, shock as a defender's volley slammed into a winded assault column. If well-timed, such a volley could so stun an attacker that his line might spontaneously reel and disintegrate, routing through supporting units to the rear and producing general pandemonium. A shock-reliant defense also entailed grave risk. Should the initial volley fail to produce sufficient shock to blunt an attacker's forward momentum, little time remained to try again. Conversely, in order for any attack to succeed, an assaulting line had to absorb a defender's initial volley and continue forward at maximum speed, spilling over and into the enemy's works like a tidal wave. The secret, Griffith explains, "was the deliberate acceptance of a higher risk in order to achieve a more decisive result." It required "an unnatural response to fear."[23]

Above all else, attackers collectively needed to believe that they could successfully make and survive an assault in order to maximize their likelihood of doing so. This degree of shared self-confidence was of greatest importance once the terrifying effects of enemy fire began to challenge the supposition. If a regiment could maintain its confidence and forward momentum through the crucible of a shock volley, the odds of a defender abandoning his position were relatively high. Attacking columns were almost never physically destroyed by fire, no matter how short the range. Instead, it was the psychological effect of a shock volley that blunted forward momentum. In the same vein, rarely would hand-to-hand fighting ensue should an attacker successfully reach a defender's parapet. Bayonet charges functioned more as psychological weapons than as tools of physical coercion, frightening the enemy out of his position. Contrary to popular belief, they frequently proved effective.[24]

There came a time in every such engagement, but most especially during frontal assaults, that historian Brent Nosworthy has termed the "penultimate moment," when combatants on both sides experienced "the beginning of a thought or emotional process, such as panic or even more reasoned thoughts, such as the need to retire." At this critical juncture, officers were well aware that "every incentive that can influence the actions of man" was necessary to sustain efficacy "even for a few moments longer [in order to] win the day." The reception of a defender's initial volley represented just such a moment for a charging regiment, and it was at this "penultimate moment" that a unit's collective self-confidence, shaped in large part by its particular history, could make all the difference.

The members of each regiment collectively encountered and experienced an engagement and its attendant penultimate moment within the specific context of their unit's particular operational heritage. For those in the ranks, every engagement was but an episode in a wartime narrative all their own, shared among all their comrades within the unit but distinct from those of even adjacent regiments. Every regimental banner represented a distinctive story, a cohort with an individual personality, character, and culture borne of all the distinctive trials that had led it to that particular place in time and space. While individual soldiers likewise inevitably forged their own personal narratives of service that allowed them to make sense of their experiences, the nature of contemporary tactics and communal military life led to high degrees of near consensus among members of a single regiment as they made sense of events.

As regiments endured successive traumatic episodes, the survivors inscribed the names of engagements upon the stripes of the unit's national flag, carried into battle alongside its regimental and state colors. This commemorative tradition represented more than a mere bid to inspire *esprit de corps*. When the men glanced upward at the ragged and torn standard of their regiment, they reflected upon a history of beloved friends lost, terror overcome, and learned strategies for mental resilience, physical survival, and tactical success. The place names themselves, though often replicated upon many banners throughout the army, represented very different things and invoked very different memories for each command, their semiotic character and value contingent entirely upon each unit's "personal angle of vision" and corresponding "face of battle" during each past engagement. Thus, as Sherman's regiments prepared themselves to meet this, their forthcoming trial by fire, they did so within the context of their own respective regimental narratives—a phenomenon that would play a powerful role in shaping both the manner in which they behaved in the crucial penultimate moment, and the ways in which the survivors made sense of the experience afterward.[25]

For this reason, the careful and thoughtful arrangement of regiments within assaulting formations by commanders was of enormous importance. While officers could not possibly anticipate what would befall a unit once it headed into the fray, they could "stack the deck" in their favor if they played their cards right. Still, even given exhaustive planning, achieving the coordinated arrival of multiple formations at their respective objectives was far easier said than done. Sherman knew better than most that "we cannot do as well on the ground as we can figure on paper." While the terrain confronting the corps at Arkansas Post as it prepared for its assault appeared, at least in most cases, far more conducive to the maneuver than it had at Chickasaw Bayou, the ground before each of the three brigades chosen to spearhead the attack was markedly different, threatening to dismantle the cohesion of the corps from the outset, just as it had along the Yazoo.[26]

At about noon on January 11, as the bombardment lifted and Sherman's batteries fell silent, Hovey's and Thayer's regiments of Steele's division came to their feet. "The enemy had ceased firing at us," Farwell of the Thirty-First Iowa later wrote, "but as soon as we raised, the shots were again sent whirring at us." Although sporadic incoming artillery fire "created considerable excitement" among the green levies, initially the Iowans had "no difficulty in keeping order in the ranks."[27] As the five hundred veterans of the

Seventy-Sixth Ohio arose, they took one last glance at the obstacles ahead. "The Rebel line of works could plainly be seen," Adjutant Charles Miller remembered. "The ground was comparatively level and partly covered with timber to our right, but in our front there was little covering save some underbrush and deadened timber."[28] Though estimating that the regiment would have to pass over nearly six hundred yards of open ground before reaching the enemy works, Colonel Charles Woods finally decided it would be most prudent to dismount along with his staff, "and go into the charge on foot."[29] He ordered his Ohioans to fix bayonets and to "make the charge without firing a shot." Emphasis had to be placed on maintaining forward momentum, and any halt to fire would slow the velocity of the attack. "The prospect looked anything but inspiring and all felt that of necessity there must be fearful slaughter in our lines," Miller remembered. While the regiment, along with the remainder of Hovey's brigade, had been spared the bloodshed at Chickasaw, Woods's veterans of Donelson and Shiloh knew well what was likely forthcoming.[30]

One of Steele's aides rode directly to Colonel Milo Smith's green Twenty-Sixth Iowa, at the front of Thayer's brigade, with orders to advance.[31] From where Smith's regiment was formed, "the enemy's line of rifle pits . . . were plainly visible," William Royal Oake wrote. "The timber that had formerly covered the intervening space having been about all cut down by the enemy, thus giving them a good view of the column coming over that comparatively level stretch of ground."[32] Though level, the "thick underbrush" to the front of Thayer's brigade, as well as "the want of space for a front of the brigade," necessitated that the brigadier advance his regiments initially in column. After the traumatic debacle at Chickasaw Bayou, such a necessity must have been difficult to swallow. Just as at Chickasaw, once through the worst of the nightmarish terrain, Thayer planned to deploy each of the regiments into line "as fast as we could get a front."[33] Having detached the bloodied Fourth and Ninth Iowa to Blair's reserve out of mercy, given their recent experiences at Chickasaw, Thayer's brigade was led by two green regiments: Smith's Twenty-Sixth and Lieutenant Colonel W. M. G. Torrence's Thirtieth Iowa. "I gave direction [to the regiment] to follow up close by the right flank of the first battalion," Torrence explained, "to form line of battle on its left, at a designated point if practicable, and, if not, to form line of battle in its rear, and advance as it advanced and halt as it halted, and in every move to act in conjunction with it."[34] He knew his rank and file remained almost entirely green, spared total destruction by Steele's error two weeks prior. If the experience through which they were about to pass could be broken into smaller, more manageable tasks, they were more likely to retain their momentum. That is, of course, provided that Smith's Iowans—themselves just as green—stayed on course.

"At a given signal," Col. Francis Hassendeubel's Seventeenth Missouri leading Hovey's brigade, comprised principally of German *Turnverein* gymnasts, were ordered to spearhead the assault on Steele's right by advancing further south "through the woods along the bayou." The Turners prided themselves on athleticism and marksmanship, both of which Hovey and Steele had been quick to perceive at Chickasaw. Accordingly, the regiment quickly became the division's dedicated light infantry force, routinely used to screen its movements from the front and flanks and earning it the informal title of "Hassendeubel's sharpshooters." The Germans had accumulated the most impressive record of achievement thus far during the war of any regiment in Hovey's new brigade. With their brother Germans of the Twelfth Missouri now detached to guard the brigade's supplies at the transports, the Turners were the only unit on the field in Hovey's command that had ever conducted a charge, having successfully assaulted the wavering Secessionist line on the second day at Pea Ridge. More recently, a brush by several companies with a contingent of Texas Rangers during the march to Helena had left several dead and the regiment fiercely embittered when word spread that most of the casualties had been slaughtered in cold blood after surrendering.[35]

Behind the Turners, Hovey deployed Colonel Isaac Shepard's Third Missouri. Shepard had never personally seen combat. A Massachusetts native, and radical Republican, his limited experience in drill during his brief antebellum command of the Boston militia had netted him a position as Nathaniel Lyon's aide-de-camp at the battle of Wilson's Creek. A kick from the general's horse, however, incapacitated him just prior to the dramatic contest that took Lyon's life. While a handful of the regiment's older members still remembered a bloodless advance of three companies against fleeing Rebel cavalry at the Battle of Carthage, most had never experienced combat. They had chased bushwhackers from hideouts in the brush, but the crucible of battle had thus far evaded them.[36]

Ideally, the veteran Turners to their front would shield Shepard's amateurs from the impending storm of Rebel fire. They, in turn, would shield the even greener troops of William Smyth's Thirty-First Iowa following behind in support. A portly Irish lawyer, Smyth along with his cohort represented the fruits of Lincoln's most recent call for volunteers. Under arms for less than six months, with the exception of a handful from older commands—many of whom were reported "ill" and remained in the rear—the regiment was barely more than a crowd of civilians with elementary instruction in drill. Even Smyth himself still had trouble remembering the proper commands on the parade field, having to rely on a low-toned inquiry to his only slightly more experienced adjutant: "Lieutenant, what shall I say?" In the interest of everyone's safety, Hovey ordered Smyth's greenhorns not to fix bayonets or affix percussion caps to their loaded rifles, but rather to follow closely behind Shepard's line awaiting further orders.[37]

Almost immediately after setting off through the woods on their approach, Hassendeubel's skirmishers were "attacked on the flank" from the opposite bank of the bayou "much more violently than was anticipated," prompting them to deploy the entire regiment. Spying a handful of Texan cavalry, their archenemies, through the trees, the Turners quickly changed front to address the new threat and, in doing so, removed the protection of their veteran experience from the assault. Piling into a ravine for cover, the Turners returned fire across the bayou. The remainder of the formation continued forward through the trees. This adjustment to Hovey's front converted the inexperienced Third Missouri into the assault's lead element.[38]

All across the line, the men of Steele's division screamed at the top of their lungs—yells "which were to be the signal for the gunboats to cease firing," one explained.[39] Shells slammed into the Arkansas mud as enemy batteries redoubled their efforts, but the Rebel infantry occupying the trenches to the front ominously held their fire.[40] In the comparative open on Hovey's left, "with alacrity and with wild yells," Woods's Seventy-Sixth Ohio launched into a double-quick toward the works, with Colonel George Stone's Twenty-Fifth Iowa following closely behind. Almost from the beginning "a tempest of canister and grape from the rebel batteries" tore into the line. The exhaustion from the previous night's forced march told on the strength of both regiments—most especially with those who had become ill during the hardships of Chickasaw. Adrenaline alone proved insufficient. "I was very week [sic] and they double quicked it about half [a] mile & I could not Keep up," Hawkeye Lieutenant Adoniram Withrow admitted.[41] Another "started with the rest but the brush were [sic] so thick and I was

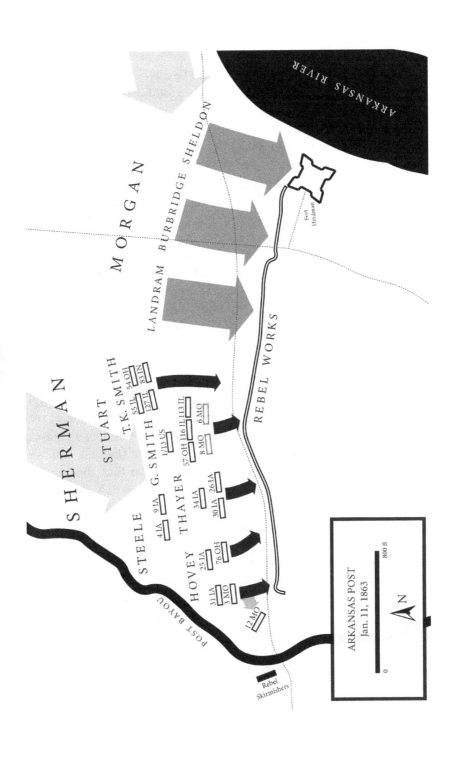

ARKANSAS RIVER

ARKANSAS POST
Jan. 11, 1863

N

0   800 ft

Rebel
Skirmishers

POST BAYOU

SHERMAN

MORGAN

STUART

LANDRAM

BURBRIDGE

SHELDON

T.K. SMITH
54 OH   83 IN
55 IL   127 IL

G. SMITH
57 OH 116 IL 113 IL
1/2/1 US   6 MO
8 MO

STEELE

THAYER
4 IA 91 IA   34 IA   26 IA
30 IA

HOVEY
25 IA 31 IA
76 OH 3 MO
12 MO

REBEL WORKS

Fort
Hindman

so weak that I was soon left behind."[42] Others who were not quite so ill also straggled. Oake, making the assault with the Twenty-Sixth Iowa, noticed "an old fashioned rail corncrib" that stood in the middle of the division's line of attack, behind which accumulated "skulkers from the different commands that had been ordered into battle." The terrified men "could not be shamed out of their place of supposed safety," he recalled.[43]

The major differences in terrain confronted by each of Steele's assault columns quickly dismantled the cohesion of his attack and carved the two brigades into three separate, if proximate, attacking pairs of regiments. As Thayer's column on the left moved through heavy brush, attempting to find an opening wide enough for more than a single regiment to deploy into line, the Third Missouri and Thirty-First Iowa on Hovey's far right struggled through the timber, skirting the bayou at a snail's pace. At the same time, Woods's Ohioans and Stone's Iowans in between them, constituting Hovey's left, outpaced both wings due to the comparatively open terrain to their front.[44] Thus the division inevitably fell upon the Rebel works in piecemeal fashion with disastrous results.

"SO HOT AS TO MAKE IT IMPOSSIBLE"

Bolting unknowingly ahead of the remainder of the division, Woods's Ohioans accidentally became the tip of Steele's spear. As the foremost prong of the attack, they also drew the concentrated fire of the enemy batteries and came into the range of Rebel infantry sooner than those on the division's wings.[45] Though most of the 600 yards covered at the double-quick was over open fields, a thin belt of trees stood roughly 75 yards from the Rebel works.[46] Just before and beyond the tree line, the enemy had constructed rude abatis out of "brush and fallen timber" in an effort to make the final approach to the only available cover exceptionally dangerous.[47] This combination of obstructions "considerably impeded the movements of the regiment," Woods noted. As the winded and now disheveled Ohioan formation reached the abatis, at about 250 yards the Rebel works finally awoke with a volley of small arms and canister.[48] While not fired at sufficient range to constitute an attritional defense, the volley was also fired too early to produce ample "shock," most especially because most of the poorly aimed Rebel rounds whizzed overhead. Opening at such distance, however, allowed for several more volleys before the Ohioans reached the works. After the Secessionists reloaded quickly, the next "fell plump into our lines," Adjutant Miller lamented, "and made considerable havoc."[49] More than a dozen Ohioans immediately fell dead, and another fifty-seven were wounded by the single fusillade—nearly 15 percent of the regiment's combat strength, "but the men kept straight on," Miller remembered.[50] The veterans of Woods's command safely endured their "penultimate moment."

Conversely, twenty paces behind, the Hawkeyes of the Twenty-Fifth immediately dropped to the ground when the shooting began. One Iowan noticed how the men instinctively sought the "slight protection afforded by the stumps and brush," and several of them nervously "commenced firing" at targets of opportunity against all orders, threatening the Ohioans still to their front.[51] Noticing immediately that their supports had gone to ground in terror, the veterans were outraged that Stone's levies had "left us exposed to the concentrated fire of the Rebel regiments." As the Seventy-Sixth now represented the lone regiment of the division still standing and visible along the forward edge of Steele's advance, they immediately attracted all Rebel fire within range. "About three regiments strong," Woods reported, "opened a destructive fire of musketry upon us from the front and right and left, extending on the left to the full extent of the range of their muskets [rifles]."[52]

Although an attacking regiment's success against a shock-reliant defense was principally contingent upon its resilient response to the impact of a defender's initial volley, the arrival of but a lone regiment to an enemy parapet was of little real tactical value. A defender's line had to be confronted along the entirety of its frontage simultaneously. If attacks arrived piecemeal, their foremost regiments would face not only the shock of a volley from the enemy to their immediate front, but also from enemy troops on both flanks for a distance of potentially hundreds of yards in either direction. It was through this enfilading fire that the increased range of rifled muskets could make the greatest difference. Defenders finding themselves unchallenged to the front could contribute their fire to an attacker far distant with much greater accuracy when armed with rifles than with muskets. Should this bloody contingency occur, an attacker would find himself, as did Woods's Ohioans, confronted with both a (short-range) shock-reliant and (long-range) attritional defense simultaneously.

While much of the fire concentrated on Woods's beleaguered regiment was still mercifully "too high," enough of it found its mark to stall the forward momentum of the veterans. Recognizing that he had outpaced both Thayer to the left and the Missourians on his right, Woods still did his best to drive his Ohioans through the tree line and across the final seventy-five yards despite the heavy fire incoming from three sides. They would have none of it. As soon as the line reached the relative safety of the trees, "the fire became so hot that the regiment faltered, but held its ground," Woods recalled. Knowing full well they were unsupported, the men instinctively "all dropped on their faces," Miller remembered.[53] Woods still did his best to urge them on, to keep them moving forward. "Finding it impossible to push the regiment over the open ground," he tried ordering them to fire "to give them confidence." He was immediately struck by the result. "After the regiment opened fire not a man flinched." The Buckeyes each fired multiple rounds from the prone or behind trees, when Woods again tried to drive them forward, "but as soon as the men raised to move forward the fire was so hot as to make it impossible," he reported.[54]

Accepting that the regiment was immovable, Woods's shifted to providing suppressive fire from the trees that might keep Rebel heads down long enough to allow adjacent units to drive home their own assaults. Though the head-logs running along the tops of the Rebel pits covered the forms of the enemy infantry and made them a difficult target for prone riflemen even at close range, the Rebel batteries and their horses were clearly visible just beyond the trenches. Here was an opportunity. Woods "ordered the men to clear and silence the guns of the enemy in our front," he reported, and the Buckeyes made short work of it.[55] "Not a single shot was fired from their two Parrott guns in our immediate front," Woods remarked, the rifle fire making the guns too dangerous to man and the killing of their horses rendering the heavy pieces immovable.[56] An enemy gun "some distance to our left" drew Woods's attention. A handpicked squad of the regiment's "best marksmen were ordered a little in advance," Miller remembered, "and, while protecting themselves as best they could behind trees, picked off the gunners of the battery which they completely silenced."[57] The remainder of the regiment continued "skimming the enemy's parapets with musket balls," suppressing the Rebel infantry and creating an opportunity for Stone's terrified Iowans to finally arise from cover behind the abatis and rush forward to join their veteran comrades along the treeline.[58] From there, they joined in the target practice. "Some got where they could see something to Shoot at and Kept popping away," one lieutenant remarked after the fight.[59] A few particularly zealous Hawkeyes "fired forty or fifty Shots," expending almost all of their ammunition.[60]

Stone made a point to "at all times" be visible "at the head of his regiment," one of the command wrote. The colonel even "made several good shots with a rifle borrowed from one of the men, who was not so good a marksman," he added. Stone's executive officer "was as cool and collected during the fight as if he had been at home," and further strove to rally the more anxious and encourage them "by his example."[61] The Ohioan command team behaved similarly. Woods "exposed himself in the thickest of the fight," Miller recalled. "His large form was a conspicuous mark, but he was perfectly cool and walked about, twisting his mustache and breaking sticks as was his habit, with an eye on all that was transpiring."[62] Even Stone's Iowans later commented on Woods's coolness under fire.[63] His brother, the regiment's executive officer, "would not lie down, but walked up and down the lines encouraging the men and exposing himself," Miller noted. "A bullet struck his revolver with such force as to bend the barrel, but it saved his life as otherwise it must have shattered his thigh fatally."[64]

Beyond the lack of further enemy artillery fire, however, the smoke made it difficult for any shooter to judge the real effectiveness of his fire. "Quite a number of men were seen to drop as if killed or wounded, but to what extent the enemy suffered from our fire I cannot tell," Woods later admitted. For many, the only viable targets were the arms and weapons of Rebels who "did not dare to show their heads," but instead "just put their arms over and fired at random," Miller wrote.[65] The two regiments remained "advanced as far as there was cover for our men" for several hours, laying down a heavy suppressive fire from cover and triaging their casualties.[66]

"OUR BOYS FELL LIKE FLIES"

The dense woods that hampered the advance of the Third Missouri and Thirty-First Iowa ended abruptly before the enemy trench, where Rebel infantry had "felled all the big trees and thrown them helter skelter in front of their rifle pits," John Buegel, the Third Missouri color-bearer later observed.[67] Sewall Farwell also remembered how, in this no-man's-land between the trees and the trenches, though the ground was "tolerably level," the Rebels "had cut the thick grass in such a way as to impede our march all that was possible."[68] Prior to the assault, one of Hovey's aides instructed the column to "advance as close as it was practicable to be before the charge was made," using the woods to shroud themselves while the skirmishers held the harassing Rebels on the opposite bank of the bayou at bay.[69]

As elsewhere along the line, the terrain made it difficult for any regiment to maintain its cohesion. Following behind the Missourians, Iowan officers and sergeants worked at "preserving as good a line as was possible under the circumstances," Farwell recalled. The column had not moved very far, however, when Rebel gunners sensed its approach and began blindly shelling the trees. As shells whirred and cracked through the limbs, the two regiments quickly halted and laid down. After the rounds detonated, the line arose again and rushed forward until the guns again were heard.[70] "We lay down on the ground and continued to advance and drop down when they would shell us untill we got within a short distance of their works," one of the Hawkeyes explained.[71] Looking around during one of these tactical pauses, Farwell "noticed trees and stumps were much sought for and those who had been in service before and honored for their bravery were among the first to seek them."[72] The inexperienced were happy to follow the lead of the few scattered veterans among them.

When the Missourians finally debouched from the trees into the open, the column charged at the double-quick "with loud cheers and the usual war cries," Farwell wrote.[73] As along Woods's front, the protected Rebels held their fire as they approached. Maneuvering the line through the abatis proved challenging, but a single "large open gap" beckoned to the Missourians.[74] Carrying the regimental colors as a marker of the column's forward progress, Buegel entered this gap. Watching the flag approach the parapet, Hovey "confidently expected they would enter the works," he later admitted.[75] At that moment, however, within about "one hundred paces," Buegel recalled, the Rebels opened fire. "The blue beans [bullets] flew into our ranks, bringing death and destruction," he wrote.[76] The Missourians were cut down not only by fire from the Arkansans to their front, but also from the right—"a quarter unexpected and therefore not guarded," Hovey lamented.[77] As they struggled to climb over the obstacles and force themselves through the gap, the Third Missouri disintegrated under fire. "It was impossible to get over the barricade," Buegel remembered. "We were all crowded into a trap, and our boys fell like flies. It was terrible."[78] Behind them, the neophyte Iowans watched in horror as the "old" soldiers they counted on to steel them fell apart. Farwell looked on as the Missourians "staggered and fell to the ground . . . when someone in their line cried that the order was to retreat." Accordingly, the regiment "sprang to their feet and with the rapidity of lightning dashed back upon us."[79] The result was chaos. "Whoever was still able to walk, ran back but most of them were killed or wounded," Buegel observed.[80]

Their veteran anchor now in full rout, the Iowans acted instinctively. "Someone in the rear called out to retreat," Farwell remembered, unsure as to the identity of the voice. "I saw that the right wing of the regiment was retreating and I also gave the order which the men were not slow to execute," he shamefully added.[81] In a desperate attempt to stem the flight, Smyth personally "dashed forward and called the men to rally." Farwell set himself to aiding the colonel in salvaging the shattered unit. As one Iowan color-bearer had been struck down by canister, and another cowered behind a nearby tree, the regiment lacked a rallying point amid the smoky chaos. To solve this, Smyth and his adjutant seized the colors themselves. Farwell cried for his company to form on the standards and "almost alone, to her honor," it began to do so.[82]

"As soon as we rallied we commenced firing," Farwell wrote, "and it seemed to have excellent effect upon the spirits of the men." As along Woods's front, the green Iowans found empowerment in returning fire. "I felt afraid until I fired my gun the first time and after that I felt no fear at all," E. Burke Wylie remembered.[83] "All became cool and went to work in earnest," Farwell explained. "The balls whirred by us but no one seemed to mind them very much." Still, a few of the junior officers "were unable to hide their trepidation," Farwell remarked in disgust, "and two had to be severely reproved for setting a bad example before their men, or rather behind them." Pushed back toward the tree line but still in the open, the men used what scant cover they could find.[84]

As casualties mounted, with at least a fragment of the regiment now under control and the other half beginning to rally in the safety of a small ravine a short distance to the rear, Smyth tried to reconsolidate his command. "An order finally came that we should retreat to [the ravine] and reform the regiment," Farwell wrote. "This was done in good order, the stragglers from most of the companies falling into their places."[85] A short distance away the shattered Third Missouri also caught its breath, having suffered a tremendous blow. Over the course of a single day, the Missourians had taken seventy-five casualties, fourteen of whom were dead on the field. The rapid retreat of half of Smyth's Iowans preserved them from a similar fate. Only fourteen Hawkeyes were wounded in the attack, none killed.[86]

"WE DISTINCTLY HEARD THE WORD 'FIRE'"

On Steele's left, trailing behind Woods's Ohioans as the column of regiments meandered through the dense underbrush, Smith's Twenty-Sixth and Torrence's Thirtieth Iowa led the equally green Thirty-Fourth Iowa in the assault. Lacking the cover that sheltered Hovey's right wing, the men did their best to move swiftly while "shot and shell flew thick," William Oake recalled. The Hawkeyes were also in the unique position of acting as the tip of Thayer's spear though neither unit had any prior combat experience whatsoever. Unlike Shepard's Missourians on Hovey's right, both had only been under arms for a little over three months' time. While many of the officers in both regiments had previously served in other units, most of the rank-and-file were entirely raw, lacking the confidence to endure a jarring shock volley. Withholding the battered Fourth and Ninth Iowa from the fight was an act of humanity, yet Thayer's merciful decision came at a cost.[87]

The Rebels patiently held their fire as the Iowans approached, allowing the gunners to their rear to hammer away at the moving target. As shell and canister cut through the brush, Torrence, rushing forward in column alongside Smith's command, continued to hunt desperately for an opening wide enough to deploy into line beside them to prevent the entire Rebel front from concentrating its fire on the Twenty-Sixth Iowa alone. He had no luck. The terrain was frustratingly uncooperative. Thayer's already undermanned attack now became a mere file of regiments streaming through the brush piecemeal to attack one of the strongest portions of the enemy line.[88]

Approaching within a few hundred yards of the Rebel works, Iowans looking anxiously ahead could clearly make out "a glistening array of steel protruding over the breastwork [and] under the headlog," Oake remembered.[89] Finally, within about 150 to 175 yards from the works, the brush dissipated into an open plain.[90] Torrence "instantly formed line of battle" and began to shift into position to support Smith.[91] At a distance of 75 yards from the works, though, the Iowans almost ceased to exist. "We distinctly heard the word 'Fire' given," Oake reflected. "To describe that moment requires an abler pen than mine."[92] As Rebel lead slammed into the line, the Iowan colors fell, rose, and then fell again.[93] Torrence's Hawkeyes were likewise stopped cold, and he instinctively screamed orders to "fire, lie down and load, and fire lying down" over the din.[94] The few surviving officers of Smith's command also screamed: "Lay down and protect yourselves, and give it to them the best you can," Oake vividly recalled.[95] Both regiments fell to the mud so quickly that Rebel officers later remarked how the Federal "ranks seemed actually to wither under our fire."[96] The cost in life among the Hawkeyes of the Twenty-Sixth rapidly mounted. Smith himself was badly wounded and carried rearward along with his adjutant who had suffered "part of his jaw . . . carried away."[97] Those still alive returned the fire from the prone.

As elsewhere along the line, the only targets still visible while laying low were Rebel batteries to the rear of the pits. "The moment that an artillery man showed himself at the embrasures fifty shots would be fired at him," Oake recalled. Meanwhile, one section of Missourian howitzers had been manhandled through the brush to within supporting range of the Iowans and "did splendid execution," Oake cheered. The suppressive fire of the German guns of Clement Landgraeber's battery likely saved many Iowan lives over the next several hours. Oake himself was fortunate enough to discover a slight depression where he and two noncommissioned officers huddled out of the enemy fire. "It seemed to us as though it were raining lead," he later wrote, "but still we were untouched."[98] Perhaps fortunately, as the full attention of each and every Hawkeye was focused on remaining close to the ground, there was little time to contemplate the human destruction in their midst. Almost a third of the regiment now lay either killed or wounded before the works.[99]

"A SERIES OF RUSHES"

The legacy of Morgan Smith's Zouave-style tactical philosophy was on full display in Second Division as it pursued its assault objectives. From his vantage point that morning, Stuart could see across what he described as a "large open field, where the enemy had their cavalry barracks," beyond which was a line of earthworks clearly manned by Rebel infantry.[100] Sherman ordered him to "advance one brigade and deploy it in line of battle across the field" in preparation for assault. Accordingly, Stuart ordered

Giles Smith's brigade into line, flanked on the left and right by his Illinoisan light batteries.[101] Kilby Smith and his brigade were "held at hand (out of sight of the enemy)" on the division's left in reserve.[102]

Gazing over the plain, Smith estimated the distance to the enemy works at about one thousand yards.[103] Unlike Steele's legions, Stuart's division enjoyed the benefit of being under the eye of their corps commander. Always anxious for recognition in spite of his obscure surname, Kilby Smith reveled in the idea that "my command was under the immediate eye of the generals." To his front he saw nothing but "a beautiful level plain, a little ascending to the fort and spacious enough to admit of three regiments in line" stretching over a thousand yards before the Rebel works. "The day [was] as bright and beautiful as ever gladdened the heart of man," he later recalled.[104]

After coming into line, the division laid down to rest while awaiting the lift of the preliminary barrage.[105] Stuart's understanding of Sherman's orders was that the division was "to advance at the expiration of three minutes after the fire from the batteries had ceased." While this interpretation was not incorrect, Stuart apparently assumed that this meant the gunboats too would fall silent for three minutes. Actually, the silence of only the army's batteries marked the signal for the assault. Thus, when the army's guns ceased firing after about half an hour of bombardment, but the gunboats continued, Stuart evidently thought little of it.[106] Suddenly, though, through the lingering smoke, he noticed Thayer's brigade on his right surging forward. Immediately anxious, he appealed for advice to Sherman, who was fortuitously nearby. "He commanded the advance at once," Stuart reported, and Second Division began its attack.[107]

As bugles rang out, Smith's brigade stepped off at the double-quick across the plain, with Kilby Smith's following 150 yards to the rear in support.[108] Just as along Steele's front, the Rebel infantry patiently held their fire. Not until Smith's front had reached within 150 yards of the works did the trenches finally erupt.[109] With this, all forward momentum stopped, but unlike with the nervous levies of Steele's brigades, Smith's seemed to drop as if on cue. The entire division promptly laid down and began to "seek the best shelter the place afforded."[110] The ground fronting the enemy works was wide open, with the exception of "logs, stumps and torn down chimneys" scattered about irregularly.[111] Having arrived far ahead of Thayer's column on his right and even the First Corps elements assigned to attack on his left, Smith, like Woods far off to his right, realized the brigade was receiving the fire of every Rebel in the vicinity.[112]

Sending back a messenger to Stuart to report these developments, Smith decided, also like Woods, that his first priority was silencing the enemy artillery. With most of his brigade behind logs or nestled in slight depressions, and still hoping that support would materialize on his left or right, he determined to spend the intervening time picking off enemy gunners.[113] The brigade had just the command for the job. "I now deployed the Eighth Missouri on the right," he reported, pulling the Zouaves out of reserve. Together with the Sixth Missouri, the two scattered behind the scant cover ahead as they formed the division's trademark skirmisher "cloud."[114] A correspondent at the rear watched as the Missourians "turned the felled timber, which the rebels intended should impede their approach, to excellent advantage as a screen from the grape of the rebels." The riflemen "crawled up within musket range of the enemy's breastwork, and, securely posted behind logs, picked off the gunners as fast as they showed their heads."[115] Stuart ordered Kilby Smith to donate the Fifty-Seventh Ohio from his brigade to plug the hole left by the deployment of the Sixth Missouri as skirmishers, retaining a veteran presence on the brigade's right flank.[116] While the "cloud" worked to silence the enemy batteries, Smith's green levies, now safely behind cover, could still fire on the works from the prone.[117]

Once the Rebel pits were sufficiently suppressed by the close-range rifle fire of the Zouaves, Stuart's command could fully apply its signature tactics. Smith ordered "a series of rushes" to restore forward momentum. It worked. "The ground gained from time to time under the hot fire was occupied by skirmishers, when the main line advanced accordingly and lay down," an Illinoisan explained. The entire division moved forward "spasmodically," covered by a screen of skirmishers dispersed behind cover.[118] As the riflemen moved carefully from cover to cover, firing at opportunity, they eventually silenced all Rebel guns in range, "not only picking off every gunner who showed himself above the works, but killing every horse belonging to the battery," Smith reported.[119] Henry Bear of the green 116th Illinois in the brigade's center, experiencing his first direct enemy fire, "shot 32 rounds" at Rebels in reply. "The Balls came close to my head but did not hit me," he later wrote.[120] Exposing oneself for long enough to acquire a visible target and pull the trigger without receiving an enemy ball in return was no simple task given the circumstances. "Protected by their earth-works, and possessing a great advantage over us, they fully appreciated it," one correspondent observed from nearby, "and no portion of flesh belonging to the Confederacy was needlessly exposed."[121] All along the Rebel lines, only "rows of dodging heads" could be seen.[122]

Even given the effectiveness of the Zouave-style tactics, without proper coordination with the remainder of the corps and army, both Smith and Stuart knew that no assault could succeed. The firefight continued for hours with no support arriving on either flank.[123] Finally, in the interest of adding firepower to the line, Stuart ordered Kilby Smith to deploy his brigade on Giles Smith's left, making up for the lack of support.[124] Amid what Kilby Smith described as "a perfect hurricane of shot and shell," Second Brigade pushed into the smoke. Tying into the 113th Illinois on First Brigade's left flank, Kilby Smith's command found cover and began to add to the din. "Had it not been for the protection of lying down and an occasional depression in the ground, the casualties would have been serious," remarked one of the Fifty-Fifth Illinois.[125] As it was, though the "fighting was quite severe & although the bullets flew around like bees swarming," another of the 127th Illinois remarked, "not a man of our Co. was wounded." After one enemy bullet "passed through Capt. Riley's hat and through a blanket that Newby carried," however, it was clear to all that the Rebels absolutely meant business.[126] In all, Second Division would suffer 24 killed and 154 wounded during the assault.[127]

Though the corps had been stopped cold before the works, and thus had failed to achieve its orders to break through the Rebel line, the volume and effectiveness of its fire had major effects on the ability of the enemy garrison to react. Colonel James Deshler, the Rebel officer commanding the mix of Texans and Arkansans to the corps's front, later reported how, while his riflemen's volleys had stopped each and every blue column short of the works, "they kept up a very heavy and unremitting fire with long-range rifles upon us" which all but eliminated his ability to make tactical adjustments and shore up gaps in his line. At one point, in an attempt to fill a hole on his left with reinforcements from the right, the incoming fire from Stuart's division forced all of the Rebels "to crawl on all fours in our shallow trench the whole distance."[128] Deshler also commented on the impact of Smith's skirmishers and First Division's efforts to silence Rebel artillery. "The enemy concealed in the timber along the front of the line kept up such an unremitting and intensely hot skirmishing fire," he reported, "that it was almost impossible for a man to show himself without being struck." Of the horses attached to the guns assigned to his support, "only one or two escaped being either killed or wounded." Along the adjacent Rebel commander's front, extending partially across Stuart's line of attack, "fire of artillery and small-arms was so intensely hot that no one could have passed from the general's position to mine without being struck."[129] Thus, despite failure to achieve their primary objective, by about 4 p.m., Sherman's corps had brought all but local Rebel command and control to a halt, achieved total suppression of enemy artillery, and neutralized vast stretches of the Rebel trenches with "very heavy and unremitting" fire from behind cover. Of course, such accomplishments could not last indefinitely. The ammunition supplies available to each regiment would be exhausted unless Sherman or McClernand could take advantage of the situation.

As both generals gradually became aware of the stalemate along the front and began to plan one final surge to seize the fort and trench by force, a white flag suddenly arose over Fort Hindman. Rebel command and control having broken down completely, with communications between the rifle pits and the fort all but severed by fire, the bastion's commander, Brig. Gen. Thomas J. Churchill, saw the writing on the wall. No reinforcements seemed forthcoming, and despite the tactical success of his infantry guarding the flank against Sherman's assault, the beleaguered Secessionists in the fort itself could not hope to hold out. Wholly unaware of the flag, many of the Rebel regiments in the pits continued to fight until panicked word finally made it to the incredulous powder-begrimed men in the trenches that the battle was over. Equally incredulous as to how the blunted assault had somehow achieved victory, Steele's and Stuart's regiments were slow in getting to their feet and cautious to advance. Finally mustering up the courage to tread out into the open and through the abatis, Second Corps claimed all the surviving Arkansans and Texans as prisoners. The battle of Arkansas Post was won.[130]

That evening and the next day were taken up with the long process of burying the dead, accounting for captured men and supplies, dismantling the fort and works, and stealing much-needed rest. Across the past month, the unique character of long-term amphibious operations had proven both a blessing and a curse. The army's operations never extended far enough from the boats to require wagon trains, and both Sherman's and McClernand's emphases on maintaining a swift operational tempo ensured that all but absolute combat necessities remained aboard the boats. Limited amounts of rations, ammunition, and medical supplies necessary to prolong the endurance of the divisions were off-loaded along the levees skirting landings, with one regiment from each brigade detached to guard them.

For those in the ranks, the absence of a supply train somewhere to the rear made little difference. Far more poignant was the continuation of Sherman's orders prohibiting knapsacks, overcoats, blankets, rubber ponchos, or any other defense against the elements, all of which were to be left on the transports so as to ensure maximum speed.[131] Most went for long stretches "without any pretense of shelter," and with clothes that "were completely wet and stayed that way on the boat."[132] Even the comparatively dry steamers had become "perfect pest houses" and cesspools of all types of pathogens that eroded numbers at roll call and on the battlefield. Companies quartered on the unprotected hurricane decks "taking storm and sun" directly had it the worst. "It is worse than Prisson [sic]," one Iowan complained.[133] Lower decks echoed with "the groans and coughs of our sick men all around," an officer remarked.[134] Even those who managed to remain in the ranks suffered terrible colds. After laying in the open with no cover under the frigid rain at Chickasaw Bayou, Private James Maxwell found he coughed so painfully at night "that it almost kills me."[135] The constant drain of effective strength from every regiment severely depleted combat power, to include the mass necessary to successfully carry out frontal assaults, while simultaneously overburdening outnumbered medical staffs.

Sherman's new corps paid a steep price for its commander's prioritization of maximizing speed. The consolidated morning reports filed by orderly sergeants across the two divisions showed an aggregate of about 18,000 men present for duty when the flotilla set off southward from Helena on December 15.[136] In just over a week that number had plummeted by more than 30 percent to 12,500 effectives. Fewer than 1 of every 5 of these losses were attributable to the fighting at Chickasaw Bayou.[137] By February, after suffering another 600 combat casualties at Arkansas Post and enduring a brutal steamer passage through the snow back toward Vicksburg, only 11,750 would answer roll call. This amounted to a loss of nearly 200 effectives from the ranks of the corps every day, or nearly one per regiment every three hours. Hardship did not spare even Sherman's headquarters. By the time the expedition was re-embarked following its victory at Arkansas Post, nearly every member of the corps staff was either suffering from illness or incapacitated and bedridden.[138]

The rapid deterioration of effective manpower over the course of the winter was most starkly evident at the regimental level. Whereas Steele's and Smith's regiments averaged about 645 effectives when the flotilla departed Helena, by January 1 they averaged only 400—a manpower loss that cost each regiment more than eighty yards from the average unit's frontage. By the arrival of the fleet at Arkansas Post that number had dropped even further, with many regiments fielding only a few hundred effectives. Several newer regiments, disastrously undergoing their customary "seasoning" period while simultaneously enduring intense hardship, were devastated by illness. The 116th Illinois, for example, boarded the steamer *Planet* on December 19, having reported more than 680 men present for duty just four days prior. By January 15, after suffering 5 killed and 13 wounded during the previous month's fighting, the regiment's effective strength had been halved. Only 280 privates answered roll call, whereas the staggering and still growing sick rolls showed an increase of nearly 300 percent from just a month before.[139] Other new commands fared similarly. The Thirty-First and Twenty-Fifth Iowa regiments, both undergoing their baptisms by fire that winter, suffered between 30 and 40 percent losses in present-for-duty strength between December 15 and January 15, despite relatively minimal combat casualties. In fact, although the Twenty-Fifth sustained 11 killed, 51 wounded, and 3 captured, mostly during its assault at Arkansas Post, the regiment suffered fewer total losses to its effective strength that winter than did the Thirty-First, which reported only 14 wounded across both battles but a nearly 40 percent reduction in turnout at roll call.[140] Over just one month the length of the battle lines of all three regiments had shrunk by nearly a hundred yards.

Despite these dramatic losses, however, the most significant changes were invisible. The brutal repulses suffered by almost every regiment of the corps at one point or another between the winter's two major engagements inspired an emergent aversion to frontal assaults that took the form of a markedly lower degree of confidence when the men contemplated assaulting enemy works. Such self-doubt represented the gravest of all possible threats in the penultimate moment of a charge. Worse yet, most of the rank and file attributed the worst of their suffering aboard the transports and under fire that winter to "mismanagement" by "our Generals." Few had yet completely lost their trust in and hope for the Republic's ultimate survival, but most agreed that, unless the Army's highest ranking officers tried a different approach to subduing the rebellion, the best blood of the western states would be poured out onto southern mud in vain.

As the corps reboarded the transports in frigid sleet that gradually transformed into a blinding snowstorm, the survivors of each regiment discussed their recent experiences together, and the winter's second phase of sensemaking unfolded. Just as in the aftermath of the Chickasaw repulse, the context in which sensemaking took place played a major role in shaping the character of its by-products. "The men have wet feet, wet blankets and overcoats and no place to dry them," Sewall Farwell complained. "They are cold and though the cabin is open to them, not one in twenty can get around the fire." Regiment by regiment sidestepped carefully down the slippery levee through the freezing rain to climb back aboard the boats. Many slid down the embankment and "carried portions of the soil of Arkansas Post for months afterwards."[141] Officers confiscated any and all contraband loot from the fort that several soldiers attempted to smuggle on board.[142] The Ninth Iowa became lost in the jumbled mass of men and animals after having spent the previous night lying on the riverbank in the rain without any protection whatsoever.[143] The exhausted regiment "had our patience tried well, for we knew not which boat we were going on and moved around in the dark," one wrote. The Hawkeyes were drenched and freezing by the time they finally climbed aboard the *Hiawatha*. Once aboard, the sounds of coughing and wheezing filled the decks of every steamer as soaked, freezing men huddled together and shivered, or tried to get what little rest was possible "on our Wet Blankets."[144] Most had enjoyed no opportunity to bathe in weeks, and many were tormented by lice acquired aboard the transports.[145] "You can imagine what a state of things we are in at present," Farwell lamented.[146] "The boys felt it was bad management," another understated.[147] Despite the victorious seizure of the fort, Cpt. Jacob Ritner had "never felt so bad in my life" as he did the day his Iowans climbed back aboard their transport. "To see the men huddled on the boat, crouching and shivering without being able to get to the fire" crushed his spirits. Not even the horrifying sight of the mangled dead strewn across the Arkansas Post battlefield had fallen with such force upon him. "When I saw the men today exposed to the storm and could do nothing for them I had to go to my room and 'take a cry,'" he confided.[148]

Historians have traditionally identified the victory at Arkansas Post as a badly needed boost in the erstwhile debilitated state of morale in Sherman and McClernand's expeditionary force following Chickasaw Bayou. Captain Farwell, shivering aboard his transport, anticipated this somewhat disingenuous conclusion. "Generals will be applauded for things which should subject them to the severest censure," he explained home. "The army will be represented to be in a condition and to possess a feeling entirely false from the real facts of the case." To be sure, most were pleased at the fortuitous victory, and while conditions might have temporarily dampened their enthusiasm, the corps was most certainly in better spirits than it had been during the departure from the Yazoo. Even so, the experience of the battle left a much more complicated mark on the command.[149]

Given the similarities between the "faces of battle" all along Sherman's corps line, the experience of Arkansas Post imparted a set of widely shared lessons that became part of the practical military education and emergent tactical culture of the corps as a whole. By far the most salient lesson learned by those in the ranks underscored one first taught amid the deadly "sharp-shooting tournament" at Chickasaw Bayou. When under enemy fire, one was most likely to survive if fighting from the prone or behind cover. Throughout the corps, men spoke and wrote about the salvation a low profile provided. "If we had stood up nearly every Ball would have cut a road through our ranks," one Iowan reflected.[150] To be sure, the inclination to lie down immediately upon the receipt of hostile fire did not have to be trained. The human body naturally reacted to danger in this manner. Still, for all its practical common-sense advantages, going prone under fire represented a blatant repudiation of the contemporary prevailing cultural discourse of battle. The lithographs adorning the covers of popular periodicals like *Frank Leslie's Illustrated* and *Harper's Weekly*, where the majority of the "fresh levies" comprising half of Sherman's corps had obtained their preconceived notions of combat, rarely if ever depicted men fighting from the prone. Instead, tightly dressed lines stood manfully under the heaviest of enemy fire, as if boldly daring the Rebels to cut them down. To reduce one's profile by cowering or sheepishly taking cover was evidence of indiscipline or even shameful cowardice.[151] Almost to a man, the experience of real combat had shorn the volunteers of these opinions. Greenhorns took comfort in observing how veterans "that have been in service since the war commenced are just as afraid of balls as those who have never been under fire," and were often just as quick—if not quicker—to lie down and seek cover. In this transformation they were helped along by the junior officers of both divisions, few of whom apparently saw any practical virtue in standing manfully before almost certain destruction. Ever increasingly, the close-order formations of the parade field were interpreted by those in Sherman's corps as being more tools of maneuver than of fighting, serving to deliver units to the point of contact, but were rarely maintained under fire. The actual exchange of gunfire most frequently took place from either the prone, individually "firing at will," or while behind cover, and usually dispersed as skirmishers.[152]

Skirmishing placed a premium on the leadership of noncommissioned officers. As only three commissioned officers served in each company (usually fewer actually present for duty), when companies dispersed as skirmishers their control was principally the duty of sergeants.[153] As the tactical culture of Sherman's corps drifted toward an emphasis on skirmishing, these enlisted leaders found themselves ever more central to the performance of their companies and regiments. In several cases, companies found themselves commanded by sergeants when the combined trials of steamer passage and campaigning robbed them of all their officers. As the hardship of amphibious life aboard the transports cut wide swaths of men from the ranks, reducing the mass of every command, the appeal of skirmishing tactics only increased. Lacking sufficient replacements, most veteran long-service regiments were fast transforming into what Sherman would soon refer to as "skeleton regiments," lacking any appreciable mass to hurl at the enemy. A preference for skirmishing over mass-based assault tactics was not merely convenient for these rapidly shrinking commands, it was obligatory.[154]

While the combined traumatic experiences of Chickasaw and Arkansas Post purged the popular image of brazen bayonet charges by close-ordered masses from the minds of most in the ranks of Steele's and Stuart's divisions, the fortuitous, if brief, euphoria of unanticipated success inspired problematic conclusions. Although both divisions had failed miserably in their primary tactical objective to seize the Rebel pits by force, the surprising surrender of Rebel forces produced the illusion that it had been the firefight itself that had prompted the garrison's capitulation. As one Hawkeye in the Thirty-First Iowa put it, the Rebel garrison must have surrendered precisely because "their artillery horses were killed . . . and all their guns on the Fort silenced" by the combined fire of infantry, artillery, and Porter's boats. What other choice did they have but to capitulate? Under the circumstances, even regiments like Farwell's Thirty-First Iowa, which had been temporarily routed after being broken by the fleeing survivors of the Third Missouri, could feel that "our regiment behaved very well all things considered." After all, the Hawkeyes had eventually rallied, gone to ground, and returned fire until the surrender. As far as they were concerned, their honor remained intact. "Had we broke and run as that regiment [Third Missouri] did, we would have been disgraced," he observed, "but I find old regiments can do with impunity what would brand new ones with cowardice."[155]

The beginnings of an altogether new tactical discourse emerged within the ranks of Sherman's corps. Certainly, many of the men assumed, "our Generals" had learned, just as they had, that frontal assaults were sheer suicidal madness. "I think experience has taught them that it is better to be a month taking it [Vicksburg], without loosing fifty men, than take it in an hour with a loss of five thousand," one Iowan considered. Sewall Farwell hoped desperately that "what has been learned" over the past two bloody contests would inspire "good management" among the high command, lest "the same fate" would await if the corps was again ordered to charge. Still, should better minds not prevail, the experience of survival and fortuitous success at "the Post" taught most of Sherman's volunteers that, if ordered to carry enemy works by frontal assault, the best way to survive with one's honor intact was to manfully endure the storm of Rebel artillery during the deadly rush forward until reaching the artificial cover of the abatis, go swiftly to ground when the shooting started, and continue a close-range exchange of gunfire. This tactic could eventually, if the lessons of "the Post" were trusted, result in Rebel capitulation. This formula for success was far more likely to ensure the survival of the rank and file than the bloody-minded tactical discourse enshrined within the popular idea of battle wherein a charging regiment would carry its assault to fruition through cold steel.[156] As this alternate discourse gradually emerged as one of the first widely shared artifacts of the corps's emergent tactical culture and was summarily combined with the widespread distrust of the martial competence of "our Generals," Sherman's command found itself organically evolving into a poorly designed tool for frontal assaults.[157]

Sherman's official "military family" likewise engaged in sensemaking based upon the experience of the battle. They placed the battle within the context of their past experience as the old Fifth Division headquarters. "The result of this affair is no doubt quite important," aide-de-camp Captain Lewis Dayton observed in a missive to his chief's wife after the battle, but "the fighting compared with Shiloh was not a good quail hunt."[158] The army had landed and "floundered around in the mud looking for roads" before finally launching its decisive assault the next morning. The Rebels proved "very stubborn, fighting well," he admitted, but with Porter's heavy guns combining with those of the army, victory was inevitable. Dayton shared Sherman's favoritism of Second Division, as well as his tunnel vision, noting proudly that "our old Division did what fighting there was" and that "if there is any credit attached to it (and I am sure there is) it belongs wholly to Genl Sherman's council, planning and execution."[159]

By Sherman's own estimation, the assault on the fort, despite the nearly six hundred casualties in his corps, "was not a Battle but a clean little 'affaire' success perfect." Like Dayton's, this judgment was based upon his past experience. Losses had been "comparatively light," and he officially reported "far less straggling than I have noticed in former battles and engagements." Privately, though, he had serious misgivings. "I have yet seen no troops that can be made to assault," he complained to Ellen. "We did not do it at the Post. We merely went through the motions."[160] Professional officers like Sherman, having received their military education at the US Military Academy, had long stubbornly embraced what historian Michael Bonura has termed the "French combat method," which deeply informed the entirety of the West Point curriculum, Army regulations, and all officially prescribed drill manuals during the war.[161] This cultural framework emphasized the absolute centrality of offensive tactical operations, ultimately resulting in the *sine qua non* of battle: the bayonet assault and "physical penetration of the enemy line." Such a penetration represented "the culmination of all battlefield operations," and thus French tactical culture "encouraged the offensive in every conceivable operation, at every level of war, [and] in every decision on the battlefield," Bonura explains. In fact, even when charged with fundamentally defensive objectives, French military thinkers urged officers to do so "only until they could launch another [counter] attack."[162] A culminating stalemate like that experienced by his corps due apparently to its failure to continue advancing through the heavy Rebel fire represented the antithesis of military effectiveness by this measure. Due to the limitations of Sherman's capacity to conceive of alternative offensive tactical paradigms that emphasized anything other than the bayonet, the event hardly even seemed a real "battle" by his estimation.

Sherman's concerns were shared among other staffers, gradually emerging as a consensus at corps headquarters. Adjutant Hammond was particularly unimpressed by the behavior of Steele's division in the fight. The assault columns attacked far too gradually, "Men & Officers very backward," he noted with frustration in his diary.[163] He shared his chief's disappointment with the seeming unwillingness of either division to drive home their assault. Both proved amply courageous in advancing under heavy shellfire to the protection of an abatis, but then promptly went stubbornly to ground as soon as Rebel infantry opened upon them. Most of this he attributed to shoddy leadership by inexperienced junior officers. "I could easily have stormed the work if there had been good company officers," he insisted.[164]

In truth, the failure of Sherman's corps to carry the Rebel pits, defended by a meager force not half their size, had far more to do with a lack of inter-brigade coordination resulting from the particularities of the terrain fronting the Rebel works than it did with the raw inexperience of half the command. Even the most combat-experienced regiments of the corps conducted themselves under fire in much the same manner as the greenhorns once they realized they had no protection on their flanks. The veterans knew well that any breach in the enemy line unsupported from the rear could be just as disastrous for an attacker as it was for the attacked. Regardless of the cause, the combined repulses at Chickasaw and "the Post" left an indelible mark on the adolescent command as its commander and those in the ranks simultaneously came to divergent conclusions as to what had happened and why. Perhaps most importantly, the combined failures significantly lessened the confidence of Sherman and his staff in their new corps's ability to carry Rebel positions head-on at the point of the bayonet. Sadly, it did not yet completely rule out the possibility in their minds.[165]

CHAPTER 4

EXPERIENCE WHICH WOULD SERVE US

Young's Point, Steele's Bayou, and Deer Creek

I think with the policy now being carried [out] that we are
crushing the rebellion and will continue to crush it though we be
repulsed from every stronghold for months to come.

—CPT. SEWALL FARWELL, THIRTY-FIRST IOWA, APRIL 22, 1863

As the flotilla crawled southward from Fort Hindman through a snowstorm, Sherman's despondent regiments shivered aboard their cramped transports. One Hawkeye worried that the "cold and exposeyer" suffered by those riding aboard the open decks would "kill more than we lost in battle." Another was convinced that if "we do much more steam boating we will all play out."[1] Overhearing alarming conversations among his coughing Missourians, Lt. Col. A. J. Seay, Thirty-Second Missouri, began to smell "signs of mutiny" in his deteriorating regiment. The brief morale boost following victory at "the Post" was proving wholly insufficient to steel the men against the hardship of prolonged life aboard the boats.[2]

Just after noon on January 15, 1863, from his perch upon the deck of the *Forest Queen,* Sherman noticed several steamers headed downstream toward the flotilla. He knew they did not belong to the fleet, but nevertheless hoped they might contain the most recent newspapers, and thus dispatched an aide to check. "You can imagine my surprise when he soon returned with Hugh [Ewing] looking as fine as possible as a Brigadier with his morning Report in hand and orders to report to me," he wrote home to his wife.[3] After months of politicking by Cump, the brigade of Brig. Gen. Hugh Ewing, his foster brother, had finally been assigned to his corps, joining Sherman's beloved "old Division" as Stuart's third brigade. Containing the Thirtieth,

Thirty-Seventh, and Forty-Seventh Ohio regiments alongside the Fourth West Virginia, Ewing's brigade came directly from duty in the Eastern Theater, and thus hailed from an operational heritage distinct from that enjoyed by the rest of the corps. Ewing's Buckeyes had not suffered through either of the recent brutal repulses. They had spent their time chasing guerrillas through the rugged mountains of western Virginia in operations not greatly dissimilar to those many of Sherman's "old" regiments had conducted in Missouri. The Thirtieth Ohio, Ewing's own original command, came with one notable distinction in that it was now the only regiment in Grant's Army of the Tennessee to have also served in the Army of the Potomac. After enduring especially bloody fighting at the battles of South Mountain and Antietam, the men of the Thirtieth had proven themselves capable of standing up to severe punishment under Rebel fire. The Ohioans were unquestionably veterans, but it remained to be seen whether the character of their prior combat experience had prepared them for the challenges they would now confront.[4]

Over the course of the late winter and early spring of 1863, the regiments of Sherman's corps would find themselves assigned a very different set of operational objectives from those they had pursued during the recent campaign. As Grant's army labored to gain access to the Rebel "Gibraltar" at Vicksburg, the Lincoln administration sought to deliver its most direct blow yet to Southern slavery, having now unequivocally identified the "peculiar institution" as a critical Rebel center of gravity. Although most in Sherman's corps had long been aware of the president's preliminary Emancipation Proclamation, in January the edict officially took effect, ordering the emancipation of all slaves in those states still in open rebellion against the government by US armies in the field. Farther South than almost any other US field army, the Army of the Tennessee became the natural spearhead for this new policy of "war in earnest." Grant wedded the administration's new tactic of proactive emancipation to his ongoing quest to pry open the "Father of Waters." As he plotted a series of ill-fated attempts to bypass Vicksburg or reach the high ground to its north and east, his army also waged extractive warfare amid the bountiful plantations of the Deer Creek Valley to its north which sustained the Rebel garrison.

Across a four-month period, Sherman's two divisions were assigned missions associated with all three of these efforts. Each of them required an adaptive response by the Fifteenth Corps. The experiences the men had

DEER CREEK VALLEY
Spring 1863

0   15 mi.

N

while engaged in these noncombat operations gave rise to an emergent "soldiers' culture" within the corps. Still reeling from the hardship and loss that defined Sherman's winter expedition, those in the ranks were ripe for an altogether new "way of war" promising greater odds of both survival and success. While their western cultural roots prevented most from ever fully embracing the revolutionary implications of the government's emancipation policy, the practical military qualities of both abolition and "war in earnest" quickly proved attractive. Sherman's volunteers were eager for the opportunity to punish the prodigiously wealthy Southern planters who inhabited the magnificent plantations of the southernmost portions of the Mississippi Valley. In the eyes of those in the ranks, these slaveholders were those they held most responsible for the war. Deeply frustrated with their inability to strike a powerful blow at the enemy on the battlefield, the chance to do at least as much damage to the rebellion without so much as firing a shot proved immensely cathartic.

"THE POINT"

Arriving along the levee at Young's Point, Louisiana, in mid-January with the rest of his army to take command of the entire force, Grant wasted no time in getting to work. The bloody results of Sherman's direct assault on Vicksburg left little doubt as to the relative efficacy of repeating such an attack. Instead, Grant hoped to bypass the "Gibraltar of the Mississippi" altogether. Restarting an abandoned project begun the previous summer by Black laborers overseen by troops under Maj. Gen. Benjamin Butler, Grant planned to cut a wide canal across De Soto Point directly across from Vicksburg which would redirect the path of the mighty river and render the city strategically insignificant. By allowing riverine traffic to pass freely beyond the range of Rebel artillery atop the Vicksburg bluffs, the plan would effectively convert the city into an inland town.[5]

Grant chose the new corps of his most trusted subordinate to lead the way in this endeavor. Sherman's miserable corps finally landed at Young's Point on January 23 and established camps along the trace of the abandoned canal ditch and upon the levee extending below it along the bend in the river. The canal, or rather its beginnings, ran a little over a mile across De Soto Point, with the spoil piled up on its eastern bank to protect laborers from the Vicksburg batteries. The ditch itself, when Sherman initially surveyed it, measured roughly ten feet wide and six feet deep, still filled with innumerable stumps. His corps was charged with widening the ditch by nine feet. Additional detachments would labor to put the few roads to and from the canal into functional condition. Employed immediately after their disembarkation from the misery of the steamers, the men did not initially appreciate the opportunity for exercise. Sherman took note of the disaffection in the details. "I have never seen men work more grudgingly," he remarked.[6]

The technical exigencies of canal construction prompted Sherman's corps to make its first substantive adjustment to force structure. Desperately short of trained engineers, Grant issued a special field order in early December prompting all divisions of the army to organize a "Pioneer Corps" of mechanically inclined men detailed from the ranks. As Sherman's two divisions were then absent from the army, it was not until Grant rejoined the command in late January that the corps's pioneers were organized. While whole regiments detailed to fatigue duty, along with increasing numbers of freedmen, could provide muscle and sweat, most volunteers lacked the technical expertise to fashion trustworthy bridges, repair levees, or dig viable canals. These tasks required men with "mechanical skill and fitness" who could "superintend Mechanical & Engineer work." Brigade commanders were to root out such soldiers from within the ranks of their regiments. Each was responsible for detailing fifty men as pioneers, further divided into two detachments, each under the command of an officer or sergeant. This armed each division with six such detachments, all under the command of a lieutenant. As soon as the detachments had been formed, they were assigned supervisory duty at the canal.[7]

The western regiments that comprised Sherman's corps were rarely hard-pressed to find such "mechanical skill and fitness" within their ranks. Men who had worked as blacksmiths, carpenters, engineers, machinists, or mechanics comprised just under 10 percent of all enlistments into the average regiment in Stuart's division, which led the way in the canal project. The Zouaves of the Eighth Missouri boasted nearly a company and a half worth of men with a technical background. By late January, it is likely that the division's camps contained more than a thousand men with relevant mechanical skills, and thus brigadiers could afford to be picky in their selection of fifty from their regiments while still leaving the majority in the ranks to assist in carrying out more technical assignments.[8] To orchestrate the unskilled labor provided by the regiments themselves, Sherman divided the canal into 150-foot segments and assigned each to a separate regiment. First and Second Divisions alternated daily in providing five-hundred-man work details, reporting each morning to the corps chief of engineers, Captain W. L. B. Jenney.[9] Twelve-hour workdays were broken into two-hour shifts in the mud. Sherman strictly required officers to be present with each and every detail. "This rule is invariable," he warned.[10]

Along with a steam pump and the promised dredges came one thousand Black laborers from Memphis, who joined other freedmen from the immediate environs already toiling in the canal at the direction of the Pioneer Corps. There is unfortunately little evidence that the two races worked amicably together. For the most part, details remained separated with the exception of white Pioneer officers charged with overseeing the Black laborers. "The darkies would be busily engaged in wheeling dirt from the canal singing their Negro melodies," one Hawkeye observed. Occasionally, when Rebel gunners sent a shell screaming over the river, he and his comrades erupted in laughter at the sight of "the darkies, wheelbarrows and all[,] roll into the mud, and water[,] and after crawling out skin [run] for some of the large cypress stumps." Chasing after them, white officers screamed, "Come back you black curs and go to work!"[11] Frustration brewed between the soldiers and laborers. David Holmes, Fifty-Fifth Illinois, thought he sensed that the "colored gents" were already "getting tired of working for Uncle Sam," having overheard a few "say they would rather be with Massa."[12] "The Negroes that are found on these plantations are unfit for free men and useless appendages to the Army," Major A. J. Seay, Thirty-Second Missouri, remarked. "We have utterly failed in almost every instant to render them useful to us."[13] Most were not quite so pessimistic, but still had reservations. "They are good for such purposes as throwing up breastworks and digging canals," one officer confided to his diary, "but I cannot think they are a class that should be armed."[14]

By March 5, optimism for the imminent success of the canal was at its height at Grant's headquarters. The ebullient commander confidently wired Washington to report his anticipation that the ditch would be ready for steamer transit in only a few more days. The very next day, however, disaster struck. When the precarious sandbag closure of the canal's entrance suddenly gave way during the night, the closure blocking the exit failed to follow suit, flooding not only the canal but nearly all of the southern half of De Soto Point, including much of the Fifteenth Corps's cantonment. Soaked engineers rushed to detonate explosives at the lower sandbag enclosure to drain the water, but Sherman's corps was forced to relocate further north, away from the flooded peninsula. The only available ground high enough to avoid the surging floodwaters was the levee itself, and thus the entire corps found itself in cramped camps atop the narrow berm. Although Grant would attempt to continue the effort once the floodwaters had partially receded, for all practical purposes the disaster marked the unsuccessful termination of the operation. By mid-March, Rebel batteries had perfected the range from the Vicksburg bluffs to the canal and rendered any additional efforts too precarious. As the Secessionist gunners grew into expert marksmen, any force detailed to work on the canal found the assignment "much like going into battle with nothing to shoot with but shovels loaded with mud."[15]

While Grant had hoped against long odds, the enlisted men who labored on the canal understood the terrible odds working against them. Around the campfire, most "prophesied that the wayward current could not be coaxed to enter the channel being laboriously prepared for it," recalled one Illinoisan.[16] This discussion inevitably led to "not much heart [being] put into the work."[17] Each and every setback to the effort came as little shock. "Every private soldier knew it was [a failure] from the beginning," Private Robert Henry, Twenty-Sixth Iowa, remarked.[18] Even so, with the trauma of Chickasaw and "the Post" still lingering in their minds, many were content with the change of pace. "It is pret[t]y hard work but I would sooner dig than fight if it will accomplish any thing," one still shaken Illinoisan remarked.[19] The survivors of Shepard's roughly handled Third Missouri agreed. "Shoveling mud was, after all, only another way of taking Vicksburg, or at least a means of getting past it," Sergeant-Major Edward Reichhelm remembered, "and preferable to another Chickasaw Bayou experiment."[20]

While ultimately a failure, the canal project offered the Fifteenth Corps opportunities to develop important skills and prompted a series of adaptations that would prove valuable in the near future. By far the most significant of these was the creation of each division's permanent Pioneer Corps. Whereas previously the brigades of Sherman's corps had lacked any formal mechanism by which to harness the expertise of their more mechanically inclined members when tasked with constructing corduroy roads, erecting battery positions, or bridging streams and creeks, the command had now consolidated the most capable of these men into pioneer detachments that could supervise not only the labor of unskilled white volunteers, but also that of the growing numbers of freedmen attached to the army. In an army lacking many professional military engineers, the creation of these detachments represented a major step forward.

There was little jollity in life at "the Point." Many felt the corps cantonment represented "the most desolate Camp on earth."[21] The sodden ground everywhere seemed on the imminent verge of sinking into a sea of river water. In many places mud was ankle deep.[22] George Browning, Fifty-Fourth Ohio, found he and his messmates "had to Build a Bridge in front of our tent to keep from drowning."[23] A shovel sunk a mere half-foot into the campground of the Thirty-Second Missouri uncovered an "abundance of water."[24]

One Illinoisan observed how, if a soldier was to "put his foot squarely down anywhere, it was questionable, when he raised it again, if the shoe would not stay behind."[25] Water was omnipresent and inescapable. "Men stand in water[,] sleep and eat in water," Robert Henry, Twenty-Sixth Iowa, observed. "It is hard for one that never had [such an] experience to imagine."[26] By late January, nighttime temperatures plummeted far enough to freeze the water in regimental wash basins.[27] Even sunny days were paired with a "cold piercing wind" that exacted a heavy toll from those already ill.[28] The deadly combination of harsh weather, flooding, "unseasoned" troops, hard labor, and in later months the hatching of malarial mosquito populations, transformed "the Point" into a veritable hell on Earth.

In his effort to cobble together an expeditionary force of sufficient size, Sherman had thought little about the character of the troops and regiments assigned to his new command. Recent experience had illustrated the cost of such willful ignorance on the battlefield as the disparate histories of each unit played a powerful role in shaping their performance under fire. But the qualitative differences between regiments extended beyond their relative tactical competency. In filling half of his new corps with freshly raised regiments, Sherman well knew that its impressive size was unlikely to last. Professional soldiers had long been accustomed to armies of fresh recruits requiring a customary "seasoning" period prior to campaigning. Ignorant of germ theory, officers and physicians presumed that the grievous losses new regiments routinely suffered from "infantile diseases" like measles and mumps were inevitable. While we now know that the predominately rural volunteers comprising the bulk of Civil War armies suffered from a lack of antibodies, Sherman and his peers remained convinced that the staggering rates of disease among "fresh levies" was due to a lack of discipline and experience with military life. New regiments "dont know how to take care of themselves and suffer unnecessarily in health," Cump explained to his brother. "They cant know how to make their camps, how to march, how to cook, how to shelter themselves so that in three months they fall away to mere skeletons."[29]

Far more frustrating to Sherman than either of his recent repulses at Chickasaw or "the Post" were the repeated repulses he suffered as he rushed the ramparts of the Lincoln administration's mobilization policy. The president remained staunchly committed to raising new regiments of volunteers instead of sending individual recruits to fill gaps in veteran "skeleton regiments," as Cump referred to them. This policy provided plentiful opportunities to award loyal Democrats with officer commissions signaling bipartisanship to a divided Northern public. Sherman bemoaned Lincoln's reasoning as "false economy." He had watched firsthand as regiment after regiment shrunk from nearly one thousand men to fewer than three hundred for duty in a matter of a few months. "This same number of men, distributed to old organizations [would] learn quickly from association," he argued, "and escape in a measure the consequent sickness and death."[30] Older regiments had "by a process of elimination weeded out the worthless and inefficient officers & non commissioned officers," rendering the remainder ideal teachers for newcomers.[31]

With the government apparently deaf to Sherman's entreaties, he and his lieutenants did their best to mitigate the anticipated losses associated with "new" regiments undergoing their "seasoning" periods while in such abysmal conditions. Commanders of both "old" and "new" regiments labored to ensure their units took advantage of dry land to attend to the lagging sanitation endemic aboard the transports. Col. George Stone ordered the officers of his Twenty-Fifth Iowa to ensure the men washed and mended their remaining clothing, and that they bathed at least once a week.[32] No member of the unit would be issued his daily rations "Unless he shall have washed his face and hands and combed his hair," Stone asserted.[33] His lieutenants shared these concerns. "If the men will take care of themselves & Keep clean, half the sickness would be avoided," one of Stone's junior officers remarked, "but as it is, there are some who do not wash once in a week, and no wonder they get sick and die." Fortunately, many were "beginning to learn Some sense, & the officers & men are taking the matter in hands."[34]

At the same time, suspicious that many complaining of illness might in fact be shirking, Stone also ordered that all reporting sick, presumably having lost their appetites, were to be issued only half-rations. The remaining surplus was divided up between those still on duty. If the "sick" were in fact "'playing off' or 'shirking,' the punishment will be a meritorious one," he reasoned.[35] Stone's quest to purge his Iowans of "play-offs" was not limited to the enlisted ranks. Officers complaining of sickness who proved incapable of procuring a certificate of disability were expected to remain on duty. "It looks very suspicious to see officers reported sick who can play Whisky Poker all day and nearly all night," Stone added sharply in his general orders.[36] Two days later, when it came to his attention that many of his exhausted men were relieving their bowels in closer proximity to the regiment's cantonment area than the authorized latrines, he opted for an even more draconian measure. "Any soldier committing a nuisance any where else near camp [than the latrine] shall be liable to have his nose rubbed therein," he boldly ordered.[37] No record of whether the punishment was ever enacted survives.

From the moment the corps landed at Young's Point, its newest units began to show alarming signs of "every conceivable variety of lice and smallpox, measles and mumps, and other diseases incident to women and children," Kilby Smith reported.[38] "It appears like one could not get well when once sick in the army," one Illinoisan observed.[39] His regiment, the 116th Illinois, was by no means unique among the "new" regiments of the corps in its loss of nearly two hundred men from resignation, desertion, discharge, and death during its four-month stay at Young's Point. Hasty funerals for the dead were marked by the somber drone of the "Dead March" and rifles fired in salute over the grave. By February, these sounds became nearly omnipresent. In March, when extensive flooding confined the corps's camps to the narrow levee itself, the men were forced to share their cantonment with the dead, and the levee was lined with shallow graves only a stone's throw from the shelters of the living. Those few who were still well found themselves picking up the slack by undertaking additional duties. "The men reported fit for duty rarely had a day of rest," Sergeant Major Reichhelm remembered.[40] The combination of exhaustion and abysmal conditions eventually disabled many of even the most physically robust specimens in every regiment.

Between January and April 1863, the Fifteenth Corps lost a staggering 3,500 men from its rolls. When its regiments finally stepped off southward on the famed Vicksburg campaign, they left behind more than 1,600 of their own in shallow graves along the levee or in crude coffins headed northward to grieving families across the West. At least another 1,000 had been discharged for disability, many of whom would perish at home in a matter of weeks or months from the same ailments which had mercilessly taken the lives of their comrades. More than 500 men deserted from Fifteenth Corps regiments during the late winter and spring, some for political reasons as the perceived meaning of the war gradually shifted, but many undoubtedly in a bid to save themselves from the omnipresent disease and death that defined life at "the Point." The frequent departure of steamers northward from the camps offered easy opportunities for those so inclined to anonymously slip away from their comrades with few if any questions asked. Finally, at least 160 officers of all grades within the corps resigned their commissions between the day Sherman's transports landed along the banks of the levee and the day the blue columns departed southward for Grand Gulf.[41]

Losses were by no means evenly distributed across the forty-one infantry regiments and six batteries that now comprised the corps. The starkest difference was between "old" and "new" previously "unseasoned" regiments. On average, "old" longer-service regiments each suffered a loss of 25 dead, 34 discharged for disability, 17 desertions, and 4 officer resignations over the four-month period. By dramatic contrast, the "new" fresh levies of Sherman's corps, comprising almost half the command, lost on average more than 100 to death, issued at least 50 discharges for disability, lost nearly 20 men to desertion, and reported an average of 9 resignations. Thus, while on average "old" regiments suffered a loss of 80 men to all causes, "new" regiments lost nearly 200—more than two full-strength companies. This disparity had the effect of converting all of Sherman's large "new" units of fresh levies into the same "skeleton regiments" that comprised his command prior to their arrival.

All told, the total loss to the corps between January and April amounted to more than twice the number lost to all causes during the recent intense fighting in the Yazoo bottoms and at Arkansas Post. More than seven times those who had fallen in battle that winter now laid silently along the levee as victims of disease, abysmal sanitation, and appalling conditions. The sheer scale of human tragedy entailed by such loss is difficult to comprehend, but the cost to the corps's operational capabilities (and, by extension, to those of Grant's army) is easier to calculate. At a point in the corps's history when most of its regiments averaged about 350 men for duty on a daily basis, the loss of almost 3,500 men was the equivalent of nearly ten regiments, or an entire division. In fact, when the corps set off on its long march to Vicksburg, neither of its two divisions could muster anywhere close to 3,500 men present for duty. Sherman would now have to do more with far less.

"EXPERIENCE WHICH WOULD SERVE US"

Accepting that the canal was a failure, Grant turned his attention elsewhere. By cutting a levee a considerable distance upriver to the north, the Army flooded backwaters leading into the Yazoo hinterland east of the Mississippi.

This increased flow, Grant hoped, would allow for a modest expeditionary force, along with an escort of Navy gunboats, to meander through the Yazoo watershed until it could reach the high ground north of Vicksburg and establish a lodgment to exploit with follow-on deployments. While the tortuous course of the vegetation-choked waterways proved challenging enough to the hard-luck combined arms force, the expedition was stopped cold in its tracks by a meager but stalwart Rebel defense of a sand-and-dirt bastion dubbed "Fort Pemberton."[42]

In part to distract Rebel attention from the logjam at Fort Pemberton, as well as to try one final roundabout approach to the heights north of Vicksburg, Grant ordered Sherman to accompany Admiral Porter in a second foray into the dark swamps of the Yazoo on March 14. This time, a joint force of five of Porter's ironclads, four tugs towing mortar rafts, and one division of Sherman's corps riding aboard steamers and in towed coal barges would ascend the Yazoo and make a left turn northward into Steele's Bayou just prior to coming into view of the Rebel batteries atop Haynes's Bluff. Porter's smoke-belching flotilla would plow the brown waters of Steele's Bayou before turning into the vine-choked gauntlet of Black Bayou to gain the slightly wider channel of Deer Creek. From there, the boats would resume their northward trajectory until making a right turn into Rolling Fork, then south again after entering the Sunflower River. Finally, at the conclusion of this labyrinthine journey, the expedition would reenter the Yazoo north of both Haynes's and Drumgould's bluffs, disembarking Sherman's one division upon dry ground after having flanked all Rebel defenses along the Yazoo River. Provided the route could be both secured and maintained, additional troops would then be dispatched through the winding bayous to the newly secured landing. At the very least, Rebel forces would be drawn off from either Fort Pemberton or Vicksburg itself to confront the new threat, growing the menu of strategic options available to Grant.[43]

It was a desperate plan, but the importance of bagging Vicksburg amid a flagging Northern war effort seemed to warrant pulling out all the stops. It was also extremely risky. Grant, Porter, and Sherman all recognized the terrifying possibility that, even barring any enemy resistance, the gambit could cost the Navy many or even all of its gunboats, and thus its only hope of ever seizing the city at all. Should a single vessel hit a snag, puncture its hull on any of the many submerged hazards, or suffer a debilitating attack by Rebel partisans, all the craft north of it would immediately be trapped.

If it sunk in a narrow portion of any of the winding bayou channels it could spell disaster for the entire campaign.

Sherman selected his beloved "old division" for the perilous undertaking, its primary mission at the canal having been nullified by the recent flooding. The multifaceted Zouaves would once again spearhead Sherman's effort. Understanding that many of the Eighth Missouri had been recruited from the St. Louis waterfront, Grant presumed that several had experience with river work. Thus, when casting about for a command to "clean out the channel" of Steele's Bayou and clear a route for the expedition by cutting away overhanging trees and vines, the Zouaves seemed a perfect fit. Along with two detachments from the Second Division's new Pioneer Corps, the regiment embarked aboard the *Diligent* on March 15 and set out on their clearance mission.[44]

In an effort to shorten the distance that the rest of Stuart's regiments had to be hauled through the challenging southern portions of Steele's Bayou, Grant thought it best to disembark the division at Eagle Bend along the eastern bank of the Mississippi and march it down a levee hugging the northern bank of Muddy Bayou until reaching transports waiting in Steele's Bayou. Accordingly, early on the morning of March 16, Stuart's twelve regiments boarded steamers at Milliken's Bend with every ax that could be found.[45] After landing at Eagle Bend, Stuart took one look at the levee running along Muddy Bayou and determined that it was utterly "impassable for the troops without the construction of rafts and bridges."[46] First, a lengthy "floating bridge" was necessary to even reach the high ground of the levee, the fields between the river and levee having been inundated with floodwaters.[47] Moreover, two crevasses had been rent in the levee by floodwaters which would require bridging before the division could reach its objective. The bayou itself was so overgrown with vegetation that considerable effort was also necessary to clear it of obstructions before it could be used as a supply viaduct. Conscious of the need for speed, he ordered the men to disassemble the slave cabins and cotton gin of a nearby plantation and use the lumber to bridge the two crevasses.[48] With this, he returned to report to Grant at Young's Point, leaving the details to Brig. Gen. Hugh Ewing.[49] Ewing assigned each regiment a separate task. Their commanders subsequently subdivided their units into even smaller details. Each of these subsequent divisions created an opportunity for junior officers and even sergeants to take initiative, growing their skills as leaders in the process.

The division of labor in Ewing's brigade as it approached its mission began with his assignment of Col. Augustus Parry's Forty-Seventh Ohio to erect two viable bridges over the gaping crevasses. As Parry's Buckeyes tore apart the nearby slave cabins for wood, just as Stuart had prescribed, Ewing set Col. Joseph Lightburn's Fourth West Virginia to clearing obstructions from Muddy Bayou. Filing into the frigid brown water of the narrow channel with axes in hand, the men started into the dirty work. Meanwhile, the division's Pioneer Corps applied its expertise in supervising the construction of Parry's bridges. Freedmen assigned to the Pioneers assisted in the heavy labor of cutting additional lumber and hauling it into place. By noon of March 19 both bridges were in place, allowing for Giles and Kilby Smith's brigades to march east to the transports awaiting them in Steele's Bayou. As the other two brigades embarked, Ewing received orders to remain with his regiments at Muddy Bayou and continue to clear the channel.[50]

After chugging northward through the winding bends of Steele's Bayou to the mouth of Black Bayou, the lead regiments of Giles Smith's brigade transferred to flatboats and coal barges which ferried them through the vine-choked stream to the relatively dry ground of "Reality Plantation." A slave on the plantation explained how the overseer, who had long referred to the Deer Creek Valley as "the Confederate snuff-box, that the Yankees could not open," had ingloriously fled.[51] To protect against attack, the men hauled cotton bales from the gins and stacked them up into impromptu breastworks.[52] The steamers meanwhile returned to Muddy Bayou to ferry the rest of the division northward in three trips spread across the next three days. By the morning of March 23, all of Stuart's division would be encamped at "Reality."[53]

Set on reconnoitering the expedition's objectives well ahead of his corps, Sherman had ascended Steele's Bayou to "Reality" alone in a tug and was waiting with the Zouaves when Giles Smith arrived with the Sixth Missouri and 116th Illinois. One look at Black Bayou and Deer Creek had been enough to convince Sherman that, as was so often the case, what looked good on a map and what was actually feasible were very different things. The route plowed by Porter's ironclads, then slashing away at trees and vines and smashing "the wooden boats all to pieces" as they attempted to ram half-submerged obstructions somewhere north of "Reality" on narrow Deer Creek, was not practicable for any sizable force. "I don't think we can make a lodgment on high land by this route," he reported back to Grant.[54]

While the optimistic Porter remained confident in his ability to continue on course to Rolling Fork, he advised Sherman to remain at "Reality" and await developments. Cump was more than happy to comply, given that it seemed a fool's errand to try and follow up the admiral on land with any more than a token force.[55]

The first signs of trouble appeared in a dispatch from Porter to Sherman at "Reality" the day after Smith's brigade had arrived. The admiral and his ironclads were still in Deer Creek, but his forward momentum was being stalled by felled trees tossed into and across the creek by slaves apparently driven by Rebels. "Hurry up to co-operate," he urged Sherman, who was incapable of doing so given that most of Stuart's regiments would still require at least another day to arrive at "Reality." Not wanting to cut off all contact with the units which had not yet arrived, he opted instead to send Smith's demi-brigade alone in advance. Before first light on the twenty-first, Sherman dispatched Smith with his eight hundred men up the east bank of Deer Creek with orders to proceed twenty miles in search of Porter's boats and provide whatever help he needed.[56] Sherman did not anticipate much fighting, and took it "for granted [that] the five iron-clad gunboats can fight anything that can be brought against them, and land forces are only needed to cover the ground, to enable them to clean out obstructions" without being hampered by harassing Rebels.[57]

As soon as the sun rose, Smith's detachment was in motion behind a "negro guide" provided by Sherman, who allegedly knew the way to Porter's most recent position.[58] Only a short distance up the creek it became clear that "the enemy had been very busy felling trees to obstruct the creek," Smith later reported. Slaves encountered along the route explained to him how all "had been notified to be ready at nightfall to continue the work." Though lacking any formal authority to seize "property" on his mission, Smith recognized that all the slaves he encountered had been made free by the president's recent proclamation. Thus, he took the obvious step, and "ordered all able-bodied negroes to be taken along," warning their masters "that they would be held responsible for any more obstructions being placed across the creek."[59] Joining the column, the freedmen converted the character of the mission from that only of tactical reinforcement to one also of emancipation.

By late afternoon, the southernmost embattled boats were in sight and the lead elements of Smith's force took sporadic fire from across the river.

Deploying his men in the usual Second Division fashion, dispersed in skirmish teams, the Missourians and their Illinoisan supports entered the fray. "Every tree and stump covered a sharpshooter," Smith reported.[60] He hastened to contact Porter, who was overcome with emotion upon seeing blue uniforms. At the admiral's behest, Smith took command of all the marines on hand along with his infantry. As his three regiments were actually only the size of a single full-strength regiment, he broke their small companies up into independent tactical units and gave them each separate objectives, just as Ewing had done at Muddy Bayou. This fragmentation actually had the effect of making the small force more difficult to drive from the field. Most companies fought to gain a tactical edge over the Rebels to their front. Others dispersed for several miles down the creek to the south "to prevent any more obstructions being placed in it."[61] Each detachment relied entirely upon itself and its junior leaders. Several lacked a single officer.

The next day, as Smith's skirmishers hammered away, Porter's boats began the painstaking process of backing down the river in retreat. As they did so, the riflemen charged with guarding their withdrawal pulled obstructions from the water. It was a laboriously time-consuming process, and even more so under enemy fire. Suddenly, in the distance, Smith noticed "a long line of the enemy filing along the edge of the woods and taking position on the creek." Slaves had warned him of these reinforcements. The oncoming Rebels opened fire on Porter's boats, which responded with little effect, their guns incapable of firing over the tall levees. Whether Smith could repel this new foe was questionable. To make matters worse, sounds of heavy musketry filtered up from the south. Concerned that two of his most distant detachments might be cut off by another Rebel force in the rear, Smith speedily organized a relief party to rescue the beleaguered contingents. After the riflemen climbed aboard one of the ironclads, the craft plowed its way through obstructions southward with abandon. As soon as it arrived, however, it came upon a welcome surprise: Maj. Gen. William T. Sherman and the rest of Second Division.

Just prior to Smith's arrival the previous day, Porter's optimism had run out. Blocked to the rear and surrounded by Rebels, the flotilla found its ability to extricate itself from the hopeless situation proving impossible, barring relief from land. He had asked Sherman for support, but none seemed immediately forthcoming. Barring a miracle, he prepared himself for the unspeakable possibility of having to scuttle all his vessels to prevent their capture. With this in mind, he made one last effort to reach Cump, scribbling an urgent message on tissue paper, wrapping it in a piece of tobacco, and handing it to "a darky who called himself a telegraph" with instructions to make haste to "Reality" plantation in exchange for fifty cents.[62]

Upon receipt of the desperate message, Cump sprung into action. Unlike at any time during the previous six months, he transformed into the leader the moment required. "I was almost alone at Hill's," he later remembered, awaiting the arrival of the rest of Stuart's command. With no time to waste, he found a canoe and paddled down Black Bayou alone until he found a steamer loaded with the rest of Smith's brigade. There was no way for the large craft to make the passage through the tree-choked bayou, so the men were transferred to an empty coal barge and towed with a smaller tug up the meandering channel. Crashing through debris with abandon, with fallen limbs "carrying away the pilot-house, smoke-stack, and everything above-deck," nothing was spared in Cump's fever for rescuing the ironclads.

By the time the tug made it to the landing nearest "Reality," the night was "absolutely black." Disembarking the barge and leading its occupants on foot, Sherman piloted the column through the pitch-black swamps to "Reality." For illumination, the men lit candles and stuck them in the sockets of their bayonets. After just a few hours' rest and the arrival of Kilby Smith's brigade (absent Smith himself), the command was moving at first light. The distant thunder of Porter's guns and growing crackle of musketry hastened the march.[63] Sherman remained at the front and on foot, wading hip-deep through swamp water in places where the road dipped. "Being on foot myself, no man could complain," he later remembered. "The soldiers generally were glad to have their general and field officers afoot," he laughed, "but we gave them a fair specimen of marching." The speeding column made twenty-one miles in five hours, or about four miles an hour—breakneck pace for infantry over such difficult terrain. Nearing the sounds of the guns, Sherman spotted Smith's southernmost detachments fighting from atop an Indian mound in the bend of the creek. Having delivered the column to its objective, the general "sat down on the doorsill of a [nearby] cabin to rest" for a moment while his subordinates took over.[64]

Second Division applied itself to the situation just as its tactical culture would have suggested, deploying skirmishers well to the front to push the scattered Rebel forces back. The engagement before the Indian mounds quickly became exclusively a battle of individual riflemen. Led independently by junior officers and senior sergeants, the "cloud of skirmishers" from a total of only seven companies from three regiments swept from tree to tree in a loosely coordinated wave, firing as they advanced. The massed remaining regiments followed safely in column a considerable distance to the rear, contributing additional skirmishers as needed. Just as at Corinth, Chickasaw, and Arkansas Post, the division's tactical approach capitalized on the individual skills of its riflemen and junior leaders while taking advantage of the terrain. Its massed main body functioned as a skirmisher reserve and potential defensive bulwark should the skirmishers have to withdraw. Second Division's tactical culture was ideally calibrated for the problem at hand, and very quickly its skirmishers gained the upper hand. Once the remaining Rebels had been driven from the field, Sherman reconsolidated the scattered elements of his relief column to ensure the continued safety of Porter's ironclads as they continued to limp southward "at a snail's pace" back toward "Reality."[65] Jubilant over the easy victory, the cocky soldiers jibed the sailors: "Better let bushwhacking out to 'Old Tecump's' boys!" they shouted.[66]

The next day, rain fell in torrents, turning the Deer Creek road to "mud, at times almost up to our knees."[67] Hoping to make something of the otherwise fruitless venture, and struck by the obvious wealth of the valley Porter called the "granary of the world," Sherman chose to make the most of the slow withdrawal. Supposed to be inaccessible to the Yankee invader, most of the Deer Creek properties had been planted with corn, and "their gardens well stocked with vegetables, which were growing most temptingly," one observer noted.[68] The slaves encountered by Smith on his initial trip northward had confirmed that most, if not all, of the plantations abutting the creek had provided "hands" to assist in obstructing the creek and capturing Porter's flotilla. All were thus deemed culpable for retaliation, and now they would pay. All properties were searched for serviceable horses to mount the officers of the command. Entire spans of mules were seized and led by the halter while other hungry infantrymen combed through corncribs, chicken coops, and smokehouses in search of eatables. Having brought only two days' rations along on the trip, Smith's brigade was famished. The slow pace of the withdrawal provided ample opportunities for practice at foraging liberally. Hungry volunteers pried open smokehouses across the valley and seized tens of thousands of pounds of cured bacon. "Chickens, eggs, mutton, veal and other delicacies . . . turkeys, geese, calves, and sheep without number" were piled into confiscated wagons and hauled along for the journey back to "Reality." Hundreds of mules, horses, and cattle were confiscated. Cotton bales, many of them stamped "C.S.A." in preparation for sale, were tumbled into the creek to float downstream for others to retrieve. Others were burned in place, frequently along with the outhouses in which they were discovered.[69] Customarily restrained in his approach to private property, Sherman now freely vented his frustration as his beloved "old Division" tried its hand for the first time at "war in earnest." In total, one correspondent estimated, Stuart's division destroyed "at least 2,000 bales of cotton, 50,000 bushels of corn, and the gins and houses of the plantations whose owners had obstructed our progress and joined in the warfare." In so doing, he confidently assumed, "we crippled the enemy."[70]

By far the most valuable "property" seized from the "granary of the world" were a large number of enslaved men and women who fell in behind the column and followed along.[71] Nearly 8,000 slaves were held within the county in 1860, and while many of the able-bodied men had been removed by nervous planters prior to the arrival of the Federal army, large numbers remained.[72] "Reality" alone was home to 127 men and women.[73] Even a staunchly conservative journalist embedded with the division had to admit that, in "every instance, everywhere, they were our friends . . . doing everything and anything in their power to assist us." Black men had carried all the crucial dispatches, guided all the critical movements, labored alongside white regiments constructing bridges and roads, alerted US forces to approaching Rebels, and even assisted in hastening fellow slaves toward the withdrawing army.[74] Undertaken in the interest of securing their freedom and that of their families, their operational contributions to the corps's efforts proved utterly indispensable.

While sharp skirmishing had been necessary to drive the Rebel host from the field, the mere arrival of the reinforcing columns, at a place and time supposed to be all but impossible, secured the closest approximation to success the expedition would enjoy. While falling well short of the expedition's original objectives, through the careful coordination of pioneering efforts, hard work, inspiring leadership, brutally hard marching, and the vital assistance of slaves, Stuart's division saved Porter's flotilla. The entire expedition had been "used in labor—constant and severe." Embedded reporters admired how the "officers and men worked with equal alacrity, whether in building bridges or making forced marches, both by day and in the night."[75] Sherman's own observation that the timing of his relief column's arrival had been "very opportune" was a profound understatement. Had the division hit any snag in its forward momentum, had any part of the division's larger system failed to fulfill its duties, and the relief column reached Porter's beleaguered craft even an hour later, it is quite possible that the boats would have already been abandoned and scuttled, and with them the campaign for Vicksburg.[76]

Crafting intelligible narratives that made sense of their unit's participation in the expedition proved exasperating for every officer charged with filing a formal report afterward. The night after returning to Young's Point, Maj. Dudley Chase, commanding the Regulars who spearheaded the relief column, came to chief engineer Jenney's cabin, quietly shut the door, and "looked around to see that we were alone," Jenney remembered. "I command a battalion of regulars," Chase whispered, "I have been on an expedition,—I must write a report,—I want you to tell me where I have been, how I went there, what I did, and if I came back the same way I went, or if not, how I did get back." Still laughing about Chase's confusion years hence, Jenney observed that the incident "serves to illustrate how little even battalion commanders knew of what was being done at this time."[77] Even so, if the larger strategic picture remained obscure to most of those in Sherman's corps, the expedition instilled a number of valuable skills and lessons to the soldiers involved. Even Porter acknowledged that the mission had provided "a lot of experience which would serve us in the future." Although in reference to his sailors, the remark was just as applicable to Sherman's footsore landsmen.[78]

The corps had been forced to fashion its own luck out of whole cloth from beginning to end. As its component units worked their way through nearly impassable terrain, each and every regiment contributed to the completion of the corps's objectives. Fragmenting into smaller units, reconsolidating when needed, and then fragmenting again to address unforeseen challenges became almost second nature as junior leaders took on more responsibility more frequently than at any prior time. Even during the fighting at the Indian mounds, all operations were controlled by junior leaders moving among their dispersed skirmishers, guiding their advance and withdrawal, and taking care to keep in touch with others on their flanks.

The unique problems of engineering, maneuver, and resource extraction had also proved easier to solve than those of the battlefield. Grit, firm resolve, and sweat proved capable of accomplishing meaningful results in ways that valor and faith had proven incapable of winning under fire. Moreover, the sight of every senior officer from regimental commanders to Sherman himself, sweating alongside their commands and often half-submerged in the same muddy water as the privates, forged a bond of familiarity that had been lacking before. In all, the expedition taught Second Division, and Sherman, that they had more up their collective sleeves than they had previously imagined.

"I WANT TO TAKE EVERY THING AWAY FROM THE DAMNED SECESH"

Stymied first at Yazoo Pass and now at Steele's Bayou, Grant began to explore an even more daring strategy to reach the high ground east of Vicksburg. On the evening of April 16, Grant and Porter sent seven gunboats and three empty transports through the dark of night down the river and directly past the batteries guarding Vicksburg's bluffs in a desperate attempt to "run the batteries." Suddenly alerted to the opportunity, the Secessionist gunners fired upon the flotilla with incredible ferocity, but most of the vessels still miraculously managed to make it through the maelstrom. Grant planned to use these vessels to ferry his army across the Mississippi some distance to the south, marching it northeastward toward the high ground east of Vicksburg in a bid to cut off the enemy garrison from supply.[79]

In preparation for the forthcoming campaign, he sought both to secure his lengthy riverine supply line and strike a blow at the breadbasket of the city's garrison which lay to the north along the Deer Creek Valley. The town of Greenville, Mississippi, several miles north of Vicksburg, had long been a source of harassing gunfire for passing steamers headed to and from Grant's army. Amid one of the richest portions of the lower Mississippi Valley, the plantations south and east of Greenville produced prodigious amounts of cotton and, of greater military value, foodstuffs that the Vicksburg garrison regularly tapped as they awaited Grant's next move. The region also contained the greatest density of able-bodied male slaves within easy reach of the army. Grant well knew that their labor had greatly benefited Rebel General John Pemberton's Vicksburg garrison, and he meant to convert those efforts to his own aims instead, offering freedom in exchange. Once again, he turned to his most trusted subordinate for the job.[80]

After meeting with Grant and learning his expectations, Sherman chose Steele's fresh division to conduct the operation. As the command would be unsupported, speed was of necessity. The column was to take only rations that could be carried by the men on their persons or upon pack mules. Barring any unforeseen contingency in the form of resistance, Steele was to march his division southward from Greenville down the Deer Creek Valley for two or three days, "clearing the country as you go of guerrillas and Confederate soldiers." If the inhabitants of the region remained at home "and behave themselves," the column was to "molest them as little as possible." On the other hand, should the division discover abandoned properties, "you may infer they [their owners] are hostile, and can take their cattle, hogs, corn, or anything you need."

These instructions left a great deal of latitude to both Steele and his lieutenants in determining the extent and character of extraction and destruction to be levied. Few clear red lines existed. Cotton "which is clearly private property" was not to be touched, but all marked "C.S.A." was to be "brought away or burned." Finally, and perhaps most importantly, any and "all provisions which are needed by us or might be used by the [Rebel] army in Vicksburg, unless needed by the peaceful inhabitants," were to be consumed, seized, or destroyed. Above all else, Steele was to ensure that the wealthy inhabitants of the valley "see and feel that they will be held accountable for the acts of guerrillas and Confederate soldiers who sojourn in their country." Beyond the denial of the valley's bounty to the rebellion, Steele was to execute a psychological operation. "Let all the people understand that we claim the unmolested navigation of the Mississippi, and will have it," Sherman ordered, "if all the country within reach has to be laid waste."[81] Embarking his command on April 2, Steele's flotilla steamed northward in search of a viable landing. After several false starts at landings that eventually proved inaccessible to the rest of the region, the column was finally on its way south into the Deer Creek Valley from Greenville on April 5.[82]

The march was hard, occasionally pushing nearly twenty miles a day. While Steele's "old" regiments stood it relatively well, for many of the "new" units the expedition represented the first hard marching they had done. "The men stumble slowly towards night," Seay observed of his Missourians, "and complain of sore feet."[83] Captain Jacob Ritner, Twenty-Fifth Iowa, though a long-service veteran now in command of "fresh levy" Hawkeyes, completely "gave out" on the first and second day's marches. By the third, he found he "stood it first-rate" and "believe[d] I could march a month now."[84] A full third of his regiment failed to keep up, "gave out and lagged behind."[85] In several regiments, at least half the privates mounted "jayhawked mules" to escape the pain.[86] By the time the column returned to Greenville, nearly every officer was so mounted.[87]

Although formal reports like those required after combat engagements were never filed by the regiments of the division in the aftermath of the expedition, a reconstruction of the tactics employed by Steele's division in the valley is possible through the triangulation of a variety of sources. Among the many plantations nestled along the usually quiet banks of Deer Creek lay the picturesque "Mount Pleasant" of the late Rhode Islander Henry Tillinghast Ireys. After Henry died in 1846, leaving his properties in a trust for his young sons, the surviving Ireys family remained absentee planters, like many of those who owned the palatial properties near Greenville. Finding Rhode Island still all too proximate to the war, the family had long since decamped even further away from Mississippi, instead riding the war out in Scotland.[88] In order to maintain what meager profits were still possible despite the blockade, and to watch over the many acres and at least fifty slaves they owned, the Ireyses employed Anderson Copeland, along with his wife, to live on the property as their overseer.[89] Well aware that Yankees were lurking in the area that warm April afternoon, Copeland was already on edge. He had taken precautions with the property he was employed to protect. Earlier that morning he ordered several slaves away from the grounds with eight mules, two full wagonloads of fresh meat, and orders to remain hidden deep in the woods until sent for. Later that afternoon, as he dutifully watched from the shade of the porch and the slaves hoed and drove mule teams plowing the dark Mississippi mud in preparation for spring planting, he noticed a group of riders in blue approaching from the Deer Creek road, and his heart began to pound. "I was so frightened that I kept at a distance and yet in full view," he later sheepishly recounted to a claims commission agent.[90]

If they too noticed Copeland, the soldiers initially showed no interest. Instead, they rode directly into the fields and approached the slaves themselves. Their foreman, slave John Lewis, looked up from his work as they approached. "Boys, put down your hoes & stop plowing," one of the riders called out. "You are all free." As Lewis and the others allowed the bluntly delivered pronouncement to set in, the mounted officer wasted no time in giving further orders to the soldiers with him. "I want to take every thing away from the Damned Secesh," another slave, Alexander Colbert, heard him say. The officer then promptly ordered the mules immediately unhitched from their plows. Turning to Lewis, he explained that he and the other slaves were "to go with us," and again insisted that they hurriedly "take out your mules!" As the slaves complied, the officer, Colonel Isaac Shepard, Third Missouri, and his entourage spurred their mounts toward the Copeland home. Having apparently fled upon the realization of what in fact was happening, the overseer had left his wife alone at the house. Announcing their intentions, Shepard received what by then the Missourians had grown accustomed to hearing from Southern women: spite. Afterward, she proudly reported to her shy husband how she had defiantly "asked them If they knew they were taking the property of Northern Men," referencing the New Englander Ireyses. "So much the worse for Northern Men owning property in the South," Shepard bluntly replied.[91]

The Missourians were merely the advance guard of Steele's division, and a long column of blue now completely filled the roadway in either direction as Lewis and the others mounted the unhitched mules bareback and fell into line. For at least two hours the dusty Yankees moved past as others rifled through the property, looking for anything deemed of greater use to Uncle Sam than to the Vicksburg garrison. They "were just passing through the country gathering up things—mules & negroes," Colbert observed. The Ireyses later reported thirty-five mules, one hundred head of cattle, and a valuable mare seized without any receipt or voucher provided. In all, they estimated the value of property lost at nearly $10,000, not including an unknown number of their most valuable "possessions"—human beings like John Lewis and Alexander Colbert.[92] As soon as word reached the slaves charged with guarding the hidden wagonloads of meat that the Yankees had arrived, the bondsmen blithely ignored Copeland's instructions and made directly for Steele's column with eight more mules and two wagonloads full of fresh provisions.[93]

As the division wound its way down the valley, similar scenes played out all along the banks of Deer Creek. At another plantation, the Missourians spotted a gang of slaves likewise preparing for planting under the much closer supervision of an overseer who sat on horseback nearby with whip in hand. At first sight of the column, the toiling slaves froze, "gazing at us as if paralyzed," Sergeant-Major Reichhelm remembered. In an instant, "they all dropped their tools and with a great shout flinging their arms into the air they came bounding over the fields towards the roadside." Their "joyful cries" were so exultant that their exact words were hard to discern. Even so, the German Reichhelm had no trouble making out "Oh, Lord," "Yankees," and "freedom." Halting the regiment for a moment while the officers hunted for forage on the property, the liberated men and women shouted and danced in the roadway "like a lot of children greeting a Santa Claus." One elderly man walked straight to the national colors at the head of the column, knelt down, and between sobs thanked God "that Thou has pleased to let us see the glory of this day." Unlike many of the more conservative western regiments in Steele's division, the Germans felt it "was an indescribable scene and we felt its tremendous significance." Still acting as the principal interlocutor between the Army and the local white population, their colonel beckoned to the white overseer "who had stood there scowling and undecided what to do," Reichhelm observed. "His occupation was gone," Shepard called out to him. For now, he should "consider himself a prisoner for the present" while the men searched the grounds.[94] Shepard promised the property owner that his home would be safe, but any provisions and willing slaves would be seized. Hearing this, those slaves nearby rushed to their quarters, rapidly gathered their few earthly belongings, and fell into line behind the regiment. As the division column swept by the indignant Mississippian's home, subsequent details from other regiments searched for anything the Missourians may have missed.[95]

While Steele's "old" regiments led the way in liberating the valley's human "chattel," the more recently raised half of his division remained far more interested in the emancipation of livestock and poultry than of human beings. By contrast with Shepard's proactive abolition efforts, officers in the Twenty-Fifth Iowa made sure that there "was no effort made to bring them along" even though inevitably "they would come." Even so, by the end of the expedition, one Hawkeye company commander counted a ratio of two "contraband" to every man in his company.[96] After watching men and women along the eastern bank fashioning rafts out of rails to cross the waters to freedom, the Hawkeyes were not about to turn them away.[97] That said, they were not always inclined to assist in their bid for liberty either. The sight of a lone slave woman attempting to pilot a flimsy handmade raft up the creek toward the column only to drift further and further away downstream elicited no pity but considerable laughter from the ranks. For all but the most radical of Steele's command, emancipation was still merely a pragmatic tactic.

Shepard's personal involvement in his regiment's search operations during the expedition was somewhat unique. For the most part, the vast majority of the division's extractive efforts were conducted by small detachments of men commanded by junior leaders. These detachments were usually ordered to set off on foot or on captured mounts to scour distant properties known only to maps or slave informants. While away from the main column, these detachments operated "on their own hook," with almost all their actions determined by their assigned leader or even the men themselves.

Private William Royal Oake was assigned to just such a six-man detail from the Twenty-Sixth Iowa commanded by a lieutenant, ordered to cross Deer Creek and search a plantation assumed to be about a mile distant on the eastern bank. As most planters in the valley owned property on both sides of the creek, many had intentionally moved all their most valuable property (including slaves) to the eastern side of the creek and summarily destroyed or burned all the bridges.[98] This did not stop the Hawkeyes. Procuring a modest craft nearby, the squad paddled across the creek and walked about a mile to their objective. The estate proved a goldmine. Turkeys, chickens, hams, and plenty of apple-jack whiskey were uncovered while rifling through the abandoned plantation, all of which was packed onto confiscated mules and horses found on the property. Much of the whiskey was consumed by the men on the spot, after which they each rode a captured mule heavily laden with forage back to the creek. Precisely how to get such volume of provender back across the water on such a meager craft took some thinking. Eventually, the squad hatched a plan whereby one would stand in the rear of the boat while the others coaxed their mounts and livestock into the water. Once across, the Iowans calculated that, given the duration of their errand and the speed of the division column, the regiment would be about three hours down the road. Steele's path was easy to trace, clearly marked by the still-smoldering cotton, gins, corn, and forage on both sides of the dirt route leading southward. Sure enough, later that afternoon the men straggled back into their regiment's bivouac.[99]

Much of the intelligence upon which such distant forays were based came from bondspeople who were eager to assist in the army's mission. Slaves were not always immediately forthcoming with information, fearful of the wrath of their masters or the Rebel partisans that shadowed the column.

"A negro generally keeps dark," one Illinoisan noted. More often than not, though, they eventually "shed much light as to where we were to look to find wagons ready loaded with supplies, and hid in the woods to be hauled away in emergency, and many other things too good to be left."[100] Foraging detachments discovered provisions hidden in the woods, in canebrakes, in locked buildings, and even "nicely boxed up & hid under the rails by the roadside."[101] Each discovery marked a lesson learned that could be applied by the men in the search for provisions at the next plantation.

In many cases, detachments from Steele's "old" regiments directly encouraged slaves to join the column. Foragers derived great satisfaction from breaking into smokehouses and corncribs, and "throwing out . . . a lot of meat to the begging and half starved darkies."[102] At almost every property, slaves lining the roadway "seemed to think that we were their friends and appeared to think they must tell us all they knew and do every thing they were told to do."[103] In other instances, their intelligence proved somewhat fantastical. Slaves who were interrogated by the Twenty-Fifth Iowa alleged Rebel cavalry to be between twelve and twenty-four miles away, numbering anywhere "from twelve hundred to twelve hundred thousand."[104]

The path to freedom was not always a one-way street. Colonel A. J. Seay's "body servant," Allen, was retrieved by his local master during the expedition. Seay had no trouble finding two others to take his place.[105] Seizing freedom by assisting the Yankees could also entail grave dangers. One particularly unfortunate man approached a group of soldiers one night he assumed to be of Steele's band to share intelligence on the location of a nearby Rebel camp. Sadly, the pickets were Rebels themselves. As the blue column swept by a plantation the next day many noted his body hanging from a tree in the yard as a warning to all other slaves in the neighborhood to keep quiet.[106] Such scenes enraged the more liberal portions of Steele's command, and seemed to increase the amount of wanton destruction meted out on the rest of the valley. By the time the column countermarched back to Greenville, every cotton gin within sight of the creek was a smoldering ruin, and enormous piles of cotton and corn still belched flames and smoke into the sky. While there is no record of a single private residence being harmed in any way, in the case of almost every other useful structure, "the work of burning [went] magnificently on," one Hawkeye proudly observed.[107]

After returning from the fiery foray back to his base at Greenville on April 10, Steele continued to send occasional patrols from Greenville into the Deer Creek environs for the next several weeks. Try as he might, he had struggled to contain the libertine spirit that his mission naturally inspired. "Steele cannot control the men as he wishes," Seay observed during the march, even as the division commander occasionally "use[d] his sword and revolver" to curb the worst excesses.[108] Upon the column's return to Greenville, Steele was appalled to learn that so many private carriages, buggies, and farming implements had been arbitrarily seized against his orders. He promptly returned the items to aggrieved families upon their pleas for mercy, reporting this decision back to Sherman. Always the conservative, Cump shared Steele's disgust. "Our men will become absolutely lawless unless this can be checked," he warned. "War is at best barbarism, but to involve all—children, women, old and helpless—is more than can be justified." While the seizure or destruction of provender represented "a well-established law of war," the national government had no right to destroy "the stores necessary for a family." Worst of all, such unbridled destruction "injures our men to allow them to plunder indiscriminately." Even so, the brief reports issuing from Greenville were sufficient to convince both him and Grant that "Deer Creek has been sufficiently chastised never again to desire a Yankee visitation," and thus the expedition had succeeded in its primary mission.[109]

The expedition had been both an illustration of signature elements of the division's tactical culture as well as an indoctrination for Steele's "new" regiments into the practice of "war in earnest." Even for veterans of Curtis's long trek through Arkansas, the expedition had imparted valuable lessons. At the most basic level, the men gained considerable experience in the rudiments of extractive warfare. They encountered a variety of schemes hatched by crafty overseers, planters, and even slaves bent on securing or hiding foodstuffs and valuables. They learned to anticipate where various items of use were usually stored on Mississippi plantations, and developed methods by which they could swiftly be procured and transported. They now also better understood the intrinsic operational value of human intelligence provided by slaves and "contraband," who had assisted materially in the success of the expedition, just as they had further south with Sherman's column. Perhaps most importantly, they recognized the anxiety, fury, and anguish on the faces of the erstwhile proud and unrepentant planters and overseers from whom they confiscated. While their actual political stances were often far more complex than Steele's volunteers were apt to recognize, the men tended to categorize them all as the rankest of "Secesh," and making them pay for rebellion felt quite good. The schadenfreude felt even better when those in the ranks reflected upon how glad they were that "the ravages of war are not visited upon Iowa."[110] In all, the men of First Division returned to Greenville "in good spirits and believe they are now in a fair way to put down the rebellion," for the first time since leaving Helena months earlier.[111]

"A WHITE MANS WAR"

While Steele's command awaited orders at Greenville, Colonel Shepard, always at the forefront of emancipation, took the opportunity to begin drilling seventy of the Black men liberated during the recent expedition. Observers fashioned Shepard's impromptu cohort the "Black Brigade."[112] Members of the Twenty-Fifth Iowa watching the proceedings thought the freedmen promised to "make good soldiers," especially because they seemed "willing to learn and [were] prompt in obeying orders."[113] By April 17, the Federal camp at Greenville had accumulated nearly six hundred previously enslaved men and women, "and more coming in every day."[114] Less than a week later, the number had risen to nearly two thousand. "It is not necessary to march through the country to get Negroes," one Iowan realized, "they come in by scores, as fast as we can provide for them."[115] Steele quartered the refugees in the buildings of abandoned plantations, issued them rations from the bounty of seized provisions, and awaited orders advising him of the next proper step to take.[116] In the meantime, two steam mills were put to work grinding captured corn "and providing for all that come."[117]

The dramatic influx of African American refugees into the corps's camps coincided with an auspicious visit from US Army Adjutant General Lorenzo Thomas. Sent on a special mission directly from Washington by Secretary of State Edwin Stanton, Thomas had orders to make a circuit throughout Army camps across the country, making speeches emphasizing the vital importance of all US officers and soldiers embracing the Lincoln administration's decision to enlist and arm Black regiments. "It was a full-scale public relations campaign," historian Kristopher Teters observes, but among predominately conservative westerners it promised to be an uphill battle from the start.[118]

Sherman was unenthusiastic about Thomas's visit. Shortly after receiving word that the adjutant general would be addressing his corps "about nigger

Regiments," he privately shared his true thoughts with Ellen. Such an obviously partisan mission seemed beyond the proper purview of Thomas's responsibilities, he thought. "I'll hold my tongue," he promised, but "if he says nigger to me, Ill show him my morning Reports, ask him to inspect my Brigades or Batteries, or ask him to Sing the Star Spangled Banner and go back whence he comes." Despite recent experience, Cump continued to "prefer to have this a white mans war, & provide for the negro after the Storm had passed." Given his "experience, yea prejudice I cannot trust them yet," especially not with arms. Even so, he admitted that "Time may change this," and understood well that "we are in a Revolution and I must not pretend to judge."[119] Accordingly, he bit his lip while Thomas spoke to the men of Second Division. "I followed & Know the men look to me, more than anybody on Earth," he later wrote. Mounting a makeshift cracker-box platform, he explained to his beloved "old Division" precisely what he had told them several times before. They knew well his ambivalence to abolition, but "we are likened to a Sheriff," he dutifully explained, and thus "must execute the Writ of the Court & not go into an inquiry into the merits of the case." He admitted his earnest hope that armed Blacks would never "be brigaded with our white men," but rather assigned "some side purpose" in the rear. After all, his experience with even the many Black cooks and teamsters attached to his regiments had soured his opinion of their military potential. "They desert the moment danger threatens," he confided to John after the speech. In the end, however, though he "wont trust niggers to fight yet," like most of those in the ranks, he did not "object to the Government taking them from the Enemy, & making such use of them as experience may suggest."[120]

As Steele's division was absent at Greenville during Thomas's visit, the consummate professional and dutiful conservative had to relay the news to his command personally. On the morning of April 23, he ordered the division arrayed in hollow square in the center of which he stood alongside his senior lieutenants. First Division listened intently to what he had to say. Much to their surprise, the erstwhile ardent conservative "came out heartily and boldly in favor of the policy of the administration in freeing and arming the Negroes." Steele argued that "all slaves should be encouraged to come within our lines and be well treated and provided for." He also warned that "every soldier or officer who refused to obey the orders of the president in this matter would be promptly punished." He knew well that many in the ranks, perhaps even most, had long been of the opinion that he was "rather too pro slavery, and too much disposed to protect rebel property," but he meant to dispel such rumors once and for all. "We [have] treated them [Rebels] as erring brethren long enough," he proclaimed, and "the time had come to throw away the gloves and use every means in our power to crush the 'infernal rebellion.'" While Steele, like Sherman, remained fiercely opposed to any indiscriminate plundering of Southern property, he was strictly a man of duty, and his orders made crystal clear that the slaves were to be freed. Just as he had always done before, Steele did not allow any of his personal political convictions to color his interpretation of these orders. He was a soldier's soldier to the last. Those officers who followed him in sharing their comments, including nearly every brigade and regimental commander in the division, echoed his sentiments exactly. While many expressed having long felt that emancipation was the correct strategy, others flatly admitted that "a year or more ago they would have opposed it, but now supported it heartily." Listening closely as their commanders and leaders made a bid to shape the cultural outlook of the division, the men issued "not the least murmur of disapprobation," and instead greeted the "most radical sentiments . . . [with] the loudest cheers."[121]

The one-of-a-kind presentation had an electrifying effect on Steele's command.[122] "The army is *now* all right," Jacob Ritner wrote, "there is no mistake about that." Listening closely to the conversations about camp after the gathering had been dismissed, he heard none express opposition.[123] That was not because no opposition existed. One Buckeye of the Seventy-Sixth Ohio "didn't like quite all they said." Most especially grating to him were expressions by several officers that "they would as leave stand by the side of a negro to fight as by a white man." This he assumed to be a lie.[124] Hearing Colonel Charles Woods, his own regimental commander, and "no nigger man," express such beliefs seemed spurious and even duplicitous.[125] While few if any were now willing to express such sentiments aloud, Steele's entreaties had by no means purged them from the ranks.

On April 18, Sherman's order to begin accepting applications for commissions in new "colored" regiments reached Steele's camps at Greenville. Accordingly, a board of three examining officers was formed to consider applications, chaired by Colonel Woods, Seventy-Sixth Ohio, arguably the most well-versed regimental officer in the division on military matters.[126] Steele encouraged all men who had interest in positions as orderly sergeants in Black regiments to apply as well. The response was explosive. Nearly a full company applied from the Twenty-Fifth Iowa alone. Woods was not about to let things get out of hand, however, and maintained a reputation for being "very strict" in his selections. "They will have none but the best of officers," Ritner understood. Still, the opportunity for the most motivated of his volunteers to depart his command concerned him. "If they all get their places I will lose some of my best men," he worried.[127]

The initial enthusiasm for appointments into the new Black regiments arose most often from motives separate from political enthusiasm for emancipation and social revolution. Several noted how the most eager volunteers were frequently "the strongest democrats in the army."[128] Many of the same political stripe still could not bring themselves to apply regardless of promises of higher pay and authority. "I have a prejudice against the color which I cannot overcome," one Buckeye admitted.[129] A few officers who had not applied for positions were offered them anyway; most of whom turned them down. "I did not accept because I knew there would be a great trouble connected with them [Black troops]," Robert Stitt, an officer in the Fourth Iowa explained to his wife.[130] Regardless of their motivations, however, the departure of many of Sherman's highest performing enlisted men to serve in Black regiments did reduce the number of experienced senior noncommissioned officers in the corps. At the same time, it also cleared the way for junior enlisted men to receive promotions into the higher echelons of their companies and regiments, thus refreshing the leadership of many units, most especially "new" regiments, with volunteers who enjoyed considerable experience serving in the ranks as privates.

For most of the still-shaken survivors of Chickasaw Bayou and Arkansas Post in both divisions, the tack toward a strategy of emancipation and "war in earnest" was well received. Not only were expeditions like Steele's Bayou and Deer Creek comparatively enjoyable affairs, but they also seemed a viable alternative for defeating the Secessionist rebellion that did not entail desperate, costly, and often futile frontal assaults against entrenched Rebels. While many still balked at the notion of arming Black men, many others came to the conclusion that "the sooner the slaves are taken away from the rebels, the sooner the war will be over and the sooner they will get to go home."[131] The volunteers knew that Secessionists could not possibly defend the entirety of their vast domain, try as they might. Their plantations and highly prized human chattel were extremely vulnerable assets. Now that the Lincoln administration proved willing to embrace the direct targeting of this erstwhile carefully avoided Rebel center of gravity, many in the ranks rejoiced. "The taking of the negroes[,] arming the men and putting women and the old and young at work on the plantations will surely have a good effect," Cpt. Sewall Farwell, Thirty-First Iowa, wrote. His regiment having suffered among the worst of those roughly handled over the past winter's operations, Farwell and his comrades thought the recent expedition was promising for the future. "I think with the policy now being carried [out] that we are crushing the rebellion and will continue to crush it though we be repulsed from every stronghold for months to come," he prophesied.[132]

Jacob Ritner noticed how the "soldiers have all got to be in favor of setting the Negroes free, and arming them too." This change was not due to any particular moral enlightenment. "There is just as much prejudice against them as there ever was," he cautioned, adding that there was nearly always "someone trying to abuse, insult, and impose upon them." Instead, the shift in what he called "the universal sentiment" concerning the liberation and arming of slaves occurred because his comrades could now clearly see how "this is the quickest way to end the war, and that is what they all want."[133]

The experiences of the late winter and early spring imparted new lessons, skills, and beliefs to the men of Sherman's corps. Novel noncombat tasks had required adaptation in everything from force structure and tactical doctrine to political ideologies and even cultural outlooks. As the strength of every unit in the command shrunk dramatically, the corps's "skeleton regiments" became increasingly tight-knit cohorts. Those still on duty found themselves with a much greater share of work assigned to them. This meant a disproportionate amount of fatigue and hardship, but also greater opportunities to grow with experience. There were far fewer chances to "shirk" hard work than had existed in the past, even after the infusion of hundreds of freedmen to assist in the backbreaking labor that defined the corps's pursuit of its objectives. This infusion increased the amount of interaction and cooperation many in the corps engaged in with Blacks, and gradually converted the command into an increasingly biracial organization. To be sure, still only white men bore arms, but freedmen increasingly took over many of the critical tasks that allowed the corps to maneuver through the bayous. Given the command's apparently intractable struggles with offensive tactics, the ability to position its regiments on ground that abrogated any need for an assault was of tremendous importance. The labor of freedmen to facilitate such maneuvering increasingly proved of far greater operational value than anything they may have accomplished toting rifles in the ranks.

Sherman's new corps continued to evolve into a tool not of attack, but of swift maneuver and area denial. Its rapid movements and mere presence within valuable enemy breadbaskets were proving of far greater potency than the physical damage its continually shrinking ranks could do to Rebels on the battlefield. While the corps was by no means combat ineffective, its recent experience had vividly illustrated a crippling lack of coordination which threatened to hobble any assault on Rebel defenses. The failures resulting from this lack of coordination had inspired a lack of confidence for many in the corps when ordered to launch an attack against works. Some of this sentiment was inspired by a lingering lack of confidence in their corps commander. A correspondent wandering the camps at Young's Point in March was struck by the "great deal of hard feeling throughout his command towards Gen. Sherman." The men he spoke with "complain that he is incapable, cruel, and malignant," still citing the Chickasaw disaster as evidence of the former and exceedingly high rates of death from disease as proof of the latter.[134]

Despite their lack of confidence in Sherman's competency in planning, the experiences of the bayou expeditions suggested a possible workaround to the men for the corps's tactical shortcomings. The now proven capacity of its divisions to move great distances through almost impenetrable terrain, convert their regiments and companies into collections of widespread detachments led by junior leaders, and quickly complete ad-hoc engineering tasks while providing for their own security began to suggest the emergence of a different corps-level "way of war." Their sense of mostly bloodless success suggested to those in the ranks an alternative recipe for victory, giving rise to an emergent "soldier's culture."

In his typology of the many varieties of "military culture," Wayne Lee describes "soldiers' culture" as shared beliefs, patterns of behavior, and assumptions that organically arise "from the shared experience of a non-elite soldiery, which often is in defiance of their elite masters but which they [see] as essential to their survival."[135] The prevailing interpretation of "war in earnest" in the ranks of Sherman's corps not merely as another tactic in their arsenal, but as a viable alternative to direct action against entrenched Rebels, was a key by-product of the emergent Fifteenth Corps "soldiers' culture," promising the men increased odds of survival. In this way it closely resembled the formula many had adopted under fire at Arkansas Post when going to ground near the enemy works and sharpshooting from cover. The men in the ranks of Sherman's corps made it ever increasingly clear through their actions that they sought first and foremost to survive the war. Their patriotic motivations to preserve the Union and defend republican government had not waned, but they could not achieve either if dead.

As this emergent soldiers' culture did not yet extend to Sherman's headquarters, it cannot be said to have represented a coherent "corps culture." The process of frustrating trial and error by which Grant had attempted to avoid a costly frontal assault on Vicksburg seemed little more than tedious to Cump. He did not blame his friend, but such forays were "bordering on the impossible, and to take Vicksburg without the deadly & costly assault is impossible," he remarked to his brother. In his opinion, "we should fight on all occasions even if we do get worsted." After all, with its bounty of available manpower, the United States could "stand it longest." His incomplete grasp of the culture in the ranks of his corps was still on clear display as late as early April. Writing to his brother John, Cump assured him that "all my soldiers are attached to me," and that every "officer of whatever Rank who arrives applies for my Corps, because they know I am truthful and will not slaughter them to build up a little personal fame." While it was true that Sherman remained uninterested in bolstering his ego or reputation with the Northern public, plenty of those in the ranks of his corps had every good reason to presume that he would take no especial pains to avoid ordering them to slaughter. It was for that very reason that many would continue to refer to him with names like "the Stormer" or "bloodhound," presumably when well out of earshot.[136]

Even so, Sherman was not so intransigent in his thinking as to escape the late winter unaffected by experience. "We are doing good," he admitted, even considering the repeated failures of the bayou expeditions. Unauthorized foraging by "skulkers" aside, the performance of his command in conducting deliberate area-denial and resource-extraction operations was promising. "We have Consumed much, and destroyed more," he wrote proudly, but remained awestruck by the sheer volume of provender his two divisions had discovered hidden in the isolated Deer Creek Valley. "I tell you tis all nonsense about the South being exhausted," he observed. "Northern papers talk about Starvation in Vicksburg," but his columns "saw every where cattle, hogs, sheep, poultry and vast cribs of corn." If the rebellion was ever to be brought to its knees, it would take much more of these kinds of operations on a much grander scale. "The war in Earnest," he decided, "has yet to be fought."[137]

CHAPTER 5

THE MEN CANNOT BE MADE TO DO IT

The Vicksburg Campaign

It was Sherman's order and that bloodhound and madman is responsible for a thousand more lives vainly and foolishly sacrificed.

—SGT. MAJ. EDWARD P. REICHHELM, THIRD MISSOURI

The operational assignments of the Fifteenth Corps throughout the campaign for Vicksburg were heavily influenced by the close personal relationship maintained between Sherman and Grant. Their mutual trust meant that Sherman's corps was often handpicked to operate independently of the others of Grant's army. Frequently, this resulted in assignment to less glamorous missions, but also to less fighting than was the case for McPherson's and McClernand's commands. The corps did not take substantive part in any of the contests that marked the route to Vicksburg: Port Gibson, Raymond, or Champion Hill. Even so, Grant trusted "Cump" more than the less experienced McPherson, and maintained little faith in McClernand, prompting him to remain nearby whenever they might run into trouble. He also felt the need to remain with the main body of his army, which meant that he required a reliable lieutenant to take care of things elsewhere. Sherman, and his corps, fit the bill.

Nearly all of the assignments Grant handed to Sherman's corps during the long circuitous march to Jackson and eventual investiture of the "Gibraltar of the Mississippi" were well tailored to its tactical culture. This happy marriage of the right corps with the right objectives ended upon the army's arrival at the gates of Vicksburg, when both Grant and Sherman once again behaved as if unaware, or at least willfully ignorant, of the corps's lack of confidence and interminable coordination struggles when assaulting fieldworks.

Prior to the onset of the campaign, the corps experienced its first major command shake-up. Following his promotion to major general in mid-March, in part due to his courageous performance at Chickasaw Bayou, Frank Blair needed a position more prestigious than that of a brigadier. Just such a position opened up when news reached the Young's Point camps that Congress had denied David Stuart's promotion. The target of considerable ire and lingering ill-repute regarding involvement in a famous antebellum divorce case, Second Division's commander had hoped that an illustrious military career might convert his reputation in the public eye. Unfortunately, though having performed admirably on every field from Shiloh to Arkansas Post, this was not to be the case. Resigning upon reception of the bad news, Stuart left Second Division with a note of thanks for its loyal service since his taking of command at Chickasaw Bayou. Grant handed the slot to Blair, the highest ranking brigadier in the corps.[1]

In addition to the change of command in Second Division, the corps temporarily gained a Third Division under the command of Brigadier General James Tuttle, attached by Grant in order to equalize the corps's combat power with those of McPherson and McClernand. Tuttle's three brigades were not destined to spend more than a single campaign with the command and struggled to integrate themselves with the other two divisions, which had already endured significant trials alongside one another.[2]

Although Grant initially planned to move his entire army southward toward Grand Gulf on April 20, the abysmal condition of the roads through the Louisiana swamps forced him to hold Sherman back until the route could be improved by McClernand's and McPherson's pioneers. Eagerly awaiting orders to follow, Cump received a note from Grant on April 28 informing him of the plan to assault Grand Gulf directly with a combined force of infantry and gunboats in order to secure a landing for the army on the east bank of the river. Grant requested that one division of Sherman's corps make a diversionary movement toward Haynes's Bluffs to distract the Rebel garrison. Cump was to take special care to ensure that those in the ranks understood that the maneuver was no more than a feint, as Grant wanted to avoid the damaging presumption that the corps was once again headed into the meat grinder of the Yazoo bottoms. While trusting that "the army could distinguish a feint from a real attack," Sherman still prudently opted to assign his more confident "old Division" to the mission, embarking it upon ten steamboats on the morning of April 29 and proceeding directly to the mouth of the Yazoo.[3]

Crawling northward toward the Rebel batteries atop the fortified bluffs, the boats passed the hallowed battlefield of Chickasaw Bayou and continued northward until in "easy range" of the enemy batteries. Accompanying gunboats opened on all enemy batteries within reach as Blair's division disembarked in view of the Rebels, taking care to "seemingly prepare to assault." In truth, the foray had more than a tinge of absurdity. Both Sherman and the Rebels "knew full well that there was no road across the submerged field that lay between the river and the bluff," rendering any assault impossible. Even so, ever faithful to Grant's wishes, the division kept up appearances until dark, when it re-embarked and started back across the river to Young's Point. Shortly after his return, a courier reached Sherman with another note from Grant. "Hurry forward," it urged. Having failed to secure Grand Gulf, Grant had instead moved the army further south and crossed at Bruinsburg, where it found the eastern bank all but uncontested. Accordingly, Cump started Steele's and Tuttle's divisions, then idling in camp, southward. On the morning of May 2, the Fifteenth Corps was finally on the road to Vicksburg. Blair's division remained behind to rest after the diversionary foray, guarding the camps at Young's Point.[4]

After four days of hard marching, Steele's and Tuttle's commands made the sixty-three miles to Hard Times, Louisiana, four miles north of the crossing at Grand Gulf.[5] Steamers ferried the two divisions across to the east bank at Grand Gulf on May 7, and the next day they marched eighteen additional miles northeast to Hankinson's Ferry on the Big Black River. By May 10, they had rendezvoused with the main body of Grant's army, then tarrying east of Port Gibson as its chief determined his next step. After much deliberation, he chose to head northeastward, aiming for Edward's Station and an opportunity to cut the vital Vicksburg and Jackson Railroad, isolating the Rebel garrison from outside support. The whole army would sweep northeast with all three corps utilizing separate routes, spread across a nearly twenty-mile front and using the Big Black River to protect their vulnerable left flank. McClernand's Thirteenth Corps would take the left, McPherson's Seventeenth the right, and Sherman's Fifteenth the center, slightly behind the others. In two days the three disparate elements would converge upon Fourteen Mile Creek, a short distance south of their objective at Edward's Station.

Keeping his titanic host fed and supplied was Grant's greatest concern. After making the long journey by boat from the depots at Memphis to Milliken's Bend and Young's Point, the army's supplies had to be hauled down the same winding route by which Sherman's corps had just made its way to the main body. While the tactical pause outside Port Gibson allowed time for the army's quartermasters to replenish supplies thus far expended, in the future such an extended lifeline would be challenging, if not impossible, to maintain. Supplies would continue to flow from Memphis and Grand Gulf throughout the campaign, but it was already clear to Grant that in the future it would be necessary to "make the country furnish the balance." While historians have celebrated this bold decision to cut from his base of supply as a feat of military genius, it came at a great cost in hardship for those of Sherman's corps habitually in the extreme rear of the army, left only scraps for forage after the passage of McClernand's and McPherson's corps. Those in Sherman's divisions fully recognized the precariousness of their logistical situation. In fact, Sherman had made sure they did, announcing in his general orders how "the officers and men of the whole army should be impressed with the real difficulty of supplying so large an army of men and horses by such a road." "Rations are hard to get and should disaster occur we will be in a bad fix," Iowan Sewall Farwell worried. "It seems to me we must be successful or be destroyed as an army we are so far from a base of supply." Most regiments found themselves restricted to two hardtack crackers per day.[6]

Arriving at the banks of Fourteen Mile Creek on May 12, Steele's division quickly secured a bridgehead. Taking personal command of the head of his corps column, Sherman ordered a battery of Steele's howitzers to shell the bushes on the opposite bank with canister while Col. Charles Woods's (originally Hovey's) brigade forded the creek and the Turner skirmishers of the Seventeenth Missouri traded shots with Rebel cavalry. Once the enemy had abandoned the east bank, Steele's pioneers set to work fashioning a crossing "in lieu of the burned bridge." Though requiring only three hours of labor, the delay was long enough for the remaining Secessionist cavalry to escape Sherman's grasp.[7]

Meanwhile, McPherson's corps on the right stumbled into a sharp fight at Raymond. While McClernand's divisions on the left discovered the advanced elements of what had originally been the Vicksburg garrison south of Edward's Station, McPherson's encounter to the east suggested that another Rebel contingent was guarding the state capital at Jackson. Sensing an opportunity, Grant now took action to attempt the piecemeal destruction of both. While McPherson's and McClernand's corps moved north in a feint to distract the westernmost of the two Rebel elements, Grant ordered Sherman's corps northeast to approach the state capital directly from the south with Tuttle's fresh division in the lead.[8]

The road to Jackson passed through "a continual succession of hills and valleys" formed of yellow clay. Dust in the roadbed was at least four inches deep in many places. "Innumerable buffalo gnats" mercilessly tormented man and beast alike. "They fly in your face and bite," one Missourian recorded in his diary while shooing them away. Fresh water was scarce, and the delays caused by balking teams and gun crews stalled in the ascent of each hill became "irksome" in the extreme. Yellow dust filled lungs, and the dry heat made breathing a chore. Finally, on the thirteenth, the dry spell was broken when the heavens opened and "it rained harder than I ever saw in my life," one wrote in awe, adding, with some exaggeration, that "the men almost drowned in the rain, mud, and water." The road deteriorated under the downpour, delays abounded, and the men were forced to stand in the rain for long stints. Road cuts transformed into veritable sloughs, and in some spots the column waded through water nearly up to their waists. After making little progress due to the weather, the miserable men "lay on the soaked ground drenched to the skin, hungry and exhausted."[9]

"A PERFECT RABBLE"

Arriving within about three miles of Jackson at ten o'clock on May 14, Tuttle's advance guard could clearly make out the thunder of McPherson's guns operating further north. It fell to his Third Division to spearhead Sherman's attack on the capital. After using his artillery to brush away a few lingering Rebel batteries watching over the Lynch Creek bridge southwest of the city, Tuttle advanced the division into a field on the east bank and maneuvered his brigades into line of battle, immediately charging Rebel skirmishers visible in a tree line beyond. The enemy having no works from which to repel Tuttle's assault, little blood was shed, and the Secessionists scurried back into their trenches outside Jackson. This changed the game.

Tuttle now confronted a tactical problem all but identical to that faced by the other two divisions of Sherman's corps at Chickasaw Bayou and Arkansas Post. "As far to the left as we could see, appeared a line of intrenchments," Sherman noted. For the first time during the long campaign, he showed signs of pause. Not wanting a repeat of the stalemate at "the Post," he ordered a staffer to take one of Tuttle's regiments "and make a detour to the right to see what was there," hoping to find an undefended flank. Steele's brigades would follow. In ordering this reconnaissance, Sherman repeated the same tactic he had ordered at Chickasaw Bayou and Arkansas Post, feeling for the Rebel flank prior to reluctantly accepting the necessity of a frontal assault. A short time later, the aide returned with wonderful news. The Rebel works on the far right were abandoned, and the city was Grant's for the taking.[10]

Although as many as six thousand Rebels had only recently garrisoned the capital, their commander, Gen. Joseph E. Johnston, had hastily evacuated the city in anticipation of Grant's arrival. While the foremost elements of McPherson's corps and Tuttle's division had run into the Secessionist rear guard, Steele's flanking division found only a wary band of state militia disinclined to put up a fight. Soon, even those to Tuttle's front had withdrawn. By nightfall, the Fifteenth Corps indisputably held Jackson, and its arrival marked a major turning point in the morale of the rank and file, boosting their trust in the army's leadership. "For once the rebels had been out generaled," one Iowan officer crowed. "We marched in with wet clothes, tired limbs blistered feet and empty stomachs but no one heeded these things." After hard marching and considerable fatigue, but fortunately little fighting, the corps now found itself unopposed in the streets of the Mississippi capital. As in the aftermath of the mostly bloodless bayou expeditions, the men again took note of what could be accomplished when "our Generals" put their minds to it. Many in the ranks quietly "thanked our stars that our exhausted vitality had not been put to a severer test." As the haggard-looking regiments of Steele's and Tuttle's divisions reconsolidated after the long march and companies stacked arms, "a race to town took place and a wild hunt for something to eat" became impossible to prevent. For the fleetest of foot, nourishment was readily available, and "immediate starvation, at least, was staved off."[11]

Hoping to catch the westernmost of the two Rebel forces off-balance, including most of the Vicksburg garrison sallied forth from its defenses,

Grant eagerly pushed McClernand's and McPherson's corps westward the following morning. Once again, he charged Sherman's corps with another independent assignment. Cump's command was to remain in Jackson and "destroy effectually the railroad tracks . . . and all the property belonging to the enemy," with an eye toward preventing the capital's reoccupation by the Rebels under Johnston still lingering nearby. Yet again, Grant leaned on his trusted lieutenant's command to carry out fiery area-denial operations while the remainder of his army pursued the enemy. Ever obedient, Sherman wasted no time in assigning the regiments of Steele's division to the thorough destruction of the railroad, the bridge over the Pearl River, and all Rebel government "property to the south and east" of the city. Meanwhile, Tuttle's division would seize or destroy all Rebel property of military value to the north and west. Destruction of the tracks was to "be extended out as far as possible, and must be complete," but above all else, "dispatch [was] of the utmost importance," Sherman emphasized. The sooner the corps could complete its work, the sooner it could rejoin the rest of the army and maximize Grant's strategic options. By destroying the strategic rail junction east of Vicksburg, Sherman's corps would prevent any Rebel relief army from threatening Grant's rear as he moved west to bag the prize.[12]

Employing the same tactics as during the recent bayou expeditions, the two divisions fragmented into smaller fatigue details, each assigned a separate mission under the command of a junior or noncommissioned officer. Details pried up rails and ties, stacked them, set the ties ablaze, and warmed the rails over the fire before warping them around trees. Starting five miles out and working their way back toward the center of town, the men worked with determination. Sweaty details had dismantled the railroad in all directions by the following morning, with some laboring all night long to meet the deadline. Their work was exceedingly thorough, and the tracks would not be operational again for months. Other groups spread out to search and destroy "everything public not needed by us." The Pearl River bridge was doused with twenty barrels of tar and set ablaze. Afterward, even the abutments "were battered down" with artillery. Several other minor bridges were destroyed in similar fashion. Ammunition beyond that which could be carried along with the army was summarily thrown into the Pearl River. Other targets included the city's arsenal buildings, a cannon and ammunition foundry, printing presses, sundry manufacturing facilities, storehouses, flouring mills, cotton sheds, warehouses, the railroad depot, rope factory, saltpeter works, and even part of the Mississippi state peniten-tiary, which had been converted into a cotton and munitions factory. Rebel tents were collected, stacked behind the State House, and set afire. "The quantity destroyed is beyond calculation," one Hawkeye put bluntly.[13]

There were in fact significant limits on the destruction. The governor's mansion and the State House were preserved. Even so, as seemed to occur so often, the destruction far exceeded Sherman's wishes. When it came to his knowledge that both a Catholic church and the local "Confederate Hotel," along with several other unauthorized structures and even a few private homes were in flames, he grew enraged. While the church and homes were likely an accident, the others were clearly acts of malice "not justified by the rules of war," he complained. Mischief was by no means restricted to arson, either. Despite the appointment of Brig. Gen. Mower's brigade to serve as temporary provost of the city, rumor inevitably made it to corps headquarters that several guards were freely "giving license to soldiers to take the contents of stores, taking things not necessary or use-ful." If true, Sherman warned, this was absolutely indefensible. "Only such articles should be taken as are necessary to the subsistence of troops, and the private rights of citizens should be respected," he insisted. Even so, what specifically was "necessary to the subsistence of the troops" proved a profoundly subjective question.[14]

In a few cases, the necessity of articles seized was obvious on its face. Food, boots, and shoes were among the most highly prized commodities. In other cases, the definition of military necessity blurred. The Twenty-Fifth Iowa scored "fine clothes of every kind, tobacco, sugar, cigars, horses, buggies, fine coaches, in fact everything imaginable," Captain John Bell exclaimed. As the city's businesses were turned upside down by looting foragers, "the niggers and workers had a rich harvest and booty" as they joined in the chaos. The offices of the local paper were "broken open, the type thrown in the street and the presses and furniture broken up," and the post office "rifled of its contents." The governor's palatial estate, while spared the torch, was likewise "broken open and pianos and furniture de-stroyed." Many private residences "were entered . . . trunks broken open, fine dresses torn to pieces, and the jewelry, silver ware and provisions taken," according to one stunned Mississippian. Medical instruments were taken from the local dentist, books and bindery seized from the local book-seller, medicine stolen from the pharmacy, and of course no shortage of tobacco and provisions liberated from the local grocery, which assessed its losses at no less than $200,000. "Intelligent gentlemen" assessed the total loss of property in the city and environs, all incurred in less than thirty-six hours' time, at $5,000,000. Mississippi Governor John Pettus doubled that figure in his own retrospective assessment.[15]

Disgust at the behavior of many in the command was not restricted to those at Sherman's headquarters. Lt. Henry Kircher, Twelfth Missouri, thought that even "war in earnest" ought to be "carried on in a deacent [sic] way, and not any one allowed to destroy as suits his notion. We are not rob[b]ers." Lt. Col. A. J. Seay, Thirty-Second Missouri, was likewise disgusted. The men had behaved like "a perfect rabble for 4 or 5 hours," he complained. No doubt fueled by confiscated alcohol, the fugitives had destroyed many unauthorized buildings, "but I am proud to say no private houses have been burned," at least not deliberately. The seizure of goods apparently bothered him far less than the pyromania. His Missourians managed to procure "an immense quantity of tobacco, some rum, whiskey, wines, etc., some clothing and some provisions," all of which Seay deemed a welcome treat.[16]

The next morning, Sherman received a message from Grant ordering the ash-covered corps in motion westward once again. The command was on the road by ten o'clock. Both sides of the route quickly became strewn with illicitly captured goods and commodities too cumbersome to carry along.[17] The column made twenty miles to Bolton Station on the sixteenth and reached Bridgeport on the Big Black River the following day. Waiting there for Cump was Frank Blair with Second Division. The division had marked time at Young's Point, improving the infrastructure of Grant's supply route west of the river before receiving orders from Sherman on May 7 to rejoin the main body. After a long march south, Blair procured transportation and crossed two brigades to Grand Gulf in the evening of May 11, setting out for Jackson in the morning. Ewing's Third Brigade remained on the west side of the river, completing a road from Young's Point to Warrenton until being relieved and marching to Grand Gulf on May 15. The brigade would rejoin Blair's division at Vicksburg on the eighteenth.[18]

Blair's primary assignment was the security of Grant's lengthy two-hundred-wagon train then en route to the main army. The train's painstaking movement greatly slowed the division's forward rate of speed, requiring three days to reach Raymond. Arriving in the midst of the rapid movement to bag Pemberton's force at Champion Hill, the command was temporarily attached to McClernand's corps with orders to support its attack. With the exception of a few Rebel shells which fell too close for comfort, and a little light skirmishing, the division was mostly a spectator to the main event. Even so, when called upon to advance to the support of other troops in contact to their front, the men conducted themselves in accordance with their division's tactical culture. Leading the column, Giles Smith's brigade deployed one company from each of its regiments ahead as skirmishers "with orders to advance and push the enemy vigorously." Meanwhile, the main body remained in the rear at its customary "close supporting distance," collecting no fewer than three hundred prisoners as it swept across the shattered forests of the battlefield.[19] Ordered north by Grant to rejoin its parent corps, the "old Division" was finally reunited with Sherman as the corps prepared to cross the Big Black River at Bridgeport. After brushing a few lingering enemy sharpshooters from the western bank with artillery, the way was clear for the corps to continue its march on Vicksburg. That night, the once-again famished regiments crawled over a flimsy pontoon bridge illuminated by bonfires on both banks.[20]

After defeating Pemberton's force at the Battle of Champion Hill with McPherson's and McClernand's corps, Grant swiftly pursued his weary prey to the west as it limped back toward Vicksburg. By ten o'clock on May 18, the lead elements of Blair's division at the head of the Fifteenth Corps had interposed themselves between Vicksburg and the long-sought-after Rebel forts atop Haynes's and Drumgould's bluffs. After nearly six months and immeasurable hardship, Grant's army was finally on the high ground in Vicksburg's rear. Pausing at a fork in the road to deploy Smith's Zouaves and Regulars as skirmishers to scout in both directions, Sherman awaited Grant's instructions on how to proceed. Upon his arrival shortly thereafter, the army commander ordered Cump to continue westward toward the northern defenses, while McPherson and McClernand headed south to approach the eastern and southern defenses respectively. Accordingly, Sherman moved Blair's division forward toward the works, left Tuttle's in support, and ordered Steele to extend further west down the road in search of the banks of the Mississippi and, even more importantly, the only road running north out of the city.[21]

By then, the hunger pangs were almost insufferable. Exhausted men stumbled out of line into the woods flanking the road in search of almost anything to satiate their stomachs. "Hungry near to the starvation point, we ate weeds, roots, leaves or anything we could get a hold of," one Missourian recalled. An officer in the 113th Illinois overheard someone in his company joking about how he planned to subsist "by chewing newspaper advertisements of provisions" cut from Rebel papers he had found in Jackson. Another in the Seventy-Sixth Ohio offered one of his privates a half-dollar for a piece of hardtack. Abandoned Rebel rifle pits discovered along the way offered a handful of skirmishers a highly coveted prize. "The rebels retreating in great haste had left us their breakfast in camp kettles filled with corn meal mush, and also bacon and corn bread and other delicacies," one remembered. These were "ravenously devoured." Even bags of raw corn intended for horse feed were slashed open and their contents pocketed by famished men, meant to "stave off starvation until relief should come from the fleet." For most in the column, though, only "filling up with water" could provide enough respite for sleep at night.[22]

By dawn on the nineteenth, the army had finally reached its objective. Despite tremendous hardship, the Army of the Tennessee had successfully outmaneuvered, and in multiple cases outfought, two Rebel armies converging to prevent it from reaching the gates of Vicksburg. "We had compassed the enemy to the north of Vicksburg, our right resting on the Mississippi River, with a plain view of our fleets at the mouth of the Yazoo and Young's Point," Sherman proclaimed in his report, "Vicksburg in plain sight, and nothing separated us from the enemy but a space of about 400 yards of very difficult ground." It was to prove "very difficult" indeed.[23]

"UNSUPPORTED ON THE LEFT OR RIGHT"

Little in the way of substantive attempts to address the corps's coordinative shortcomings or lack of confidence in frontal assaults had been attempted by Sherman or his lieutenants since the spectacular failures at Chickasaw Bayou and Arkansas Post. This was mostly due to a lingering divergence of explanations for these failures prevailing at headquarters and in the ranks. Sherman and his chief subordinates remained convinced that failure had been principally due to a lack of experience, discipline, and spirit within attacking regiments, most especially among their junior officers. Little to no consideration was apparently given to their own coordinative failures as a command team. The men, on the other hand, most especially those of Steele's hard-luck division, were of the opinion that orders for frontal assaults against works were themselves evidence of a grave incompetency in the higher echelons of command. "Our Generals" seemed to suffer from a severe lack of creativity, and for that reason repeatedly ordered what amounted to suicide missions. Lacking confidence in their ability to succeed, most of those in the ranks had instead devised practical strategies to survive such futile assignments without sacrificing their personal or regimental honor, by obediently advancing to an enemy's abatis or into his initial shock volley, and subsequently going to ground to "sharpshoot."

The long campaign of maneuver to Vicksburg gave hope to many that "our Generals" might have perhaps finally learned their lesson, and a germ of renewed confidence began to spread as the army again found itself in view of the Mississippi. That confidence was perhaps highest in the ranks of Sherman's corps, having been spared much fighting during the circuitous march, unlike the other corps of Grant's army. Even so, on the morning of May 19, it was once again the Fifteenth Corps's turn to bleed. Grant was confident that Pemberton's army was still reeling from its defeat at Champion Hill, and thus would crumble under minimal pressure. Accordingly, he planned to use the entire army to assault the Rebel works in hopes of collapsing what little fighting spirit the garrison still retained and seizing the city without having to resort to a lengthy siege. After all, with Johnston's force still hovering near Jackson, there was no telling how long he had to bag the "Gibraltar" before having to fight in both front and rear.

The mostly slave-prepared Rebel defenses of Vicksburg extended for a distance of more than eight miles, encompassing the northern, eastern, and southern portions of the city completely. Scarring a succession of hills that ringed Vicksburg, the irregular and jagged line of works appeared "exceedingly tortuous" to the eye, but this gave it additional strength, allowing for a crossfire of rifle, musket, and artillery fire at almost every point. To the immediate front of Blair's division on the northeastern shoulder of these defenses, blocking the route of what locals called the "old grave yard road," were the looming ramparts of "Fort Beauregard," known today as "Stockade Redan." As the slopes of the region's hills were so steep, and the intervening valleys so filled with tangled thickets and dense underbrush, relatively few viable avenues of approach existed for attacking the imposing salient. In fact, along Sherman's front only one immediately presented itself: the "Graveyard Road." Visible from Rebel defenses for several hundred yards in either direction, assaulting columns would almost certainly remain under a deadly fire for their entire journey down the road toward their objective. Whether any body of troops could endure such a fusillade while still maintaining ample force to penetrate the fort's parapet upon arrival was an open question. Grant meant to find out.[24]

Although Grant issued orders on the evening of the eighteenth for all three corps to "push forward rapidly, and gain as close positions as possible to the enemy's works" in preparation for an army-wide assault at two o'clock in the afternoon, by that time Sherman's was still the only corps in position. Moreover, of his three divisions, Blair's was the only command poised to assault the Stockade Redan complex, and thus Cump charged it with the mission. All three of Blair's brigades would participate in the assault arrayed in line of battle, forming behind a hill to shroud their preparations from prying Rebel eyes. On the left, Blair ordered Kilby Smith's regiments to aim directly for the Stockade Redan, attacking along the Graveyard Road but split into two wings by its raised embankment. The right wing of the brigade, including the Eighty-Third Indiana and 127th Illinois, Smith placed in the independent command of Col. Benjamin Spooner, "in whose ability and dauntless courage I repose[d] fullest confidence." Spooner was to drive his pair of regiments "forward as rapidly as possible" in the customary Second Division fashion—not worrying so much about well-dressed formations, but rather surging forward "in such order as he could best get over the ground."[25]

In Blair's center, Giles Smith's brigade would assault down a steep slope and directly through the Mint Spring ravine, aiming at the Rebel line running between a prominent lunette to the east and Stockade Redan. On his right, Ewing's brigade, having yet to participate in an assault with the corps, would likewise attack through the ravine, doing its best to cut through the entangling abatis while aiming directly for the lunette. Having never before conducted a frontal assault against Rebel works, but assuming that the army's recent victories at Raymond and Champion Hill indicated that it was truly "irresistible," Ewing's Buckeyes "expected another complete victory." The advance would constitute "a short job," Ewing proclaimed to the assembled command. "We would be inside of the works, in less than ten minutes after receiving the order to move," he promised. Finally, in cooperation with Blair's brigades, Sherman ordered Steele to advance Thayer's Iowa brigade in an attack on the Rebel works to the west of Second Division to prevent enfilading enemy fire on Ewing's regiments from that sector.[26]

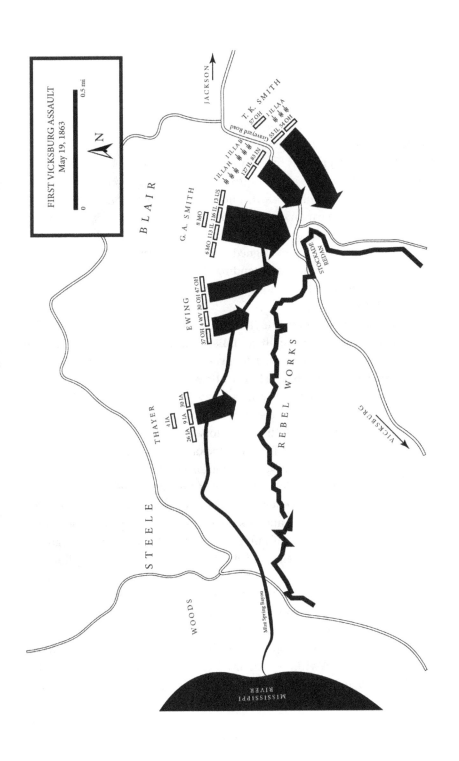

FIRST VICKSBURG ASSAULT
May 19, 1863

N

0   0.5 mi

JACKSON

T. K. SMITH

54 OH
127 IL
83 IN
116 IL
113 IL
8 MO
6 MO
30 OH 47 OH
4 WV
37 OH
30 IA
41 IA
9 IA
26 IA

Graveyard Road

STOCKADE
REDAN

VICKSBURG

BLAIR

G. A. SMITH

EWING

THAYER

STEELE

WOODS

REBEL WORKS

Mint Spring Bayou

MISSISSIPPI RIVER

In hopes of keeping Rebel heads down behind the parapet during the assault, Blair ordered the division's Zouave skirmishers advanced as far forward as possible "with a view of obtaining a closer position and of reconnoitering the ground" prior to the attack. In this, he displayed a basic grasp of the division's habitual skirmisher-centric approach to assaults, despite having only recently taken command. The guns of Battery A, First Illinois Light Artillery, registered five rounds on the parapet to find their range, shouting their findings aloud to the gun teams in a manner that nearby skirmish teams must have heard, adjusting their own sights accordingly.[27] At nine o'clock, Sherman ordered a preliminary bombardment in hopes of easing the job of the assaulting force, and thus all available guns along Blair's line opened on their assigned targets. The bombardment continued unabated for five full hours, extending throughout the morning and into the early afternoon. Almost no return fire was received from Rebel batteries behind the works.

At precisely two o'clock, the Illinoisan guns fired three salvos in quick succession to signal the assault, and Blair's division "dashed forward" into the deadly valley. The dispersed Zouaves poured a heavy fire from behind cover onto the top of the parapet in an attempt to suppress the enemy. While the effectiveness of their fire was, as always, difficult to judge, the small numbers of effectives still in the regiment, as well as the necessity of firing upward toward the crest of the steep slope from the ravine bottom, likely limited their impact. The defense of Stockade Redan proved more akin to that confronted by Blair's brigade at Chickasaw Bayou than it did the shock tactics confronted at Arkansas Post. As at Chickasaw, near impenetrable terrain, dense abatis, and enemy fire dismantled the assault long before it reached the base of the parapet. As the mass of each brigade "dashed over stumps and tangled limbs of fallen trees, struggled through deep gullies bristling with brush and cane, and climbed the steep slopes," one Illinoisan observed how "men dropped by tens [from enemy fire], stopped behind some sheltering log or bank, [or] slackened speed for sheer want of breath" until finally "all the momentum of the start had worn itself out; and a thin line of panting, staggering humanity pressed on."[28]

Trees felled with their tops toward the attacker, their branches sharpened and entangled with telegraph wire, presented a formidable abatis. Rebel slaves had dug deep pits covered with dry grass designed to swallow whole portions of assaulting lines unaware of their presence. In several spots, these obstructions proved "an almost impenetrable mass," forcing men to cut narrow pathways through the trees and wire that quickly drew "a murderous cross fire" as they tried to surge through the tight defiles. In other places, most notably along the right flank of Ewing's brigade, whole regiments discovered that passage through the abatis was utterly impossible, and they were forced to halt, go to cover, and add their fire to the suppression of the works with the Zouaves instead.[29]

Even for those who managed to cut their way through the obstructions, maintaining alignment proved impossible, shattering the concentrated mass necessary for the assault to succeed. "A line of battle could no longer be preserved," one Regular remembered, "but the flag steadily advanced, and each man earnestly strove to keep within its shadow." Recognizing this, the captain of the color company called to the ensign to keep the banner well ahead of the battalion, as "we shall not be able to preserve much of a line." Col. Hamilton Eldridge, leading his 127th Illinois alongside Spooner's Hoosiers, also noted the tendency of terrain and Rebel fire to scatter the men "to a considerable extent," with only the colors serving as rallying points for those making their way forward independently. Even Kilby Smith was forced to admit that it "was almost vain to essay a line." As at Chickasaw Bayou, the visibility of bright regimental colors through the smoke proved crucial to maintaining any vestige of cohesion in the chaos.[30]

After making upwards of four hundred yards across the ravine, the surviving members of both brigades paused under the defiladed cover of the southern slope, "where they were comparatively sheltered from the small-arms of the enemy," Kilby Smith reported. An additional deadly seventy-five yards of almost vertical embankment still separated the command from its objective, but Smith quickly recognized that the men around him "were thoroughly exhausted" and his brigade was "alone, [and] unsupported on the left or right, save by a portion of the Thirteenth Regulars." Even most of Giles Smith's adjacent command was impossible to see from the southern side of the road. Rising from his prone position along the slope to gaze southward, he was disheartened to find "not a soldier to be seen" and absolutely no evidence "that we had friends near us outside of our division." Something must have gone awry, he assumed, and sent a runner to find Blair and ascertain the facts. While they waited, many scrambled to find cover from which to ply their skills as marksmen—just as they had from the abatis at Arkansas Post. Quickly spotting a group of Rebel skirmishers "picking off our officers with devilish skill," several crack shots worked to silence the enemy riflemen as they awaited further orders.[31]

Though invisible to Kilby Smith, First Brigade was in fact making some progress, none of its regiments more so than the small indomitable band of Regulars. Their national standard was by then "yards in advance of anyone," making it a natural target for every Rebel in the immediate vicinity. A special kind of madness fired the enthusiasm of the men to keep the flag aloft. Despite a withering fire that cut officers and five successive color-bearers down as they ran, much of the yelling blue swarm nearly made it to the foot of the parapet, but at a tremendous cost in blood.[32] The survivors huddled behind cover only twenty-five yards from the redan, doing their best to return fire and praying for the darkness of night so they might retire. By the time it finally came, more than half of the Regular officers were dead or wounded, their commander Captain Edward Washington, grand-nephew of the nation's first president, mortally. A comparable proportion of those in the ranks had also fallen before the redan. Morning roll call at first light on May 20 showed a loss of more than 43 percent in the battalion. For all practical purposes, after only three major engagements, it ceased to be a combat force, and would spend the rest of its service guarding Sherman's headquarters. The shaken survivors inscribed the regiment's colors, riddled with more than fifty-five bullet holes but somehow successfully evacuated from the field, with the phrase "First at Vicksburg"—a motto still enshrined in the Thirteenth Infantry's crest today.[33]

When his exhausted aide completed the perilous journey from the rear back to Kilby Smith, between breaths he parroted instructions not from Blair, but directly from Sherman. Smith was "to get my men as close to the parapet as possible and be ready to jump in when they began to yield." The rest of the army would soon attack in support, Cump assured him. Accordingly, Smith cried out for the men to cease firing, fix bayonets, and await the command to charge. Even so, every time he glanced up at the steep slope, ever deepening doubts stirred within him as to whether the command could even make it up the embankment at all without ladders. It might be possible to fashion an impromptu ladder by driving bayonets into the parapet, he considered, but any isolated individual or small group that hazarded such an ascent would have been immediately captured or cut down at the summit.

Beginning to dread Sherman's order to drive his brigade's assault to its bloody fruition, Smith instead chose mostly to ignore it, and instead continued employing his brigade's firepower from its current position. After all, perhaps his location already represented "as close to the parapet as possible." His brigade quickly shifted to what it knew it could do well. After dispatching runners to the rear for ammunition, "the most accurate marksmen were thrown forward, with *carte-blanche* to select the best cover." Individual companies from each regiment pushed a short distance forward to skirmish at closer range until their ammunition was exhausted or guns fouled beyond their ability to reload, when they were summarily replaced by others. Once again, just as at Arkansas Post, the brigade managed to achieve almost complete fire superiority at close range, "and none of the enemy ventured his head above the wall who failed to pay the penalty."[34]

Just how long the two brigades could hold on to their hard-won forward positions remained an open question. As during prior assaults, while success in gaining fire superiority at close range was no small feat, it remained mostly tactically insignificant unless it could be exploited by a coordinating maneuver element. With no such force available, there could be no breakthrough. Communicating via aides with Spooner across Graveyard Road, Smith started to receive troubling reports from all along his brigade frontage. "Their loss had been fearful, falling upon their best line and noncommissioned officers," he reported. "Captain after captain had been shot dead; field officers were falling."[35]

As the fearful hours dragged on and daylight began to fade, it gradually became evident to those still hugging the southern wall of the Mint Spring ravine that neither reinforcements nor assault orders were likely forthcoming. The wholly unsupported division's attack had failed, and it was time to begin thinking about how to escape the potential total destruction or capture that might accompany a Rebel counterattack. Although Kilby Smith had already started to consider how best to fortify his newly won ground, even going so far as to begin sighting potential battery positions under the slope, an aide from Sherman arrived at his position near nightfall with orders to fall back whenever he thought he could. After confirming the order with Blair, Smith somewhat reluctantly began the retrograde movement as soon as darkness blanketed the battlefield, in many cases one company at a time. By three o'clock the next morning, nothing but a few skirmishers still resided in no-man's-land, and Blair's battered division was once again behind the crest from which the bloody assault had begun.[36]

In contrast to the Rebels guarding Stockade Redan, the Secessionists responsible for repelling Thayer's and Ewing's assaults on Blair's right at the Twenty-Seventh Louisiana Lunette opted for a more conventional shock-reliant defense. Ewing's Buckeyes, arrayed in line of battle, advanced into the ravine with a screen of skirmishers deployed well to the front, instead of ensconced upon the north ridge to their rear as the rest of the division had done. Ensnared by felled trees and telegraph wire and incapable of further forward movement, the stalled half of the brigade "retired to the first cover, laid down," and peppered the parapet with "a heavy fire" to help keep Rebel heads down as the rest of the brigade approached. The left wing continued forward. As Col. James Dayton's Fourth West Virginia neared the parapet, the Louisianans opened with a fearsome shock volley that felled every member of the color guard. Urging the men on from the front, the regiment's major was likewise cut down. Only a portion of the men reached the ditch at the foot of the parapet, but the enemy fire they encountered even there proved "too strong to be resisted" anyway, prompting them to sprint back to a bluff about seventy-five yards from the parapet to await orders. Attempts to coordinate a renewal of suppressive fire from the batteries in support of a final push broke down. Unaware of the plan, those of Ewing's command still lodged for safety in the ditch at the base of the scarp took the fire of the Federal guns as a signal not for assault, but as cover for their withdrawal to salvation. Those who made it back to the cover of the brigade's jumping-off position left fifty of their dead behind. Nearly two hundred of Ewing's command were wounded, and six wholly unaccounted for.[37]

The experience of Thayer's brigade, assaulting the redan from a position four hundred yards west of Ewing, was little different. With the still decimated Fourth Iowa in reserve, the Hawkeyes of Thayer's Twenty-Sixth, Ninth, and Thirtieth Iowa charged down the northern slope of the ravine with a cheer at the sound of the artillery signal. Their brigade frontage mangled by the intervening smaller ridges, draws, and fingers of higher ground that filled the ravine, the Iowans received a Louisianan shock volley while still attempting to make their way across the bayou itself. Only the veteran Ninth, which had yet to face such a volley in its history, withstood the fire without halting behind cover in the ravine bottom. Lacking any obvious support visible to the right or left, and facing a steep rise to their front, the Iowans opted to pursue survival with honor. Taking cover under the protection of the defiladed southern slope, they did not budge until dark allowed for a cautious withdrawal. The assault had failed.[38]

In his formal report, Blair attributed the failure of his division to a combination of the "insuperable" terrain in many places along his command's frontage and the enemy's ability to reinforce the main point of attack due to his not being engaged simultaneously at any other location.[39] In reality, the terrain itself had not been "insuperable" for any but Ewing's right-wing regiments. Instead, it was the capacity of the dense abatis, intervening bald ridge lines, and sharp Rebel fire to cause total breakdowns of command and control that had utterly dismantled Blair's assault, just as the same factors that had disrupted the corps's maneuvers in every previous assault it had attempted during the war.

While Blair's division and Thayer's brigade futilely flung themselves at the Rebel works, the remainder of Steele's division hunted the Mississippi and the long-sought-after northern road out of Vicksburg. Though they were ordered to participate in the general assault at two o'clock, this contrasted with Sherman's previous orders to close with the river and secure the army's new vital supply line back to the Yazoo. Accordingly, while dispatching Thayer to participate in the assault, Steele sent Manter's (originally Blair's) and Woods's brigades westward through a dense forest and canebrake to complete Grant's northern encirclement of the city. Proceeding the furthest west of any command in the army, Woods's lead regiments found the road, and were within 150 yards of the river when they debouched from the timber upon a bald ridge line and immediately drew the fire of Rebel batteries to the south. Deploying to counter this threat, Landgraeber's howitzer teams sprinted into the open at a full gallop under fire, unlimbered, and began to respond to the Rebel battery, mostly without effect. Meanwhile, Woods's infantry cleared a house on a nearby prominent vista and recognized that they could silence the battery themselves.[40]

Lieutenant Colonel Seay led his Missourians into the house and ordered the riflemen to the windows to keep up a steady fire on the Rebel works and all batteries within range. "We are fighting at long range, losing but few men," he proudly reported, as the regiment "kept the Rebs so completely driven from their guns they could not use them." His Thirty-Second Missouri was proving "hard to beat as sharp shooters." Seay himself grabbed a rifle to join in the fun. "I shot till my shoulder was sore from the kicking muskets," he laughed. All along the line, Steele's regiments found cover and practiced their sharpshooting on Rebel works and gun teams. Accurately estimating the distance between himself and the Rebel guns to be about three hundred yards, Pvt. Calvin Ainsworth, Twenty-Fifth Iowa, elevated the rear sight on his rifle before he and his Hawkeye comrades each fired twenty carefully aimed rounds into the Rebel positions. Lt. Alonzo Abernathy's company of the Ninth Iowa fired sixty per man during the day. While usually remaining silent behind cover, the Rebel guns did respond at opportunity. One enemy Parrott, thought to be silenced, suddenly let loose a fury of grapeshot that killed and wounded several Hawkeyes in the Twenty-Fifth Iowa. Despite these losses, the regiment remained sheltered under the brow of the hill, firing at targets of opportunity until its ammunition was completely exhausted.[41]

"FORLORN HOPE"

As the corps awoke on the morning of May 20, word passed through the ranks of Blair's bloodied division "that an assault would be again made upon our left; and that we would make a demonstration in favor of the attack." That afternoon, Sherman's batteries again thundered their deep notes, and most of the division crowded into protected positions along the crest of the northernmost ridge in the ravine, peppering the Rebel parapet with rifle fire. "The ruse" continued for four hours, without any actual assault ever taking place. Even so, all had plentiful opportunities to find the range to the Rebel works. The men of the Thirtieth Ohio fired no fewer than thirty thousand cartridges during the day—more than a hundred per man—"and would have fired more, had they been furnished in time." Moving rearward from the firing line that evening, the Buckeyes were covered in powder, with "blackened lips . . . and blackened hands." Orderly sergeants discovered that only a mere three men had been wounded during the day's operations, prompting several to grow "loud in expressing their preference for always fighting just such kind of battles." In sharp contrast to the previous day's maneuvers, "they were so safe, and pleasant . . . had all the excitement of a real battle, without any of its dangers." They also produced much the same in the way of results: very little.[42]

During the day, Grant met with his three corps commanders, and after comparing notes the officers came to a consensus that the previous day's assault had failed "by reason of the natural strength of the position, and because we were forced by the nature of the ground to limit our attacks to the strongest parts of the enemy's line." Along the Fifteenth Corps front, that meant the deadly Graveyard Road, which still remained the only viable route left open to reach Stockade Redan. Beyond this, the greater problem had been the failure of any but Sherman's corps to attack, the others not yet having reached their jumping-off positions when Blair surged forward. After much deliberation, and no little reluctance, Grant determined they would try again. This time, though, the enemy would be attacked simultaneously all along the line, preventing another Rebel concentration against any single assaulting force.[43]

Sherman personally reconnoitered the area to his corps's front after the meeting. He knew that the narrow Graveyard Road was still the only clear route to the redan, but this time he also noticed "another point in the curtain about a hundred yards to its [the redan's] right (our left)" that might prove viable if an attacker could cut his way through the abatis. He ordered his staff to prepare general orders announcing Grant's intentions to the corps. Blair's division, with all its officers on foot, would again assault down the Graveyard Road, this time in a narrow column "preceded by a selected, or volunteer, storming party of about 150 men." Simultaneously, Steele's division would "in like manner attack, by any route he may select." So as to avoid the confusion of Arkansas Post and the Nineteenth, he ordered all division assaults to be coordinated "by the watch, and not depend on [artillery] signals." Commanders were not to sacrifice momentum when fearful of lacking support on their flanks. "All must presume that others are doing their best," he instructed, "and do their full share."[44]

Prior to any of this, skirmishers along the entire corps front would "during the night, advance within 100 yards of the enemy's works," and use shovels or axes to "prepare pits, or fallen trees, so as to give them cover from which to kill artillerists who attempt to load the guns, [and] also to keep down the fire of the enemy's infantry in the rifle-pits during the assault." Experience at Chickasaw Bayou and Arkansas Post had taught "Cump" the vitality of establishing fire superiority with skirmishers prior to and during any major assault. It had also impressed upon him the importance of pummeling Rebel positions with artillery before any attack. Starting at daylight, all the corps's batteries were to open "with great care and precision" on the portions of the Rebel works that were to be targeted by the assault columns. Only one hundred rounds of canister and shrapnel "for service after passing the parapet" were to be retained as a reserve in battery caissons.[45]

The volunteer detail charged with leading the attack down Graveyard Road, referred to by the contemporary military term "forlorn hope," consisted of two officers and fifty men from each of the three brigades of Blair's division placed temporarily under the command of Captain John Groce, Thirtieth Ohio. Together, they would carry their guns, axes, boards, and hand-fashioned ladders to enable the main body to scale the steep scarp of the redan. Both Grant and Sherman visited the detachment personally and promised a sixty-day furlough upon completion of their deadly mission.[46]

The rest of the division would follow close on the heels of the "forlorn hope," directly down the Graveyard Road in column. Ewing's brigade, "by right of rank" and having suffered the fewest losses on May 19, would lead the way, followed up closely by Giles Smith's and then Kilby Smith's. If all went according to plan, the skirmishers would keep Rebel heads down while the "forlorn hope" rushed across no-man's-land to the redan and established a breach. Ewing's brigade would subsequently mount the parapet and drive a wedge into the Rebel line that could be exploited by the other two brigades.[47]

Although this time the corps's assault would fall on the Rebel works simultaneously with Grant's other two corps, thus preventing the enemy from sending reinforcements to bolster their line to his front, Sherman's own tactical-level plans failed to replicate this logic. Witnessing the last assault had convinced him that the only realistic approach was the narrow Graveyard Road. At the same time, the moment any attacking column was spotted by any Rebels who were not adequately suppressed, it would immediately draw fire from the front and both uncontested flanks. While Grant's plans ensured that Sherman would face no more Secessionists than currently held the works to the immediate front, Sherman's plans ensured that nearly all of those in the area would be able to concentrate their fire on the head of his single attacking column.

At "precisely two o'clock" on May 22, the dauntless volunteers of the "forlorn hope" debouched from the cover of a berm along the northern slope of Mint Spring ravine and took off down Graveyard Road toward the redan. It took the party three minutes to sprint for their lives the full distance down the road and into the ditch before the rampart of Stockade Redan. Under a heavy fire for the entire distance, many fell—all posthumously awarded the brand new "Medal of Honor." Others simply lost their nerve. Overcome with fear only twenty yards from the base of the redan, one lieutenant of

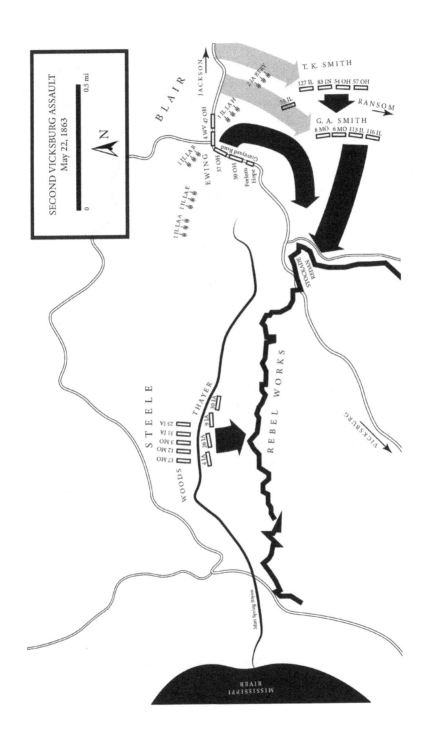

SECOND VICKSBURG ASSAULT
May 22, 1863

N

0   0.5 mi

BLAIR

JACKSON

T. K. SMITH

2 IA BTRY   127 IL   83 IN   54 OH   57 OH

55 IL

RANSOM

4 WV   47 OH

1 IL L-H

EWING

G. A. SMITH

8 MO   6 MO   113 IL   116 IL

1 IL L-I

37 OH

Graveyard Road

30 OH

Forlorn
Hope

1 IL L-A   1 IL L-B

1 IL L-E

STOCKADE
REDAN

STEELE

REBEL WORKS

THAYER

25 IA

31 IA   9 IA   30 IA

4 MO

12 MO

26 IA

17 MO

4 IA

WOODS

VICKSBURG

Mint Spring Bayou

MISSISSIPPI
RIVER

the 127th Illinois dove off the roadway for cover along with ten others. The squad refused to budge for the remainder of the fight. A surprising number of the party successfully reached their objective in one piece. Sadly, just after survivors leaped into the trench and started to catch their breath, two shots rang out from afar, and two officers of the Sixth Missouri fell severely wounded. One Zouave lodged the detachment colors into the loose dirt of the parapet. Looking up the ten-foot-high rampart "for a head to shoot at," and then back toward Federal lines, the survivors anxiously awaited support. Fortunately, although the preliminary bombardment had failed to erode the slope of the parapet, it had "pretty well pulverized" the scarp so as to ease the process of digging with bayonets for cover. From above came frequent Rebel cries to "Surrender, Yanks!" which elicited the defiant reply: "Come and get us."[48]

Ewing chose his own original command, the veteran Thirtieth Ohio, having been in reserve during the previous assault, to spearhead his attack. Behind them would follow the German Thirty-Seventh Ohio. In a customary display of his considerable personal courage, Blair stood near the head of the column, head uncovered, awaiting the moment to assault. Ewing, in shirt sleeves, was at his side. Behind him, the German Lieutenant Colonel Hildt stood at the head of his regiment, silently observing the forlorn hope's sprint to destiny. Finally, after what seemed an eternity, Blair ordered the division to attack, Ewing screamed "Forward!" and Hildt, through a thick accent, echoed the call, starting the Buckeyes forward at the double-quick.[49]

Immediately upon the column's coming into sight, the Rebels, then focused on eradicating the surviving members of the forlorn hope, shifted their fire to the Ohioans hurdling down Graveyard Road. Once again, Blair found himself confronting a defender attempting to erode his division from four hundred yards before it could even approach its objective. "To the right of us, to the left of us, and to the front, a perfect sheet of flame issued from the enemy's fortifications," one Buckeye recalled. Confronted by no other proximate advancing column—as Grant's original plans had contemplated—the Secessionists manning the works for a considerable distance on both flanks were free to concentrate their fire against the head of Hildt's lone regiment. Veterans of brutal handling at the Battle of South Mountain the previous year, the Buckeyes had "stood up against a front fire . . . for forty-five minutes," only to spend the following night crowded around campfires wondering "how could a single man escape?" This, though, was different.

"It is difficult to describe the horrors of a cross and concentrated fire," one Ohioan wrote. "Forward, forward!" Hildt and Ewing cried through the din. The sight of the Stars and Stripes of the forlorn hope, waving from the scarp of the parapet, was encouraging. The sight to the rear was not. Although the entirety of Ewing's Kanawha Brigade had been ordered down the road, the Lieutenant Colonel von Blessingh's German Thirty-Seventh Ohio, formed in column behind the Thirtieth, had not followed Hildt's Buckeyes in the charge. In fact, watching the Rebel fire seemingly converge from all points of the compass onto the lone embattled regiment, the lead German companies stubbornly, and disastrously, refused to budge.[50]

Blair was confounded. Most of the Rebel fire still seemed to be focused on the surviving lead elements of the Thirtieth, yet the Germans positively would not advance. Fewer than ten had been killed, and just over thirty would receive wounds over the entire course of the day, yet "the men lay down in the road and behind every inequality of ground which afforded them shelter," he later angrily reported. "Every effort" of Blair, Ewing, von Blessingh, the regiment's junior officers, and even its sergeant major proved ineffectual to move them. In any assault, even if the majority of a regiment maintained its confidence, the nerves of a few inevitably gave out. At Chickasaw Bayou and Arkansas Post, as most brigades had attacked in line of battle, these men were those observed dropping from the ranks and taking cover as their comrades continued on. This time, as Ewing's column attempted to wedge itself through a tight defile, the breakdown of even a handful at the front of the formation had brought the entire division to a sudden halt.[51]

Suddenly finding themselves in a position not at all dissimilar to that confronted by Williamson's bloodied Fourth Iowa at Chickasaw Bayou, the Thirtieth promptly halted and took cover on the southern slope of the ravine, still more than 150 yards from the parapet before attempting one final surge toward the works. The thick Rebel fire from front and both flanks quickly dismantled the unit as it struggled alone through a narrow defile near the salient. Casualties literally piled up within the defile, blocking the way. "The second company forced its way over the remains of the first, and a third over those of the preceding," Ewing observed in horror, "but their perseverance served only further to encumber the impassable way." While a small number of the Thirtieth made their way all the way into the ditch at the foot of the scarp, the ranking officer present determined that their numbers were hardly "sufficient to warrant my thrusting them over the ramparts, to be either slaughtered or taken prisoners." Barely underway, Blair's attack had already stalled.[52]

Showing far more flexibility than at Chickasaw, while his terrified Germans balked, Blair quickly adapted by ordering the rest of Ewing's command, the Forty-Seventh Ohio and Fourth West Virginia, to bypass their traumatized comrades, forego the Graveyard Road completely, and continue directly into the tortuous ravine. Giles and Kilby Smith's brigades followed closely behind. Enraged by the sight of the insubordinate Germans, Colonel Augustus Parry instructed the privates of his Forty-Seventh Ohio to shoot any officer they saw halting to take cover behind a tree or stump, then told the officers to do the same with balking privates. While offering far more protection than the road, the new route through the ravine quickly proved "almost impassable with abatis of felled timber," and would not "admit of anything like a charge," Blair later reported with frustration. The best he could now hope for was to use the protection of the ravine to gradually move his division close enough to the parapet to organize a final lunge at the redan. The stall of his brigade in the captured trenches at Chickasaw Bayou and the intractable tarry of the corps at Arkansas Post had shown how effecting such a lunge after the men had found good cover would be exceedingly challenging, but Blair had little choice. Once again, a combination of nightmarish terrain and Rebel fire had eradicated Sherman's best laid plans and broken up the cohesion and momentum of his corps's assault.[53]

With the division's cohesion rapidly deteriorating in the chaos, Blair again adapted by handing control of the finer details over to his subordinates. Ewing's two remaining regiments took up positions along a ridge of higher ground halfway through the ravine and began adding their fire to suppress the Rebels behind the redan, still about seventy yards distant. Feverishly pouring lead into the enemy position "as fast as we could load and fire," some Ohioans discharged as many as 240 rounds during the attack. Though well intentioned and at close range, much of this fire fell short and into the backs of comrades ensconced in the ditch or sheltering against the parapet. On at least one occasion, this prompted a few of those now under fire from both directions to fire back toward the rear in anger.[54]

Making his way to Giles Smith, Blair ordered the veteran brigadier "to go forward as rapidly as the nature of the ground would admit, and to assault whenever he found it practicable to do so" under the cover of Ewing's fire. Kilby Smith was to follow on his heels.[55] Struggling through the vine-choked ravine at the head of his column, Smith was pleased to find Ransom's brigade of McPherson's neighboring corps, likewise mired in the morass of vegetation and telegraph wire en route to the works. The two brigadiers agreed to work together and coordinate their assaults, scaling the cluttered slope of the hill until within striking distance of the Rebel works. As the rounds zipped by and cut into the dirt, Smith boldly rose and shouted over the din to his Zouaves. "Boys, they'll give us one volley," he screamed, "before they can reload, we'll be inside their works!" The men of both brigades rushed up the slope toward the redan with abandon. Immediately visible all along the line, their attack prompted a redoubling of fire from Blair's batteries and Ewing's riflemen, still peppering the crest of the parapet as fast as possible.[56]

Those few of Smith's brigade who were able to mount the parapet found themselves engaged from front, flank, and even rear, as the Rebels holding the salient of Stockade Redan, then unchallenged to their front, turned to assist in repelling the assault on their flank and rear. The brigade "met so severe a fire from my front and left by both musketry and artillery that I found it absolutely necessary to order the brigade to fall back," Smith later reported. Yet again, terrain had nullified Sherman's numerical advantage, and funneled his brigades into piecemeal assaults that confronted an overwhelming volume of Rebel fire from almost every direction. "It was found impossible to advance," Blair somberly admitted.[57]

As the survivors took shelter behind whatever cover they could find and continued to take shots of opportunity at hats and heads peeking over the parapet, Grant found Sherman watching the disaster from the rear, and the two concurred that their assault had failed yet again. Just then, an orderly from McClernand's corps arrived and handed Grant a hastily scrawled message. McClernand's assault to the south had been successful, broken through the enemy line, and "the flag of the Union waved over the stronghold of Vicksburg." He urgently requested a renewal of the attack all along the line so as to prevent a Rebel concentration against him. Both Grant and Sherman were skeptical, but if there was any truth to the claim, it would have been criminal to withhold support. Grant departed to learn what he could in person, telling Sherman that "if I did not receive orders to the contrary, by 3 o'clock P.M. . . . try it again." No follow-on orders ever arrived from Grant, but the sounds of heavy fighting to the south did. Assuming these echoes to be those of McClernand's supposed breakthrough, Sherman reluctantly opted to order a renewal of the assault.[58]

Tuttle's Third Division would repeat exactly the same plan which had just gone bloodily awry. This time, however, the Graveyard Road column would hopefully benefit from the suppressive fire of the first assault's survivors, still dispersed behind cover all along the Mint Spring ravine. Alas, just as with that of Blair's skirmishers ahead of the first assault, such fire was fated to be mostly ineffectual, given the steep slope of the ravine and parapet and exhaustion of both the men and their ammunition. At exactly three o'clock, Mower's brigade surged forward down the road, with its commander striding brazenly at the head of the column. The brigade advanced "closed up beautifully," with "no running, [and] no excitement."[59] All of the pomp and circumstance of the ostentatious approach came to a screeching halt a short distance from the works under the weight of a Rebel shock volley. More than 150 casualties resulted from the single fusillade, prompting Sherman to immediately call off the attack. "This is murder," he exclaimed to a staffer, "order those troops back."[60]

Sherman had always intended for the attack on Stockade Redan to represent the corps's main effort. But, in the spirit of Grant's intent, he also ordered Steele's division to launch "a strong demonstration" against the Twenty-Seventh Louisiana Lunette to the west to prevent the Rebel reinforcement of Stockade Redan from that direction. This time, Steele was to employ the entirety of his division against the lunette. Thayer's Hawkeyes would again spearhead the attack, followed closely by Woods's brigade, with Manter's in reserve. The brigade had advanced in the darkness of night and expected to attack at 10 a.m., yet nothing happened. It took the arrival of Steele himself and Woods's brigade from the right to commence the attack up the steep southern slope toward the lunette.[61]

The lengthy delay of Steele's "strong demonstration" was principally caused by the deadly challenge of getting Woods's brigade from the far right to a jumping-off position alongside Thayer's brigade—a problem that Sherman apparently had given no consideration. Much of this maneuver necessarily took place across an all-but-bald ridge in full view, and minimal range, of the Rebel works, "through gullies, single file, over hills, fallen trees, etc." The unforgiving terrain and lack of cover made it necessary for each regiment to sprint through enemy rifle and artillery fire in single-file lines on multiple occasions, "running the blockade," as many sardonically called it.[62]

Once the two divisions had finally reached their combined jumping-off positions, one Hawkeye predicted grave results should they be ordered to advance further. "They can fire at us from their fort, from their front and from their right and left," he scribbled in his diary, "it is folly in my opinion to make this charge."[63] Moreover, with Blair's division already repulsed, it was highly questionable what, if anything, such a charge could even achieve. Steele could never hope to carry the lunette. Instead, his orders instructed him to launch a diversionary attack in support of another assault elsewhere—an assault which, by the time his command was in position to make it, had already failed. Tragically, this did not stop him.

"We found ourselves on a very steep hillside, slanting, as it seemed to me, at an angle of 45 degrees," Sgt. Maj. Reichhelm later observed. "Some distance back of it stood the rebel fort, so that we were directly under and in front of it, but sheltered from its fire until we should reach the crest." The brow of the ridge was too narrow to support even an entire regiment in line of battle; the brigade would have to charge in column in groups of two or three companies at a time.[64] Half of the Twenty-Fifth Iowa were deployed along the ridge as sharpshooters to suppress the Rebel works at long range until the rest of the brigade column had rushed past.[65]

At about four o'clock in the afternoon, just as Steele was beginning to scan the foreboding terrain to his front, an artillery salvo thundered across the Mint Spring ravine. Mistakenly taking this to be the signal for Tuttle's renewed assault on Stockade Redan—one that, by that time, had already been repulsed—Steele hurried his brigades into position.[66] After what seemed like hours of waiting, his shrill voice cried out: "Forward! Charge!" Beside him, Thayer echoed the command, screaming "Forward, forward!" The Hawkeye skirmishers attempted to provide some vestige of suppressive fire from behind the brow of the northern hill but found "the rebs behind their rifle pits could seldom be touched." Because of this, as soon as the division's foremost companies crested the hill, they were butchered mercilessly. "As the men rose to a level with the crest a terrific fire seemed to sweep the front rank away as the wheat falls before a mower blade, and the colors went down almost instantly," one mourned. "Whoever poked his head over the hill was a dead man," another observed. "Forward, forward! Follow me, boys!" officers screamed, often moments before being cut down. "We struggled forward against the weight of dead and wounded who fell backward into our ranks, and the ground on the steep incline gave way under our feet," Sergeant Major Reichhelm remembered. From the rear, Steele watched as his division was fed piecemeal into a veritable gauntlet of death. Finally, those regiments not yet to the crest decided that "to mount the crest of the hillside was certain death . . . and it seemed impossible to pass beyond it alive." Steele's and Thayer's ceaseless cries of "Forward! Forward!" gradually lost their effect. "Rank had lost its power," Reichhelm remembered. "The column refused to move and our repulse was accomplished."[67]

In fact, a handful of Thayer's brigade had managed to rush through "the terrible hail," steeled by the confidence of the veteran Ninth Iowa in its center, a few making it all the way to the cover of the Rebel parapet. "Terribly thinned out," the Hawkeyes anxiously gazed back through dense smoke for Woods's supporting regiments, but in vain. Only the Germans of the Twelfth Missouri had rushed ahead "hard on their heels." "To our disappointment & chagrin none [other] came," Lt. Alonzo Abernathy observed with disgust. Still balking behind the brow of the hill, Steele's lieutenants urged, cursed, and shoved men over the crest and into the fire "only to meet death." The remainder of Woods's brigade, still traumatized from their repulse at Arkansas Post, simply refused to advance. The brigade's aversion to frontal assaults held it in place. Only the German Twelfth Missouri, having avoided the debacle at "the Post," moved forward.[68]

The survivors, huddled beneath the parapet, awaited their fate until dark, long after Steele had accepted defeat and called off the "strong demonstration." Thayer's and Woods's brigades had sustained a combined 345 casualties during the charge—almost double the total number of effectives in several of their regiments. Seventy-two of the division's officers and men were dead on the field, and nothing was gained. Yet again, the Fifteenth Corps had been brutally repulsed.

Spared the worst of the engagement due to the breakdown of its lead regiment, Ewing's brigade lost only about half the men it had during the May 19 assault, reporting a total of 25 dead and 116 wounded. Giles and Kilby Smith's brigades also suffered fewer casualties the second time around, though combined the two still sacrificed 158 men in the futile assault, 31 of whom were killed. Four of Blair's regimental commanders were seriously wounded, and two of Steele's killed. Mower's brigade of Tuttle's division also paid a heavy price for their brief contribution. Nearly 200 of the command fell. Altogether, Sherman's corps suffered 1,570 total casualties, including 283 dead, across the two fruitless charges. Since most regiments in the corps had reported fewer than 200 men for duty that bloody week in May, the losses in aggregate represented the loss of nearly eight regiments' worth of effective manpower.[69] Worse yet, McClernand had not in fact made any breakthrough. The heavy losses suffered by Mcpherson's and Sherman's corps in attempting to support his imaginary success "caused great feeling with us, and severe criticisms on General McClernand," Sherman later remembered.[70]

In many cases resignation to one's ultimate fate had carried men considerable distances toward the Rebel works. "I have been left constantly to think how entirely we are dependent upon God for our preservation," one Hawkeye reflected. During the assault "it seemed as though human thought[,] reason[,] and intelligence was of no avail." There seemed no good reason to cross the expanse in maximum haste, as "by so doing perhaps the fatal bullet would penetrate the body that otherwise might fall harmlessly at the feet," he reasoned. "There was but one way to do and that was to go forward," he concluded, "and trust in God." While a sound strategy for coping with the likely prospect of imminent death, the Iowan's statement was simultaneously an admission of his lack of confidence in the likelihood of success. The corps had obediently advanced, but few thought it even possible that the Rebel works could be carried.[71]

Indeed, in the aftermath, the widespread consensus in the ranks of both divisions had it that the assault could never have succeeded, "knowing these works to be manned by veteran soldiers of similar blood to our own." Watching the whole nightmare unfold from the relative protection of his battery's fortified position, one Illinoisan gunner thought it "almost if not entirely impossible to have ever taken those Bluffs from the front." Others found it hard to even refer to the action as an assault. One Hawkeye preferred the word "slaughter . . . for I can call it nothing else." Another chose "destruction, [for] I don't call it a battle." One of Steele's Missourians thought it "a wonder that the whole division was not destroyed on the spot." Just as in the aftermath of the Chickasaw repulse, the survivors were left regretting "that so many lives were thrown away and so much danger incurred when it was not necessary and no good accomplished." The only bright lining seemed to be that the men were now, yet again, "richer in experience." All now had unquestionably gained "satisfactory proof that Vicksburg cannot be taken by storming it," one reasoned.[72]

Those in the ranks were well aware of the grave lack of coordination which had hamstrung both assaults from the beginning.[73] "The common soldier does not ascertain who was responsible for this murder," Private Buegel, Third Missouri, admitted. Beyond rumors of "jealousy and betrayal," his comrades sensed "that a general attack was supposed to take place on the whole line, but was not carried out." Thus, as usual, "the enemy could throw his troops against this division." "The troops have only a portion of them been engaged at a time," another Hawkeye complained. Yet another merely noted somberly in his diary: "Bad management somewhere. Don't want to see another one."[74]

Many found themselves consumed with the same outrage that had dominated discussions after Chickasaw Bayou. "Today the most deplorable event in this campaign occurred—the vain assault of the enemies [sic] works," Sergeant Major Reichhelm recorded ruefully. "It was Sherman's order and that bloodhound and madman is responsible for a thousand more lives vainly and foolishly sacrificed."[75] This, Reichhelm later asserted, was the "sentiment of every man with whom I came in contact that day and the day following." It was certainly the sentiment of Lt. Henry Kircher, Twelfth Missouri. As far as he could tell, a third of his regiment had been "murdered, only because Sherman thinks that everything can be forced by the stormers without knowing the terrain or testing it out."[76] The notion that these tactics were the best "our Generals" could devise seemed impossible to believe. "Why did not the great charger S[herman] come and lead it himself," Kircher wondered. "But no, only orders are given to charge up the hill and take the pits." He prayed that "this be the last fit of insanity that our commanders will ever have."[77]

Inevitably, recent experiences were compared with past experiences. "I thought we had to work at the 'Post,'" Captain Jacob Ritner, Twenty-Fifth Iowa admitted, "but that was a mere nothing to this." The "terrible hail of bullets" had been like nothing "I nor anybody had ever heard before," Kircher, a veteran of hard fighting at Pea Ridge, observed. One thing was beyond any doubt—Sherman's corps had reached a new low in the deterioration of its confidence in assaulting works. Many officers, in fact, were convinced that the loss of efficacy was now total. "I do not think there will be any more charges made," Ritner predicted. "The men cannot be made to do it."[78]

While opinions vary as to the wisdom of Grant's second assault on Vicksburg, historians have rightfully been sharply critical of Sherman's handling of his corps's operations.[79] In his three-volume history of the campaign, Ed Bearss attributed Sherman's failure on May 22 to his having completely "lost control of his corps." Contrary to the logic of Grant's larger plan, "he had launched three separate and disjointed attacks," allowing the Rebels to swiftly reinforce any embattled portion of the works without worrying about weakening another still under attack. "It is clear," Warren Grabau, another historian of the battle, observed, "that Sherman did not fully understand the reasoning behind Grant's decision." Overawed by the vexing abatis that had ensnared Ewing's brigade on May 19, and the lack of effective artillery support during that attack, he opted to attempt another "by ramming an assault column right down the road."[80]

Even given the benefit of years' worth of reflection, Sherman always remained of the opinion that the failure of both assaults was due exclusively to the unique strength of the Vicksburg defenses. The attacks had failed "by reason of the great strength of the position and the determined fighting of its garrison," he asserted. No mention of his failure to coordinate the attacks even of his own corps, let alone Grant's struggles to accomplish the same across the army, were ever acknowledged by either officer. Both attacks had been necessary, they maintained, because without them the army never could have known if such an assault was possible. In fact, Grant later spuriously asserted in his memoirs that the May 22 assault had been required in large part because "the troops believed they could carry the works in their front, and would not have worked so patiently in the trenches [afterward] if they had not been allowed to try."[81]

Members of the press who had witnessed the prosecution of both attacks were more honest in their assessment of the failure. One embedded journalist of the Chicago Tribune thought both operations had broken down chiefly because of either "bad management or disobedience of orders on the part of those to whom high commands were entrusted, or from the dreadful character of the work to be performed, I will not attempt to decide." One way or another, it was undeniable that there had been "a want of co-operation between subordinate and superior officers and commands." Assault columns "went gallantly forward, but were left to perish for want of support." Individual units charged valiantly, "only to be disappointed in their expectations of receiving success and help."[82]

Despite their repeated failures to seize the bastion by storm, or perhaps even because of them, most of the officers and men in Sherman's corps were confident of the efficacy of the forthcoming siege. "We are sure to take Vicksburgh," Captain Farwell wrote confidently. "We have them surrounded with an army that cant be whipped in a fair fight and victory is sure to come sooner or later." Now that "our Generals" had finally come to the same conclusion as those in the ranks, "all that is necessary is to wait patiently . . . instead of charging upon works that have been built upon the best military knowledge and principles," and victory was all but inevitable. "This is the only way in which the place can be reduced without immense loss of life," another Hawkeye remarked. "If we cant storm them we can starve them out," Private Henry Bear, 116th Illinois, wounded in the side during the May 19 assault, proclaimed. On the far opposite flank, Lieutenant Colonel Seay agreed. "I have no doubt that we will have a long, bloody siege," he prophesied. "Those of us who survive will be able to stand anything."[83]

The men of the corps were well aware that the only reason a siege was even possible was because of the arduous feats of endurance they had performed during the long campaign of maneuver from Young's Point to the gates of Vicksburg. They prided themselves on their capacity for swift long-distance movement on an exceedingly tight logistical budget, just as they had after the risky bayou expeditions of the previous months. By an indirect campaign of maneuver, the army had positioned itself so that there was no need for bloody assaults. Those ordered anyway, in their eyes, represented grievous errors of judgment—just as they had at Chickasaw and Arkansas Post. The experience solidified their sense of the corps's coordinative failings and deepened their aversion to assaults. After witnessing once again the defensive advantages naturally accruing to well-planned and soundly constructed earthworks, both the Fifteenth Corps and its commander took to the spade themselves as they underwent their most complete evolutionary adaptation yet.

CHAPTER 6

ONE OF THE BEST TRAINING SCHOOLS

The Sieges of Vicksburg and Jackson

It is astonishing how soon we become accustomed to things.

—CPT. JACOB RITNER, TWENTY-FIFTH IOWA

With characteristic understatement, Sherman began his report to Grant on the evening of May 22 with an admission that his corps "had a hard day's work, and all are exhausted." Two brigades of Blair's division, Giles Smith's and Ewing's, remained ensconced along the ridge between their jumping-off positions and Stockade Redan. These he ordered to dig in and fortify their positions, ordering a thousand picks and shovels delivered to assist them in the labor. Certainly, it would be possible to cut a mine underneath the Rebel redan, he considered, and blow the position sky-high. But this would have to wait. "My men are too exhausted to do all this to-night," he confessed.[1]

General orders composed at Sherman's headquarters that evening set the stage for the next phase of operations. The Fifteenth Corps would hold what little ground it had won during the second assault. Smith's and Ewing's commands were to "construct in their front a rifle-pit or breast-height of logs, and lay out a covered road to their rear."[2] More instructions followed the next day, finally acknowledging the Rebel works as "too strong to be carried by assault," requiring reduction "by a system of regular approaches." Just like the enemy works themselves, these "approaches," zig-zagging across no-man's-land, would be hand-fashioned by the corps "according to the well-established principles of the military art." On May 25, Grant confirmed Sherman's assessment by ordering the entire army to begin cutting the approaches immediately under the supervision of the army's chief engineer, Cpt. Frederick E. Prime.[3]

Lacking more than a handful of officers with training in military engineering, Grant's siege would represent both the final "Vaubanian" siege in Western military history and a departure from contemporary US Army custom in siegecraft. As historian Justin Solonick has observed within his masterful treatment of the Vicksburg siege, the Army of the Tennessee "embraced conventional engineering maxims and adapted them" based upon what they considered common sense and the many lessons they had derived from the experience of past campaigns. The experience of the siege was to in turn leave an indelible mark on the tactical culture of the command.[4]

The eagerness of those in the ranks to turn toward siegecraft was in large part derived from the realization that there would be no more suicidal assaults. Just as historian Steven Sodergren has observed of an Army of the Potomac emerging from its fierce bloodletting during the 1864 Overland Campaign into the comparative safety of the Petersburg trenches, siegecraft "was welcomed by those in the ranks for the escape that it offered from the frontal assaults and charges" which characterized high-intensity combat. "The boys now seem perfectly willing to siege the place," one Illinoisan sensed, "being confident that storming will not do it." The army had gone "to work and built forts as well as the rebs and we are going to let them come out and fight us when they get hungry enough," another added. It seemed to all that "Gen. Grant deems the game caged and he does not want to sacrifice life" in any more fruitless assaults.[5]

"SHOT UNTIL MY SHOULDER IS BEAT VERY SORE"

In accordance with Sherman's orders, each of the three division commanders set his pioneer detachments to constructing covered roads aiming for prominent Rebel salient, taking advantage of any and all natural cover along the way. In places where such cover was unavailing, zigzag approach trenches were necessary. Cpt. W. L. B. Jenney, the only staff officer of Sherman's headquarters who enjoyed any training in military engineering, roved between divisions providing "general supervision" in light of his understanding of Captain Prime's intent. While the lion's share of the labor was conducted by fatigue details drawn from each regiment, Sherman made clear that "negro labor, when organized," would also be employed to save the sweat of his bloodied veterans.[6]

While Steele retained the Black laborers of First Division's pioneer corps, Blair's "negro force" was assigned duty maintaining the crucial supply route back to Chickasaw Bayou and the Yazoo. Those relatively few white pioneers serving alongside these Black men noted, with some racist derision, how "some are very easy to learn, [but] others are slow." While unfortunately no record of how the Black pioneers felt about their white counterparts survives, the ceaseless and efficient flow of supplies across the old Chickasaw Bayou battlefield throughout the siege is evidence of the indispensable contributions of these ex-slaves to the campaign.[7]

Captain Jenney sited and ordered the establishment of covered approaches along the fronts of each brigade in Blair's division immediately after the receipt of Sherman's orders. From left to right, or west to east, these were Smith's, Ewing's, and Lightburn's approaches, along with another cut by Tuttle's pioneers. On the right, Cpt. Herman Klostermann, commanding Steele's pioneers, superintended two additional approaches along Woods's and Thayer's fronts. Second Division's white pioneers were responsible for maintaining the roads between the works of the corps's brigades. The remaining pioneers constructed siege materials and supervised the erection of fortified battery positions all along the line. Gabions and fascines, neither of which most in the ranks were familiar with, were hand-fashioned from vines, cane, and saplings growing along the crest and rearward slope of the Walnut Hills. In at least one case, Sherman himself had to instruct junior officers in the novel art of manufacturing such siege materials.[8]

Although many of the "old" regiments of Blair's division had experience with constructing modest field fortifications during Halleck's campaign for Corinth, the complicated works and "regular approaches" at Vicksburg were "more elaborate than any we had yet seen," one Illinoisan later noted.[9] On the far right of the corps line, Thayer's Iowans first cut into the Mississippi loess soil on the night of May 30 to begin down the meandering path toward the Rebel works approximately three hundred yards distant. Surveying the route, Klostermann marked out the pathway for the approach trench so as to reduce the task of the unschooled volunteers to mere digging—much as had been done along the canal. As the approach ran by necessity down the steep northern slope of the ravine before climbing the southern embankment toward the Rebel works, daily details from Thayer's regiments and the division's pioneers found themselves inevitable targets of Rebel sharpshooters. To solve this deadly problem, the men fashioned fascines out of cane, and placed them over the six-foot-deep and six-foot-wide trench, forming "a roof which hid the movements of our men, and [which], where well constructed, [was] impenetrable to musket balls." Rebel shells would have obliterated the cane roof, but the inability to sufficiently depress the guns and the perpetual volume and accuracy of covering fire from Steele's riflemen usually kept the enemy batteries silent.[10]

Off to Thayer's left, the approach of Ewing's brigade just north of Graveyard Road was the corps's primary focus. Still convinced that Stockade Redan, blocking access to Graveyard Road's path into the city from the north, remained the primary objective of his corps, Sherman focused maximum attention on this approach. Ewing's regiments had begun cutting what would become the sap the day after the failed assault, two days before even receiving Grant's orders to begin the siege. Having established an impromptu forward rifle pit only a hundred yards from Stockade Redan as cover for the survivors of the attack, Ewing's approach was initially started as a mere shallow "covered road" by which to provide ammunition to skirmishers rotating in and out of the advanced position. Once Grant and Prime ordered them on May 25 to commence siege work, the men began converting the covered road into a proper zig-zag approach. Mechanically skilled men from the Thirty-Fifth Missouri, erstwhile assigned to the pontoon train and not members of the corps, were charged with the technical aspects of the work while the regiments of Ewing's brigade provided rotating fifty-man daily details to move earth.

Just south of Graveyard Road, Giles Smith's battered brigade began its own approach toward the right flank of the redan, more or less concurrently with that of Ewing's to the north. Beginning in the ravine bottom secured during the assault, Smith's Zouaves alongside the Sixth Missouri and 116th Illinois cut multiple approach trenches which converged when nearing the redan. Smith's approaches measured eight feet wide, intended to allow for a column four-men abreast to debouch from their confines and spring violently onto the redan parapet.[11]

Despite cane fascine roofs and sap rollers, labor on the works and approaches during daylight hours quickly proved more dangerous than it was worth all along the line. Instead, most brigades alternated between sharpshooting and artillery barrage during the day and siegecraft during the night. The necessity of laboring on approaches under the cover of darkness forced the men to accustom themselves to working, communicating, and coordinating operations at night. This was a novel experience for most regiments. While a handful of Sherman's expeditionary force had found themselves digging battery positions in the rain through the night following the repulse at Chickasaw Bayou, and Steele's division had made its miserable tramp westward in the darkness of night at Arkansas Post, corps operations had usually come to a halt following "Taps" and the extinguishing of lights in camp each evening. Work now continued in one capacity or another at all hours of the day and night.[12]

On June 9, Sherman ordered a permanent and unbroken "continuous chain of sentinels" to be established across the entire corps front, to "act as sharpshooters or pickets" after being instructed to allow "no human being [to] pass into or out of Vicksburg, unless on strictly military duty, or as prisoners." Individual sentinels on duty were to connect with those to their left and right and remain in close contact with others massed in reserve to the rear. In effect, this "continuous chain" was to function as a permanent "cloud of skirmishers" meant to harass the Rebel works continually and provide covering fire for those working in or on the approach trenches during the dangerous daylight hours.[13] Regiments often divided companies into five reliefs, each spending two hours in forward sharpshooting pits cut perpendicularly off the approaches during each day, providing all effective manpower in the corps a daily opportunity to practice their marksmanship.[14]

Sharpshooting details quickly found they could "see the town from where we are . . . but the rebel sharpshooters can see us also so we have to keep close [down]."[15] Duty in the forward pits was exceedingly hot in both senses of the term: air temperature and enemy fire.[16] Regiments converted empty grain sacks into sandbags, just as they had done to dam the entrances and exits of Grant's ill-fated canal, and stacked them along the forward edge of trenches in a manner that produced "port holes" out of which to aim and shoot "at the unlucky head that hap[p]ens to appear above the other works." At night, details covered the pits with roofs of rails and brush, both to hide the riflemen during the day and protect them from the merciless rays of the summer sun.[17] Although some regiments erected "head-logs" to protect their shooters, for others, "it had not yet occurred to us to use logs on top to protect our heads when firing, as became the custom later on."[18]

Riflemen had to take extra care when scanning for targets and exposing themselves behind the portholes, as many of the Secessionists proved crack shots themselves. "The enemy have Squir[r]el rifles' which are very accurate," one Iowan observed, "[and] they watch these 'port holes' and when they see the flash from our gun [they] put a bullet general[l]y right through." Very quickly, the men adapted accordingly, and "learned to get down as soon as we fire." Unfortunately, this tactic also reduced their ability to judge the accuracy of their fire. "If we stand to see what effect our shot has had we are all most sure to share the fate of one of our boys of Co. D," Private Robert Henry, Twenty-Sixth Iowa, observed of a comrade recently shot through the head. Another Hawkeye explained to his wife how he and his comrades had to learn how "to dodge and where to stand up, and so keep pretty well concealed."[19] At night, officers worked to identify "the best and most concealed places" in which to place detachments so as to maximize coverage and the potential effectiveness of their fire the next day.

Although judging the accuracy of sharpshooting fire was difficult for the men in the pits, in retrospect it is clear that the riflemen of the corps exacted a fearsome toll on the Rebel regiments to their front. The Twenty-Seventh Louisiana, charged with holding the works to the immediate front of Ewing's brigade during the siege, lost every field officer it had, either killed or wounded, to the fire of sharpshooters. In fact, on June 27, Brig. Gen. Martin E. Green became the highest ranking casualty of the corps's "chain of sentinels" when he boldly shouted to his men that "a bullet has not been moulded that will kill me" just prior to rising up to check the progress of Smith's sap, only to be cut down immediately by a ball fired from the 116th Illinois.[20]

At first, Henry and his comrades found themselves "a little timid" on sharpshooting duty, exposed to the snap and buzz of incoming Rebel lead overhead in a continual stream throughout the day. The young Hawkeye "involuntarily dodged at every Whiz but they were so frequent that it became tiresome and I soon got so I could stand the racket," he proudly reported. By the time his company's daytime rotation was complete, "I was as mindless of them [Rebel bullets] as of the hum of flies."[21] Most men assigned to the task armed themselves to the teeth with ammunition, in almost giddy anticipation of expending all of it over the course of a day. Private John Mains, Sixth Missouri, routinely took at least a hundred rounds along with him on duty in the pits. Private Arch Brinkerhoff, Fourth Iowa, regularly fired until his "shoulder is very much bruised, where my gun kicks me," frequently expending between thirty and sixty-five rounds per day.[22] By mid-June, at

the height of the siege, Brinkerhoff estimated that his company fired approximately one thousand cartridges per day when assigned to the forward
pits.[23] One Buckeye estimated that he alone fired "at least one thousand
rounds" over the course of the siege.[24] While unfortunately reliable numbers
are all but nonexistent, if Brinkerhoff's estimates are even remotely correct, Sherman's corps likely fired tens of thousands of cartridges per day.

The rate of this fire was contingent upon each shooter's ability to identify
potential targets, find the range, and take careful aim. Each day his company made its way forward to sharpshoot, Brinkerhoff would set himself
to carefully "looking for Rebs." The availability of such targets was often
dependent upon the weather. On intensely hot days, the men rarely spotted Rebel heads to shoot at. On cooler days, however, "our game stirs about
more and we have some pretty fair shots." The range to targets likewise varied significantly dependent upon how far advanced each brigade's forward
pits were at the time of assignment to them—most progressively advancing
week by week and day by day until shooters were within a hundred yards
or less of the enemy works. Some riflemen even established their own
personal positions from which to partake in their routine sharpshooting
assignment. Private Charles Willison, Seventy-Sixth Ohio, happened upon
a particular piece of terrain that allowed him visibility into a highly vulnerable portion of the Rebel line at almost a thousand yards' distance. "My rifle
was sighted for one thousand yards and practice enabled me to get accurate
range of the spot so I could see the dust fly just where I wanted to hit," Willison explained. The Buckeye became so good at such extreme long-range
firing that it was at this very spot "I hit the only man I was *sure* of during
the war," watching as the Rebel threw his hands into the air before being
evacuated by stretcher.[25]

On the occasion of general artillery bombardments, entire companies
blazed away "pretty fast to keep the rebels down, so the Battery men can
work the cannons," sometimes even firing by volley. On other days, the
enemy did his best to contest the corps's fire supremacy. "Sometimes the
Johnnies shoot pretty close," Brinkerhoff observed. "We have to take good
care of our heads." A few of the Thirtieth Iowa took to holding their hats up
on ramrods to draw Rebel fire and "see how quickly some Johnnie would
fire at them; and they would nearly always hit it if above the log." The
Hawkeyes learned, just as their enemy counterparts did, to look carefully
for targets immediately after the shot, and "if they saw a rebel put his head

up above their works to see if he had hit some Yank . . . they would pull on him." Others less interested in taking such risks to get a clear shot merely watched for the darkening of Rebel artillery embrasures—an occasion which would inevitably draw "five to ten ready to shoot into it."[26]

Although individual companies and even whole regiments regularly rotated to and from the forward pits, many also selected rearward positions at the crest of the southern lip of the Mint Spring ravine where men could practice their marksmanship on the Rebel works at more or less personal whim. This surprising liberality in ammunition expenditure represented the bountiful supply that Grant's army enjoyed. It also converted the enemy works into a kind of "free-fire zone" where even junior enlisted men needed little to no authorization from superiors to engage at will. On days when Brinkerhoff's Hawkeye company was not assigned to sharpshooting duty, the young private found he enjoyed shooting so much that he frequently climbed the ridge to the embrasures of the First Iowa Battery and shot "till I get tired." Firing from more than four hundred yards' distance, it was difficult to tell if he "hit any one body," but he nevertheless continued "until my shoulder is beat very sore." The safety of long-range sharpshooting even allowed for photography, and Brinkerhoff and his comrades "got our pictures taken in a group standing skirmishing . . . Some loading some firing in all positions." Sadly, these images do not survive.[27]

Unlike the dismal swamps of Young's Point or the Yazoo bottoms, the Walnut Hills were "high, healthy, and good . . . in direct and easy communication with our supplies," offering substantial cover for those in the rear from the intermittent fire emanating from the Rebel works. Most regiments established camps on the reverse slope of the ridge from which both major assaults had been launched. If not assigned to sharpshooting duty, most did their best to stay out of the sun and "lie by in the middle of the day as much as we can."[28] Still, the static monotony of siege life inevitably eroded discipline and cleanliness, just as it had in the camps at Young's Point. Regimental commanders found themselves frequently issuing and reissuing sharp-toned general orders threatening punishment if companies failed to maintain well-policed encampments. In the Twenty-Sixth Iowa, many junior enlisted men who failed to painstakingly care for their quarters and clothing drew the ire of their commander, Colonel Milo Smith. Inspecting his regiment behind the works, Smith was astounded to find several "exceedingly filthy," a few of whom were so infested with lice "that these vermin can be seen 'even at a distance' crawling upon their persons at all hours of the day." Smith warned his junior officers that failure to address such a sad state of affairs would soon result in "details . . . made for the purpose of washing such men." The Hawkeyes of the neighboring Thirtieth Iowa were ordered to concern themselves with an altogether different sort of cleanliness. Lt. Col. W. M. G. Torrence, after observing how "the Great God" had bestowed upon the regiment "blessings" of "good health and cheerfulness" throughout the campaign, did not want to risk alienating His benevolence. Accordingly, Torrence ordered "everything which might prove offensive" to God be immediately removed from camp.[29]

Sherman required commanders of every company and battery in the corps to conduct three daily roll calls, ensuring that familiarity with orderly sergeants would not produce spurious reports that erroneously inflated the army's perception of available manpower. The unusually honest reports that reached corps headquarters daily were rarely uplifting.[30] Hard work each night and stifling heat each day took a heavy toll on the health of the corps.[31] Constant details to picket duty or fatigue parties left little free time remaining to bathe or wash clothes.[32] Watching his men bake in their camps to Steele's rear, one Hawkeye noted how "the sun pores its rays of heat down upon them," producing widespread "fever and ague" in the ranks. By the first of July, the men present for duty in his regiment, the Twenty-Fifth Iowa, had decreased by more than 23 percent since the opening of the campaign in May. Still a "new" regiment, the Twenty-Fifth suffered considerably greater losses to its effective strength during the siege than did the "old" veteran Fourth and Ninth Iowa regiments of Steele's division. On the whole, First Division suffered a decrease of 8 percent in available effective on-duty strength between May and July. Blair's Second Division, in no small part due to the grievous losses sustained during its two ill-fated charges, suffered far worse, losing 21 percent of its effective strength across the three months of the campaign. Including Tuttle's Third Division, Sherman's corps experienced a decrease of more than 14 percent of its already heavily depleted effective manpower during the campaign, leaving it with only 14,644 of the 27,116 men borne on its rolls (54 percent) in the works atop the Walnut Hills with their companies on July 1.[33]

The 410 infantry companies and nine artillery batteries assigned to Fifteenth Corps headquarters averaged about 35 effectives each by July, though many rarely mustered even half that number. Company I, Twenty-Sixth Iowa, reported 14 privates, 5 corporals, 3 sergeants, and a first lieutenant for duty on July 1. Their brother Hawkeyes in Company E, Thirty-First Iowa, counted only 8 privates, 3 corporals, 2 sergeants, 1 lieutenant, and their captain for duty on the same day—only one less leader than the total number of privates still able for duty. While these represented some of the more extreme cases of company-level attrition within the corps, they were by no means singular. Very few companies could boast more than 30 aggregate men of all ranks for duty by the beginning of July. This shrinkage naturally transformed most companies into increasingly tight-knit groups, as the survivors bonded ever more closely over the course of the siege. By the summer of 1863, even within the ranks of the newer regiments, those who remained understood that "the weak members [had] been left behind or winnowed out" of their companies.[34] After the combined bloodlettings of Chickasaw Bayou and "the Post," the protracted nightmare of Young's Point, the long slog to invest Vicksburg, and the two desperate assaults, all that was left of Sherman's "skeleton regiments" were the lean sinews and connective tissue that constituted each unit's true combat power. While all the regiments of the corps would continue to leach men from their rolls throughout the rest of the war, the rugged and wiry cohorts that filled the Walnut Hills works that summer would represent the veteran core of each command for the duration.

By mid-June, many began to tire of the monotony of siege life. "Just the same old programme," John Gay, Twenty-Fifth Iowa, jotted in his diary. "Some firing but not much[,] can't see why they dont pitch in and I think twentyfour hours firing would be more than the reb's can stand as it would be a fire from every quarter."[35] Unsubstantiated and erroneous rumors that "our army corps is to make another assault upon the rebel works" rustled the feathers of many in Steele's division. Cpt. John Bell, Twenty-Fifth Iowa, was aghast at the news. "I hardly believe it," he scribbled in his diary. "It is fool-hardy and useless in my opinion." While most agreed that assaulting the works again would be suicidal, some thought that, if the parapet itself could be breached by artillery, it might be possible to exploit the gap. "All say the third time is to prove the charm," one Illinoisan in Blair's division asserted, somewhat singularly.[36] While still confident that such rumors of a forthcoming assault were untrue, Bell's brother officer Cpt. Jacob Ritner began to worry considerably about the growing rates of sickness sapping his company's effective strength. "If we have to lie in these rifle pits another month," he fretted, "we will lose as many men by sickness as we would by a charge." While the Rebels remained all but silent during the day, it was the "continual excitement and strain on the nerves" that Ritner feared the most. It would "wear out any set of men" eventually.[37]

On clear evenings, moonlight usually offered ample illumination for digging approaches and gun positions and gradually inching the saps ever nearer the Rebel works. Skirmishers maneuvered through no-man's-land in the darkness to provide protection and early warning for fatigue details toiling in the trenches.[38] While both sides occasionally attempted nighttime raids between trenches to capture pickets and gain intelligence, far more frequently an informal "common understanding" existed between Federal and Rebel pickets that "musket firing ceases at dark," leaving work details comparatively safe to push forward the saps and improve the works.[39] The cover of night also frequently brought Rebel deserters into Federal lines, bearing tales of woe from within the beleaguered city that significantly boosted confidence in eventual success. "They all told the same tale of being worn out with sleeplessness and fatigue," one Illinoisan of the Fifty-Fifth Illinois recalled, "of hospitals crowded with sick and wounded; of women and children slain in the city by fragments of shells." The emaciated Secessionists "bitterly complained that their daily ration of meat was but a mouthful of bacon, and half spoiled at that; that beef and flour and even corn meal had long been exhausted . . . [and] that raw pork and musty pea-meal bread formed a monotonous diet."[40]

Despite the apparent dejection of Vicksburg's inhabitants, Grant grew increasingly concerned about a Rebel relief force under General Joseph E. Johnston supposedly coalescing in the Federal rear. On June 11, he ordered Sherman to detach Tuttle's Third Division from behind the corps lines for duty along the Big Black River to the east. Its departure left the entirety of the siege work along the corps's front to Steele's and Blair's divisions alone. Moreover, when Grant assigned Sherman to command of all detached divisions forming along the Big Black on June 22, in preparation for a potential enemy onslaught, Steele—as the senior division commander—assumed temporary command of the corps.[41]

Shortly before Sherman's departure, Cpt. William Kossak took charge of the trenches and saps of Ewing's approach, then extending to within twenty feet of the Stockade Redan parapet. To the right, Colonel Oskar Malmborg, Fifty-Fifth Illinois, superintended a new approach by Lightburn's brigade aiming at the stockade itself. Malmborg, a product of some formal education as a military engineer in Sweden prior to immigrating to America, cut an eight-foot-wide trench to allow for a column four abreast to assault the works from its head.[42] Employing a combination of pioneers, a company of miners drawn from a Missouri regiment, and regularly rotating fifty-man details from various others, Kossak was charged with advancing the approaches close enough to the enemy works to allow for a point-blank plunging fire to be poured directly into the Rebel trenches. While constructing "trench cavaliers" to achieve this, some of Kossak's pioneers thought they heard sounds of tamping, a tell-tale sign that "the enemy was mining to blow up the head of my sap," Kossak reported. Frantically digging counter-ditches in multiple directions, Kossak hoped to strike the Rebel mine chamber, but to no avail. Early in the morning of the twenty-sixth, explosives in two of these enemy mines were detonated, throwing gabions into the air and collapsing several of Kossak's counter-ditches. Undeterred, the details continued to shovel Mississippi dirt by both day and night, even as Rebels threw shells with lit fuses over the parapet amid the fatigue parties. Fortunately, none were killed by these bombs, nor even by the detonation of the Rebel mines. "A few men were covered by earth and gabions falling on them from the parapets," Kossak observed, "but they extricated themselves without material injury." To return the favor, his details flung their own grenades over the redan parapet.[43]

"ONE OF THE BEST TRAINING SCHOOLS"

By late June, the saps had reached such a near proximity to the outlying Rebel works that many again began to wonder if yet another bloody assault was likely to be ordered. Fatigue details working at the saps were "within Ten steps of the rebs if not Closer," Private John Mains, Sixth Missouri, observed. "They will soon bee close enough to eat off the same dish."[44] Many of the foremost pickets had ceased exchanging fire even during the day.[45] Given the short distance now necessary to cross under fire, even some of the most recently pessimistic members of the corps wondered if such a maneuver might now meet with success. Even still, "it would be attended with losses very great and I think Gen Grant desires that the place be taken without further loss of life," Sewall Farwell explained.[46] While many found relief in this assumption, they were also wrong.[47]

All of the corps's saps were now well within one hundred yards of the Rebel works. Ewing's was within twenty feet of Stockade Redan and Light-burn's twenty-five. All realizing that further forward progress was both unlikely and probably imprudent, on the evening of July 3, Captain Prime instructed all to turn to mining operations in preparation to explode mines underneath the enemy works prior to a direct assault from the approaches on the morning of July 6.[48] "Little farther progress could be made by digging alone," Prime considered. "We could put the heads of regiments under cover within from 5 to 100 yards of his line," thus avoiding what most of Grant's headquarters believed to be the primary cause of failure in May: "Long-continued exposure" to enemy fire. Now, with assault columns debouch-ing simultaneously from the ten approach trenches no more than twenty feet from the enemy parapet, Rebel defenders would struggle to get even a single volley off as the men crested the works and fell directly upon them with the bayonet. Instead of a Rebel shock volley, each attacking regiment's crucial "penultimate moment" would come either as stunned (and starved) Secessionists fled in terror, or in the throes of hand-to-hand combat.[49] Not knowing much of anything about mining, Malmborg, Ewing, and Smith were at a loss until Kossak recalled that many in Lightburn's Fourth West Virginia were "old coal miners." A detail of sixteen Appalachian miners were drawn from its ranks and distributed to each brigade's approach to superintend the process, but they were never put to work. The very next day, the Rebel garrison of Vicksburg surrendered.[50]

Many found the euphoria of victory ineffable. After suffering through every traumatic step of the campaign from the Yazoo bottoms to the sur-render, Private Burke Wylie, Thirty-First Iowa, was filled "with feeling al-moste too full for utterance." Robert Henry could only exclaim, "What relief! What pleasure! No pen can ink or painter paint . . . the thrilling pleasure."[51] Even so, instead of cheers, most merely turned to their filthy comrades to offer "hand shakes of mutual congratulation, [with] moist eyes and silent prayers of thankfulness."[52]

The long-awaited fall of the city served to revive the army's confidence in Grant's generalship. "Every body likes Genl Grant & well they may, for he has done well," one Hawkeye pronounced on the day of the surrender.[53] "He has gained a greate victory here," another wrote home, "and consequently is the greatest General of the time."[54] One of the Fifty-Fifth Illinois thought that Grant had "shown himself to be one of the very best planning and maneuvering generals that we have in the service."[55] In fact, he was certain that in coordinating the circuitous campaign to invest Vicksburg, the army commander had "displayed the best generalship yet shown since the beginning of the war," and hurrahed for "Grant and W. T. Sherman, long may they live to lead our armies." In truth, such celebrations of Sherman were comparatively few and far between within the corps. Even so, while the command had by no means yet developed the passion and love for "Uncle Billy" that they would later exhibit, by the conclusion of the siege little of the disgust and hatred that had accompanied his name in late May still lingered on the lips or pens of the men.[56]

Looking back with the benefit of hindsight, it was clear to all who had endured and survived the protracted siege that the experience had imparted many lessons and skills which would later prove invaluable. Foremost among these was the sheer volume of marksmanship practice the siege provided. "While we lay there fighting our men were given a better opportunity for becoming good marksmen than they would have had without such practice," one Iowan later recalled, "and it helped our army ever afterwards."[57] Adjutant Charles Miller, Seventy-Sixth Ohio, likewise observed how the companies daily rotating in and out of the sharpshooting pits eventually "became almost perfect in [finding] their range."[58] Overall, he thought the siege "presented one of the best training schools for engineering and gunnery known to modern times."[59]

The riflemen taking their turn in the foremost pits were not the only members of the corps provided unprecedented opportunities for marksmanship practice during the siege. Each gun crew in every one of Sherman's batteries likewise capitalized on the opportunity to hone their skills on Rebel targets and "became almost perfect in range and center shots," Miller observed.[60] In fact, according to most accounts and analyses, the accuracy of Federal artillery fire far exceeded that of the "sharpshooting" riflemen of Grant's army.[61] Sending individual shells from the corps's Parrott and James rifles sailing directly through narrow embrasures to silence Rebel guns from a distance of often more than seven hundred yards was no small feat, but after weeks of opportunities for trial and error, the crews had mastered their craft and learned much about their weapons in the process. While howitzer crews were usually incapable of matching the accuracy of the rifled guns, they found a separate niche in battering down earthen Rebel parapets and habitually setting fire to cotton bales used to bolster the enemy works. Once the approaches had been advanced adequately to maneuver howitzers to within three hundred yards of the enemy works, they too began to take aim at the embrasures.[62] Over the course of the siege, the Fourth Ohio Independent Battery of Steele's division fired a total of 1,865 rounds from its two 12 lb. Howitzers and four James rifles while supporting the advance of Thayer's approach.[63] Artillery practice was far more plentiful along Blair's front, where the gunners of Battery A, First Illinois Light Artillery, expended an astounding 9,690 rounds from their two Parrott rifles and five 12 lb. Napoleons over the course of the siege.[64]

The amount of firing a given battery might accomplish each day often had to be gauged by the volume of incoming rifle fire that filled the air, and thus the opportunity for such extensive artillery practice was almost entirely contingent upon the ability of the corps's sharpshooters in the trenches to suppress their Rebel counterparts. Crews learned the hard way to stay low while sponging their barrels and loading the guns. As Charles Affeld was sponging the bore of his crew's piece while supporting the May 22 assault, a fellow crew member was shot through the heart and killed instantly while thumbing the vent and "standing erect." Had he "been more careful he would probably [have] been living yet," Affeld observed.[65] Another member of Battery A was killed well behind his gun's embrasure while washing his hands during the siege. "Getting some soap in his eyes, he called for a towel and holding out his hands, he raised himself a little too high and a rebel bullet went through his heart," a comrade lamented.[66]

Occasionally, riflemen waiting their turn in the approaches or forward pits were detailed to man the guns so as to give their crews a rest. In doing so, they "became expert artillerists," Miller noted, and "after getting their range, planted some remarkable shots into the works." Those fortunate enough to earn a chance to work the guns found the detail "a great deal better than . . . [the] infantry." One Hawkeye earnestly hoped "to try and stay in the artillery till the war is over."[67] Although infantry details were routinely assigned to establish or improve gun emplacements, many artillerists found their work insufficient, unimpressive, or worse. When Battery B, First Illinois Light Artillery, was moved at night to a new position dug by infantry details in preparation to support the May 22 assault, gunner Charles Affeld and his team were aghast at what they found. "The infantry had done a poor job, either on account of poor management or not enough tools," he griped. In an attempt to manhandle their piece into the shoddy earthwork before the sun arose along with the Rebel sharpshooters, they found there was barely enough room for the gun alone, let alone its crew. After feverishly scraping away at the dirt "so the gun would at least stand straight," they hurriedly "cut brush to screen us from observation . . . so as to be protected from sharpshooters."[68]

While all in the corps maintained a subjective sense of fire superiority throughout the siege, the true extent to which the command had succeeded in winning and defending its fire supremacy was not apparent until the Rebel surrender. After the capitulation of the city, Grant's chief engineer, Captain Prime, was astounded at the discovery of more than 40,000 rounds of yet unused Rebel artillery ammunition. "If at almost any point they had put ten or fifteen guns in position, instead of one or two to invite concentration of our fire, they might have seriously delayed our approaches," he observed. During the course of the siege, he and others had remained of the apparently erroneous opinion that the comparative silence of the Rebel guns had been due "to the lack of ammunition." Even a "small portion of this [ammunition], judiciously used, would have rendered our app[roach much slower," he thought.[69] Those who had enjoyed an opportunity to grasp the tactical realities of the daily situation from the forward pits well understood why the enemy's guns had been so comparatively silent. "We have so many batteries that can be brought to bear on one point that they dare not fire," one observed.[70] More accurately, the tactical symbiosis of suppressive sharpshooting fire from the forward pits and surgical precision fire from the corps's batteries marked a major advance in the command's tactical capabilities on the battlefield—one that the corps would apply with deadly effectiveness on future fields.

The success of the siege had, to a truly unique extent, been the product of the adaptive "native good sense and ingenuity" of the men. "Whether a battery was to be constructed by men who had never built one before, a sap-roller made by those who had never heard the name, or a ship's gun-carriage to be built, it was done," Prime observed in his report, "and, after a few trials, was well done." It astounded him how quickly the veteran regiments of citizen-volunteers had accustomed themselves to the novel labor despite having received no specialized training. "Officers and men had to learn to be engineers while the siege was going on," he wrote.[71] This proved no problem at all for Sherman's corps. "It is astonishing how soon we become accustomed to things," Captain Ritner reflected.[72]

"A MINIATURE VICKSBURG"

The Fifteenth Corps was not to immediately enjoy the fruits of its momentous victory. The evening after the city fell, orders from Sherman reached both Steele and Blair instructing them to prepare to move at short notice.[73] By five o'clock the next morning, the corps was already out of its works, in column, and headed east toward the Big Black River with orders to join Sherman's Expeditionary Force and pursue Joseph Johnston's ragged Rebel band all the way to Jackson if necessary.[74] On July 6, both divisions crossed the river and continued eastward through oppressive heat and dust. Armed with their recent experience of success in siegecraft, most expected to employ much the same tactics against Johnston. "The intention is to surround his Army and 'bag' them all as was done in Vicksburg," one Hawkeye wrote.[75]

Despite a thunderstorm on the evening of July 7, the insufferable dust of the road east made the remainder of the journey trying in the extreme. "The dust rose in suffocating clouds about the sweltering columns," one Illinoisan recalled, "and the men suffered wo[e]fully." Very quickly the "men and horses were of the same color as the ground." Many fell dangerously ill with heat exhaustion and sunstroke, "and others were constantly seen dropping out of the ranks and lagging behind from exhaustion." Potable water proved all but nonexistent as groups of parched volunteers wandered listlessly away from the column in desperate attempts to parch their thirst. "We were obliged to use w[h]at water to drink that in peaceable time would not make good answer for washwater for your feet," one Iowan admitted, and even that "was very scarce." Most that could be found nearby was "covered with a green scum and warm." In other places, Johnston's retreating army had intentionally poisoned springs and wells with the carcasses of livestock so as to prevent their use by Sherman's onrushing force. On frequent occasions details were forced to haul water to camp from miles away just to boil for cooking. Those who managed to find it often sold full canteens for as much as fifty cents apiece, with great success. After the minimal rations brought along from Vicksburg were expended, most regiments sustained themselves exclusively on blackberries and green corn, stripping whole acres near encampments. Corn still in its husk was laid atop rails over a fire, and once "the husks were burned off the corn would be cooked by the steam and be in a delicious state to be eaten."[76]

By the ninth, the foremost elements of Steele's column were within sight of Jackson's outskirts. The next day, at about ten o'clock in the morning, a Rebel battery caught sight of the advance guard and sent a fusillade as a warning.[77] Remarkably level by comparison with the Walnut Hills, the ground sweeping ahead of Steele to the Rebel works had been mostly clear-cut by enemy pioneers in an effort to establish clear fields of fire. Most of Sherman's force, including Tuttle's division, was already investing the city by the time of Steele's and Blair's arrival. Shuffling the two newly arrived commands into the center of his lines of investiture, it was clear to all that "Sherman had evidently no intention of ordering any hasty or unnecessary assaults," which came as a great relief to the corps.[78] "The batteries and long lines of rifle-pits could have enfiladed and swept the wide, open space in front with a murderous fire," an embedded journalist with the *New York Times* observed. "It is well that an assault was not ordered."[79]

Although frequently brushed over by historians of the Vicksburg campaign, the subsequent siege of Jackson, while brief, provided powerful evidence of an evolutionary shift in Sherman's tactical philosophy. While Johnston, with every good reason, seems to have assumed that his opponent would squander his numerical advantage once again by hurling it against the well-prepared Rebel works ringing the city, for perhaps the first time, Sherman thought twice. This time, as he later explained to Admiral Porter, "the forts and lines were too respectable to venture the assault," and instead, he opted to employ what he termed—in language that made clear how the strategy was a direct product of learning from experience—"a miniature Vicksburg." In fact, he not only "made no assault—indeed—I never meditated one," but instead progressively enveloped the city by maneuver while the men engaged chiefly in sharpshooting from rifle pits.[80]

Just as at Vicksburg, many regiments almost automatically set to digging in "to protect ourselves."[81] Once again, most work on the fortifications took place "in the shades of night," whereas skirmishers and batteries dueled with Rebels at considerable range during the day.[82] The gunners of Battery A, 1st Illinois Light Artillery, immediately put to work the experience of preparing gun positions at Vicksburg and established "the safest works we ever occupied." "Sinking our guns into a pit," the crews threw the dirt ahead of the breastwork while others fashioned an embrasure of cotton bales. With such defilade, enemy fire "invariably shot over us." Moreover, the distance to the Jackson works being much greater than that at Vicksburg, the battery was able to post a spotter well ahead of the guns while still within audible shouting distance. Whenever smoke billowed out of one of the Rebel embrasures, before the sound of the shot could even reach the position, the spotter would scream "Down!" and Illinoisan crews instinctively hit the ground until the shot struck or passed. After several close calls, the men responded in the same fashion even if in the middle of loading their guns. Fortunately, such dangerous encounters were relatively rare given that the teams had mastered their aim so well at Vicksburg that enemy crews were almost always silenced by the long-range rifled guns long before they could do much damage.[83]

Other batteries were assigned far less precise targets. The four James Rifle crews of the Fourth Ohio Independent Battery found themselves ordered to "throw all the projectiles in the direction of the State House, so that the[y] may be destructive in the town." Initially conservative in their ammunition expenditure prior to resupply from Vicksburg, the battery eventually increased its rate of fire until July 14, when it was "ordered to fire one shot every five minutes day or night in the direction of the State House or . . . into the enemy Rifle Pits" at a distance of about 850 yards. At no point were the battery's howitzers engaged, both the town and enemy being beyond the effective range of the smoothbore guns.[84]

Once again, nearly all the powder the corps's infantry expended during the siege was burnt by sharpshooting details. Because the volume of fire called for was significantly lower than at Vicksburg, and because targets were generally at much greater range, frequently such details were more impromptu affairs conducted by a handful of "picked marksmen." Just such a squad was thrown together by the First Sergeant of Company A, Fifty-Fifth Illinois, on July 11 in the interest of silencing a frequent harassing fire from nearby Rebel skirmishers. Selecting six men to join him, the team maneuvered into a dry creek bed and "crept on within shorter range of the rebel lines" to positions behind cover. Employing a single Colt Revolving Rifle—the only one of its kind in the regiment—the first sergeant "cleaned out a whole picket post," cutting down several unsuspecting Rebels and scattering the remainder.[85] Such small unit actions, though they usually went unrecorded, illustrated many of the particular strengths of the corps's tactical culture: high degrees of initiative by noncommissioned officers, the capacity to operate in impromptu groups, considerable marksmanship experience, and small-unit maneuver through difficult terrain.

After a last-ditch effort to raid Sherman's supply lines with Rebel cavalry, Johnston came to the same conclusion Pemberton had in Vicksburg. There was no escaping the grip of such a leviathan, and now veteran, Federal force. Accordingly, on July 16, he opted to evacuate Jackson and escape northward with his "Army of Relief" in hopes of employing it more fruitfully elsewhere within the embattled Confederacy. Vicksburg and Jackson, and with them the Mississippi River, following the nearly contemporaneous fall of Port Hudson to the south, were now firmly in Federal hands. Well aware that his army was utterly exhausted, Sherman prudently chose not to pursue the fleeing Secessionists, instead ordering his victorious legions back into Jackson for a second time that summer.[86]

Unlike during the corps's brief visit to the capital in May, when it bore orders from Grant concerning the specific extent of destruction he wished meted out on the city, this time the army commander instructed Sherman's command to "do the enemy all the harm possible" and "inflict on the enemy all the punishment you can." In fact, he added that he had "no suggestions or orders to give" and that Cump was to deal with Johnston "in your own way."[87] On July 13, just before the fall of the city, he sent follow-on orders for Sherman to "destroy . . . everything valuable for carrying on war." This lack of specificity in orders for targeted destruction has been identified by historian Mark Grimsley as altogether "something new" in the war and "unmistakably different" from prior Federal policies even of "war in earnest." In the wake of Vicksburg's capitulation and Johnston's flight, the strategic dynamic of the campaign changed dramatically. Grant was no longer in fear of a Rebel relief army falling upon the rear of his siege lines, and thus there was "little need for such destruction [of Jackson] if the objective were the 'pragmatic' one of preventing an enemy force from operating . . . in the area," as it had been along Deer Creek, Grimsley notes. Instead, the corps's second visit to the Mississippi capital was intended to "destroy the region's economic value to the Confederacy," plain and simple.[88]

The corps most certainly went about its mission in its "own way," perhaps to an extent well beyond what Grant had originally contemplated. The lack of clear boundaries delimiting Grant's definition of what constituted "everything valuable for carrying on war," Sherman's habitual incapacity to control the destructive tendencies of libertine volunteers, and the lessons derived by the rank and file during their recent experiences of "hard war" in the Deer Creek Valley all combined to produce the swift and unequivocal erasure of Jackson, Mississippi, as a strategic point on any military map.

In truth, however, much of Jackson was already either in flames or ashes by the time Sherman's force entered the environs. Fires started by Johnston's retreating army in an attempt to keep valuable stores out of Sherman's hands spread to adjacent blocks of homes and shops and proved resistant to efforts to put them out. The corps's brigades fragmented into smaller details and went to work dismantling the capital with a vengeance. What railroads had been crudely repaired during the Federal absence were once again demolished for a distance of ten miles in every direction. All rolling stock discovered in the city was burned along with four thousand cotton bales utilized in the Rebel earthworks, and the sky over Jackson turned black with smoke.[89] While leaders attempted to corral their work details and prevent straggling, some excesses were inevitable. "Our men in spite of guards have widened the Circle of fire" begun by the Rebels, Cump lamented.[90] As working parties continued their punitive work in the capital, Sherman dispatched Steele with three brigades of the corps eastward thirteen miles to Brandon, Mississippi, where he was to continue the destruction of the railroad in that direction. When combined with the prior efforts of Woods's detached brigade at Canton, by July 18, the Fifteenth Corps had effectively "ruined the main arteries of travel and communication in the heart of Mississippi," and thus its work was done.[91] Looking on as "the skies are illuminated by a fire in the northern portion of the city," one journalist had trouble feeling much sympathy for the Rebel city. "Nothing is safe or respected here, but everything destructible seems doomed to destruction," he wrote. "Such is war."[92]

"The place is ruined," Sherman reported bluntly. His command had "desolated this land for 30 miles round about."[93] Far more impressive to him, however, was the apparent reaction of its dejected inhabitants as the Fifteenth Corps quartermaster began distributing rations to the destitute citizens of the city in an effort to "relieve the immediate wants of suffering humanity."[94] "The people are subdued," he wrote, "and ask for reconstruction." All across the city he encountered Mississippians admitting "the loss of the Southern cause." While, as usual, abhorring the fiery excesses of "stragglers" in his ranks, Cump simply could not ignore the clear psychological, and thus strategic, impact their heavy-handed tactics appeared to have on erstwhile rebellious Southerners.[95]

Finally granted a well-deserved respite, Sherman's expeditionary force departed Jackson en route westward to the banks of the Big Black River in late July to establish long-term cantonments. Once occupied, "Camp Sherman" would allow the corps to catch its breath, reorganize its shrunken battalions, and begin the long process of preparing for the next campaign. When Grant suggested deploying Sherman's corps south to Natchez to conduct a similar operation to that which the command had just conducted at Jackson, Cump showed a keen awareness of the tendencies of his command, as well as his inability to control them. "As he left it to my option I preferred to stay here for good reasons," he explained in a letter home. Unlike the agriculturally rich hinterlands of Natchez to the south, "This land is stripped of niggers, and Every thing" by virtue of the recent campaign. Indeed, all the area between Vicksburg and Jackson had been effectively "cleared out and all the mischief done." "Were we to go to Natchez it would be one endless strife about run away Negros, plundering and pillaging soldiers and I am sick and tired of it," he asserted. The still quite conservative Cump had "had my share of this trouble and am willing others should try it." In truth, while he would always remain ashamed that so many in the ranks of his corps had become "Expert thieves, sparing nothing not even the clothes of women, children & Negros," he began to understand how the sheer destructive capacity of the volunteers, even when bridled to the minimal extent he and his lieutenants could achieve, could itself prove a powerful strategic weapon.[96] In fact, if the experience of the long campaign for Vicksburg had been any indication, such a weapon might even have a greater potential to put down the rebellion than did direct confrontation with Rebel armies on the battlefield. Commanding a corps which had yet to find success in the attack, but which had frequently shown a profound capacity for swift long-range maneuver and frighteningly efficient destruction of enemy assets, Sherman's "slow evolution," as B. H. Liddell Hart called it, only slightly trailed that of his corps's tactical culture.[97]

The long Vicksburg and Jackson campaigns nearly disintegrated many companies in Sherman's corps. Cpt. Sewall Farwell found only nineteen men in his company of the Thirty-First Iowa well enough for the march to Jackson, and he left the remainder in the trenches before Vicksburg. After the tough movement to the state capital and the pursuit of Johnston to Canton, the company could muster only five men, including Farwell himself, for daily duty. Another Hawkeye company "had no one able to march, except a Sergeant and Corporal—no privates," Farwell remarked.[98] The experience had likewise disintegrated the clothing of most in the corps. Private Charles Willison, Seventy-Sixth Ohio, "was down to hardpan in the way of clothing." By the time Vicksburg capitulated the one shirt he had left "was gone all but the front and one sleeve," and before the regiment went into camp after the fall of Jackson, he had no shirt at all, and "my pants were in an indescribable condition, my blouse all rags, and my only fairly respectable covering a forage cap." The uniforms of several were in such poor condition that they had even taken to donning captured Rebel uniforms, likely seized at Jackson. Understandably alarmed at this practice, regimental commanders promptly condemned it by general orders.[99]

Once the corps's new camps were comfortably established, Sherman charged Hugh Ewing with compiling brief historical reports from each regiment in the corps with an eye toward awarding authorizations for the adornment of each unit's national colors with the names of battles in which it had honorably taken part. The duty required the staff of each regiment and battery in the corps to reflect upon their experiences in service and forge a coherent narrative that emphasized the most salient episodes in the careers of their units. For the most part, reports consisted of little more than a brief paragraph highlighting each battle in which the unit had fought. Details were limited to when the unit arrived on the field, what had been expected of it, its most signal successes, and the casualties it sustained. The embattled Seventy-Sixth Ohio's trials at Arkansas Post were reduced to a single sentence: "Charged Rebel works on the Right to within 75 yards silencing 2 Parrott Guns and musketry fire untill the surrender." Its entire participation in the long and bloody Vicksburg campaign was likewise summarized: "Were under fire and in the front and sharp shooting with the enemy during the entire Siege." Because neither the Steele's Bayou nor Greenville expeditions, to say nothing of the ill-fated canal project, had constituted major battles, regimental reports ignored these experiences completely despite their being among the most salient influences on the development of the corps's tactical culture.[100]

The Fifteenth Corps and its commander emerged from the lengthy struggles for Vicksburg and Jackson molded by experience in specific and indelible ways. The beliefs, assumptions, predispositions, and habits of thought and action concerning operations that predominated throughout the command were all direct by-products of the particular experiences through which it had passed over the previous eight months since its organization. As would always be the case, each regiment and battery within the command had developed its own distinctive unit-level tactical "micro-culture" due to the limitations of its "personal angle of vision" and lessons learned from its experiences across each campaign. Even so, the many cultural differences between the regiments of the corps, which had been so striking upon the formation of Sherman's flotilla, were ever increasingly subtle. The component units of the corps were becoming ever more culturally alike. As the corps's units accrued ever more experience alongside one another, enduring the same trials in pursuit of the same objectives, their members naturally arrived at similar conclusions as to the key lessons of their experiences, developed confidence in their relative capacity to successfully achieve certain missions, and gained varying levels of skill in conducting certain tasks due to disproportionate opportunities for practice. In this fashion, a coherent and easily discernible corps-level tactical culture took shape.

Perhaps the signature element of this tactical culture was the corps's deeply ingrained aversion, widespread lack of confidence, and proven incapacity to charge Rebel breastworks. Crucially, this aversion to assaulting works did not extend to a lack of confidence in all attacks. Many within the ranks yearned for what they called a "fair fight" against Rebels in the open—a fight they both were certain they could win and, at the same time, had almost never experienced. Instead, the men had developed a greatly inflated respect for the defensive advantages accruing to infantry fighting from behind works, and thus for field fortifications themselves. It was in large part this profound respect for entrenchments, coming from the corps's recent painful experiences charging them, that inspired Sherman's corps to dig so ardently themselves over the course of the campaign.

While Blair's division, still bearing the influence of Morgan Smith, remained far and away the most effective light infantry force in the corps, the ongoing sharpshooters' war that unfolded across the siege gradually converted even Steele's division into expert riflemen. The extensive marksmanship practice that Sherman's regiments had enjoyed set them, and the rest of Grant's army, apart from all other field armies, whose regiments rarely fired their weapons outside of major engagements. Moreover, the experience the corps accrued operating as fragmented details led by junior leaders charged with a variety of tasks made it extraordinarily flexible in approaching novel tactical challenges. From digging earthworks in the dark, coordinating the fire of sharpshooters and artillery against Rebel embrasures, swiftly tearing up railroad tracks, or hunting water and sustenance to sustain the punishing daily march, almost everything that the corps did at the tactical level it conducted in small groups guided by junior leaders. This competence and confidence in detached small-unit operations represented a defining element of the corps's tactical culture that would prove vital in future campaigns.

Finally, though often much to its commander's chagrin, the corps continued to show an especial skill in the efficient and occasionally excessive destruction of Rebel property. When such violence to Secessionist military articles was ordered, the corps had proven itself to be among the most effective and swift commands in the US Army for destroying valuable enemy resources and infrastructure. Due to Grant's habitual reliance on Sherman to conduct his "dirty work" distant from the remainder of the army, the corps developed a cultural affinity for raiding operations due in large part to its past experiences of success. As in the Deer Creek Valley, the reactions of Mississippians, whom the men all but uniformly presumed to be among the rankest Secessionists, to the destruction of their property signaled a special kind of victory to those in the ranks. If the Rebels chose to hide in their impenetrable rifle pits, then the enlisted men and an increasing number of their officers determined that they would instead effectively "smoke them out" by dismantling the rest of the so-called "Southern Confederacy" left unguarded.

Despite what several historians have claimed, neither Sherman nor Grant was wholly responsible for imparting this panoply of cultural elements. Neither officer had molded the command by hand, nor imparted their unique personalities to the subordinate units serving under their headquarters. In fact, in many ways the exact opposite had occurred, and continued to do so. The real process of first genesis and then evolution of the corps's tactical culture was one of constant interaction between the command, its commanders, and the experiences through which they passed together.

Grant exerted his primary influence on the evolution of the Fifteenth Corps through his assignment of particular objectives to it as a subordinate component of his army. Thinking of Sherman as an avatar of the corps when contemplating these assignments, Grant rarely showed evidence of any special contemplation of the organization's proven tendencies, strengths, weaknesses, or even recent history when determining which tasks to assign to it. Instead, he almost instinctively reached for Sherman to conduct those operations furthest away from his immediate supervision, feeling a constant need to shepherd the other two inexperienced corps commanders through the trials of the campaign.

The manner in which Sherman chose to prosecute the missions that Grant handed down to his corps was always a by-product of an ongoing feedback loop of experiential learning. Sherman's unique personality and tactical philosophy mixed with empirical evidence of what his still young command either could or was not likely to accomplish. As the disasters of Chickasaw Bayou and Arkansas Post had suggested, and the bloody repulses before Stockade Redan and the Louisiana Lunette only dramatically reified, he still commanded "no troops which can be made to assault." Although he and his senior lieutenants still disagreed with most of the rank and file as to why the corps seemed to be habitually hobbled in offensive operations, its chronic inability to carry Rebel works from the front was indisputable.

Though commanding more than just his own corps at Jackson, Sherman's striking departure from his habitual reliance on bloody assaults was powerful evidence of his learning from experience. It also hinted at the somewhat singular personality trait that would eventually propel Sherman into the ranks of American military history's great commanders. While plenty of bayonet assaults launched by both sides during the war did in fact succeed, Sherman had never witnessed nor commanded such successes, and thus could only reflect upon and learn from his uniform experience of failure. That he eventually did reflect upon it allowed him to learn vicariously from those in the ranks of his command, gradually imbibing the culture that saturated the force he commanded borne of its particular history. By way of their successes and failures, the men of the corps transmitted their culture from the bottom up to their chief.

For all its unfortunate shortcomings in the assault, the corps's successes off the battlefield imparted a new confidence in Sherman's perception of the organization's true capabilities. The corps proved time and again that it could sweep across unforgiving terrain at impressive speed, endure lengthy marches on extraordinarily tight logistical budgets, swiftly and efficiently dismantle Rebel infrastructure, construct fieldworks worthy of admiration by the most professional military minds of the era, and fight in small teams as skilled marksmen with both small arms and artillery to deadly effect. As Sherman's own thinking about the root causes of the rebellion and the ideal strategy to put it down started to transform, he realized, like so many in the ranks of his corps had done months prior, that the inability to coordinate frontal assaults against entrenched Rebels across nightmarish terrain might not be so debilitating a liability after all. Perhaps the tactical culture that emerged from experience within the ranks of his corps was something he could work with.

CHAPTER 7

JUST IN FROM
THE MISSISSIPPI

Missionary Ridge and Tunnel Hill

If you like, if you can.

—SHERMAN TO EWING, NOVEMBER 25, 1863

By the fall of 1863, Col. Adin Underwood was a hard-bitten veteran of the fiercest fighting the Army of the Potomac had seen in the Eastern Theater of the Rebellion. After fighting in the Valley, Second Bull Run, and Chancellorsville, and being wounded at Gettysburg, he and his veteran Thirty-Third Massachusetts, along with fifteen thousand men of the hard-luck Eleventh and Twelfth army corps, were transferred west to Lookout Valley just outside Chattanooga, Tennessee, as the War Department hurriedly consolidated a force to raise the Rebel siege. After pushing the enemy out of Chattanooga, the three dispersed columns of Maj. Gen. William S. Rosecrans's Army of the Cumberland had been caught off guard that September by retreating Secessionists at the battle of Chickamauga in northern Georgia. Only narrowly averting disaster, Rosecrans managed to fall back to the relative safety of Chattanooga to await reinforcement. Gen. Braxton Bragg, commanding the Rebel forces hot on Rosecrans's tail, subsequently laid siege to the town that fall from the heights of Lookout Mountain and Missionary Ridge frowning down upon it from the south. Judging any frontal assault of Rosecrans's defensive works too risky, Bragg settled in to starve the Federals out that fall instead.[1]

Despite their lengthy journey, Underwood's Bay Staters, along with their comrades in other Potomac regiments, took pride in the tidiness of their new camps, the sharp appearance of their fresh uniforms, and all the "general marks of Eastern trimness and setting up," as Underwood put it.

These traditional hallmarks of martial professionalism had long been an important part of the Army of the Potomac's culture, first instilled by Maj. Gen. George B. McClellan in the aftermath of the Bull Run disaster and scrupulously maintained by each of his successors.[2] On November 20, however, what appeared to the Potomac men to be the very "slouchy" antithesis of military bearing came trudging into the valley from off the mountains to the west. "Just in from the Mississippi," Underwood observed, the advanced elements of Sherman's Fifteenth Army Corps tramped down the muddy road and past the eastern encampments, "dusty and dirty, ragged and shoeless." While having never met the westerners in person, the Bay Staters were well apprised of the exploits of Grant's "Vicksburg rats."[3] Crowding the sides of the roadway to catch a glimpse, the spit-and-polished Massachusetts men quickly drew ridicule. "What elegant corpses they'll make in those good clothes!" one of the ragged westerners shouted. "We prided ourselves upon not having a superfluity about us," an officer in the Fifty-Fifth Illinois explained, "not an ounce of weight that did not mean business—the business of the campaign." After all, "clothes were of minor consequence." The only possession of real importance was one's weapon, "always in perfect order and readiness, and the powder kept dry."[4] Though donning the same uniform and enrolled in the same US Army, the eastern and western veterans seemed culturally worlds apart. "Each one thinks their army is best," Cpt. Jacob Ritner observed of the interactions. "For my part I don't see what the Army of the East has to be proud of. If I belonged to it, I should be ashamed to own it," he added.[5]

"What's your badge?" one of the Potomac men shouted out, frustrated at being unable to identify the column by the characteristic corps badges worn by all soldiers in the Army of the Potomac. "Badge is it?" an Irish westerner replied. Thinking quickly, he patted his cartridge box. "Why fourty rounds to be shure, besides twinty in me pocket," he crowed with arrogant confidence. Rugged westerners had no time for foppery like corps badges, the response implied. Grant's "Vicksburg rats" had been too busy winning the war to spend time designing corps badges with which to adorn their hats. Though probably apocryphal, the story eventually made its way to corps headquarters, where it was so heartily appreciated that it inspired the corps's only official badge. Although it was adopted at nearly the end of the war, all of those still serving in the Fifteenth Corps in the spring of 1865 would adorn their chests with a cloth or metal badge marked by nothing more than a symbolic cartridge box inscribed with the words "40 Rounds"—the individual rifleman's standard load of ammunition.[6]

Much has been made since the war of the supposedly major cultural differences between eastern and western volunteers during the war. For the most part, eastern troops thought of their western counterparts as "crude, undisciplined and slovenly"—all characteristics frequently attributed to the inhabitants of the antebellum western states. Likewise, westerners assumed that the Potomac army was filled with exactly the same kinds of "effete, liquor-soaked, money-mad" dandy frippery and extravagant display that they attributed to life "back East." Too much attention to appearances, they thought, led to the production of "'bandbox' troops, fit only for parade and garrison."[7] Some historians have tacitly accepted these sociocultural explanations.[8]

In truth, little of the Fifteenth Corps's appearance that crisp fall day had anything to do with the western origins of its men. Had Underwood instead first encountered Sherman's legions while they were ensconced in their snug camps along the Big Black River a few months prior, he would have had difficulty telling them apart from his Massachusetts comrades. Wearing fresh uniforms (in some cases even white parade gloves), under orders to appear "neat and clean" at all times and toting brightly polished weapons, with their shoes "properly cleaned and blackened," the "Vicksburg rats" had regained much of their proper military bearing and appearance after only a brief respite from the prolonged trials of the Vicksburg campaign.[9] Much had transpired since then to dramatically deteriorate their outward appearance once again.

After receiving urgent instructions from Halleck to send reinforcements to Rosecrans, Grant turned to his most trusted subordinate before heading northward to assume command of all Federal forces in Chattanooga. Sherman was to take the three divisions of his and one of McPherson's corps upriver from Vicksburg to Tennessee. Disembarking at Memphis in early October, the command set out eastward toward Chattanooga, repairing the Memphis and Charleston Railroad along the way so as to alleviate Rosecrans's supply problems while sparring with Rebel cavalry intent on preventing such repairs from taking place. On October 27, an exhausted courier arrived at Sherman's headquarters with a note from Grant, ordering him to "hurry eastward with all possible dispatch" and abandon repairs. He needed his dependable Army of the Tennessee to break the siege in Chattanooga, and he needed it fast.[10]

Stripping down the army's trains dramatically and determining to live off the land to furnish the balance of rations he lacked the transportation to haul, Sherman rushed his four divisions over more than two hundred miles, often averaging more than fifteen miles a day.[11] Forced to take a meandering route due to a combination of abysmal roads, burned bridges, and impassable fords, the columns frequently found themselves headed almost every direction but east toward their objective. While the weather largely proved amenable to the march, at other times it slowed or even halted the advance entirely. Having fine-tuned their extractive capacity throughout the Vicksburg campaign, Sherman's men had few compunctions about foraging liberally when hungry.

After nearly a full month of marching and countermarching, the bedraggled Army of the Tennessee finally stumbled off the eastern slope of the Cumberland Plateau and into Lookout Valley.[12] The corps had withstood the more than two-hundred-mile march remarkably well. Surveying his exhausted but hardy Sixth Missouri, Maj. Delos Van Deusen noted how, although there was "not a sick man in our regiment," those in the ranks were "nearly all out of shoes," many traipsing barefoot past the Eastern camps.[13] Cpt. Jacob Ritner, whose company was also barefoot by the end of the march, was similarly impressed at the forbearance with which his Hawkeyes stood the march. "It does my heart good and I feel proud of my company when I see with what fortitude and good will they bear hardship and fatigue," he commented. "They don't talk now like they did in the 'dark days' at Young's Point."[14] His veteran Iowans had matured markedly over the course of a year. While their rough appearance had much more to do with the circumstances of the long, grinding march than their regional origins, Underwood's observation that Sherman's columns were "just in from the Mississippi" was more heavily freighted with significance than he knew. Unlike the two corps of the Potomac army, the Fifteenth Corps and its tactical culture were direct by-products of the war in the lower Mississippi Valley. The command's distinctive "way of war," its tactical strengths, weaknesses, assumptions, and predispositions, had all been forged in the particular assignments it had pursued there as a component element of Grant's Army of the Tennessee. The degree of success which its regiments would enjoy while pursuing the many diverse missions and objectives Grant assigned them during the forthcoming campaign was in no small part contingent upon this distinctive tactical culture.

Due to the nature of the campaign, the men enjoyed relatively few opportunities to write. What little does survive, mostly in the form of formal reports, memoirs, and hurried but illuminating entries in pocket diaries, still offers a vivid glimpse at the degree to which the men and officers of the Fifteenth Corps had become powerfully aware of their distinctive tactical strengths and weaknesses by the end of the command's first year. By the winter of 1863, this self-awareness began to extend well beyond those in the ranks, all the way up the chain of command to Sherman's headquarters. Over the long course of the Vicksburg campaign, Cump and his corps had mutually molded one another into powerful but limited instruments of warfare: nearly unmatched masters of certain operational tasks while all but completely incapable of others. In requesting his most trusted subordinate and the corps he still nominally commanded to assist in breaking the Chattanooga siege, Grant thought almost entirely in terms of aggregate numbers. Just as Sherman had given little thought to the nuanced qualitative differences between the various units comprising his flotilla a year prior, Grant likewise paid little attention to the major differences in past experience and thus tactical culture within each of his field armies and corps. Just as Sherman had learned the hard way, Grant ignored such nuance at his own peril.

"CAMP SHERMAN"

For three months, the shady billets at "Camp Sherman" along the banks of the Big Black River in Mississippi had provided Sherman's exhausted corps with an invaluable opportunity to recuperate, refit, and reorganize after the hard trials of the Vicksburg and Jackson sieges. Fatigued officers and many enlisted men received brief furloughs home to renew their health and spirits. A few used the opportunity to try and recruit fresh blood to replenish their "skeleton regiments," though usually with little success.[15] While regimental strengths would fluctuate some over the course of the coming Chattanooga campaign, most of the corps's units rarely fielded more than 250 officers and men on any given day, nearly all of them veterans. Even so, of those regularly present with their units, an average of 83 percent would be reported as "for duty" that fall—the highest rate the corps would ever achieve during the war.[16] Those veterans still in the ranks after the hard trials of the Vicksburg campaign represented the resilient core of each unit, and short of illness, injury, or death, little would manage to shear them away from their formations until discharge.

The officer corps at the regimental level had matured along with the corps's units. Of the twenty-eight infantry regiments serving in First and Second divisions, only five had been commanded by the same officer since enlistment. All those currently at the helm of the corps's regiments had learned their trade, and in most cases gained the entirety of their military experience, as junior officers within the regiments they now led. The Army's policy of internal promotion of field officers maintained the integrity of regimental culture by avoiding contamination by outsiders. A regiment's commander had typically experienced the same events from the same particular limited "angle of vision" as all those in his charge, and thus the tactical choices he made and the manner in which he comprehended his orders were both products of his regiment's particular combat experiences. This naturally led in most cases to leaders at the regimental level who were well aware of what they could realistically expect their commands to accomplish, and what they could not. While not every commander would (or could) always take such factors into consideration, none were ignorant of their regiment's true capabilities.

The same could not necessarily be said of Sherman's highest ranking lieutenants. Shortly after the establishment of "Camp Sherman," First Division's chief was called westward to command Federal forces culminating at Helena, Arkansas, for a new campaign. Having loyally served alongside his friends Sherman and Grant throughout the struggle for Vicksburg, "Fred" Steele was off to punish a different corner of the Rebellion. In his place, Brig. Gen. Elias Smith Dennis, an outsider from McPherson's corps, temporarily administered First Division's operations at "Camp Sherman" until the first of September. On that day, a stern-looking redheaded officer strode into division headquarters and took the command he would hold for the next thirteen months before taking over the entire corps.[17]

Maj. Gen. Peter Joseph Osterhaus came to First Division with a distinguished military history. A native of Prussia and an infantry veteran of the 1848 revolutionary conflict, he had come to America shortly thereafter to evade arrest. After raising the Twelfth Missouri in St. Louis after the outbreak of the war, Osterhaus had risen rapidly through the ranks as a result of his proven tactical acumen on every field from Wilson's Creek to Pea Ridge to Vicksburg. After the fall of the latter bastion, he had explicitly requested a new command encompassing the veterans of his old regiment, the Twelfth Missouri. Heartily recommended by multiple of Grant's highest ranking lieutenants, Sherman accepted the request and assigned the Prussian command of the First Division in Dennis's place.[18]

To hear the veteran Germans speak of him around the campfires of "Camp Sherman," one could reasonably form the impression that Osterhaus was anything but a nuanced tactician. "*Späne Peter*" they called him—"Chips Peter"—in reference to orders he had shouted over the din at Pea Ridge just prior to launching them into a frontal assault: "Strike them so as to make the chips fly!"[19] They had done so with great success, making the Twelfth Missouri one of the few regiments in the Fifteenth Corps to have ever successfully conducted a frontal assault. Needless to say, the Germans were elated at Osterhaus's appointment. "Wherever the Red One can go, we can go too," Henry Kircher wrote confidently home. "The assurance that General Osterhaus will lead us wherever we are going satisfies me."[20] He had other nicknames, too. "Red Peter," in reference to his flaming red hair, or occasionally even just "the Red One." The latter moniker took on even greater meaning due to First Division's bright red guidon marking the command's headquarters in the field.

While anti-German nativism continued to thrive in mid-nineteenth-century America, even within the Army, Osterhaus managed to quickly overcome any reservations the command might have had about his ethnic background by consciously exhibiting the highest possible standards in his personal military bearing and perpetually earnest appearance. "Everyone in the division loved the General," one native-born Hawkeye remembered, "and would cheer when he rode by." The Prussian, he estimated, "was a fighter to the finish."[21] Osterhaus's natural capacity for charismatic leadership contrasted sharply with the reserved professionalism of Steele, who at no point during his lengthy tenure of division command had earned even a fraction of the same esteem from the men.

Specific experiences in Arkansas and during the long campaign for Vicksburg had led Osterhaus to embrace a tactical philosophy remarkably similar to that of Morgan Smith. Like Smith, "the Red One" had come to appreciate the capacity of relying heavily on skirmishing tactics to conserve lives in the main body of an attacking force. This tactical conservatism was mirrored in the Prussian's passion for artillery—the heavier the better. Whenever a tactical problem could possibly be solved exclusively with artillery fire and an open-order skirmisher "cloud," Osterhaus had continually shown an inclination to avoid risking any more lives than necessary. He understood well that effective artillery could spare his veteran infantrymen, and joked about wishing he could "put bayonets on the guns and make charges with them."[22] Even during the occasional frontal assault, as conducted by his division on the second day at Pea Ridge, *Späne Peter* frequently ordered the same Zouave-style rushes that Morgan Smith cherished to preserve the integrity and ensure the survival of his command.[23] While some historians have occasionally criticized this tendency as excessively cautious, the men in the ranks unsurprisingly did not share this opinion. In all of these tactical tendencies, Osterhaus could not have differed more dramatically from the hard-charging direct-approach of Steele. Instead, Osterhaus's tactical philosophy paired perfectly with the evolved tactical culture of First Division in the wake of the Vicksburg campaign, most especially its aversion to frontal assaults and recent extensive experience with both rifle and artillery marksmanship practice. For the first time in its service, the division stood to benefit from the leadership of a commander who, though an outsider, was perhaps the perfect officer to command it.

Steele took Brig. Gen. John Thayer along with him to Arkansas, prompting Osterhaus to consolidate the division's three "skeleton" brigades into two, each commanded by the division's two most accomplished colonels: the indomitable Buckeye Charles Woods and veteran Iowan James Williamson. This represented the first shuffling of regiments the division had yet undergone. Moreover, for the first time, these brigades were organized almost exclusively along state lines. Woods's new command, with the exception of his own original Seventy-Sixth Ohio and the hard-luck Thirteenth Illinois, included every Missouri regiment in the division. Williamson's, unsurprisingly, retained its exclusively Hawkeye character. The command's artillery, just as it had been across the Vicksburg campaign and siege, remained consolidated and independent of the two infantry brigades.[24]

Immediately recognizing the "depleted condition of our ranks," Osterhaus took steps to maximize combat strength in each unit. Noticing several able-bodied white volunteers employed by regiments as teamsters shortly after taking command, he promptly ordered them "replaced by good Negroes."[25]

He also ordered the smaller units in each brigade to pair up "for all tactical purposes" with another regiment from the same state to form what he called "tactical battalions." Woods's brigade would contain six of these battalions, and Williamson's five. Seven of the division's largest regiments were to operate as independent tactical battalions. Regardless of the regimental identities of their members, the battalions were subdivided into four equal "divisions" and eight equal "companies," commanded by the senior officer in the battalion. When in camp or on the march, each regiment would retain its independence under the leadership of its original commander, but under fire it would become half of its respective "tactical battalion."

This innovation, apparently of Osterhaus's own invention, allowed veteran regiments to maintain their *esprit de corps* and distinctive identities while simultaneously maximizing their combat potential by increasing the modularity of the division as a whole. Though his heavily depleted veteran commands obviously could not muster the raw firepower of a full-strength 800-man regiment, Osterhaus understood the maneuverability advantages of smaller units. In his native Prussia, infantry companies with strengths of no more than 250 men were routinely given independent tasks in combat, consolidating with the three others in their battalion as necessary. The "tactical battalion" concept mirrored this logic. When needed, individual "skeleton regiments," usually of fewer than 250 men, could be maneuvered quickly and tasked independently to perform a particular mission, only to later be paired with another in a tactical battalion to maximize defensive firepower. First Division's officers had long struggled with the command-and-control dynamics of moving large regiments and lengthy columns through nightmarish terrain. The "tactical battalion" concept promised to help alleviate these challenges in the future. Whereas Second Division's shrunken "skeleton regiments" maintained about the same available manpower strengths as Osterhaus's, the "tactical battalion" idea appears to have been instituted only in Osterhaus's division.[26]

In late July, Frank Blair departed on a lengthy leave, prompting the shuffling of Second Division's command structure as well. On October 6, while the tired blue column trudged eastward across Tennessee en route to Chattanooga, electrifying news spread through the ranks. "The Zouave" had finally mended sufficiently from his gory Chickasaw wound to return to command, and Morgan Lewis Smith once again took over his beloved Second Division.[27] Although the men had long been separated from their chief,

Smith's impress on the evolution of the division's tactical culture had always been on display. Despite orders to launch frontal assaults, the division's leadership had routinely relied upon the Zouave-style tactics that had long been Smith's trademark. Added to this foundation was a panoply of skills and increased confidence in light infantry combat embodied in regiments now barely half the size since the last time Morgan Smith had led them. He announced his return with characteristic humility. "Having been debarred the privilege of being with you in your last and most brilliant campaign, I feel very much like a recruit upon joining an old Regiment," he admitted in his first general order, read aloud to each company. He earnestly hoped for "the disposition of every officer and man to look upon my mistakes as errors of the head and not the heart," remaining confident that "we shall have no difficulty in resuming our former pleasant relations." Indeed, they would not. With the return of Morgan Smith and the appointment of Osterhaus to command of First Division, both of the corps's original divisions were now led by officers whose tactical philosophies were perfectly calibrated to the tactical cultures that had organically arisen within their commands.[28]

Smith's brother Giles remained in command of First Brigade while Lightburn retained the Second. Like those of First Division, both brigades consolidated their "skeleton" regiments, though not along state lines like in Osterhaus's command. Tuttle's Third Division, briefly attached to Sherman's corps during the Vicksburg campaign, would remain at Vicksburg and never again rejoin the command after it headed northward. Instead, three brigades of the old Sixteenth Corps division of Brig. Gen. William Sooy Smith, veterans of the Jackson siege but not the battles for Vicksburg, were transferred into the corps to operate as a new Fourth Division. Sherman assigned this division, comprised of the brigades of Col. John Loomis, Brig. Gen. John Corse, and Col. Joseph Cockerill, to his foster brother Brig. Gen. Hugh Ewing, representing his first division command. The brigades were by no means a *tabula rasa* of tactical culture. They all joined the corps bearing the cultural impress of their own distinctive past experiences. Most strikingly, they lacked the deeply ingrained aversion to frontal assaults shared by the remainder of the corps, having avoided the same experiences of bloody repulses suffered by First and Second divisions across the past year.[29]

Ironically the least significant command change occurred at the very top. Having been called east to Chattanooga to take the reins of all beleaguered

Federal forces in the area, Grant could not simultaneously command his beloved Army of the Tennessee. On October 24, that task passed to Sherman, leaving formal command of the Fifteenth Corps to Frank Blair upon his return to the army en route to Chattanooga on October 29. A changing of the guard at headquarters immediately prior to a major campaign typically carries major implications, but Blair was not fated to play much of an active role in forthcoming operations. In fact, he would ultimately take so little ownership over the command that he never even filed a formal report in the aftermath of the campaign. Instead, Sherman and his spartan entourage of staffers, along with the same headquarters culture they had developed over the years, would remain nominally at the helm of the corps throughout the battles for Chattanooga. For at least a few more months, the command remained, for all intents and purposes, Sherman's corps.[30]

"YOU WILL ATTACK THE ENEMY"

On November 15, Sherman personally arrived at Chattanooga ahead of his army and participated in a hurried conference wherein Grant explained his plans to break the siege. Having successfully reopened his supply line to the west via a series of daring maneuvers in Lookout Valley, the hero of Vicksburg now turned to the much more daunting problem of removing Bragg from Lookout Mountain and Missionary Ridge to the south. Aware that Bragg had recently detached one corps of his army to threaten Federal forces under Maj. Gen. Ambrose Burnside at Knoxville, Grant knew he needed to quickly finish up with Chattanooga and respond to the new threat. Frantic dispatches from Washington constantly underscored that fact. Things needed to move expeditiously, but given that nearly all of the Army of the Cumberland's horses were dead of starvation after the prolonged siege, it was unlikely that it would be doing anything expeditious anytime soon. Despite the recent arrival of the Eleventh and Twelfth corps of the Army of the Potomac into Lookout Valley, Grant still hoped, as usual, to rely on his most trusted subordinate to achieve the most critical portion of his plan.

Sherman's divisions would cross the Tennessee River at Brown's Ferry, west of Chattanooga, and then march into the hills behind the city to screen their movements and give the impression to Rebel onlookers atop the heights that they were in fact headed northward to reinforce Burnside at

Knoxville. Instead, the columns would slip eastward, away from the city, again using the hills as a screen, until arriving at a creek feeding into the northern bank of the river, where they would find pontoon boats waiting for them. Under the cover of darkness one brigade would utilize these boats to cross the river, silently secure a bridgehead on the opposite bank, and allow for the rest of the command to be ferried across until a pontoon bridge could be laid down. Once Sherman had the entirety of his force on the south bank of the river, he would proceed southward, skirting the banks of North Chickamauga Creek until reaching the "northern extremity" of Missionary Ridge and, presumably, Bragg's extreme right flank.[31]

"The general plan," Grant explained in a note to Thomas on November 18, was merely for Sherman to "secure the heights on the northern extremity [of Missionary Ridge] to about the railroad tunnel" (see map) and threaten Bragg's sole supply line before he could shift forces northward in response. Beyond that, the plan would evolve fluidly based on the behavior of the Rebel foe.[32] A month after the battle, Sherman also confirmed this interpretation in a letter to his senator brother. "The whole philosophy of the battle was that I should get by a dash a position on the Extremity of Missionary Ridge from which the enemy would be forced to drive me," he explained. Once ensconced upon "the extremity" of the ridge, he fully "expected Bragg to attack me at daylight," when he could repel him from works in the same bloody fashion he himself had been repelled so many times before.[33]

In his own subsequent orders to division commanders, Sherman made clear that the corps's objective was merely to secure "possession of the end of Missionary Ridge," which it was to "hold, and fortify." No mention was ever made by him of any "assault," "sweep," or even "attack" of Bragg's lines, nor of any movement against Rebel positions further south than the "northern extremity to about the railroad tunnel."[34] The Fifteenth Corps's officer corps must have breathed a sigh of relief given the command's habitual incapacity for such maneuvers. Grant's orders seemed perfectly calibrated for the corps's tactical culture. Making "a dash" over difficult terrain after a risky amphibious landing, followed by the rapid fortification of key terrain, were tasks the corps had mastered over the course of its year in service, and thus its men and officers had every reason to be confident about the assignment.

As usual, things quickly became more complicated. Under a deluge of cold rain on November 20 and 21, Cump's ragged-looking legions crossed the Tennessee at Brown's Ferry. Morgan Smith's brigades along with John

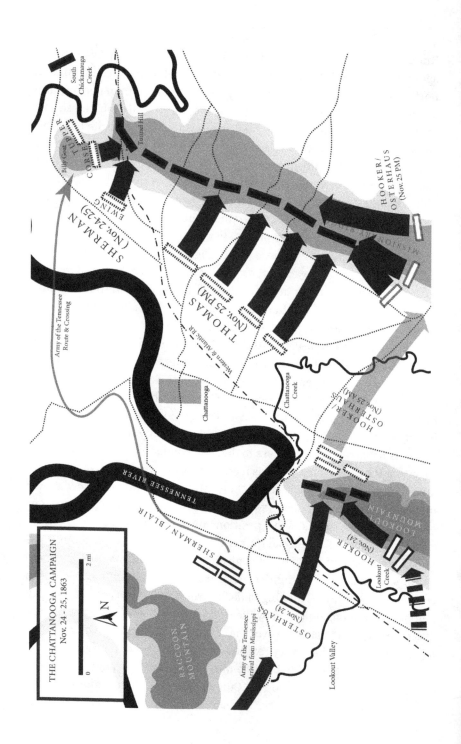

THE CHATTANOOGA CAMPAIGN
Nov. 24 - 25, 1863

N

0   2 mi

RACCOON MOUNTAIN

TENNESSEE RIVER

SHERMAN / BLAIR

Army of the Tennessee
Arrival from Mississippi

OSTERHAUS
(Nov. 24)

LOOKOUT MOUNTAIN

HOOKER
(Nov. 24)

Lookout Valley

Lookout Creek

HOOKER /
OSTERHAUS
(Nov. 25 AM)

Chattanooga Creek

Chattanooga

Western & Atlantic RR

THOMAS
(Nov. 25 PM)

MISSIONARY RIDGE

HOOKER /
OSTERHAUS
(Nov. 25 PM)

Army of the Tennessee
Route & Crossing

SHERMAN
(Nov. 24-25)

EWING

CORSE

Billy Goat Hill

TUPPER

Tunnel Hill

South Chickamauga Creek

Smith's Seventeenth Corps division led the way, followed shortly thereafter by Hugh Ewing's new division. In truth, the crossings themselves had proven a bit perilous, given the proclivity of the river's rushing current to dismantle the rickety pontoon bridge. Before Osterhaus could push First Division across, the bridge fell apart yet again, leaving "the Red One" stranded on the west bank. Anxious of any further delay, Grant promptly ordered Sherman to do without. The First Division would be detached from the rest of the corps, remaining in Lookout Valley and reporting to Hooker instead. Sherman, the two Smiths, and Ewing trudged northeast, away from Brown's Ferry and into the hills beyond. Halting at a hidden camp, the three divisions bedded down in preparation for the next move.[35]

On November 23, Sherman ordered Giles Smith's brigade to the waiting pontoon boats in preparation for the nighttime crossing. After dark, the brigade would board the boats and "drop down silently to a point above the mouth of South Chickamauga [Creek], then land two regiments" which would "move along the river quietly and capture the enemy's river pickets." It was an exceedingly perilous endeavor. Should the south bank of the river be held by more than just a few scattered Rebel outposts, the two "skeleton regiments" could easily prove more a sacrifice than an advance guard.[36]

That night, cloud cover reduced visibility to nearly zero, and a steady drizzle made for an unpleasant evening. All of Smith's regiments carried a hundred rounds of ammunition per man—a signal that a desperate fight for the opposite bank might be in the offing. Each of the craft was loaded with twenty-five men and manned by four oarsmen who self-identified as having past experience on the water. Having chosen his own Zouaves of the Eighth Missouri to spearhead the landing, followed close-up by the veteran Fifty-Fifth Illinois, Smith boarded a boat himself for the journey. "All guns were loaded but not capped," one Illinoisan remembered, "and no one was to fire on any pretence whatever, unless by orders." Talking above a whisper was strictly prohibited, and even the oars were "carefully muffled."[37] Silently drifting down the swollen river, oarsmen hunted a bonfire on the northern bank which marked a point opposite the area designated by Sherman as the landing site. Those along for the ride nervously eyed a string of fires on the southern bank that "glimmered through the mist," accompanied by the shadows of Rebel pickets. Finally, after the lead bateau came abreast of the signal fire, it turned hard to the left against the current, and deposited its load of anxious Zouaves onto the south shore.[38]

Although no formal regimental report survives, enough anecdotal evidence is extant to suggest that the twenty-five Zouaves on each boat likely operated more or less independently under the direction of their junior officers once ashore. After all, the vast majority of the Eighth Missouri's operational experience had been conducted in just such a fashion, scattered across a wide front in small skirmish teams. The command also enjoyed considerable amphibious experience, having served with distinction during the Steele's Bayou expedition. With their vast experience and training moving stealthily and carefully from tree to tree in combat from Fort Donelson to Arkansas Post to Vicksburg, the Zouaves were the ideal candidates for the mission.

Creeping silently through the dark along the riverbank toward the nearby outpost fires, a captain and his contingent of Zouaves managed to get close enough to overhear the idle conversation of one Rebel group. "It would be a good joke if the Yanks floated down the river some night and took us in," he later remembered hearing one of them say. "Boys, that's just what Uncle Billie has done," the Zouave captain allegedly shouted out, springing from the darkness upon them. "Guess you'll surrender, won't you?" All along the riverbank, desperate looking Zouaves startled unprepared Secessionists without any bloodshed. Only one shot was fired over the entire course of the operation, and that by a startled Rebel picket. Another frantic mounted Rebel "came up at full speed, shouting, 'The Yanks are coming!' only to be "promptly dismounted and invited to join his comrades just captured."[39]

Elated by the news of the safe landing, Sherman quickly ordered the shuttling of the rest of his force to the south bank. After consolidating their prisoners and ensuring that no greater enemy force was in the immediate area, those on the south bank began, in typical "Vicksburg rat" fashion, digging in and securing their newly won position. "At this point we expected to have a desperate struggle," Major Thomas Taylor, Forty-Seventh Ohio, wrote, "and it took strong nerves to bear up under the contemplation of this prospect." If the stray shot from the startled Rebel's musket had drawn the attention of those atop Missionary Ridge to the south, only a handful of boats remained on the bank with which to escape. "We had no artillery," he worried, "and only the ground we stood upon." Accordingly, he and his fellow officers "put a spade in the hands of each man . . . with instruction to 'bury himself' in the shortest possible space of time."[40] The gravity of the situation was not lost on any present. "Every man worked with a will," an Illinoisan recalled.[41]

The extensive experience of Smith's brigade with preparing earthworks from Corinth to Vicksburg to Jackson paid off. Within less than five hours, the command had established "a line of pits over a mile and a half long, almost four feet deep and the same wide, with good parapet capable of resisting shell and shot from ordinary sized guns." As the rest of the corps focused on the laborious process of moving across the river, Second Division turned the south shore of the Tennessee into a "miniature Vicksburg," just as it had the outskirts of Jackson, Mississippi, five months earlier. Even Sherman, an especially stern critic of field fortifications, pronounced the fruits of their labor "very respectable."[42]

It took the rest of the morning to get the remainder of Sherman's army across the river. Most historians of the campaign still remain sharply critical of this delay, arguing that Cump ought to have sent Smith's division southward to occupy Missionary Ridge immediately after landing, alone if necessary.[43] While there is no way of knowing for sure just how much blood and toil might have been spared by such an audacious maneuver, historians continue to ignore the full weight of past experience and thus ingrained tactical culture that informed Sherman and his command at dawn on November 24, when the decision to entrench along the bank was made.

Both the Eighth Missouri and the Fifty-Fifth Illinois were filled with veterans of the near-total disaster at Shiloh in the spring of 1862. With their backs to the very same river, the entire army had been surprised by a sudden Rebel onslaught without the benefit of any earthworks from which to repel the attack. Cump, ever the consummate paranoiac, was not about to commit the same blunder again. Neither were his men. Over the long course of the Vicksburg campaign, they had routinely witnessed the powerful advantages accruing to even vastly outnumbered defenders when fighting from behind the most rudimentary of works. All of those veterans in the regiments huddled along the south bank of the river that morning still maintained vivid memories of having been brutally repulsed by a force less than half their number at Arkansas Post from behind a rifle pit prepared in a manner of a few hours using only fence boards. If an enemy counterattack was forthcoming, and there was every reason to believe it might be, they meant to be prepared. Their behavior, and Sherman's decision, were the direct by-products of their tactical culture.

While Smith's veterans cut into the Tennessee mud, Sherman rallied his division commanders and explained the details of his plan to seize the "northern extremity of Missionary Ridge." The three divisions across the river would array themselves *en echelon* from left to right facing south toward the ridge. Morgan Smith's command would form the left wing, sweeping south with its own left flank skirting the steep western bank of South Chickamauga Creek. In the center, John Smith's Seventeenth Corps division would advance alongside, with Ewing's division in column on the right flank, "prepared to deploy to the right on the supposition that we would meet an enemy in that direction." The 20-lb. rifled Parrotts of Lt. Francis De Gress's Illinois battery, already installed in positions prepared for them by Second Division, would send a salvo southward to signal the coordinated advance of the command.[44]

Before the conference had ended, the dense fog of the early morning was already converting into a light rain. Sounds of heavy fighting echoed across the valley from the west, apparently from the far slope of Lookout Mountain. Finally, at about noon, De Gress's guns thundered, and the Fifteenth Corps stepped off with its customary "cloud" of skirmishers screening its front. From the beginning, the fog paid dividends. While the base of Missionary Ridge to the south was unmistakable, its crest was shrouded in clouds, and thus the corps's advance was invisible to the Rebels atop the height. Although meeting with no resistance, the corps still moved with caution, edging its way forward behind the skirmishers until pausing briefly around three o'clock along a railroad track "to correct our lines." Nearing what appeared to be the steep rise of the "northern extremity" of Missionary Ridge, Morgan Smith ordered Lightburn's brigade to "carry the ridge." E. W. Muenscher, a captain in the Thirtieth Ohio then on the skirmish line, received orders to "go ahead with my company" and seize the heights. Obediently, Muenscher "gave the order, and up we went on the run."[45] The Ohioans reached the crest unopposed and caught their breath briefly before continuing southward to clear the rest of the hill. After cresting himself, Lightburn recognized immediately that the summit was "not . . . the [crest of the] hill designated" in his orders, perceiving that another point to the south was in fact the real objective. Accordingly, he dispatched the Forty-Seventh Ohio to seize the wooded eminence.[46]

The Buckeye skirmishers moved carefully through the fog and mist until reaching their objective atop the southern hill. Shortly after their arrival, however, the woods erupted with fire. A single Rebel regiment, also maneuvering as dispersed skirmishers, had rushed to the hill after receiving word from an anxious scout that a massive Federal host was en route to Missionary Ridge. As surprised to find Federals already atop the height as the Ohioans were to meet them, the Rebels quickly gave way under the full weight of Lightburn's brigade, falling back off the hill to the west. As the fog still hindered visibility, the precise location of the brigade remained somewhat of a mystery to all present. What topography could be made out in the fading light did not seem to match anyone's expectations.[47]

While the lingering clouds and the angle from which both Sherman and Grant had originally observed the "northern extremity of Missionary Ridge" from afar had suggested that the furthest hilltops east were in fact an organic and unbroken extension of the ridge, Lightburn's brigade had actually crested a freestanding height known locally as Billy Goat Hill. Between Billy Goat and the real Missionary Ridge was a deep saddle nearly 300 yards across and at least 150 feet deep. Frustrated at learning this, Sherman also recognized that Billy Goat "was so important that I could leave nothing to chance." With night coming on quickly, and still concerned about the same imminent counterattack the corps had worried about since the beginning of the operation, Cump "ordered it to be fortified during the night." After all, the command had successfully reached "the northern extremity of Missionary Ridge," even if it was not technically on the ridge itself. Grant's original plans had made clear that Sherman was to "hold, and fortify" just such a position. Given the surprise saddle to his front, Sherman must have wagered that it was tactically better to have the saddle between himself and the Rebels likely atop Tunnel Hill than to have it at his back. Moreover, as the men hauled Second and Fourth divisions' heavy guns up Billy Goat with ropes by hand, the corps's batteries would soon have a perfect elevated position from which to pummel Tunnel Hill. Despite these advantages, historians since the end of the war have been unmerciful in their criticism of Sherman's "uncharacteristic caution" in choosing to consolidate his gains by again digging in. "Normally more aggressive," Larry Peterson suggests, "Sherman had erred on the side of caution," and in so doing, "undermined Grant's entire plan of action."[48]

A few historians do cut Cump some slack, given a brief and often overlooked episode that occurred that evening on the corps's left flank, then resting along the steep banks of South Chickamauga Creek. While Lightburn's skirmishers fought off the unsuspecting Rebels atop the crest, the rest of Morgan Smith's division continued its sweep southward along the creek bank, moving around the back side of Billy Goat with its skirmishers advanced well to the front. At about four o'clock, the lead elements of Giles Smith's brigade suddenly took both sporadic musket and artillery fire from across the creek to the east. Rushing a battery into position to counter the unanticipated Rebel threat, Smith hurried forward on foot to ascertain the true nature of the situation. Suddenly, "the peculiar whir of a charge of canister shot coming straight for us filled the air," wrote one officer standing nearby, who also heard one of the iron balls "strike the General as plainly as one would hear a ball of putty thrown against a wall, and it sounded much as that would, too." The wounded Smith "was staggered, but did not fall, and was supported by his companions and led from the field."

The ambushing Rebel force proved meager and uninterested in pressing any significant attack, withdrawing shortly thereafter out of range of the brigade's guns. Frantic shouts filled the air. "Where is Col. Tupper? Where is Col. Tupper? Where in hell is Col. Tupper?" Following Smith's wounding, the ranking officer on the field, Col. Nathan Tupper, 116th Illinois, suddenly found himself at the helm of First Brigade. Crippled in one arm, Tupper had ignored his disability and quit his law practice to raise a regiment the moment he heard of his brother's death at Shiloh. Having commanded the regiment since Chickasaw Bayou, Tupper had accrued considerable experience with leading the Sucker cohort, but none at the brigade level. Now, as dusk faded to night, Tupper and First Brigade struggled to regain its balance and adapt to the change while attempting to find themselves on the map.[49]

Despite the temporary discomfiture rendered by Smith's incapacitation, the corps as a whole had performed admirably in achieving the limited objectives Grant had assigned to it. Its success was in no small part a product of the mission's near-perfect compatibility with the tactical culture of the command. The vital skills necessary to complete the corps's assigned objectives just happened to be those with which it had experience. About midnight, however, a courier arrived at Sherman's headquarters with a directive from Grant that shifted the operational paradigm in a dramatically disadvantageous direction for the Fifteenth Corps. "You will attack the enemy at the point most advantageous from your position at early dawn tomorrow morning," it read. Thomas and his "Cumberlanders" would likewise assault "early tomorrow morning," aiming either to seize the Rebel rifle pits at the foot of the ridge or "move to the left to your support, as circumstances may determine best." As before, Grant's instructions left considerable room for flexibility, leaving even the precise hour for Sherman's forthcoming assault up to his own judgment.[50]

Grant's initial orders had contemplated a mission that Cump knew was ideally suited to the capabilities and tactical strengths of the divisions he had on hand. Probing ahead to secure what Sherman and his lieutenants all presumed to be the "northernmost extremity" of Missionary Ridge, with an eye to fortifying the same and bringing on a presumably futile Rebel attack, the tables seemed to have finally been turned. For once, the corps would have the chance to repel hopeless charges from behind the protection of works instead of being repelled itself. The intervening valley that ran between Billy Goat and Tunnel Hill was just one more obstruction to a Rebel counterattack Sherman fully expected would come. Alas, it was not to be. Grant's follow-on orders to assault the Secessionists atop Tunnel Hill effectively converted a mission erstwhile perfectly calibrated for the Fifteenth Corps to one monstrously out of step with its operational heritage and tactical culture.

As Grant had no way of seeing the tortuous and confusing tangle of thickets, marshland, ridges, saddles, hills, and spurs to Sherman's front, he also could not have known how unrealistic his orders were. To be sure, the deep saddle between Billy Goat Hill and the real Missionary Ridge, somewhat counterintuitively, would ultimately have little bearing on the course of the fight. Instead, it was the combination of Missionary Ridge's exceedingly narrow crest along with an additional Rebel-held eastward-projecting spur that made Sherman's attack all but impossible from the very beginning. Assaulting the narrow rise from the north end would dramatically reduce the available frontage for any attacking force. Little more than a "skeleton regiment" or two could ever manage to pack themselves into the limited ground before those on the wings were no longer able to engage Rebels atop the crest. Moreover, though Sherman did not yet know it, attacking the ridge from its rear or eastern slope would also prove impossible due to a combination of nightmarish terrain and enfilading Rebel fire from the eastward-projecting spur. As Steven Woodworth suggests, the hesitation and delay to carry out his orders for which so many historians have castigated Sherman was more likely evidence that he fully grasped the impracticality of Grant's expectations—most especially given his perceived lack of "troops that can be made to assault." Cump's hesitancy was less a blunder and more a powerful expression of his growing awareness and understanding of both his own weaknesses and those of his corps combined with a veteran's eye for truly impossible terrain.[51]

At dawn, Sherman and his staff surveyed the entire front prior to issuing his orders, "catching as accurate an idea of the ground as possible by the dim light of morning." Across the deep saddle, he could see Rebels preparing "a breastwork of logs and fresh earth, filled with men and two guns" atop the crest of Tunnel Hill.[52] Even more Secessionists appeared to be forming beyond. The likelihood of pushing them off must have seemed exceedingly small, but with positive orders from his close friend and superior, Sherman had little choice but to commit to disaster. He evinced anything but confidence when he delivered the attack orders to his adoptive brother. "I guess, Ewing, if you're ready, you might as well go ahead," a nearby journalist overheard him say without even so much as a shred of conviction. Ever the consummate theater connoisseur, Sherman had seen this show too many times. Two of Ewing's brigades, those of Corse and Loomis, would attack the ridge from opposite directions: one from the northern end and one from the western face of Tunnel Hill. They would be supported to the limited degree possible on the eastern slope by elements of Lightburn's brigade, which had not been engaged the previous day. Almost as an afterthought, Sherman added that Ewing ought to try and maintain his formational cohesion "till you get to the foot of the hill." Whatever awaited the men at the crest, he knew it would require cohesive mass to punch through—cohesive mass that terrain and Rebel fire had routinely conspired to rob from his assault columns in each and every previous attack long before they reached their objective. "Shall we keep it after that?" Ewing asked. "If you like," Cump responded somberly. "If you can."[53]

Although Sherman intended that at least three coordinated assault columns would strike Tunnel Hill at more or less the same moment, nightmarish terrain would, as so often before, dismantle Federal coordination and cohesion. Just as deep bayous and meandering tributaries had done at Chickasaw Bayou, smoke and dense woods had accomplished at Arkansas Post, and the maddening maze of hills caused north of Vicksburg, the terrain confronted by the corps's attack exacerbated its lingering struggles with coordination and destroyed its cohesion in the assault. Worse, Ewing had never commanded a division in combat, and the challenges of attempting to learn how to do so while operating across an extended exterior line against a concentrated Rebel foe was altogether too much to for him to handle. Sherman likely knew and understood all of this prior to giving his brother the orders to attack, but evidently could imagine few alternatives.

At about 9 a.m., Sherman rode to the left to find Lightburn and order him to support Ewing's main effort by sending "200 men to occupy Tunnel Hill." Presumably, he meant for these men to step off at roughly the same time as Ewing's lead brigade, but alas these specifics seem to have been left out. Instead, Lightburn ordered the detachments across the deep intervening valley immediately. The Forty-Seventh Ohio he left in reserve, it having seen the brunt of the skirmish the preceding afternoon. While an order for two hundred men would have accounted for less than two companies a year prior, by the fall of 1863 it encompassed the entirety of the "skeleton" Thirtieth Ohio along with two additional companies of the Fourth West Virginia in support. "It was the understanding that they were to advance firing, then halt behind trees, load and advance again," Captain Muenscher recalled, alluding to what had by then become the standard Second Division manner of attack. Encountering little resistance, "this was forgotten, and they went on a dead run down one side of the ravine, across the valley and up the other side . . . in less than five minutes." A few Rebel videttes cowering in a rifle pit were scooped up in the process at the point of the bayonet, but little in the way of enemy fire was met until the Ohioans neared the crest of the hill's northward protruding bench. Flattening out before rising again after a few hundred yards, the lip of the bench provided some cover from the Rebels waiting behind their log works atop the summit. Catching their breath, and then working their way east around the hill so as to approach the works from the more densely wooded portion of the slope, the Buckeyes mustered a brief and meager probe toward the breastworks alone. Unsurprisingly, given their woeful lack of numbers, the attempt was very limited, and they fell back to the cover of the trees still within rifle shot of the works and began sharpshooting. As they peppered the Rebel logs with fire in an attempt to keep their heads down, the Ohioans awaited the next assault column to try its luck. Anyone who had seen the Fifteenth Corps assault before would have found the scene painfully predictable.[54]

The next phase of the bloody performance brought Corse's brigade of Ewing's division hurdling off Billy Goat with a yell of confidence and the thunderous applause of every one of Sherman's batteries. Although commanding four understrength regiments, the exceedingly narrow ridge precluded Corse from deploying any more than one to his front, dispersed as skirmishers so as to take advantage of every last inch of available ground. Once again, the inability to mass the firepower of more than a single regiment as skirmishers against the Rebel breastworks proved decisive. While a handful reached within a stone's throw of the works before being cut down mercilessly by both musket shot and canister, the brigade fell back to the protection of the lip of the bench to regroup. Once sufficiently rallied, the bloodied command made a second attempt, only to meet with precisely the same fate and the severe wounding of its commander. Even worse, smelling blood, the Rebels sallied briefly from their works, sweeping the survivors from their positions and chasing them back to the shallow pit captured by the Buckeyes earlier that morning.[55]

By 11 a.m. things were going poorly, but they were about to get much worse. Finally managing to get Colonel John Loomis's brigade underway on its attack route west of the ridge, Sherman and Ewing shifted their attention to that front. Originally intended to fall upon the Rebels simultaneously with Lightburn's and Corse's attacks, instead Loomis's regiments debouched from a tree line and into a broad field in clear view of every Secessionist atop Missionary Ridge. Moreover, these Rebels were unoccupied after having already repelled the prior two brigade attacks. Hurdling his brigade forward through a dense fire, Loomis managed to reach the slight protection of an elevated railroad embankment near the foot of the ridge, but immediately required additional units deployed from John Smith's Seventeenth Corps division, and even more from an attached brigade of Pennsylvanians to secure his left flank from harassing Rebel sharpshooters. These reinforcements attacked eastward up the slope independently so as to get out of the raking fire in the bottomland, only to be halted in their tracks halfway up by Rebel guns in exactly the same manner as Lightburn, Corse, and Loomis. Once again, inspiring bravery and intrepid obedience to orders by the men and junior officers of the corps was squandered by a complete failure of command, control, and coordination, due in large part to the complex terrain and expansive distance between maneuvering elements.[56]

Fortunately, at Arkansas Post and during both Vicksburg assaults, Rebel forces ensconced snugly behind their protective works had never yet attempted the *coup de grâce* of any successful defensive effort: a bayonet counterattack. The peculiar contour of Tunnel Hill and Missionary Ridge, however, offered unique opportunities for adept Rebel leadership, embodied in Maj. Gen. Patrick Cleburne, to land a devastating counterpunch. After all six of the brigades Sherman had committed piecemeal to the attack had been forced to ground by Rebel fire, and after nearly four hours of close-range sharpshooting began to exhaust supplies of ammunition, at about four o'clock disaster struck.[57]

Watching from the slopes of Billy Goat Hill as his regiment idled in reserve, Maj. Thomas Taylor, Forty-Seventh Ohio, stood anxiously near an equally nervous Sherman, who "chewed the stump of his cigar earnestly." Suddenly, the command team distinctly heard the yipping Rebel yell through the din, followed by a handful of blue-coated men sprinting from the trees off the hill. "Anon others and whole regiments came flying back," Taylor saw. Shortly thereafter entire Federal brigades came flying off the ridge—the victims of a brutal Rebel counterattack that swept across the face of Tunnel Hill and took each of them in the flank. The result was pure pandemonium. "Oh, what a stampede—each one for himself," Taylor lamented. "I was mad and uttered a few expletives," he admitted, but took solace in an explanation he overheard for the disgraceful behavior before him. "I was informed they were of Chancellorsville, Va. and not from the 15th A.C.," he wrote, referencing the Army of the Potomac men the corps had first encountered in Lookout Valley a few days prior. Certainly, these could not have been rugged "Vicksburg rats" routing ingloriously from the hillside. "The rebels followed, shrieking like fiends," he observed, as the disaster continued to unfold. "The poor, cowardly devils run over that space," he added. "I never saw such a sight before." Fortunately, the "boys of the 15th [Corps] held their own." While indeed the fugitives were exclusively men of John Smith's Seventeenth Corps and the lone Pennsylvanian brigade, the Fifteenth Corps had only barely "held their own," and very shortly thereafter began to withdraw from their sharpshooting positions. Sherman's assault had failed, at a cost of nearly two thousand men killed, wounded, and captured.[58]

"ONE OF THE SORRIEST EPISODES"

In his history of the campaign, Peter Cozzens deems the attack on Tunnel Hill "one of the sorriest episodes in this or any other battle of the war." The failure of the Fifteenth Corps to succeed in turning Rebel lines "defies explanation," he argues. That Sherman "had the forces needed to do it is undeniable." Still, while Sherman's piecemeal deployment of only a small fraction of his thirty thousand total men available still routinely receives condemnation by historians, given the extremely limited viable frontage atop Tunnel Hill, combined with the nightmarish terrain and prohibitive enfilading fire to its east, it is hard to see how he could have possibly done better.[59] While Cozzens argues that Sherman "had the forces needed to do it," such an assertion is based entirely on quantitative measurements. Qualitatively, the general himself had every good reason to believe that, in fact, he did not.[60]

To be fair, the odds of success were by no means improved by Sherman's selection of brigades to make the assault. As at Chickasaw, Arkansas Post, and Vicksburg, successfully assaulting entrenched Rebels called for high levels of confidence, which the regiments of Ewing's new division did not obtain. None of the regiments in Corse's brigade had ever before assaulted enemy breastworks, let alone fortified rifle pits and gun positions perched atop such a foreboding height. The very same could be said for Loomis's command. In fact, the only Federal units then on the field who could claim past success in frontal assaults were those of John Smith's division, resting idly in reserve to the rear of Billy Goat Hill for most of the battle, and finally committed only when it was too late to have much effect.

Even so, whereas most histories of the battle have focused on the bloody assault and repulse of Ewing's and Smith's brigades, relatively little effort has been made to explain the lack of any simultaneous coordinated attack by Tupper's First Brigade on the backside of Tunnel Hill. This trend is especially curious, given that many historians continue to blame Sherman's failure, to a significant degree, on the lack of any such attack. Had Tupper assaulted the hill along his front, they argue, Cleburne's position atop the crest would have been doubly enveloped, if not completely surrounded, likely routing it in its entirety and collapsing the whole right flank of Bragg's army. As such a Rebel disaster probably would have occurred almost simultaneously with contemporaneous breakthroughs on Bragg's left, the maneuver may very well have secured the total destruction of the Army of Tennessee, and perhaps even the end of major operations in the Western Theater.[61]

This specific criticism of Sherman's handling of the battle first began with an operational narrative penned by Brig. Gen. William F. "Baldy" Smith shortly after the war. Sherman ought to have "put in all his force to turn Bragg's right, instead of attacking the strongest place on the right," he insisted.[62] Nearly every subsequent historian has agreed. Tupper's brigade had been "within rifle range of cracking the fragile shell of Cleburne's defenses to the right of Tunnel Hill," Cozzens argues. Neither Sherman nor Morgan Smith nor Tupper had apparently given "any serious thought to the brigade or what it might accomplish." Although tantalizingly proximate to the rear of Rebel defenses atop Tunnel Hill during the day, the brigade had never been ordered to attack. Had things gone otherwise, the brigade "might have changed the outcome of the fight," Cozzens argues. The fact that the veterans had not even been "permitted to try" was, by his estimation, "unconscionable."[63] Even so, although long castigated by historians as all but incomprehensible, Sherman's reluctance to employ Smith's brigade in a heavier attack up the backside of Tunnel Hill is far more easily explained when historicized within the broader context of the Fifteenth Corps's operational history and its tactical culture.

One artifact of that tactical culture which had, by the winter of 1863, become so firmly held as to approach dogma, was the habitual norm of unit rotation on the front lines. Those commands which had most recently been employed in an arduous mission or under fire were customarily held in reserve during the next phase of operations. This principal of using the "freshest" troops to spearhead each operation had been standard practice since Chickasaw Bayou, so much so that the men and their officers had come to expect it. Those in Second Division outside of Lightburn's brigade openly assumed that Sherman's reluctance to employ them more directly in the assault had been motivated by this very tradition. "They were held back for the reason that they were the brigade which risked so much in the start, and performed the feat of crossing the river in boats and landing right under the enemy's works at night," one explained. The nighttime crossing of the Tennessee had been exceedingly dangerous, the brigade had hardly slept in nearly forty-eight hours, and its beloved commander of more than a year had been lost to it only the night before. Thus, Sherman respectfully held the command in reserve the next day. Tupper's brigade also contained the greatest number of regiments which had comprised Sherman's much beloved "old Division." For this reason, he may very well have been moved by an even unconscious, if quite vain, urge not to destroy them in a maneuver he had every reason to believe would not, indeed could not, succeed.[64]

Not all historians have been as merciless toward Sherman's decisions as others. Several undeniable practical factors also precluded any dramatic charge launched up the rear slope of Tunnel Hill by Smith's brigade. By far the strongest of Sherman's defenders, B. H. Liddell Hart, in his 1929 biography of the general, argued that to throw more men into the narrow corridor between Tunnel Hill and the South Chickamauga Creek—Tupper's front—"would not only lead them to a well-blocked end but would have massed his troops along a defile under the fire of the Confederate guns on the heights and on other heights beyond the river." Indeed, aside from the nearly impossible terrain in the sector, Giles Smith's command would have likely become the victims of enfilading fire from nearly every direction had it continued to advance. "Compressed cannon-fodder, indeed," he added grimly.[65]

In the end, a number of interacting factors, some endogenous and others exogenous to the Fifteenth Corps, culminated to prevent any decisive attack by Tupper's brigade during November 25, 1863. While historians continue to debate whether such an attack may have, at the very least, destroyed or captured an entire division or more of Bragg's army, such alternative histories are less helpful to understanding the Chattanooga campaign than are more holistic explanations for the decisions and actions that did occur. Such explanations are only possible by placing the events of that day within the broad context of the particular histories of the individuals and commands involved and considering them within the separate but related context of the particular operational situation and terrain confronted at the time.

While Sherman never said so explicitly, his behavior left clues that suggest an evolution in his awareness of the true capabilities of the men, officers, and regiments of his Fifteenth Corps. For a year, "the great charger S[herman]," as a dejected Henry Kircher once referred to him, had seemed to maintain "that everything can be forced by the stormers without knowing the terrain or testing it."[66] His nuanced approach to the "miniature Vicksburg" at Jackson had suggested to many that a change of heart, if not yet of mind, may have been in process. Given the liberty of independently determining if or when to employ a bloody frontal assault, he happily chose not to. Given Grant's positive orders to attack at Tunnel Hill, his hand had been forced. Still, despite the destruction of Ewing's and John Smith's divisions strewn across the northern and western slopes of Tunnel Hill, it seemed that Cump was nearing the apex of his learning curve. While never willing to consider insubordination, he also knew better than any other living officer what his corps was capable of, and what it was not. From this point on, though not without occasional missteps, he began to act accordingly. He had finally become one of them.

CHAPTER 8

THE WAY IN WHICH
THEY ATTEMPTED TO GO

Lookout Mountain and Ringgold Gap

The effect was the same as we had seen at Arkansas Post and Vicksburg.

—JOHN BUEGEL, THIRD MISSOURI

Divorced from their native corps, Osterhaus's First Division experienced a quite different series of engagements while operating under the command of Maj. Gen. Joseph Hooker. Initially charged by Grant with making a feint toward Lookout Mountain (considered by all to be less tactically important than Missionary Ridge, despite its greater elevation), Hooker was slated to play a bit role in the coming drama by comparison with Sherman. This was by design. After "Fighting Joe's" lackluster performance at the Battle of Chancellorsville in May, the entire nation remained ambivalent about his command capabilities. Grant shared their skepticism, and thus planned for Hooker and his Potomac veterans to do little more than hold the attention of the Rebels atop Lookout Mountain while his trusted friend Cump landed the key blow.[1]

At a height of 2,388 feet, Lookout Mountain commanded the region. Between Hooker's camps and the mountain itself lay a wide valley through which ran the waters of Lookout Creek. Only four viable crossing points were evident on the map, at least two of which would need to be secured before any force could even begin to address the immense challenge of scaling the mountain while simultaneously confronting its Rebel defenders. No feint toward the mountain would convince anyone if conducted only on the west bank of the creek.[2]

Conferring with his new temporary commander at Hooker's headquarters on the night of November 23, as Second Division piled into the pontoon boats miles away to the east, Osterhaus was present when an urgent dispatch from Grant arrived near midnight. The message ordered Hooker to "abandon the scheme of a feint," Osterhaus recalled, "and with the assistance of my Division to attack and dislodge the Rebels from their Lookout positions."[3] Accordingly, late into the night the two officers hatched a plan by which Hooker's Potomac brigades would cross Lookout Creek some distance to the south, scale the mountain beyond the Rebel defenses, and sweep northward along its slope as if to brush the unsuspecting Secessionists off the heights and into the river. Meanwhile, Osterhaus would keep up appearances in the valley and repair the bridge he required to add his own weight to the attack. Acting as the anvil for Hooker's hammer, Osterhaus would advance against the mountain face at the moment he perceived the easterners as being immediately adjacent to his front. By that point, the Rebels would be on the run, and First Division would have little left to do but collect prisoners and apply additional pressure wherever needed. It was the kind of parsimonious plan the Prussian could appreciate, and thus early the next morning things were set in motion.[4]

"AH, COLONEL, THIS IS GLORIOUS!"

In customary fashion, Osterhaus planned to fulfill his part of the operation in a manner most conservative with the blood of his division. Recent experience in skirmishes during the march to Chattanooga had illustrated to him how adept his new command was at combining accurate artillery gunnery with small-unit maneuver as skirmishers without any need for massed bayonet assaults. This style of attack differed dramatically from that employed by Hooker's Potomac veterans, who were to conduct nearly the entirety of the operation without even so much as a skirmisher screen, massed shoulder-to-shoulder until the terrain made such tactics impossible, just as their own particular experience in the Eastern Theater had taught them to do.

As Hooker's legions started southward toward their respective crossing points, the Prussian mounted the division's fourteen heavy guns atop a string of hills skirting Lookout Creek, which afforded overwatch of all the viable crossing points in his sector and a clear shot to the still fog-shrouded western slopes of Lookout Mountain. Detaching a few of the "skeleton" regiments from both Williamson's and Woods's brigades to support these batteries in the event of a Rebel surprise, Osterhaus set the guns to suppressing enemy pickets on the east bank of the creek while his pioneers toiled to repair the bridges. The rest of Woods's brigade fanned out as skirmishers along the west bank to add their own covering fire to that of the batteries and prevent any Rebel suppression of the pioneers.[5] The veteran gunners of First Division's batteries employed their Vicksburg-borne skills with deadly effect. "The rebels can scarcely move," one Hawkeye supporting the guns observed. "We see them dodge from rock to rock, the shot and shell is poured into them directly in front of Hookers advancing column so they have but little to oppose them."[6] From the perspective of a nearby Missourian, the frantic Rebels looked "so small, like ants swarming on the mountain."[7] The coordinated combined fire of riflemen and artillery, just as it had done at Vicksburg, achieved complete fire superiority while also distracting those Rebels further south from the comparatively silent advance of Hooker's columns up the slope. The fog also assisted in this, shrouding the maneuvers in the valley just as it hid the approach of Sherman's ill-fated columns toward the northern end of Missionary Ridge.

By ten o'clock, the veteran pioneers had already finished with the bridge, and all that remained was to await the arrival of the Potomac men herding frantic Rebels from the right at the point of the bayonet. After only another hour, sounds of heavy musketry made clear that Hooker would not disappoint. As the fog began to dissipate, all in the valley caught a glimpse of the operation unfolding precisely according to plan. "Up, up, they go in a straight line," one Hawkeye watched, "a long unwavering line of blue" sweeping across the face of Lookout Mountain.[8] Another was awed by the sight of rigid discipline under fire. "How steadily and with a fine alignment [did] the Potomac veterans face that storm of lead," he wrote.[9] As thinly manned Secessionist defenses were rolled up from the south by the easterners, Osterhaus knew it was First Division's moment to strike. On his command, the batteries redoubled their fire to exacerbate the chaos whirling around the surprised Rebel lines, and Woods's Missourians crossed the creek and started toward the western face in line of battle, with a dense skirmisher "cloud" advanced well to the front.[10]

Pushing forward up the steep slope from tree to tree, Woods's skirmishers encountered sharp resistance from dispersed Rebels, but also enormous numbers of willing prisoners.[11] Added to those who had been surprised in the valley by the sudden rush over the creek, Woods's "skeleton" regiments were quickly overwhelmed by the need for detachments to watch over the bountiful prisoners. In fact, by the time the command had made it halfway up the slope, so many regiments had been detached from their "tactical battalions" that both Woods and Williamson (having advanced his Hawkeyes over the creek and into connection with Woods's right) were rapidly running out of manpower to contribute to a fight which continued to escalate in ferocity as their battalions climbed the slope. Indeed, the grade itself posed serious challenges. "It was not an easy task and not much fun," John Buegel, Third Missouri, later remembered. "If one took a step forward he slipped back two."[12]

Identifying the front line quickly became difficult. Scattered in small groups behind cover, just "as they had fought at Vicksburg," each of the scattered riflemen of First Division fought his own independent battle to gain the initiative in the firefight, coordinating individually with his comrades to combine their fire and maneuver. "Each man fought his own way," one Hawkeye observed, "here and there a squad but all with faces up the Steep [slope]."[13] One "Potomac officer" nearby, anticipating that the lack of any discernible battle line would spell disaster for the westerners, later spoke with surprise about how the division fought "like rats . . . broke all up, but the pieces kept a going."[14]

Upon receiving word that a nearby Potomac brigade was rapidly running out of ammunition, "the Red One" sprang into action, gathering together two hundred men from the Third Missouri and about the same from the Twenty-Seventh, forging an impromptu battalion from the dispersed pieces of his modular division and rushing up the slope to the rescue. Consolidating behind the cover of a rock wall situated on a bench of flat land running along the northern slope of the mountain, the riflemen arrived just in time. Sensing that the easterners had run out of ammunition, Rebels rushed to launch a desperate counterattack. Unbeknownst to the yipping Secessionists, Osterhaus's "Vicksburg rats" awaited them. For the first time in the Fifteenth Corps's history, the tables were turned.[15]

Kneeling behind a rock wall with their rifles loaded, the Missourians immediately recognized the situation from their own painful experience. "We were well protected and knew the game," John Buegel wrote, "so we let Johnny Reb approach within a hundred paces, and then gave them hot fire. The effect was the same as we had seen at Arkansas Post and Vicksburg." This time, there was "death and destruction in the ranks of the enemy" instead of among those of First Division. After only "a few more salvoes of the same sort, those who were still alive ran in wild flight," and that "put an end to the slaughter."[16] Having learned their own lesson, the repulsed Rebels fell back and took cover, just as Buegel and his comrades had done in the aftermath of their repulse at Arkansas Post. The irregular opposing lines of skirmishers strung out along the slopes hunkered down as dusk turned to night.

Riflemen continued to exchange sporadic fire through the dark for the entire chilly evening. Others simply lay on the ground, "wet to the skin, without fire, and hungry without anything to eat."[17] A few attempted to kindle small fires behind boulders until the dim light drew the fire of sharpshooters further up on the mountain.[18] By midnight, many in Osterhaus's division had expended all the hundred rounds issued to them earlier that morning.[19] Eventually, however, the enemy fire slackened and then silenced altogether. At dawn the cause became evident: the Rebels were gone. Hooker had successfully seized Lookout Mountain.[20]

While their successes would have been impossible without the valiant and able efforts of Hooker's main effort, Osterhaus's veterans had proven their tactical prowess when employed in close accordance with their tactical culture and allotted the independence to operate in their own inimitable fashion. Tasked with a mission well calibrated to their particular capabilities as a combined arms team that coordinated the effects of long-range, accurate artillery gunnery with dispersed skirmishing, those in the ranks gained markedly in their self-confidence. The opportunity to return the favor of repeated brutal repulse at the hands of entrenched Rebels increased the intense respect their history had imparted for the advantages accruing to defenders behind works.

As the sun rose and Sherman began his preparations to launch his assaults far away on the "northern extremity of Missionary Ridge," Hooker began his own preparations. The men found the air atop the mountain "pure and fine as in paradise," and the sun quickly became so warm "that our clothes soon dried on our bodies."[21] At ten o'clock, Osterhaus received Hooker's orders to prepare First Division to lead the way off Lookout Mountain eastward into Chattanooga Valley, toward Rossville Gap and the southern end of Missionary Ridge in pursuit of the fleeing Rebels. As the division trudged off the mountain and eastward into the valley, the desperate fighting on Tunnel Hill was audible to the northeast, even at considerable distance. "I think it is the heaviest I ever heard," one Hawkeye considered.[22]

Discovering the bridge across Chattanooga Creek, halfway through the valley, burned by retreating Rebels, Osterhaus once again set his small seventy-man biracial pioneer detachment to work. Just as at Lookout Creek the day before, they were protected by skirmishers from Woods's brigade who crossed over a narrow "hastily constructed" foot bridge of driftwood and fanned out among the trees along the east bank. Immediately coming under fire, the skirmishers of the Twenty-Seventh Missouri once again leaned on marksmanship skills honed at Vicksburg to keep the Rebels at bay while the pioneers worked.[23]

In the time it took to cross the rest of Osterhaus's infantry over the impromptu bridge, an enemy battery managed to unlimber in the middle of Rossville Gap, supported by two regiments of infantry, intent on making a last stand to protect the vulnerable extreme left of Bragg's army atop Missionary Ridge. Osterhaus once again tapped into what he knew to be the division's proven acumen for maneuverability and pursued a double envelopment of the enemy guns. First Division split into two separate brigade columns. Woods's command headed to the right to scale an exceedingly steep slope on the left flank of the Rebel battery, and Williamson's column cut left to scale the southern end of Missionary Ridge. While the frustrated Rebels managed to fire a few salvos in the direction of Woods's flanking regiments, they quickly ascertained the extreme threat posed by their being outmaneuvered on both flanks and abandoned the gap entirely, fleeing to the east and out of the battle. At almost zero cost to his division, Osterhaus had single-handedly captured the strategically vital Rossville Gap and, as no Rebel forces now held the terrain east of Missionary Ridge, the thinly defended extreme rear of Bragg's whole army.[24]

Climbing back off the steep slopes, both commands rallied at a crossroads east of the gap to await Hooker's orders. They arrived in short time. Osterhaus would continue northward along the road running behind Missionary Ridge toward Chattanooga, pushing any and all Rebel resistance aside and collecting prisoners while the Potomac men simultaneously swept across the crest and northern slope. In effect, the plan contemplated a repetition of the previous day's tactics. Due to the nature of the terrain, Hooker urged Osterhaus to act independently "as circumstances might demand," with an understanding of the larger plan. This loose leash once again represented Hooker's confidence and respect for the Prussian's tactical acumen, as well as a perfect opportunity for the division to continue to operate in a manner maximally calibrated to its strengths.

As Hooker's divisions battled through consecutive lines of Rebels atop the ridge, taking each in the flank, Osterhaus pushed his two brigades northward "as fast as the column of infantry could move" along the backside of the ridge. Once he had ascertained that both brigades had outflanked all the Rebel units confronting Hooker, he changed front to the west, shifted the brigades into line of battle with skirmishers well to the front, and charged up the back slope. Lt. Col. A. J. Seay, long a critic of shoddy generalship, was floored at the sight of "our men running, yelling, shooting with furious impetuosity" as they hurdled confidently toward the Rebel rear. Falling almost entirely upon Secessionists distracted by Hooker's threat to their front, the charge was fantastically successful. "We've got 'em in a pen!" the bareheaded Prussian shouted above the din, eagerly urging on both brigades.[25]

Bragg's flank had been effectively converted into "a swirling, struggling mass of panic-stricken men, signaling frantically to make us understand they surrendered," one Buckeye wrote. "Each ran for himself as best he could to get out of range of our bullets," another Missourian crowed.[26] Continuing to surge northward through the confused masses of surrendering Rebels, the division was surprised to meet Thomas's "Cumberlanders" atop the crest of Missionary Ridge. Sent by Grant in a probing assault against the enemy pits at the base of the height to support Sherman's flagging efforts on the northern end, the Army of the Cumberland had taken it upon themselves to continue all the way up the ridge that afternoon despite an absence of orders. Now, their impromptu actions were fortuitously coinciding with those of Hooker and Osterhaus to dismantle the Rebel army. Despite the total ignorance of Sherman and the remainder of the Fifteenth Corps to the north, shrouded from all visibility of these developments by the lay of the land, the battle for Chattanooga was rapidly nearing a victorious conclusion for Federal arms.[27]

As the massive attack of the "Cumberlanders" all across the western face of the ridge swept thousands of Rebels from their positions, Osterhaus's veterans merely held their positions and collected prisoners. "The troops on the other side of the ridge had shaken the tree and we were holding the bag to get the fruit," one Illinoisan later wrote. Overawed at the gravity of their success, the men of First Division let forth loud hurrahs while "the

Red One" rode up and down the lines atop a captured Rebel horse, shouting, "Two more hours daylight and we'll destroy this army!" Turning to an aide, the beaming Prussian pronounced, "Ah, colonel, this is glorious!"[28]

"FROM THE FRONT WE COULD NOT DO ANYTHING"

Those Rebel commands on Bragg's right that had avoided utter destruction or rout during the day escaped from Sherman's front during the night, pulling out from their works silently. Limping eastward, the severely damaged Army of Tennessee attempted to avoid total catastrophe by hurrying toward Ringgold, Georgia, and a critical mountain gap of the same name. Hoping to bag or destroy the remainder of Bragg's army, Grant somewhat belatedly ordered Hooker's ad-hoc corps to pursue.[29]

In the afternoon of November 26, First Division was on the road toward Ringgold. After making a distance of about six miles from Missionary Ridge, the division encountered its third burned bridge of the campaign at a critical crossing of Chickamauga Creek. A nearby ford served the purposes of ushering the infantry across the water, but there was no time to repair the main span adequately for the division's batteries to join. Instead, the guns would have to wait for the time-consuming repair of the original bridge. The prospect of stumbling into more than a fleeing enemy force without the benefit of artillery must have produced considerable heartburn for those veterans of Arkansas Post still in the ranks. Ever the consummate artillerist, Osterhaus was among their number. Even so, when Hooker advised the Prussian that he intended to place First Division in the lead the next morning, and that contact with Bragg's rear guard was likely near Ringgold, Osterhaus had no choice but to operate without his precious guns.[30]

By that time the vast majority of the battered Rebel force, with the exception of the tail end of its baggage train, had already escaped through Ringgold Gap, leaving behind a token force commanded by none other than Maj. Gen. Patrick Cleburne, who had only two days prior brutally repulsed Sherman's legions from the works atop Tunnel Hill. The recent success of his regiments had left them quite confident in their ability to do so again. Now, on the morning of November 27, the veteran Rebels would try their hands against the only remaining division of the Fifteenth Corps they had not yet encountered. Their defense, though meant to be little more than a delaying action, would be considerably eased by the heights of White Oak

Mountain, towering over the gap on its northern flank. Covered with dense woods and pock-marked with massive boulders and irregular undulations, the western slopes of the rise offered ample opportunities for defensive positions, and Cleburne planned to use the mountain to prevent Federal efforts to flank northward while placing all his available artillery in the gap itself. As the gap's southern flank was naturally protected by the waters of Chickamauga Creek, no double envelopment (like Osterhaus had conducted at Rossville) would be possible.[31]

Those in the ranks of First Division arriving in Ringgold west of the gap that morning took one look at the looming ridge they assumed held Rebels and immediately "knew the game." Any direct assault would inevitably lead to the same bloody results as so many times before. "From the front we could not do anything," John Buegel, Third Missouri, survivor of every one of the division's failures from Arkansas Post to the Louisiana Lunette, scribbled in his diary. The enemy certainly "had all the heights fortified and well manned." The only option was to advance "by flanking movements" in an attempt to dislodge the Secessionists from their strong position. Unfortunately, such was not to be the case.[32]

With nothing more than suppositions that the heights of White Oak Mountain contained hidden Secessionists, Osterhaus judged that little more than tacit Rebel resistance held the gap itself. Cleburne's guns had been carefully masked from prying eyes by brush. After a brief conference with Hooker, the Prussian, in his typical tactically conservative fashion, offered that only a swift cavalry rush toward the gap was likely necessary. With no cavalry immediately on hand, and eager to bag Bragg's trains, Hooker was not interested in delay. Instead, Osterhaus would launch a two-pronged frontal attack directly against the face of the mountain and into the gap itself, he explained, to be supported by an additional flanking movement by his Potomac veterans on the left if absolutely necessary. Despite his division's heritage of failure in frontal assaults, despite the dread already recorded within the diaries of some in the ranks, and despite the absence of his heavy guns, Osterhaus acceded to Hooker's request.[33]

To their credit, Osterhaus, Wood, and Williamson approached the grim problem at hand with a nuance from the tactical culture of First Division. Despite a sweeping open plain extending for some distance before the mountain that offered plenty of room for a wide frontage of close-order formations, the command trio instead approached the terrain from the

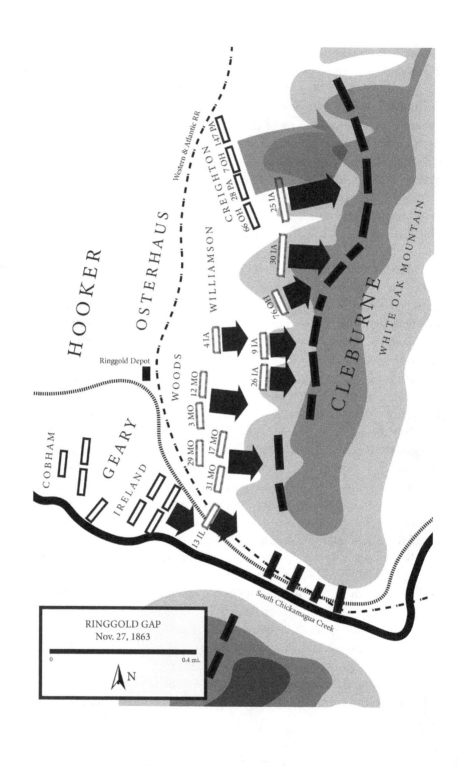

HOOKER

OSTERHAUS

Western & Atlantic RR

CREIGHTON

66 OH 28 PA 7 OH 147 PA

25 IA

WILLIAMSON

30 IA

76 OH

41 IA

9 IA

26 IA

CLEBURNE

WHITE OAK MOUNTAIN

Ringgold Depot

WOODS

12 MO

3 MO

29 MO 17 MO

31 MO

COBHAM

GEARY

IRELAND

13 IL

South Chickamagua Creek

RINGGOLD GAP
Nov. 27, 1863

0   0.4 mi.

N

perspective of "Vicksburg rats." Through the middle of the plain, from north to south, ran the tracks of the Western & Atlantic Railroad, elevated on an earthen embankment that represented a natural breastwork almost identical to the levees the men had encountered at Chickasaw Bayou. Advancing in column and deploying behind the embankment, the two brigades quickly established themselves in a defensive posture in preparation for Osterhaus's orders to advance.

At about nine o'clock, those orders came, and Woods's Third, Twelfth, and Thirty-First Missouri—now fewer than six hundred men in total—sallied over the embankment and toward the gap, screened by the Turner skirmishers of the Seventeenth Missouri, as usual. This manner of advance, premised in part upon the erroneous assumption that no enemy artillery was present, proved terribly inappropriate when Cleburne's gunners suddenly rushed from hiding, tore away the brush from their pieces, and fired blasts of canister and shell toward the brigade. The deadly salvo felled several of the Missourians and prompted a stunned Woods to immediately fall back to the protection of the embankment. Uninterested in risking mass casualties in an assault against the guns, Osterhaus took a more dynamic approach, concentrating on driving the gunners from their guns with rifle fire. Harassing enemy batteries by sharpshooting was something the division had considerable experience at doing, and thus the plan was in close accordance with its tactical culture. Ordering the veteran Thirteenth Illinois to rush forward from the embankment and occupy a cluster of farm buildings that would allow them to employ their Vicksburg-borne sharpshooting skills to silence the guns, the fewer than three hundred remaining survivors of Blair's desperate charge at Chickasaw Bayou once again flung themselves into the fray.[34]

Surprised at a sudden silence of Rebel arms as they approached the cluster of houses, the Illinoisans quickly closed the distance to the gap. The Secessionists having again masked their batteries, only when the regiment had neared the farmhouses did the gunners again return to their posts and send forth a blast of canister that tore directly into the left flank of the command. "This was a surprise and a severe test of our nerve and power of concession as a regiment," one veteran later recalled, and "at a word from the officers, all the men lay flat on the ground but stayed in place."[35] Hard won lessons for survival from past experience thrust the Suckers to the ground for protection. After a short time under fire, they worked to suppress the Rebel batteries long enough that the regiment could sprint to the cover of the nearby farmhouses. Many never made it. Those who did immediately began to sharpshoot from the windows of the barn and outhouses "in the most determined way." Robbed of a consecutive series of commanding officers by Rebel fire, the men were mostly left to coordinate the desperate fight among themselves.[36]

Meanwhile, hoping to flank northward and seize the northern end of the mountain from Rebel units he had spied moving in that direction along the crest, Osterhaus ordered Woods's Seventy-Sixth Ohio along with Williamson's Fourth, Ninth, and Twenty-Fifth Iowa to advance in a northeasterly direction and confront any Rebels they discovered on the western slope. While Williamson personally went forward with his Hawkeyes, Osterhaus retained the two hundred men of the Thirty-First Iowa in reserve, deploying two of their companies as sharpshooters along the embankment to pepper the mountain with long-range covering fire as their brother Hawkeyes crossed the open expanse. Despite this support, Williamson's advance faced harassing fire for the entire distance to the base of the hill, at which point the Buckeyes and Col. George Stone's Twenty-Fifth Iowa began the long climb up the steep slope dispersed as skirmishers.[37]

Despite the rugged nature of the mountain, good cover for riflemen proved somewhat sparse. "A few large rocks and scattering trees and logs were the only places of safety," Private Calvin Ainsworth observed. Having now spent more than a year fighting mostly as skirmishers across all types of terrain, Ainsworth and his fellow Hawkeyes were experts at sniffing out any viable protection along a line of advance. Maneuvering across the unforgiving broken ground of the bayous and hills of Mississippi had imparted a preference for fighting "Indian fashion," as Ainsworth called it, "each man for himself, dodging from tree to tree, from rock to rock, advancing in the meantime."[38] Such a tactic seemed to them the only viable method by which the Rebels ensconced along the crest could safely be challenged. "Every time we would expose ourselves the bullets would rain around us," Ainsworth explained.[39] Thus, each Iowan sought first and foremost "to get a tree between myself and the rebel bullets."[40]

A considerable distance behind the Hawkeyes creeping up the slope was Williamson's massed battle line. The veteran general had no intention of storming the ridge with a bayonet charge. His Iowans had attempted such futile maneuvers too many times before. He had no idea whether the Rebels hiding in the brush at the crest were already entrenched, but he refused to find out the hard way. Those Iowans not with the skirmishers could be deployed incrementally to support their dispersed comrades, but barring any unforeseen contingency, he planned to fulfill his mission with the least possible risk to his brigade.[41]

As the skirmisher battle on the northern end of the mountain ebbed and flowed, seesawing Williamson's lines alternatively further up or down the western slope of White Oak Mountain, Cleburne made a bold move. Hoping to break through Woods's line at the railroad embankment in a counterattack similar to that which they had enjoyed so much luck with against Sherman at Tunnel Hill, several Rebel battalions came hurdling out of the gap and into the open. Comfortably situated behind the embankment, Woods's veterans still "knew the game," just as they had proven on Lookout Mountain. Waiting until the Secessionists had come within easy range, the Missourians let loose several "well-directed volleys" that promptly dismantled the assault and sent the survivors rearward.[42]

Hooker was as unimpressed with this defensive feat as he was frustrated with the lack of forward progress. Bragg's trains were escaping, and Osterhaus seemed apparently less than up to the task at hand. Greatly annoyed at the sight of Woods's initial repulse from the gap, and with Williamson's apparent lack of obvious momentum on the left, he decided it was time to add more weight to the northern flanking effort. Casting about for available troops, he chose Brig. Gen. John Geary's Second Division, and more specifically Colonel William Creighton's brigade of Potomac veterans, for the maneuver. The manner in which Creighton's command approached its mission, in stark contrast to its Fifteenth Corps counterparts, illustrated dramatic differences in tactical cultures derived from vastly different operational heritages.

Delivering his orders to Creighton in person, Geary instructed the brigadier "to charge up the ridge and drive the enemy from it."[43] Without pause, even given the obvious difficulty Williamson's Hawkeyes were having with accomplishing the same objective, Creighton ordered his four regiments into two tightly packed lines of battle, each with orders to maintain a strict distance of one hundred yards from the other. Leading off abreast were the Twenty-Eighth and 147th Pennsylvania, with Creighton's own original Seventh Ohio and the Sixty-Sixth Ohio following behind in support.[44] The brigade crossed most of the intervening open ground between the railroad embankment and the foot of White Oak Mountain without issue, given the preoccupation of most of the Rebels atop the height with the sharp skirmish along its slopes. Creighton maneuvered the brigade slightly to the left of Williamson's massed reserve waiting at the base of the mountain for the results of the skirmisher battle. One look at the tightly packed battle lines of the Potomac regiments shocked the Hawkeyes, who had rarely seen any experienced veteran command approach combat in such a fashion. Worse, on their current trajectory, once upon the slope they would risk breaking up the cohesion of the Hawkeye skirmisher "cloud" which extended some distance beyond the flanks of the massed Iowans to the rear.[45]

Spurring his mount hurriedly over to Creighton's formation, Col. George Stone "ordered and begged" the onrushing regiments to shift their formation further to the left so as to avoid breaking up the integrity of his skirmishers, but "the officers in command said they had orders for doing as they did," Williamson later reported, "and persisted in their course." At the very least hoping to reduce what seemed their all-but-inevitable imminent destruction, Stone warned the intransigent officers that, should their battle lines continue approaching the slope "in the manner they were going," massed in tight formation "as if on parade," and without even the benefit of a skirmisher screen, the hidden enemy would cut them to pieces as soon as they came within close range. Indeed, he and his Twenty-Fifth Iowa had learned that very lesson the hard way at Arkansas Post. He advised breaking up the ranks and deploying companies as skirmishers as his Hawkeyes had done. The Potomac men would have none of Stone's entreaties, brushing him aside with a cocky rebuff about how they intended to "teach 'Western troops a lesson.'" Another Iowan overheard one of Creighton's officers shout out to his men that they would "show these western boys how to fight."[46]

Approaching the base of the slope, Creighton halted his Pennsylvanians and fired a volley blindly toward the crest, as if to announce his arrival on the field. After this ineffectual fire, the supporting Potomac veterans continued boldly up the slope, still with no skirmishers to their front.[47] By the time the line had crawled within sight of the Rebels atop the heights, the men were exhausted. "It was as much as we could do to climb the rough and steep mountain-side without having to fight," one remarked. Creighton ordered his men to fire by carefully controlled volleys into the dense woods without knowing precisely what was to their front. The results were less than spectacular. "We were tired," one admitted, "and our fire was not delivered with that accuracy and effect that might have been hoped for."[48] Though the brigade had unquestionably "advanced beautifully," its effectiveness left much to be desired.[49]

Recognizing the need to attempt to turn the Rebel line, but still wanting to do so with a flourish, Creighton ordered his own Seventh Ohio out of reserve and up a draw to the left. "Boys, we are ordered to take that hill," he shouted, characteristically adding that he wanted "to see you walk right up it." Struggling mightily to maintain their formational integrity in the ascent, the Ohioans maneuvered into column and made their way up the ravine the best they could, "not stopping to return the fire" that emanated from every Rebel who suddenly noticed the opportunity to pour lead into an unprepared Federal column blindly groping its way up the slope. This fire rapidly grew in intensity until finally it reached a pitch altogether "too heavy and effective for flesh and blood to withstand."[50] The Buckeye commander, Lieutenant Colonel Orrin Crane, was among the first to fall. Perceiving that the same fate might befall themselves, the Pennsylvanians fell back in confusion. It was only a matter of moments before the valiant Creighton shared Crane's fate, and soon the entire brigade found itself in a panicked rout down the slope. Creighton pleaded with those nearby to "Tell my wife I died at the head of my command," as his brigade fled for its life off the slope of White Oak Mountain.[51]

Even during the hottest moments of the engagement, the Hawkeye skirmishers had watched with great interest what seemed the almost exotic tactics of the easterners. "I noticed that when one of their officers fell half a dozen men would break ranks to carry him off the field," Ainsworth observed. "That is something we never did."[52] Indeed, the Potomac regiments operated almost as if part of an altogether different army from that in which the Hawkeyes served. When Creighton's line broke, however, there was no time for fascinating ethnography. The Potomac veterans, so recently filled with bluster, ran directly through the scattered Hawkeye skirmish teams, carrying them all in a blue tide rushing down the steep slope "like an avalanche, carrying everything before them," Williamson later grieved. Fleeing his scant cover, Hawkeye Calvin Ainsworth "never ran, or tried to run so hard in my life. Bullets were flying about my head and I could see the dust rise whenever the ball struck the ground."[53]

Halting at the foot of the mountain, where Williamson managed to rally his command, the brigade gave up on its orders to seize the mountain and determined to merely hold its position instead. Hooker's attack had failed. Left alone near the crest, the remnants of the Seventy-Sixth Ohio's skirmisher teams rallied to form a defensive perimeter and fought off successive Rebel counterattacks until finally disengaging and withdrawing down the slope. Finally, at about one o'clock, the exhausted and disoriented brigade heard the distinctive thunder of Maj. Clement Landgraeber's howitzers echo through the valley. The artillery had arrived at long last, but it was too late. Cleburne and his Rebel rear guard, along with the tail of Bragg's army, was already gone.[54]

"BY SKIRMISHING AND CAUTIOUSLY ADVANCING"

Few officers or soldiers in Williamson's command came away from the battle at Ringgold Gap with the impression that Creighton's regiments had failed in their mission due to cowardice. "The fault of these regiments seemed to be more in the way in which they attempted to go up the hill than in anything else," Williamson determined. His Hawkeyes had naturally "preferred the method of taking [the ridge] by skirmishing and cautiously advancing." The Potomac men, in sharp contrast, "tried to go up as if on parade where the men could barely have gone up by clinging to the rocks and bushes."[55] Williamson's remarks represented one of the clearest and most concise elaborations of the Fifteenth Corps's historically derived approach to offensive operations, while also highlighting the profound differences between the tactical culture of his own brigade and that of Creighton's veterans of other fields.

With the sole exception of the 147th Pennsylvania, most of Creighton's regiments had been under arms for longer than those of Williamson's. His own Seventh Ohio, organized during the first spring of the war, had undergone upwards of nine major engagements by the time of its arrival at Ringgold Gap, including six frontal assaults. Those who fell upon the slopes of White Oak Mountain, and those who led them to their fate, were anything but neophytes to combat. Instead, just as with Williamson's Hawkeyes, it was the specifics of their past experience which shaped "the way in which they attempted to go up the hill." Unlike his Iowan counterpart, William Creighton had little relevant experience when it came to assaulting fortified Rebel positions in rugged terrain—an environment which robbed commanders of their ability to read the battlefield problem before them.[56]

With the exception of skirmishing in the mountains of western Virginia during the first months of the war, the Seventh Ohio's prior experiences with offensive operations had almost all unfolded across open ground, with an enemy clearly visible to the front. At the battle of Kernstown in March 1862, the Ohioans had launched their first assault. After maneuvering to within close range of the Rebel host and enduring a punishing artillery bombardment, the Buckeyes charged Secessionists who were ensconced behind a stone wall "in double column for some distance as if upon the drill-ground." As had befallen Williamson's Hawkeyes at Arkansas Post, a close-range shock volley dismantled the command and forced survivors to ground and into a firefight from the prone. Only the sudden retreat of the Rebel infantry due to attacking Federal reinforcements on their flank eventually decided the day.[57]

Unlike Williamson's Iowans, the men of the Seventh Ohio did not emerge from the experience with a diminished confidence in the efficacy of serried ranks in offensive operations. Indeed, given the failure of defending Rebels to deliver a decisive countercharge from behind their breastworks, "victory to our arms followed," one Buckeye wrote, and thus the attack could be interpreted as a success. Four months later, at Port Republic, the regiment again charged in close order to retake a captured battery in an open field, losing five color-bearers to Rebel musketry in the process. To support its advance, just as it would at Ringgold Gap, the command intermittently halted to pour "volley after volley" upon the enemy. The regiment's officers reported satisfaction at the unit's conducting itself "in perfect order" and "in gallant style," immensely proud of its growing reputation "for gallant fighting in the open." Later that summer, at Cedar Mountain, the regiment was praised by superiors for its "regular and well-directed fire upon the enemy" during an assault, again delivered in volleys like those ordered at White Oak Mountain—volleys which Williamson's Iowans had never employed during any of their own assaults. Once again, the advancing Ohioans bore punishment stoically in the open, caught under Rebel guns "without protection or support . . . in an open field" that survivors referred to as a "terrible furnace of fire." Even so, the command "never faltered in this march of death, moving cooly on, regardless of the missiles that were tearing through its bleeding ranks." Despite sustaining greater than 60 percent losses in the engagement, survivors took pride in the fact that "the line wavered not." By late 1862, this impressive capacity for stalwart endurance in the face of such a bloodletting was central to the emergence within the regiment of what historian John Lynn has termed a tactical culture of forbearance reminiscent of eighteenth-century European armies.[58]

A product of the social and cultural realities of early modern Europe, Enlightenment-era European tactical trends prior to the dramatic changes of the French Revolution encouraged the tight control and discipline of the lower classes filling the ranks of infantry regiments while under fire. Close-order serried ranks of soldiers were drilled to march in lockstep under the watchful eye of aristocratic officers bent on controlling their every move so as to maximize the effects of massed musketry and prevent shirking from the ranks. Though brutalized by enemy artillery while advancing toward their objectives at a measured pace, Lynn explains how regiments were expected "to absorb the punishment and keep advancing without responding." This widely prevalent tactical norm in eighteenth-century Europe "emphasized not so much inflicting casualties as demonstrating that one could absorb enemy fire and continue to fight and advance without breaking or flinching." The paramount achievement of any regiment was not the destruction of an enemy by fire, but rather to "appear to be unshakable" and thus "overthrow him [the enemy] psychologically," following up his flight with the bayonet. In the end, such an approach was "based less on fury than on forbearance." While this "culture of forbearance" dissipated in Europe during the French Revolutionary and Napoleonic eras as a result of the tactical, cultural, and social developments of the early nineteenth century, the widespread lack of modern martial expertise among American volunteer officers frequently resulted in a renaissance of such anachronistic norms during the Civil War. This was especially the case when the particular experiences of particular officers and regiments upheld these archaic beliefs.[59]

Yet again at Antietam in September 1862, the Buckeyes went forward in line of battle, "as cool and regular as on drill." Despite the pummeling of first Rebel artillery and then rifle fire, the regiment's advance "was made steadily, and in slow time," with officers mounted and trotting forward alongside. After closing within short range of Rebels behind a rail fence, the command disgorged several volleys, killing or wounding nearly all of the Sixth Georgia before receiving the order to charge. "We started, with levelled bayonets," one participant later recalled, when unlike during Williamson's brigade's many traumatic past experiences, "terror-stricken, the rebels fled." Following after the foe "like hounds after the frightened deer, we pursued them fully three-fourths of a mile, killing, wounding, and taking prisoners almost every rod." Although subsequent Rebel counterattacks eventually forced the Ohioans rearward, they "retired from the front, lacerated but cheerful, feeling that our duty was faithfully performed."[60]

By the fall of 1863, in nearly every instance in which Creighton and his Seventh Ohio had been called upon to launch a frontal assault, it had been conducted in tightly massed ranks "with levelled bayonets," and had almost uniformly resulted in "terror-stricken" Rebels flying from their positions—if not immediately, then after a brief close-range exchange of fire. The conclusions to be drawn from such regular experiences of success, though almost diametrically opposite to those of Williamson's battered Iowans, were obvious. Unfortunately, given the death of the young colonel, his explicit reasoning for prosecuting his orders in the manner he did at Ringgold Gap is lost to history. Despite this silence, by evaluating the past experiences of Creighton and his original command, his blustering refusals and those of his lieutenants to heed Stone's anxious entreaties to approach the tactical problem differently or court disaster is evidence enough of the power of learned tactical culture.

At the same time, the matter-of-fact tone in which both Stone's and Williamson's observations were conveyed similarly illustrates just how normalized the Fifteenth Corps's own tactical culture had become within the ranks of its component regiments. The same or remarkably similar experiences had produced a shared collection of habitual preferences which informed and shaped "the way in which [its member units] attempted to" prosecute their assigned objectives. A year's worth of particular ordeals had forged a fondness for "the method of . . . skirmishing and cautiously advancing" within the corps, as opposed to boldly storming enemy positions at the point of the bayonet, "as if on parade," in the manner of Creighton's serried ranks. The command's preference for tactical conservatism had little to do with its western sociocultural origins. After all, most of Creighton's regiments were comprised of westerners as well, having been raised in the same state as Woods's Buckeyes of the Seventy-Sixth Ohio. The differences in "the way in which they attempted to go up the hill" at White Oak Mountain were far more closely related to a much more recent history: the experiences each brigade had undergone while in uniform, the meanings they had attributed to those experiences, and the specific lessons derived from them. The resultant tactical culture that thrived within each organization shaped the manner in which its members collectively interpreted the orders they were given, prepared themselves for what was likely to occur, and responded to it when it did.

If there had been any doubt about the Fifteenth Corps's particular strengths and weaknesses, the long Chattanooga campaign had removed all lingering ambiguity. From the rank and file of both divisions to Sherman's headquarters, a now mature and coherent set of beliefs, assumptions, and predispositions informing tactical-level decision-making, behavior, and performance had emerged in the aftermath of the Vicksburg campaign and remained indelibly etched in the ranks of the corps's regiments and batteries. Among the most prominent aspects of this corps-wide culture were (1) a preference for fundamentally conservative tactical choices (even when assigned less than conservative missions), with an emphasis on the use of artillery and open-order skirmisher "clouds" and sharpshooting details as the main effort in almost all offensive operations, (2) a glaring lack of confidence in the capability of massed bayonet assaults to successfully overcome even modest breastworks, (3) an affinity for indirect over direct maneuver solutions, and finally (4) a strategic preference for long-range maneuver and resource denial over direct armed confrontation with Rebels.

The battles for Chattanooga ultimately had little new to teach the veterans of Sherman's corps about the nature of combat that it had not already gleaned over the previous year. Instead, the campaign reified for the corps, and for Sherman, precisely what they had already suspected about themselves and their capabilities as a military organization. Many of those in First and Second divisions, who had long ago suffered through repeated confirmation of their beliefs regarding the impossibility of successful assaults against works, learned that those lessons still applied. At the same time, first at Lookout Mountain and later at Ringgold Gap, Osterhaus's command learned firsthand that the intrinsic power of defensive works and shock volleys worked both ways. If assaulting fortified Rebels had again proven to be futile, the survivors of First Division remained more than willing to allow the enemy to try his own luck against works. By painful experience, their respect for the defensive power of breastworks had been strengthened in a manner that would pay great dividends in the future.

In the aftermath, all across the corps those in the ranks tended to focus more on their successes than their failures when constructing retrospective narratives of the campaign, usually seizing on a particular moment as the essence of the whole. Delos Van Deusen and his comrades of the Sixth Missouri celebrated their daring nighttime crossing of the Tennessee as the "great success" of the campaign. "Sherman knew it would turn their right and make us masters of the position," he wrote home excitedly, "which proved correct," ignoring entirely the rest of the bloody story.[61] An Ohioan of Lightburn's brigade, writing after the war, still considered it "one of the most strategic manoeuvers of the war, and have always felt a glowing pride in the conspicuous part my regiment bore in that night's work."[62] Thaddeus Capron, a quartermaster in Smith's First Brigade, likewise interpreted the operation as a total success from start to finish. "The Confederates finding that we had flanked them, thought to drive us off, but 'Tecumseh' Sherman was prepared, and drove them from their outermost works, and cut their railroad to Richmond," he crowed in a letter home.[63] While George Hildt admitted to having been "despondent at Chattanooga before the battle as they were so nicely fixed," now the victory seemed "only second to Vicksburg." To his eye, no Rebel army could "stand up against Grant with his Western army," and he looked forward to spring when the mighty host would "move forward again."[64]

The disaster at Ringgold shook First Division to the core, and thus their reflections on the recent victory at Chattanooga were more subdued. "This was one of the sharpest battles that I was ever in," Calvin Ainsworth, a survivor of both Arkansas Post and the Louisiana Lunette assault remarked in his diary the evening after the fight. "It was a very foolish thing to charge the hill," he added.[65] Hard facts were few and far between. "As to particulars I cannot give you any," another Iowan scribbled home. "You will get them in the papers long before we do here," he added. "All we know is that we have gained a glorious victory, but in doing So have lost many noble men and many hearth stones will be desolate and many hearts bleed for the events of the last week."[66]

Despite the pain of loss that hung like a pall over First Division, the net positive tone that emanated from the corps's regiments was incontrovertible evidence of one final salient element of the command's culture: a nearly unshakable confidence in their abilities to crush the Rebellion, provided that "our Generals" stuck to what they knew from experience worked, and avoided all they knew from experience did not. "We have driven the enemy from another strong hold[,] have to a considerable extent destroyed his army and means of injuring us, have reflected great honor upon our corps and its commanding Officers Genl Grant & Sherman and all this with but little loss of life," one Missourian proclaimed.[67] He and his comrades felt "as though we never could tire [of] talking and writing about our great success." Grant's "Vicksburg rats" had struck a blow which "opens up Georgia to us, and bids fair to split the rebel states in two again."[68] Cpt. Jacob Ritner, wounded at Ringgold Gap, expressed matters succinctly. "Of all the fights where we have been, no one man here knew what has been done, except the general result." The "general result," as far as he could tell, was that "the rebels have been out-generaled by Grant, and defeated, routed, demoralized, and the whole army gone to the devil where it belongs."[69] That was enough for the men of Sherman's corps, who were already preparing themselves for new fields.

CONCLUSION

Veteran Character

It was this veteran character that utterly dominated Sherman's army, . . .
[and] made the March to the Sea and through the Carolinas possible.

—JOSEPH T. GLATTHAAR, *The March to the Sea and Beyond*, 1985

After five frigid months huddled in winter quarters in northern Alabama,
on May 1, 1864, the veteran "skeleton regiments" of the Fifteenth Army
Corps departed for their final combat campaign. Despite the infusion of
a handful of replacements, few regiments could muster more than 250
effectives for duty in the ranks. In many, fewer than 200 still answered
roll call.[1] For the most part, those who remained had been present at the
original formation of their regiments. The initial terms of service having
run out during the winter for those in the oldest regiments, the majority
had reenlisted as "Veteran Volunteers" for three more years or the duration
of the war. Now commanded by Maj. Gen. John A. Logan, following Frank
Blair's departure for command of the Seventeenth Corps and Sherman's to
command of the entire Military Division of the Mississippi, the Fifteenth
Corps was very much a veteran's corps.[2] Moreover, it was the command's
"veteran character," which Joseph Glatthaar identified as having enabled its
exploits during the later March to the Sea, that would likewise enable its signal contributions throughout the forthcoming bloody campaign for Atlanta.

In between leave, drill, and occasional patrols into the Alabama hills,
the corps had spent much of the winter and early spring honing its tactical
skills. After three months of inaction after Ringgold, in mid-February all
of First Division's infantry conducted target practice so as to refresh their
hard-won marksmanship skills. Each rifleman fired a total of twenty rounds

on the range—five rounds apiece at targets 200, 300, 400, and 600 yards' distance.[3] While the necessity of husbanding ammunition often hobbled efforts to conduct regular rifle practice, even rare exercise provided invaluable opportunities for volunteers to hone their skills. The fact that more than forty thousand rounds of ammunition were required to conduct the practice underscores the prominent place marksmanship enjoyed within the division's tactical culture. Moreover, the opportunity to fire upon targets presented at predetermined distances provided all of those within the ranks a chance to practice manipulating their sights and estimating the distance to a target—skills initially developed in the trenches at Vicksburg.

In preparation for the forthcoming campaign, First Division's veteran officers took steps to integrate the corps's light infantry–centric tactical culture into its operational structure. A month prior to stepping off, the division established its own permanently detailed "Corps of Sharpshooters." While all of the division's "skeleton regiments" would lean on their skirmishing skills throughout the campaign, this detachment would provide Osterhaus with a contingent of skilled riflemen who could be deployed independently of any particular regiment. The sharpshooters were to be commanded by "very energetic Officers with a thorough administration and tactical knowledge," and who were also "well acquainted with skirmishing practice." Along with three sergeants and six corporals, the detachment was composed of seventy-five veteran privates who proved themselves "the very best marksmen" during target practice. No evidence exists to suggest they were armed differently from the rest of the division. Moreover, as Special Orders from the same period do not survive for the corps's other divisions, it remains unknown whether such detachments were forged across the corps. Nevertheless, their existence in Osterhaus's division represented a novel innovation in the structure of US volunteer infantry forces, as well as a powerful expression of the Fifteenth Corps's tactical culture. While many brigades of the Army of the Potomac would eventually form their own impromptu sharpshooting detachments later that summer, after enduring heavy skirmishing across the forthcoming Overland Campaign, that such details emerged first in the Fifteenth Corps is testament to the impress of its combat experiences on its tactical evolution.[4]

Just as past experience had taught the corps the vital importance of rifle marksmanship, its time in the trenches at Vicksburg and its victories at Chattanooga had likewise illustrated the salient contributions of dependable and accurate artillery support to infantry operations. Instead of simply opening engagements with heavy bombardments designed to pulverize enemy positions prior to infantry assaults, the Vicksburg siege had taught the corps how infantry and artillery could effectively work together in rudimentary ways to support one another. For this reason, Osterhaus's efforts to hone his division's skills were not restricted to the infantry. All the division's batteries were also to "so arrange the Target practice as to be productive of the greatest possible benefit in the instruction of the men," with all loading and firing "made in strict compliance with the prescribed Manual." Battery commanders were to continually order the crews to limber, move, and redeploy their guns "as soon as the men become habituated to the range, in order to accustom them to estimate distances correctly and quickly." The loss of artillerists to Rebel rifles at Vicksburg impressed the artillerymen with the danger accompanying the maneuver of batteries prior to going into action. "Experience has shown that most of the casualties occur during this critical period," Osterhaus cautioned, "[and] it becomes therefore of the highest importance to shorten the time so occupied." After training on quickly limbering and unlimbering the guns and ensuring "proper discipline" was maintained at all times, the division's batteries would be able to deploy and redeploy quickly and safely in order to support the infantry. Officers kept meticulous records of the target practice and submitted them to division headquarters for review. The speed and accuracy with which the batteries could provide support had proven itself of great value at Chattanooga, and Osterhaus sought to refine these skills for the benefit of future operations.[5]

"ONE UNIVERSAL SKIRMISH"

The campaign for Atlanta, arguably the most strategically important of the war, was to prove well calibrated for the Fifteenth Corps's evolved tactical culture. This was in no small part due to the similarity of the rugged and unforgiving terrain of northwestern Georgia with that which the corps had confronted before at Chattanooga and Vicksburg. Nearly 70 percent of the area over which the armies clashed during the campaign was still covered in dense pine forests as late as 1870, all but prohibiting the kinds of large-scale textbook bayonet assaults arrayed in massed lines of battle that the corps had habitually proven itself incapable of achieving.[6]

Instead of pummeling successive Rebel lines of defense arrayed between Chattanooga and Atlanta with frontal assaults, Sherman's southward progress was marked by an adept marriage of the strategic offense with the tactical defense. Digging earthworks to defend part of his army group while the men skirmished constantly all along the line in an effort to hold their Rebel counterparts in place, another element launched repeated "whiplash" turning movements designed to outflank fortified enemy positions and plunge ever further southward toward Atlanta while avoiding direct confrontation. Through this "indirect approach," forward momentum toward the army's objective was still possible despite the avoidance of major battles between the two competing forces.[7] Cump habitually relied upon his trusted Army of the Tennessee and Logan's Fifteenth Corps to conduct these "whiplash" turning movements, perhaps in hopes of reducing the amount of fighting they might have to endure. His choice leveraged the corps's proven capacity to move swiftly across difficult terrain. Its parent Army of the Tennessee, then under the command of Maj. Gen. James B. McPherson, amounted to what one historian has termed "Sherman's prize pedestrians," and their dependable capacity for arriving at every assigned objective on time allowed Cump to hone the "tedious and risky process" of maneuver warfare "to a fine art."[8]

In large part because of Sherman's initial avoidance of major clashes with the Rebels to his front whenever possible, rolling firefights between skirmishers scattered behind natural cover quickly defined the character of infantry combat during the campaign. After the first full month of fighting and maneuvering, Sherman concluded that the campaign had yet to be distinguished by any "real battle," but rather constituted "one universal skirmish extending over a vast surface" or even "a Big Indian War." Another member of his army thought the almost perpetual contact with Rebels in densely wooded terrain ought to have been described as a "skirmisher's war." Indeed, as Earl Hess observes, more than any other campaign of the war, the drive to Atlanta "offered skirmishers their best opportunity to shine." The consistent forward momentum of Sherman's columns through the pine woods of northwestern Georgia was entirely contingent upon the ability of dense "clouds" of skirmishers to screen the army's front and maintain the tactical initiative. Even when Rebels managed to blunt forward progress, "aggressive skirmishing . . . helped to shape the contour of operations," Hess argues, as Sherman's veterans habitually dug in and relied upon skirmishers to hold Rebel attention while turning movements unfolded on the flanks. The consistent success of US skirmishers to maintain this initiative enabled Union forces to exhaust and degrade the Rebel capacity to resist the inexorable advance toward Atlanta. "Federal skirmishers were seriously degrading the stamina and fighting effectiveness of troops on the Confederate battle line," Hess observes. As a direct result, many Secessionist commands gradually found themselves "too weakened to fight effectively."[9]

Few of Sherman's several corps performed as adeptly along the skirmish line as his original Fifteenth. If the Atlanta campaign was defined by its character as a "skirmisher's war," John Logan commanded what, by 1864, had evolved into a veritable skirmisher's corps. Each of its "skeleton regiments" had been molded by experience into a premier light infantry force. Moreover, Sherman's operational art and the tangled terrain of the region played to the greatest strengths of the command's tactical culture. "With years of experience behind them," Hess observed of Federal skirmishers during the campaign, the veteran riflemen utterly "dominated no-man's land."[10] In a similar vein, historian Andrew Haughton has observed how the relative willingness of Federal and Rebel forces in the Western Theater to be "flexible and innovative" in their tactics played a major role in determining victory and defeat on the battlefield. Whereas, by the spring and summer of 1864, the Fifteenth Corps conducted nearly all of its offensive operations arrayed in strong skirmisher "clouds," the Rebels they confronted still emphasized the use of massed battle lines bristling with bayonets in the assault. This intransigence is even more striking given their innovative embrace of dedicated sharpshooter detachments years prior to their creation in any US command. Thus, while the western Rebels cannot be accused of neglecting the employment of light infantry entirely, their own tactical culture played a major role in allowing Sherman's riflemen to gain the initiative at most every turn.[11]

To be sure, there were dramatic missteps. On two separate occasions during the campaign, the corps was once again forced to launch frontal assaults against entrenched Rebel positions. As at Missionary Ridge, Sherman and his lieutenants always showed considerable reluctance when ordering such maneuvers, but in both instances the assaults seemed all but unavoidable. Also, as upon earlier fields, uncooperative terrain dismantled the cohesion and coordination of massed formations. While during the first of these attacks, undertaken by the corps at the Battle of Resaca, skirmisher "clouds" screening the corps's main assault formations proved mostly capable of carrying thinly held Rebel trenches by themselves, this fortuitous success proved dangerously misleading.[12]

When again charged with launching a frontal attack against supposedly thinned Rebel lines at Kennesaw Mountain in late June, the corps paid a heavy price. Although screened by skirmisher "clouds," which managed to brush away outlying Rebel pickets, this time the veterans dispersed in open order proved insufficient to overcome the much more formidable works atop Pigeon Hill at the base of towering Kennesaw Mountain. Passage of the main body of three brigades over intractable terrain marked by every conceivable natural obstacle from creeks to forests to bogs dismantled the corps's cohesion prior to its arrival at the enemy abatis. "The underbrush through which we advanced was so thick that it was impossible to preserve a line," Brig. Gen. Lightburn later observed with frustration. "The consequence was the entire line was broken . . . which was impossible to reform."[13] One Hoosier in his brigade described the tangled thickets as "indescribable confusion," adding that "it was difficult to tell our position, or see from what quarter danger threatened us." Attacking adjacent to Lightburn's brigade was Giles Smith, returned from convalescing after his Chattanooga wounds. "The ground advanced over proved to be worse than anticipated," he later reported. The "steep and rugged [hillside], covered with brush and felled trees, ledges of rock, and an abatis ingeniously and firmly constructed . . . render[ed] the advance in the line of battle entirely impracticable." Just as so many times before, the rugged terrain eradicated the coordination of the attack, again giving most participants the perception of being entirely unsupported. "There could be no concert of action and little leadership," one Illinoisan later lamented. "Nothing we had surmounted at Vicksburg equaled it in natural difficulties."[14]

After suffering 571 men killed or wounded, the Fifteenth Corps fell back from its final repulse of the war. Sherman would never make the same mistake again. Still, his private reaction to the brutal rebuff at Kennesaw proved that, while he had a firm grasp of the command's lingering incapacity for frontal assaults, he still retained an incomplete understanding as to why. "Had the assault been made with one-fourth more vigor," it would have succeeded, he later asserted, echoing the same conclusions he had arrived at in the aftermath of Chickasaw Bayou and Arkansas Post. The extensive bloodletting seemed "small, compared to some of those (battle[s] in the) East," he wrote to General George Thomas (who was himself aghast at the casualties). The result at Kennesaw "should not in the least discourage us" from future frontal assault, he wrote, citing his own imperfect remembrance of Arkansas Post as supposed evidence of their potential success.[15]

The men needed to become hardened to loss, as he had been, he explained to his wife. "I begin to regard the death & mangling of a couple thousand men as a small affair, a kind of morning dash," he casually noted.[16] Of course he knew that this most recent repulse had seemed anything but "a kind of morning dash," and had indeed been exceedingly discouraging to those who had suffered through it firsthand. "I was forced to make the effort, and it should have succeeded, but the officers & men have been so used to my avoiding excessive danger and forcing back the enemy by strategy that they hate to assault," he explained in a letter home. Despite the exceptional experience of the Fifteenth Corps at Resaca, it appeared that Logan, like Sherman, still had "no troops which can be made to assault," even if, as Cump pronounced, "to assault is sometimes necessary, for its effect on the Enemy." Indeed, Sherman was correct in his perception of the corps's evolved tactical culture having been partly sustained by his recent efforts to "avoid excessive danger and force back the enemy by strategy," but in his frustration Cump misunderstood the true causes of his perpetual tactical failures in the attack. Even so, from Kennesaw onward, Sherman would do everything in his power to avoid direct assaults on fortified Rebel positions if at all possible.[17] Despite his bold pronouncements that Kennesaw ought not to have discouraged him or the army from attempting such attacks again, in the end it did just that.

In between the two bloody assaults at Resaca and Kennesaw, another even more nightmarish engagement in the dense woods outside Dallas, Georgia, marked the most chaotic contest of the campaign. After launching one of its characteristic "whiplash" turning movements, McPherson's "skeleton" army stumbled into nearly two weeks of an intensely traumatic siege-like gridlock with entrenched and desperate Rebels less than thirty miles from Atlanta. Fortunately for Logan's veterans, their experience with field fortifications and skirmishing paid off in the "Hell Hole" despite several close run-ins with massed Rebel assaults through the thickets.[18]

Despite the immense hardship and bloodletting of the first three months of operations, the true crucible of the corps's participation in the campaign came at the very eastern gates of Atlanta on July 22. After approaching the apparently abandoned outlying works of the city from the east, the men had not yet enjoyed an opportunity to establish respectable defensive works like those at Dallas before an entire Rebel corps fell upon two of Logan's most advanced brigades. Although the veterans of Morgan Smith's Second Division, caught in the open, did their best to repulse the sudden onslaught, their complete inexperience with defending a position outside the protection of a trench, along with an unfinished railroad cut on the division's flank, combined to catalyze total disaster. As wildly yipping South Carolinians and Alabamians poured from the railroad cut onto the Federal flank, much of Smith's veteran division routed in pandemonium to the rear. Only the combination of the urgent support of First Division's massed artillery to the north—"accurate in the extreme," according to one Rebel officer—a frantic counterattack led by Logan in person, and bungled Secessionist orders ultimately saved the corps from complete destruction. While ultimately a victory for US arms, the close call deeply impressed upon the survivors of Logan's battered corps the importance of fieldworks and carefully protected flanks when defending against a charging foe.[19]

Both of these tactical lessons were on clear display during the final two major engagements of the campaign. Slung westward around Atlanta by Sherman in yet another "whiplash" maneuver designed to cut the city's final remaining rail lifelines, the Fifteenth Corps led the Army of the Tennessee. Diligently entrenching at each and every nightly halt, the corps's still-traumatized veterans refused to be caught unprepared again. On July 28, less than a week after their ignominious rout, these tactics paid off. Sensing Sherman's bid to isolate the Rebel bastion, General John Bell Hood launched a counterstroke aimed at destroying the Army of the Tennessee west of the city near Ezra Church. Arrayed in massed lines of battle, several successive waves of Secessionist infantry hurled themselves at Logan's riflemen, ensconced snugly behind log breastworks and church pews packed with bulging knapsacks. As at Dallas, the veterans fired volley after volley into the Rebels at near point-blank range, utterly destroying their formations. Sherman, too, had learned his lesson. With the tables now finally turned, and his own beloved original corps now unleashing the same punishment it had so often painfully received, Cump knew precisely what was on the menu. "Just what I wanted, just what I wanted," he shouted reflexively aloud to staffers: "Invite them to attack, it will save us trouble, save us trouble, they'll only beat their brains out, beat their brains out!" Indeed, the Rebels did just that, suffering more than 3,000 casualties compared to 562 (50 killed) across the entire Fifteenth Corps. One in every 3 Rebels making the attack had been cut down in a battle that lasted only two hours. The morale of the Atlanta garrison having been all but completely destroyed by the losses of July 22 and 28, Hood's attempt to assail Logan's corps once again at Jonesboro on August 31 came with even less vigor. Once again suffering mightily in sequential uncoordinated frontal assaults, the Secessionist defense of Atlanta was decisively crushed. On September 1, the Rebels abandoned the city and took with them much of any hope for the so-called Confederacy's bid for independence.[20]

"THE DAWN OF THE TACTICS OF THE PRESENT DAY"

The campaign for Atlanta marked the apotheosis of the Fifteenth Corps's combat effectiveness on the battlefield. Despite occasional misadventure, the corps performed well due to the calibration of its tactical culture with the objectives it was called upon to pursue. Just as at Chattanooga, when the corps was required to conduct operations for which its operational heritage had prepared it, its veteran regiments performed admirably. On the other hand, when required to launch frontal assaults across intractable terrain, its signature weaknesses were on vivid display. While Logan and his "veteran volunteers" were proud of their accomplishments for the rest of their lives, soldier scholars had much to learn from the experience of the Fifteenth Corps during the campaign as it related to the future of infantry warfare.

More than any other factor, the particular terrain upon which the Fifteenth Corps had confronted its enemies during its early campaigns shaped the command's tactical culture. Both its penchant for open-order skirmishing and its perpetual struggles with the coordination of frontal assaults were direct by-products of its traumatic experiences fighting Rebels over the broken ground and dense woods of Mississippi, Arkansas, and Tennessee. Reflecting upon his own "Military Lessons of the War" within his 1875 memoirs, Sherman drew upon his experience of commanding the corps:

Very few of the battles in which I have participated were fought as described in European text-books, viz., in great masses, in perfect order, maneuvering by corps, divisions, and brigades. We were generally in a wooded country, and, though our lines were deployed according to tactics, the men generally fought in strong skirmish-lines, taking advantage of the shape of ground, and of every cover. We were generally the assailants, and in wooded and broken countries the "defensive" had a positive advantage over us, for they were always ready, had cover, and always knew the ground to their immediate front; whereas we, their assailants, had to grope our way over unknown ground, and generally found a cleared field or prepared entanglements that held us for a time under a close and withering fire.[21]

This passage has come under a close and withering fire itself by historian Earl Hess. Europe's battlefields were also "cluttered with obstacles," he argues, and Sherman "generalized far too recklessly" about Civil War tactics based almost exclusively upon his army's experiences fighting for Atlanta.[22] These criticisms ignore the fact that Sherman's observations of "the battles in which I have participated" were limited to his own "personal angle of vision," just as the tactical culture of the Fifteenth Corps had likewise been forged by the content of its own specific experiences. Never having witnessed the titanic "open field fights" of Antietam or Gettysburg in the East, or even their rare counterparts in the West, the entire corpus of combat experience Cump and his corps developed over the course of the war neatly matched his description. Much the same could have been said of Grant. "Our old systems of tactics were translations from the French, and altogether not adapted to territory such as that in which the greater part of the rebellion was fought," he told a *New York Times* reporter in 1881. "In wooded country with narrow roads, we might as well have had no tactics at all, so far as the old system served us. Indeed, it was not infrequently the case that we were obliged to entirely abandon the system and depend upon plain common sense," he added.[23] Of course, there were plenty of cleared fields in Mississippi, Tennessee, and Georgia, but the Fifteenth Corps, like both Grant and Sherman, rarely if ever encountered the Rebel enemy upon such ground. Instead, combat came primarily within "wooded and broken countries," and the corps's tactical culture represented a powerful expression of that fact.

Even by 1870, the first postwar census to tabulate cleared versus wooded acres of land in the United States, the difference between eastern and western areas of operations remained stark. In Virginia, Maryland, and Pennsylvania, where the majority of the major battles of the Eastern Theater took place, only 45 percent of the land was still covered in forest. Within the eight counties of northern Virginia that experienced the most bloodshed during the conflict, that number dropped to 38 percent. By contrast, in Missouri, Arkansas, Mississippi, and Tennessee, where the Fifteenth Corps had fought its battles, 65 percent of the ground in these much younger states remained densely wooded as late as 1870. In stark contrast, less than a quarter of the acres of Adams County, Pennsylvania, where the Army of the Potomac fought its most climactic engagement at Gettysburg, were still forested at the time of the battle. While the nightmarish bloodletting of the James Peninsula and the Wilderness obviously represented major and important exceptions to the rule, western battlefields were on average far more heavily forested and cluttered with vegetation than were their eastern counterparts.[24]

The terrain of American battlefields had long proven far more vexing than those in Europe, and European armies had been forced to adapt their tactics to this environmental reality since the era of initial colonization. Much of prevailing eighteenth- and early nineteenth-century Western tactical art having been first devised during the Enlightenment era of "limited war" in Europe, theorists assumed that most major clashes between armies would take place upon mostly open ground. Even by the early nineteenth century, although much of Europe remained blanketed with dense woodlands, most of the fields upon which Napoleon I fought his great battles were distinguished by "relatively open, gentle countryside where both armies could manoeuvre with ease."[25] The contrasting lack of such expanses of cleared terrain in the Americas forced Europeans to adapt their tactics accordingly. For the most part, they did so with remarkable effectiveness, few quite so adeptly as the British.

At least as early as the Seven Years' War, the British Army had adapted to the exigencies of congested American terrain by leaning heavily on colonial militia with their especial skill in light infantry combat when fighting upon heavily wooded battlefields. Habitually extending the distance between the files of their battle lines, the Crown's infantry learned from experience that "no maneuvers may ever be carried out in serried ranks in these districts that are so terribly wooded."[26] Matthew Spring has recently shown that British infantry during the American Revolutionary War once again learned quickly from experience to emphasize open-order skirmishing and a consistent pursuit of Rebel flanks in order to avoid frontal attacks across cluttered ground against an often entrenched enemy. Many conservative British tacticians worried about this trend, arguing that skirmishers had, in America, "instead of being considered an accessory to the battalion . . . become the principal feature of our army."[27] Although the Continental Army eventually achieved victory for reasons that extended well beyond infantry tactics, the natural evolution of British infantry deployments during the conflict was powerful testament to the impact American geography could have in shaping tactical culture.[28]

While both European and American officers across the late eighteenth and early nineteenth centuries consistently sought to master maneuvers "as described in European text-books, viz., in great masses, in perfect order," the geography of the United States routinely refused to comply.[29] The unforgiving terrain of American battlefields dismantled the cohesion of "touch of the elbow" infantry formations learned and practiced on small manicured parade fields.[30] While the much smaller commands of earlier conflicts could often conceivably wedge themselves into the meager acreage cleared for planting on American farms, as the sheer size of formations and armies ballooned exponentially during the Civil War, the same small plots could never hope to play host to even a small portion of battles that involved tens of thousands of men. In the still mostly uncleared portions of Arkansas and Mississippi, where the Fifteenth Corps faced its baptism by fire, the terrain itself spurred what amounted to an American tactical renaissance in infantry warfare as armies of volunteers trained on the drill field to operate in massed formations learned the same lessons their European counterparts had perennially derived from experience before.

Contemporary military professionals had long anticipated that such a renaissance was coming, though they had incorrectly judged it a "revolution," and had fundamentally misjudged its cause. They had harbored grave concerns about the mass arrival of the rifle musket onto modern battlefields for decades prior to the Civil War. While there remained much heated and contentious debate as to what impact the weapon's increased range and accuracy would have on infantry tactics, most agreed that infantrymen armed with rifles would open engagements at distances far greater than those common to the predominately smoothbore Napoleonic era. Formations massed in "serried ranks" assaulting with bayonets across open ground would be butchered by rifle fire long before they could strike with cold steel. Only by either speeding up the pace of forward movement or loosening formations could the effects of prolonged exposure to fire be avoided. For this reason, theorists prophesied, future battlefields would necessitate a heavier reliance upon open-order formations and skirmishing tactics. Even so, others argued that the complicated process of accurate long-range firing would ultimately prove beyond the comprehension for the dullards who often filled the ranks of European armies. These critics argued that engagements would continue to unfold at the same distance they had for the last several centuries. Massed bayonet charges following point-blank offensive volleys would continue to define the traditional attack, and relatively little adaptation would be required.

The experience of the American Civil War indirectly proved both parties correct. As episodes like Blair's charge at Chickasaw Bayou made clear, on occasion defenders did pepper onrushing attackers with rifle fire from distances nearing the maximum range of their weapons. This attritional tactic eroded the cohesion of an assaulting force long before its arrival at the abatis, just as many theorists had argued it would. At the same time, far more frequently defenders still relied upon massed "shock volleys" at smoothbore range. Historians continue to debate the range at which the "average" engagements (if such a thing existed) unfolded, but as the corps rarely encountered long-range fire on the assault, the fact that the Rebels it confronted were frequently armed with rifles cannot itself explain the corps's learned tendency to rely upon open-order skirmishing in battle.[31]

Although antebellum writers had emphasized the capacity of the rifle to revolutionize defensive infantry tactics, the experience of the Fifteenth Corps suggests the weapon had a far more significant impact on offensive maneuvers, most especially in cluttered terrain against an enemy hidden behind field fortifications. If the landscape itself motivated the first vestiges of what historians have deemed an "open-order revolution" during the Civil War in the Western Theater, the arrival of the rifled musket played a powerful role in enabling it. While the difference of accuracy between smoothbore and rifled muskets at close range when firing at a massed target in the open was negligible, when engaging an enemy behind cover or hidden in the depths of a rifle pit, exposing only his face and forearm below a head log, the increased accuracy of a rifle could make all the difference. When firing close-range massed volleys at an infantry line arrayed in "serried ranks" before driving home a bayonet charge, the performance disparity between smoothbore and rifled muskets mattered little. When attempting to strike fleeting and mostly shrouded targets from the protection of a forward trench amid a prolonged siege or sniping the gunners of an artillery battery from hundreds of yards away, the rifle was irreplaceable. Indeed, the impressive ranges at which several members of the corps reported engaging Rebel targets with their rifles during the Vicksburg siege suggests that, in the capable hands of experienced veterans, the rifle's full capabilities could be and often were realized on Civil War battlefields. Moreover, as the men of the Fifteenth Corps almost never fired massed volleys while on the offensive, their particular experience taught them little about the rifle's relative utility in such circumstances. Instead, when ordered to attack an entrenched enemy that routinely proved resistant to frontal assault but still vulnerable to a skilled rifleman's ball, the rifle's increased range and accuracy paired with a veteran's skill, honed over months of practice, frequently proved the ideal tools for the task.[32]

The offensive advantages organic to such tools were squandered when employed within massed formations. In order to take full advantage of the rifle's capabilities, individual shooters needed cover, opportunities to take careful aim, considerable experience behind the sights, and the independence to improve their positions. Just as Sherman's loose leash would soon allow his army's "veteran character" to flourish during the forthcoming raids through Georgia and the Carolinas, only by leveraging individual freedom and hard-won marksmanship skill on the skirmish line could Sherman's veteran skirmishers achieve, secure, and maintain the critical tactical initiative that facilitated his "indirect" way of war.[33] While the broken and rugged Mississippi, Tennessee, and Georgia terrain regularly destroyed the cohesive mass and critical coordination of their frontal assaults against Rebel works, by 1864 most of the men and officers of the Fifteenth Corps had determined that such assaults were futile anyway. By instead learning to use the same cluttered Southern terrain, their learned tactical skills as skirmishers, and their modern rifled weaponry to maximum advantage, the volunteer regiments of the corps had naturally evolved into expert skirmishers who enabled Sherman's drive toward Atlanta.

While military professionals had long recognized the tactical utility of skirmishers in infantry combat, few anticipated that they would ever wholly supplant massed lines on the battlefield. As historian Rory Muir observes, Napoleonic contingents of riflemen and light infantry were meant to play an exclusively "negative role" in combat, screening and protecting massed main bodies while "preparing the way for the decisive attack" with the bayonet.[34] In his *Elementary Treatise on Advanced Guard, Outposts, and Detachment Service of Troops* (1847), widely read by officers on both sides before, during, and after the Civil War, Dennis Hart Mahan identified two basic forms of infantry: light and line. The two were meant to habitually support one another in the attack. Light infantry led as skirmishers, opened engagements, and kept the enemy suppressed with fire while massed line infantry maneuvered for advantage. Once in striking position, the line would launch its bayonet assault, covered on the flanks by the fire of the skirmishers.[35] Only if the foe proved particularly meager would light infantry ever constitute the main effort.[36]

On the defense, both light and line infantry combined their firepower to repel enemy assaults with volleys of fire before launching a counter-charge when the exhausted attacker "shows, by the wavering or confusion of his line, a want of confidence."[37] While Mahan acknowledged that infantrymen only capable of operating exclusively as either line or light would prove "inconvenient, at the least," he still admitted that "perfection is more easily reached by confining the individual to one branch of his art, than by requiring him to make himself conversant with the whole."[38] Sherman and his subordinates learned this lesson from experience as their corps, drilled to act as both line and light infantry, organically transformed into a corps of almost exclusively the latter.

Their transformation probably would have come as little surprise to Mahan, given the corps's particular experiences while under arms. After all, the success of line infantry, he explained, "depend[ed] upon the action of the mass, *ensemble* [coordination], coolness, and determination."[39] Packed elbow-to-elbow in line, they fired by volley, maneuvered in column, and habitually "attack[ed] with the bayonet."[40] The *"ensemble,"* or coordination of an attacking line, was the key to its success. As the corps had painfully learned on many occasions, attacks that fell upon works in piecemeal fashion never had any hope of decision. Each assault column needed to arrive simultaneously all along the enemy line in order to effectively overwhelm defenders. Routinely incapable of effecting such cohesive assaults due to difficult terrain, its successive failures eroded the confidence of its regiments whenever ordered to assault. That very lack of confidence—Mahan's "coolness, and determination"—when added to the lack of any concerted attempt by their officers to remedy the command's coordinative failings, sustained the corps's signature tactical disability throughout the war.

On the other hand, light infantry, Mahan instructed, fighting habitually in "the dispersed order," relied upon effective small arms fire for success in its much more limited offensive role. Each skirmisher, though supported by others to his right and left, regularly found himself "thrown upon his own resources, being obliged to take cover where he can most conveniently find it." To become a master of his trade, he needed to "be a good marksman, cool, deliberate, and circumspect."[41] The Fifteenth Corps enjoyed plentiful opportunities to develop these skills throughout the war. Continually required to fragment into small groups, the men and officers were more than comfortable operating independently without direct oversight. Cluttered terrain had broken their massed lines into skirmisher "clouds," even when officers did everything in their power to prevent it. The very ground and vegetation of the lower Mississippi Valley had thrust small units and individual soldiers upon their "own resources." Pairing the natural fruits of these experiences with the opportunities the corps enjoyed to master the art of rifle and artillery marksmanship during the Vicksburg and Jackson sieges, along with the veteran's "cool, deliberate, and circumspect" approach to combat, Sherman's command matured into a premiere skirmisher's corps. That it did, however, also meant that its tactical capabilities were markedly limited, forcing its commanders either to adapt their operational art accordingly or to neglect doing so at great peril.

By the final year of the war, the Fifteenth Corps could reliably be expected to march great distances at impressive speed, sustain itself entirely off the countryside, denude a region of valuable foodstuffs, and swiftly destroy Rebel railroads and strategic infrastructure. In combat, it could reliably gain and maintain fire supremacy and the tactical initiative on the skirmish line. It could also rapidly construct "hasty" field fortifications from which it could repel even the most savage of Rebel assaults with great confidence. On the other hand, nothing in its operational heritage suggested that it could or should have been reliably expected to carry enemy positions at the point of the bayonet by frontal assault. Nor could it dependably stand up against an enemy in the open without the benefit of protective works. To be sure, these two capabilities represented crucial tactical skills, but nevertheless had proven time and again to be irrepressible handicaps for the Fifteenth Corps. Successful prosecution of the corps's assigned objectives was in no small part contingent upon the relative calibration of assignments with the manner in which the command had learned from specific past experiences to operate—its organically evolved tactical culture. Sherman commanded the corps during the formational period of his lengthy career as a tactician and strategist, and so his own operational art during the latter years of the conflict as an army group commander showed the indelible impress of the Fifteenth Corps's tactical culture. Although historians have long lauded Cump's mastery of the "indirect approach" during the latter years of the war, avoiding battle with Rebel forces when threatening enemy logistical means would suffice, his own personal evolution into a practitioner of maneuver warfare came initially at a great cost in blood and suffering paid by his corps. Sherman's place in the annals of America's "great captains" was only earned due to his intellectual malleability and a capacity to learn from experience what he could realistically expect his corps (and later army) to achieve given its specific past experiences. While he always retained an incomplete understanding of why the command chronically suffered from an inability to carry works from the front, he did ultimately accept it, and aside from a particularly bloody miscalculation at Kennesaw Mountain in the summer of 1864, acted accordingly.

The same perfect marriage between the Fifteenth Corps's tactical culture and the specific operational tasks it was called upon to perform during the Atlanta, Savannah, and Carolinas campaigns of the conflict's final years was not initially enjoyed by those corps serving within the eastern Army of the Potomac during the final year of the war. The dense thickets, Rebel entrenchments, and relentless tempo of the Overland Campaign to capture Richmond introduced most Eastern Theater veterans for the first time to a much enlarged and prolonged version of the Fifteenth Corps's earlier 1862 experiences fighting at close quarters in the tangled Mississippi bayous. Even so, by the end of the war most units within even the Army of the Potomac had cultivated a tactical culture remarkably similar to that which the Fifteenth Corps had years prior.[42]

Attempting to retrospectively survey the tactical significance of the Army's wartime experience during the fall of 1865, military critic John Watts De Peyster spoke with an "officer of experience" who had served in the Army of the Potomac. While most of the Eastern Army, as evidenced by the behavior of Creighton's brigade at Ringgold Gap, maintained a tactical culture which emphasized the efficacy of massed bayonet assaults, often without even a protective screen of skirmishers, even the Potomac men had started to evolve into expert light infantry by the end of the war. As during the Fifteenth Corps's experience in the West, this evolution was likely more the result of the terrain confronted by the army during the bloody Overland Campaign than it was the effect of modern weaponry. "In actual conflict, unless our lines formed behind a barricade or protective work of some kind," the officer told De Peyster, "they very soon resembled, as to relative formation, a 'Virginia rail-fence,' or a skirmish-line where squads of fours, distinct and irregularly placed, kept up relatively the direction or emplacement of a line." Reflecting later upon this statement, and others similar in tone, De Peyster concluded that the veteran "soldiers from experience" in both Western and Eastern theaters of the Civil War, though at different rates, had stumbled upon an important truth of modern infantry combat.[43]

The rigid linear doctrine of Napoleon I, still enshrined in the Army's drill manuals, needed to go and fast. Such rigid drill seemed "the very reason why it took four years to make our soldiers what they should have been at the outset," he complained. "Experience alone taught them that the success of battles depends more on intelligent individual action properly combined, than the hurling of large masses forward to slaughter." Moreover, given the extreme challenges confronting the command, control, and coordination of attacks in difficult terrain, such "hurling of large masses" was almost always ill-fated. Fortunately, by virtue of experience, most "became accustomed to act for themselves, when the actual circumstances of battle or duty found them alone and distant from support." Indeed, "the very word veteran," he emphasized, "actually expresses that the soldier has become more or less perfectly self-reliant."[44]

De Peyster remained convinced that the experience of the war proved that the "conversion of the customary main 'line of battle,' which is a continuous line of mutually dependent combatants, into a vast dislocated skirmish line of independent marksmen, should be a prominent feature in the infantry tactics of the future."[45] If rugged terrain and modern weaponry were to disperse massed lines anyway, it was best to build a doctrine that accepted this reality as fait accompli. His visionary conclusion was borne not of the somber hindsight of battalions maneuvering with antiquated tactics while being cut down in windrows by an enemy at long range, as antebellum theorists had prophesied, but rather a logical conclusion drawn from observation of what veteran "soldiers from experience" had already fashioned into their own informal tactical doctrine by the end of the war. It was now up to the Army to catch up to innovations in the ranks, just as Sherman had. After several decades of careful study, tactical theorist Colonel Arthur Lockwood Wagner determined, like De Peyster before him, that the war had represented a veritable "turning-point of tactics, there being scarcely a feature of the tactics of the present day that did not have its germ, its prototype, or its development" during the conflict. The first of these developments, infantry "attacks by rushes," Wagner credited to Morgan L. Smith. First employed by his Zouaves at Fort Donelson, later by all of Second Division at Arkansas Post and Vicksburg, and eventually by the entire Fifteenth Corps, the Zouave rush was deemed by Wagner a "brilliant movement . . . far in advance of the tactics then generally in use."[46]

Since at least the mid-eighteenth century, skirmishers had been utilized "merely to feel and develop the enemy," but the lessons of the Civil War, most especially in the West, made clear how light infantry had become "the most important element in modern tactics," Wagner observed.[47] He credited the "wooded country which formed the theater of so many of the principal campaigns" much more than rifled weaponry for the habitual reliance on skirmishers "to a degree before unknown" in western warfare. He took especial notice of Sherman's command in particular for having "habitually fought in strong skirmish lines, the men taking advantage of every feature of the ground."[48] By 1864, the army's massed lines had become primarily reserves of light infantry "ready to reinforce the skirmishers." This dramatic change marked "the dawn of the tactics of the present day," he predicted.[49] In the future, as within the Fifteenth Corps, the effective employment of skirmishers would remain "the prime consideration in tactics."[50]

In 1891 the US Army finally caught up with these tactical lessons. New infantry regulations included nearly every aspect of the informal tactical doctrine the "soldiers from experience" of the Fifteenth Corps had organically developed during the war. They also, for the first time in Army history, instructed readers in more than just linear maneuver, providing guidance to commanders at every level on how to actually conduct combat operations. As Upton had written to Sherman in 1880, drill manuals up to that point "have been simply a collection of rules for passing from one formation to another. How to fight has been left to actual experience in war." Now, they would offer explicit guidance on "how to fight."[51]

Dispersed "extended order" lines were to thenceforth be the primary mode by which US infantry deployed in combat. Instead of tightly packed lines of battle, eight-man squads commanded by noncommissioned officers became the primary units of maneuver under fire, much as had become the case for the Fifteenth Corps's "skeleton regiments" as early as 1863. Instead of manicured fields, drills were to be conducted "on varied ground, making use of the accidents of the surface for cover," and the regulations included an entire page of suggestions for how riflemen should use various forms of cover. When cover was not availing, firing from the kneeling and prone positions were emphasized in training, just as they had been for Smith's Zouaves. Also like the Zouaves, recruits were trained to practice "advancing from cover to cover" against their comrades, as the rest of their squad counted the number of times they caught a glimpse long enough to take aim. Soldiers were advised to "stoop and even creep or crawl" when necessary, just as the riflemen of the Fifteenth Corps had done in every engagement since Chickasaw Bayou. Maintaining proper alignment in tight formations was all but abandoned, and "close order" marching relegated exclusively to what officers called "maneuver tactics," meant to carry a command into battle, wherein loose-order "fighting tactics" were employed once a unit was actually engaged.[52] When advancing across open ground, squads were to cross the dangerous expanse "by rushes of about thirty yards," going prone in between, "and raising the head in order to see the enemy," just as Second Division had done since Corinth. By no means were these rushes to exceed fifty yards, "else the skirmishers will be winded and unable to aim accurately," as Steele's division had learned the hard way in their charge at "the Post." Finally, the doctrine included explicit instructions for how to coordinate suppressive fire elements detached from a battalion with a charging main body by bugle—representing the Army's first substantive attempt at authentic "fire and maneuver" tactics.[53]

As the men and officers of the Fifteenth Corps knew well, this light infantry–centric tactical doctrine came with both advantages and disadvantages that the Army would encounter on future fields. While relying on dispersed skirmishers to carry the main effort of an attack reduced the dangers posed by enemy fire, such open-order lines were unlikely to overcome a well-entrenched foe by themselves. Prior to the invention of indirect artillery and aerial bombardment to support the advance of open-order infantry, overcoming a dug-in enemy fighting from behind an abatis still required either outflanking their position or overwhelming them at the point of massed bayonets. While dispersed riflemen could suppress entrenched defenders to an extent that made it dangerous for them to reply in kind, the unavoidable break in their fire requisite for the safe passage of a charging friendly line across the front proved ample time for defenders to reply with a brutal shock volley. The Fifteenth Corps had learned this the hard way during both Vicksburg assaults. Once survivors were forced to ground, they could begin to apply their own suppressive fire to keep enemy heads down, but at the expense of any and all additional forward momentum.

Although every man in the corps was made to understand the concept of what would eventually be termed "alternating bounds"—during which one soldier in a pair fired to cover the advance of another—pairing suppressive fire with maneuver at the regimental or brigade levels proved mostly beyond the capabilities of even the most veteran commands during the Civil War. Indeed, even coordinating the simultaneous advance of adjacent formations across broad fronts of challenging terrain consistently proved impossible. The problem of cohesively "crossing the deadly ground" would continue to vex the Army until the era of indirect artillery support, radio communications, and the machine gun, but was always far more a problem of coordination than of weapons technology.[54] Once the firepower of an entire Civil War regiment could be replaced by a single machine gun crew, the potential for combining suppressive fire with an open-order advance of light infantry increased dramatically. Even so, as late as 1918, many of the old guard still bemoaned failures of unsupported frontal assaults they attributed to the very same crippling lack of spirit and confidence among the attackers that Sherman had decades prior. Not until the Second World War would the manifold advantages of the "indirect approach," learned by experience in the ranks of the Fifteenth Corps, finally become standard fare among American tacticians. Armed with the myriad mobility advantages provided by the internal combustion engine and aerial transport, by the mid-twentieth century most military professionals agreed that, if the "deadly ground" did not absolutely have to be crossed in order to defeat an enemy, unless ample supporting firepower was available, it was best to avoid it altogether.[55]

"THE DIABOLICAL 15TH"

The affinity of the Fifteenth Corps for "avoiding excessive danger and forcing back the enemy by strategy" arose from its traumatic experiences on the confusing battlefields of the lower Mississippi Valley. This tactical predisposition played a powerful and erstwhile overlooked role in seeding the ground for their embrace of "hard war" and the government's strategic turn toward a more direct assault on the South's "peculiar institution." Scholars continue to highlight the ways in which military reversals, most especially that suffered by the Army of the Potomac during the 1862 Peninsula Campaign, provided inspiration for the Lincoln administration's belated decision to target Southern slavery directly. Apparently incapable of decisively besting Rebels on the battlefield, the formerly conservative Lincoln government, goaded on by countless acts of self-emancipation by slaves themselves, added aggressive exploitation of the Rebellion's real center of gravity to its arsenal of strategic methods. This revolutionary policy shift occurred at almost the exact moment of the Fifteenth Corps's organization: the winter of 1862–63.[56]

Much ink has been spilled in debating precisely when, why, and to what extent the US military effort to put down the rebellion transformed from a conciliatory "kid glove" approach to a "hard hand" of "war in earnest" bent on destroying slavery as a means by which to crush the rebellion. The definitive account of this evolution remains Mark Grimsley's *The Hard Hand of War* (1995). Arguing that a "series of Union military reversals convinced many Northerners to abandon conciliation," Grimsley asserts that the US government gradually and reluctantly embraced "actions against Southern civilians and property made expressly in order to demoralize Southern civilians and ruin the Confederate economy" by the second winter of the war. At the heart of this transformation was not so much rational calculation by the Lincoln administration, but rather "tens of thousands of Union soldiers—toughened by war, hungry for creature comforts, and often angry at the civilians in their midst" who embraced "hard war" because they "understood the logic" of the indirect strategy. First emerging in the logistically strained and sparsely inhabited Western Theater, Federal tactics of foraging liberally off the country naturally evolved over time into the explicit targeting of Southern economic infrastructure more broadly, including most importantly the liberation of millions of slaves. Grimsley argues that this transformation was due in no small part to the perpetual inability of Federal commanders to control hungry, chronically undersupplied, and ill-disciplined volunteers who consistently showed an almost insatiable urge for the theft and destruction of private property, whether loyal or "Secesh."

Indeed, it seems "quite likely that the zest with which soldiers embraced foraging pulled the generals along farther than they might otherwise have gone," Grimsley asserts.[57]

While Grimsley has most likely accurately identified the origins of "hard war" policies as laying within the enlisted volunteer ranks of the Union Army, his insightful assessment missed an opportunity to address the vital connections between the apparent penchant of Western Theater US volunteers for "hard war" and the tactical imperatives of mid-nineteenth-century infantry warfare within the "wooded and broken countries" of the "Old Southwest." Highlighting these connections allows historians to bridge the operational history of the war with the historiography of its broader political contours. Moreover, the experience of the Fifteenth Corps provides a vivid example of these very connections. Just as the frustrating and somber experience of military reversal after the Peninsula campaign convinced many Northern civilians, those in the ranks of McClellan's Army of the Potomac, and the Lincoln administration that only "war in earnest" stood a realistic chance at defeating the so-called Southern Confederacy, the near contemporaneous traumatic experience of successive and brutal repulse at the hands of entrenched Rebels protected by apparently impassable terrain convinced the men and officers of the Fifteenth Corps that only an alternative strategy of defeating the Rebellion could ever succeed.

While most remained reluctant emancipators throughout the war due to their prevailing anti-Black attitudes and fundamentally conservative politics, the westerners of Sherman's corps evolved into "practical liberators" and hard warriors in large part because of their traumatic experiences of tactical failure and rebuff on western battlefields. When such failures were paired with the striking and comparatively bloodless successes of the Deer Creek and Steele's Bayou raids, those in the ranks emerged from their experiences convinced that "we are crushing the rebellion and will continue to crush it though we be repulsed from every stronghold for months to come." While what happened on the battlefield would always of course remain important to the men of the corps, their hard-won understanding of the inherent limitations of mid-nineteenth-century land warfare in the heavily wooded American South spurred their embrace of "war in earnest" against Southern slavery far more powerfully than any pyromania or wartime transformation of moral convictions.[58]

While the long and bloody "skirmisher's war" for Atlanta represented the culmination of the Fifteenth Corps's tactical culture on the battlefield, its original commander's legendary raiding campaigns through Georgia and the Carolinas during the final months of the conflict proved likewise perfectly calibrated for the command's strengths. Once again, this was no coincidence. Sherman had been forged as a strategist in the very same fires that produced his original Fifteenth Corps's tactical culture, and thus by the fall of 1864 the two shared an understanding of how the war ought to be prosecuted and won. Although Southern civilians like those of Columbia, South Carolina, bemoaned the "diabolical 15th" as it wrecked the so-called Confederacy's capacity for self-sustainment, just as it had done in the Deer Creek Valley; in Jackson, Mississippi; and across a wide swath of Georgia only months before, the corps was in reality not composed of demons. Instead, it was made up of men who, as Sherman would later assert, would throughout the rest of their lives prove "first rate men—farmers and mechanics, and men who are to-day as good citizens as we have in our country, but who went to war in earnest." There was nothing naturally malevolent about their character. They had been forged into expert skirmishers, hard warriors, and "practical liberators" in the very same manner they had transformed from citizen-soldier western recruits into "Veteran Volunteers." They were, after all, only "soldiers from experience."

NOTES

INTRODUCTION

1. Caudill and Ashdown, *Sherman's March in Myth and Memory*.
2. US, *Who Burnt Columbia?* 82; Miers, ed., *When the World Ended*, 43.
3. US, *Who Burnt Columbia?* 82–83.
4. Sherman [WTS], *Memoirs*, 879.
5. WTS to Halleck, Dec. 24, 1864, Simpson and Berlin, eds., *Sherman's Civil War* [*SCW*], 776.
6. WTS to John Sherman, Dec. 14, 1862, *SCW*, 345.
7. In fact, the US Army did not adopt a corps-based organization of its field armies until the spring of 1862. Kreiser, *Defeating Lee*, 4–7. Army corps during the American Civil War have enjoyed increased historiographical attention in recent years. See Wipperman, *All for the Union*; Rafuse, ed., *Corps Commanders in Blue*.
8. Glatthaar, *March to the Sea*, xi–xii.
9. Glatthaar, *March to the Sea*, 15.
10. Glatthaar, *March to the Sea*, 28.
11. Glatthaar, *March to the Sea*, 30, 32.
12. Glatthaar, *March to the Sea*, 38.
13. Glatthaar, *March to the Sea*, 157–58.
14. Glatthaar, *March to the Sea*, 157.
15. To be sure, neither are human beings necessarily expert in consistently deriving objectively accurate lessons from experience. March, *The Ambiguities of Experience*.
16. Jamieson, *Crossing the Deadly Ground*, 93, 108.
17. Griffith, *Battle Tactics of the Civil War*, 51.
18. US Army, *Infantry Drill Regulations*, 6.
19. Schein, *Organizational Culture*, 197–218.
20. This strategically offensive use of tactically defensive field fortifications is well elaborated upon in Hess, *Fighting for Atlanta*, 4.
21. Swidler, "Culture in Action," 73–286.
22. Hull, *Absolute Destruction*, 2; Lynn, *Battle*; Lee, ed., *Warfare and Culture in World History*.
23. Tony Ingesson's dissertation, "The Politics of Combat," carries this research into a study of military subcultures at what is most appropriately termed the branch level (though he refers to these as "unit" subcultures).

24. WTS to John Sherman [JS], Jan. 17, 1863, *SCW,* 362.

25. Konijnendijk, *Classical Greek Tactics,* 117–18, 124.

26. Vegetius, *De re mlitari,* 84.

27. Saxe, *Reveries,* 304–5.

28. Griffith, *Battle Tactics of the Civil War,* 145.

29. Schein, *Organizational Culture,* 55–56.

30. WTS to Grant, June 2, 1863, *The War of the Rebellion* [OR], III, 3, 387.

31. Keegan, *The Face of Battle,* 128–29.

32. Powell, *Learning Under Fire,* 186.

33. S. S. Farwell to Brother, Apr. 22, 1863, S. S. Farwell Letters, State Historical Society of Iowa–Iowa City [SHSI Iowa City].

1. SOLDIERS FROM EXPERIENCE

1. Thomas Kilby Smith [TKS] to Wife, Dec. 26, 1862, Smith, ed., *Life and Letters,* 250–51.

2. Abraham J. Seay [32 MO] Diary, Dec. 24, 1862, Sigler and Sigler, eds., *Diary of Col. A. J. Seay,* 13; Catton, *Grant Moves South.*

3. G.O. 14, HQ Department of the Tennessee, Dec. 22, 1862, *OR* I, 17; I, 461.

4. Halleck to Ulysses S. Grant [USG], Dec. 5, 1862, *OR* I, 17; I, 473. Halleck to USG, Dec. 9, 1862, *OR* I, 17; I, 474.

5. WTS to JS, Dec. 14, 1862, *SCW,* 345; WTS to Ellen Ewing Sherman, Dec. 14, 1862, *SCW,* 342.

6. WTS to JS, Dec. 14, 1862, *SCW,* 345; WTS to EES, Dec. 14, 1862, *SCW,* 342.

7. Work, *Lincoln's Political Generals,* 78–81.

8. WTS to Gorman, Dec. 13, 1862, *OR* I, 17; II, 409.

9. WTS to Gorman, Dec. 12, 1862, *OR* I, 17; II, 402–3. WTS to EES, Jan. 4, 1863, *SCW,* 350.

10. WTS to Gorman, Dec. 12, 1862, *OR* I, 17; II, 402–3.

11. WTS to Gorman, Dec. 13, 1862, *OR* I, 17; II, 409.

12. WTS to EES, Dec. 20, 1862, *SCW,* 348. In reality, the Rebels guarding Vicksburg then numbered less than 14,000 men.

13. WTS to Charles Ewing, July 8, 1862, *SCW,* 249.

14. Hardee, *Rifle and Light Infantry Tactics,* 14, 26, 87; Casey, *Infantry Tactics* 2: 3; US, *Revised United States Army Regulations.*

15. Freidel, *Union Pamphlets,* 1028. Unfortunately, the tendency of military officers and analysts to measure a force's capabilities through primarily quantitative means has not abated much in the past century and a half. In his groundbreaking approach to the measurement of *Military Power* in a book by the same name, Stephen Biddle argues that effective and "holistic assessments" of the true capabilities of any given military force or organization require both rigor and breadth, as well as "a systematic treatment of both material and non-material variables." This chapter seeks to provide such an assessment of the capabilities of the regiments assigned to Sherman's future Fifteenth Corps. Biddle, *Military Power,* 2.

16. Glatthaar, *Partners in Command,* 135–61. See also Flood, *Grant and Sherman.*

17. "General Morgan L. Smith," *Inter Ocean,* Jan. 2, 1875, 10; "Correction," St. Louis *Daily Missouri Republican,* June 1, 1861.

18. H. W. Smith to B. F. Wade, Mar. 22, 1862, "Morgan L. Smith," M619, National Archives and Records Administration [NARA].

19. Heitman, *Historical Register,* 902. The *Register* incorrectly identifies Smith's pseudonym as "Martin L. Sanford," when in fact it was "Mortimer L. Sandford," Register of Enlistments in the U.S. Army, 1798–1914, July 19, 1845, RG 94, NARA; "Smith, Morgan Lewis," Tenkotte and Claypool, eds., *Encyclopedia of Northern Kentucky,* 839.

20. Nosworthy, *Bloody Crucible of Courage,* 53–58, 97–101.

21. Hyde and Conard, eds., *Encyclopedia of the History of St. Louis* 3: 1499; "The Parade and Drill of the Chicago Zouaves," *Daily Missouri Democrat,* Aug. 13, 1860, 2.

22. "The Parade and Drill of the Chicago Zouaves," *Daily Missouri Democrat,* Aug. 13, 1860, 2.

23. Most Civil War military historians have observed that the vast majority of Zouave regiments on either side during the war (and there were many) tended to adopt the gaudy uniforms but not the tactics of the *chasseurs-à-pied* in any meaningful way on the battlefield. Griffith, *Battle Tactics of the Civil War,* 101–2; Hess, *Civil War Infantry Tactics,* 33. Hess, however, observes that Smith's Eighth Missouri, along with Lew Wallace's Eleventh Indiana—with whom the Eighth would soon be brigaded—may have been the only regiments of the war who were trained from the beginning as, and actually fought like, Zouaves. Hess, *Civil War Infantry Tactics,* 70.

24. "Our St. Louis Correspondence," *New York Herald,* June 2, 1861, 9; 8th Missouri Volunteer Infantry Descriptive Rolls, RG 133, Missouri State Archives. "Suckers" was a common period slang term for Illinoisans.

25. David Monlux [8 MO] to Parents, undated, 1861, Monlux Letters, Missouri History Museum [MHM].

26. David Monlux [8 MO] to Parents, undated, 1861, Monlux Letters, MHM.

27. Dyer, *A Compendium of the War of the Rebellion* 2: 1326.

28. Wallace and Leeke, eds., *Smoke, Sound & Fury,* 88.

29. Walter Hunter [8 MO] to Thomas Hunter, Feb. 19, 1862, Walter Hunter Letter, Trempealeau County Historical Society.

30. Walter Hunter [8 MO] to Thomas Hunter, Feb. 19, 1862.

31. Wallace and Leeke, eds., *Smoke, Sound & Fury,* 89.

32. H. W. Smith to B. F. Wade, Mar. 22, 1862, "Morgan L. Smith," M619, NARA.

33. Thomas Wise Durham [11 IN], Patrick, ed., *Three Years With Wallace's Zouaves,* 72.

34. Wallace and Leeke, eds., *Smoke, Sound & Fury,* 89.

35. Walter Hunter [8 MO] to Thomas Hunter, Feb. 19, 1862.

36. David Monlux [8 MO] to Father, February 1862, Monlux Letters, MHM.

37. Walter Hunter [8 MO] to Thomas Hunter, Feb. 19, 1862; Smith's Zouave assault at Donelson was considered by military theorist Arthur Wagner to have been a "brilliant movement . . . far in advance of the tactics then generally in use." Wagner, *Organization and Tactics,* 266. See also Mahon, "Civil War Infantry Assault Tactics," 63–64.

38. Stephens, *Shadow of Shiloh,* 95.

39. Stephens, *Shadow of Shiloh,* 97.

40. Stephens, *Shadow of Shiloh,* 98.

41. Stephens, *Shadow of Shiloh,* 98.

42. Stephens, *Shadow of Shiloh*, 98.

43. Stephens, *Shadow of Shiloh*, 95.

44. *OR* 1, 10; I, 193.

45. "Gen. Morgan L. Smith. A Generous Tribute from Gen. Sherman," *New York Times,* Jan. 5, 1875, 6.

46. Stephens, *Shadow of Shiloh*, 111.

47. Dyer, *A Compendium of the War of the Rebellion* 1: 481.

48. Frank and Reaves, *Seeing the Elephant.*

49. Smith, *Corinth 1862*, 49.

50. USG, *Personal Memoirs*, 171; Hagerman, *American Civil War,* 168–69.

51. Crooker et al., *Story of the Fifty-Fifth*, 144.

52. Hagerman, *American Civil War,* 173.

53. David Grier [8 MO] to Annie, May 12, 1862, Grier Letters, MHM. In many ways, this transformation is akin to that observed among the Army of the Potomac two years later as it transitioned from the intense fighting of the Overland Campaign to the much more conservative approach of siegecraft at Petersburg. Sodergren, *Army of the Potomac.*

54. Crooker et al., *Story of the Fifty-Fifth*, 140.

55. "Report of Col. Morgan L. Smith," May 19, 1862, *OR* I, 10; I, 841.

56. "Late from Corinth," *Western Reserve Chronicle,* May 21, 1862, 2. "From Pittsburg Landing," *Cleveland Daily Leader,* May 19, 1862, 3. "Report of Maj. Gen. William T. Sherman," May 19, 1862, *OR* I, 10; I, 840.

57. "Report of Lieut. Col. James Peckham," May 17, 1862, *OR* I, 10; I, 843.

58. "Report of Lieut. Col. James Peckham," May 17, 1862, *OR* I, 10; I, 843.

59. "Report of Maj. Gen. William T. Sherman," May 19, 1862, *OR* I, 10; I, 840.

60. "Report of Maj. Gen. William T. Sherman," May 19, 1862, *OR* I, 10; I, 840. Crooker et al., *Story of the Fifty-Fifth*, 140.

61. "Endorsement of Report of Col. Morgan L. Smith," May 19, 1862, *OR* I, 10; I, 842.

62. "Report of Lieut. Col. James Peckham," May 17, 1862, *OR* I, 10; I, 843.

63. Long after the war, Brig. Gen. Arthur Wagner noted how dispersed skirmish lines tended to attract almost all enemy fire, even when close-order battle lines arrayed in their support were visible and within range. He attributed this to the tendency of "soldiers in battle [to] instinctively and invariably fire at those who are shooting at them." Thus, "clouds" of skirmishers like those Smith habitually deployed, when actively engaged with the enemy, could effectively shield the advance of close-order lines, dramatically lowering casualties within them as they seized ground moving forward. Wagner, *Organization and Tactics,* 65.

64. "Report of Col. Morgan L. Smith," June 1, 1862, *OR* I, 10; I, 856.

65. "The Field of Battle," *Wauwatosa News,* Aug. 9, 1902, 5.

66. Wallace and Leeke, eds., *Smoke, Sound & Fury,* 56.

67. Crooker et al., *Story of the Fifty-Fifth*, 151.

68. Wallace and Leeke, eds., *Smoke, Sound & Fury,* 58.

69. David Monlux [8 MO] to Parents, undated, 1861, Monlux Letters, MHM.

70. Davidson Leatherman to Andrew Johnson, Mar. 14, 1866, Bergeron, ed., *Papers of Andrew Johnson* 10: 255.

71. MLS to Wallace, Apr. 17, 1862, Simon, ed., *Papers of Ulysses S. Grant* [*PUSG*], vol. 5: 357.

72. Wallace and Leeke, eds., *Smoke, Sound & Fury*, 58.

73. USG to Stanton, Mar. 14, 1862, *PUSG* 4: 356–57.

74. USG to Henry H. Wilson, July 1, 1862, *PUSG* 5: 184–85.

75. Crooker et al., *Story of the Fifty-Fifth*, 151.

76. "Spirit of the Contests," *National Tribune*, June 27, 1901.

77. Crooker et al., *Story of the Fifty-Fifth*, 153.

78. David Monlux [8 MO] to Father, July 26, 1862, Monlux Letters, MHM.

79. David Holmes [55 IL] to Family, July 7, 1862, Holmes Papers, Abraham Lincoln Presidential Library [ALPL].

80. Crooker et al., *Story of the Fifty-Fifth*, 156.

81. Crooker et al., *Story of the Fifty-Fifth*, 157.

82. Crooker et al., *Story of the Fifty-Fifth*, 157.

83. David Monlux [8 MO] to Father, July 26, 1862, Monlux Letters, MHM.

84. "Compliment to Brig. General Smith," *Daily Missouri Democrat*, July 30, 1862, 2.

85. Crooker et al., *Story of the Fifty-Fifth*, 170.

86. Unfiled Dispatches, RG 393, 15 AC, 2 DIV, Box 2, NARA.

87. Grecian, *History of the Eighty-Third*, 15–17; Bearss, *Campaign for Vicksburg* 1: 59–94; Woodworth, *Nothing but Victory*, 243–60.

88. Regimental Descriptive Books, 6th Missouri, 8th Missouri, 54th Ohio, 57th Ohio, 55th Illinois, 113th Illinois, 116th Illinois, 127th Illinois, 83rd Indiana, RG 94, NARA.

89. USG to Steele, Dec. 8, 1862, *PUSG* 6: 408.

90. Hess, "Confiscation and the Northern War Effort," 68.

91. Teeters, *Practical Liberators*, 38.

92. Watson, *Jackson's Sword*, 282–85.

93. Hess, "Confiscation and the Northern War Effort," 56–75; Teeters, *Practical Liberators*, 38–39.

94. Steele to USG, Dec. 13, 1862, *OR* I, 17; II, 410.

95. Steele to USG, Dec. 13, 1862, *OR* I, 17; II, 410.

96. USG to WTS, Dec. 15, 1862, *PUSG* 7: 41. WTS to USG, Dec. 18, 1862, *OR* I, 17, 426.

97. Forsyth, *Camden Expedition*, 38.

98. Forsyth, *Camden Expedition*, 39.

99. Piston and Hatcher, *Wilson's Creek*; "Report of Maj. S. D. Sturgis, First U.S. Cavalry," Aug. 20, 1861, *OR* I, 3, 70; Lacey, "Major-General Frederick Steele," 424–38.

100. Grimsley, *Hard Hand of War*, 98; Schultz, *March to the River*.

101. Committee of the Regiment, *Military History and Reminiscences of the Thirteenth*, 27.

102. Committee of the Regiment, *Military History and Reminiscences of the Thirteenth*, 27.

103. Committee of the Regiment, *Military History and Reminiscences of the Thirteenth*, 27.

104. Thomas Coleman [6 MO] to Parents, Jan. 6, 1862, Coleman Correspondence, State Historical Society of Missouri–Rolla [SHSM Rolla].

105. The term "household war" refers to the network of support which Missouri bushwhackers utilized to maintain their insurgency. Beilein, *Bushwhackers*. See also Lane, "Challenging the Union Citizen-Soldier Ideal," in McKnight and Myers, eds., *Guerrilla Hunters*, on how Federal troops fighting guerrillas struggled with making sense of their unique experiences.

106. Committee of the Regiment, *Military History and Reminiscences of the Thirteenth*, 79.

107. Dyer, *Compendium of the War of the Rebellion* 1: 498.
108. Kohl, "'This Godforsaken Town,'" 109–44.
109. Kohl, "'This Godforsaken Town,'" 123.
110. Kohl, "'This Godforsaken Town,'" 135.
111. Hess, "Confiscation and the Northern War Effort," 68.
112. Hess, "Confiscation and the Northern War Effort," 72.
113. Hess, "Confiscation and the Northern War Effort," 73.
114. Kohl, "'This Godforsaken Town,'" 110.
115. Kohl, "'This Godforsaken Town,'" 126.
116. Baker, *The Sacred Cause of Union*, 150.
117. Parrish, *Frank Blair*, 146–58.
118. WTS to USG, Dec. 15, 1862, *PUSG* 7: 41.
119. WTS to JS, Dec. 14, 1862, *SCW*, 127.

2. DISCOURAGED BY SUCH MANAGEMENT

1. Grecian, *History of the Eighty-Third*, 18.
2. Ballard, *Vicksburg*, 101–33.
3. "Special Orders No. 36," HQ RW 13 AC, Dec. 26, 1862, *OR* I, 17; I, 621–22. Ballard, *Vicksburg*, 129–35.
4. Ballard, *Vicksburg*, 135–40; Crooker et al., *Story of the Fifty-Fifth*, 193.
5. Bearss, *Campaign for Vicksburg* 1: 186–87.
6. "Special Orders No. 37," HQ RW 13AC, Dec. 28, 1862, *OR* I, 17; I, 622. WTS, *Memoirs*, 314.
7. Committee of the Regiment, *Military History and Reminiscences of the Thirteenth*, 243–44. "Report of Brig. Gen. Frank P. Blair," Dec. 30, 1862, *OR* I, 17; I, 655. Hall, *Story of the 26th*, 46.
8. "Reports of Brig. Gen. Stephen D. Lee," *OR* I, 17; I, 682. Hall, *Story of the 26th*, 46, 31–32, 47. The Rebel strength of 600 is a very rough estimate based upon Hall's recollections on p. 37 and from Sept. 10, 1862 returns in *OR* I, 17; II, 699.
9. "Report of Brig. Gen. Frank P. Blair," Dec. 30, 1862, *OR* I, 17; I, 655.
10. Warmoth, *War, Politics, and Reconstruction*, 15.
11. T. C. Fletcher [31 MO], undated, in WTS, *Memoirs*, 443–44.
12. "The Vicksburgh Failure," *New York Times*, Jan. 19, 1863; *Thirteenth Regiment*, 246; Seay [32 MO], Dec. 24, 1862, Sigler and Sigler, eds., *Civil War Diary*, 15–16.
13. "The Battle of Chickasaw Bayou," *New York Herald*, Jan. 18, 1863; "From Vicksburg," *Cincinnati Enquirer*, Jan. 15, 1863; Woodworth, *Nothing but Victory*, 275–77.
14. *Thirteenth Regiment*, 247–48; Wilson E. Chapel [13 IL] Journals, Northern Illinois University Digital Library.
15. Chapel [13 IL] Journals; "Orders No. 17, HQ 'Blair's Brigade,'" Dec. 21, 1862, 30 MO Regimental Order Book, RG 94, NARA; Gilham, *Manual of Instruction*, 39.
16. Fletcher [31 MO] in WTS, *Memoirs*, 444; The 31st Missouri reported a strength of about 750 effectives on Dec. 21. *OR* I, 17; I, 604. Adjusting for probable attrition in the bayous, the regiment likely went into the assault with around 700 muskets. It reported a loss of 151 men

to all causes while in the bayous, the vast majority of whom were lost during the attack. *OR* I, 17; I, 625.

17. Blair's Report, *OR* I, 17; I, 656. Woodworth, *Nothing but Victory*, 277. While it is impossible to know the precise strength of Blair's surviving contingents at this point in the assault, the number 1,000 is a reasonable estimate based upon the reported strengths of the 13th Illinois and 29th Missouri on Dec. 21 (*OR* I, 17; I, 604), adjusted by assumed attrition in the bayous and casualties reported after the battle (*OR* I, 17; I, 625).

18. "The Vicksburg Failure," *New York Times*, Jan. 19, 1863; "The Battle of Chickasaw Bayou," *New York Herald*, Jan. 18, 1863; Chapel [13 IL] Journals, NIU Digital Library; "From Vicksburg," *Chicago Times*, Dec. 30, 1862.

19. "Special Orders No. 37," HQ RW 13 AC, Dec. 28, 1862, *OR* 622.

20. John M. Thayer to 13th Illinois Committee, Sept. 18, 1891, *Thirteenth Regiment*, 264-66. Steele later remembered Morgan providing Thayer with finer instructions on "the route which his brigade should take and sent a guide to lead him," but no other reference to a guide is extant.

21. "Report of Brig. Gen. John M. Thayer," Dec. 31, 1862, *OR* I, 17; I, 658-59.

22. "Report of Col. John M. Thayer," Apr. 10, 1862, *OR* I, 10; I, 193.

23. "Report of Col. Charles H. Abbott" [30 IA], Jan. 12, 1863, *OR* I, 17; I, 661. Thayer to 13th Illinois, Sept. 18, 1891, *Thirteenth Regiment*, 254-56.

24. Abbott's [30 IA] Report, *OR* 661.

25. Abbott's [30 IA] Report, *OR* 661.

26. Thayer to 13th Illinois, Sept. 18, 1891, *Thirteenth Regiment*, 254-55.

27. 28th/29th Louisiana Infantry Ordnance Reports, Col. Allen Thomas, C.S., Combined Service Record, RG 94, NARA; Col. Joseph Octave Landry, C.S., Combined Service Record, RG 94, NARA; "Address by General G. M. Dodge," *Proceedings of Crocker's Iowa*, 266; IA AG, *Report of the Adjutant General*, 10; Kerr, "Wall of Fire," 26; US, *Reports of Experiments*.

28. Unknown [4 IA], Feb. 14, 1863, private seller, www.railsplitter.com/sale12/grant.html (accessed Feb. 26, 2018). Copy in author's files.

29. Logan, *Roster and Record* 1: 525-672.

30. Randolph Sry [4 IA] to Mrs. Miller, Jan. 4, 1863, Miller Widow's Pension Application, RG 15, Department of Veterans Affairs, NARA.

31. Henry Ankeny [4 IA] to Wife, Dec. 31, 1862, Ankeny Papers, State Historical Society of Iowa-Des Moines [SHSI Des Moines].

32. US, *Revised United States Army Regulations*, 9; Thayer to 13th Illinois, Sept. 18, 1891, *Thirteenth Regiment*, 255.

33. "Report of Brig. Gen. Frederick Steele," Jan. 3, 1863, *OR* I, 17; I, 652; Thayer to 13th Illinois, Sept. 18, 1891, *Thirteenth Regiment*, 257.

34. Nosworthy, *Bloody Crucible of Courage*, 40-60; Gibbons, *Destroying Angel*. It was this very defense that avant-garde Zouave tactics were designed to overcome.

35. Nosworthy, *Bloody Crucible of Courage*, 599-607; Wagner, *Organization and Tactics*, 63.

36. "General Sherman and His Old Regiment," *Soldier's Casket* 1, no. 10 (October 1865): 631.

37. Henry C. Bear [116 IL] to Parents, Jan. 2, 1863, Temple, ed. *Civil War Letters*, 23.

38. Bear [116 IL] to Parents, Jan. 2, 1863, 24.

39. "Report of Giles A. Smith," Jan. 5, 1863, *OR* I, 17; I, 633.

40. Smith, *OR Report*, 633.

41. Smith, *OR Report*, 633.

42. "General Sherman and His Old Regiment," *Soldier's Casket* 1, no. 10 (October 1865): 631.

43. Giles Smith, *OR Report*, 631; Bear [116 IL] to Parents, Jan. 2, 1863, Temple, ed., *Civil War Letters*, 23–24.

44. Giles Smith, *OR Report*, 631.

45. Bear [116 IL] to Parents, Jan. 2, 1863, Temple, ed., *Civil War Letters*, 23.

46. 6th Missouri Company Morning Reports (Fragments), 6th Missouri Regimental Books, RG 94, NARA.

47. Woodworth, *Nothing but Victory*, 274; Bear [116 IL] to Parents, Jan. 2, 1863, Temple, ed., *Civil War Letters*, 23–24.

48. Smith, *OR Report*, 634.

49. John B. Mains [6 MO], Jan. 20, 1863, John Mains Letters, SHSM Rolla.

50. Smith, *OR Report*, 634.

51. Mains [6 MO], Jan. 20, 1863; Bear [116 IL] to Parents, Jan. 2, 1863, Temple, ed., *Civil War Letters*, 24.

52. Bear [116 IL] to Parents, Jan. 2, 1863, 24.

53. "Report of Capt. Peter P. Wood," Jan. 16, 1863, *OR* I, 17; I, 628.

54. George Browning [54 OH] to Wife, Jan. 2, 1863, Browning Papers, Nau Civil War Collection.

55. Bear [116 IL] to Parents, Jan. 2, 1863, Temple, ed., *Civil War Letters*, 24.

56. Smith, *OR Report*, 634; Woodworth, *Nothing but Victory*, 274–75.

57. Bear [116 IL] to Parents, Jan. 4, 1863, Temple, ed., *Civil War Letters*, 26.

58. Bear [116 IL] to Parents, Jan. 4, 1863, 24.

59. Bear [116 IL] to Parents, Jan. 3, 1863, 24.

60. "Return of Casualties in the Union forces," Jan. 3, 1863, *OR* I, 17; I, 625.

61. "Return of Casualties," *OR* I, 17; I, 625; Bear [116 IL] to Parents, Jan. 2, 1863, Temple, ed., *Civil War Letters*, 24.

62. Seay [32 MO], Dec. 30, 1862, Sigler and Sigler, eds., *Civil War Diary*, 16. Farwell [31 IA] to Brother, Jan. 4, 1863, Farwell Letters, SHSI Iowa City; Crooker et al., *Story of the Fifty-Fifth*, 196; Woodworth, *Nothing but Victory*, 281–83.

63. Ballard, *Vicksburg*, 145–47; Ambrose, *Halleck*, 111–12; Meyers, *McClernand and the Politics of Command*.

64. G.O. 12, HQ RW 13 AC, Jan. 4, 1863, *OR* I, 17; I, 535.

65. Schuyler Coe [1 IL LA] to Mr. and Mrs. Henry Hicker, Jan. 29, 1863, Taylor's Battery Digital Collection.

66. G.O. 12, HQ RW 13 AC, Jan. 4, 1863, *OR* I, 17; I, 535.

67. Keegan, *Face of Battle*, 128; Nosworthy, *Bloody Crucible of Courage*, 247.

68. TKS to Wife, Jan. 3, 1863, Smith, ed., *Life and Letters*, 251–53.

69. Jacob Ritner [25 IA] to Emeline, Jan. 7, 1863, Larimer, ed., *Love and Valor*, 98.

70. Bear [116 IL] to Parents, Jan. 2, 1863, Temple, ed., *Civil War Letters*, 24.

71. Bear [116 IL] to Parents, Jan. 3, 1863, 25–26.

72. James Maxwell [127 IL] to Sister, Jan. 5, 1863, Past Voices Digital Collection·

73. Wilson E. Chapel [13 IL] Journals, NIU Digital Library.

74. Iowa, *Roster and Record* 1: 527–672.

75. Henry Ankeny [4 IA] to Wife, Dec. 31, 1862, Ankeny Papers, SHSI Des Moines.

76. In fact, Morgan did not even accompany his single assaulting brigade across the bayou, instead remaining behind.

77. "The Battle of Chickasaw Bayou," *New York Herald*, Jan. 18, 1863. Thayer's *OR* Report, 659; WTS, *Memoirs*, 315. "Report of Col. James A. Williamson," Dec. 30, 1862, *OR* I, 17; I, 660.

78. William T. Seaward [9 IA] Diary, Jan. 1, 1863, Seaward Papers, SHSI Des Moines; Enos Whitacre [30 IA] to Sister, Jan. 26, 1863, Enos Whitacre Papers, SHSI Iowa City.

79. Farwell [31 IA] to Brother, Jan. 4, 1863, Farwell Letters, SHSI Iowa City.

80. Farwell [31 IA] to Brother, Jan. 4, 1863.

81. "From the Reserves," R.P.S. [31 IA] to *Cedar Falls Gazette*, Jan. 5, 1863, published Jan. 23, 1863.

82. Farwell [31 IA] to Brother, Jan. 13, 1863, Farwell Letters, SHSI Iowa City.

83. Farwell [31 IA] to Brother, Jan. 4, 1863.

84. Farwell [31 IA] to Brother, Jan. 13, 1863.

85. Farwell [31 IA] to Brother, Jan. 13, 1863; "From the Reserves," *Cedar Falls Gazette*, Jan. 23, 1863; Kircher [12 MO] to Mother, Jan. 3, 1863, Hess, ed., *German in the Yankee Fatherland*, 50; Willison [76 OH], *Reminiscences*, 39; Charles Dana Miller [76 OH], Bennet and, eds., *Struggle for the Life*, 71.

86. WTS to Porter, Dec. 30, 1862, *OR* I, 17; II, 879.

87. J. H. Hammond to WTS, Feb. 5, 1876, WTS, *Memoirs*, 439.

88. Hammond to WTS, 439.

89. Hammond to WTS, 440.

90. Hammond to WTS, 440–41.

91. Hammond to WTS, 440–41.

92. "Return of Casualties in the Union forces," Jan. 3, 1863, *OR* I, 17; I, 625.

93. WTS to Halleck, Jan. 5, 1863, *OR* I, 17; I, 613.

3. NO TROOPS THAT CAN BE MADE TO ASSAULT

1. Farwell [31 IA] to Brother, Jan. 13, 1863, Farwell Papers, SHSI Iowa City; William T. Seaward Diary (1863) [9 IA], Jan. 10, 1863, Seaward Papers, SHSI Des Moines, 13–14; Alonzo Abernathy [9 IA] Diary, Jan. 10, 1863, Abernathy Papers, SHSI Des Moines.

2. Farwell [31 IA] to Brother, Jan. 13, 1863; "Report of Brig. Gen. Charles E. Hovey," *OR* I, 17; I, 765–66.

3. "Report of Brig. Gen. Charles E. Hovey," *OR* I, 17; I, 765–66.

4. Seaward [9 IA] Diary, Jan. 10, 1863, Seaward Papers, SHSI Des Moines, 14–15.

5. W. R. Oake [26 IA], Allen, ed., *On the Skirmish Line*, 68; Miler [76 OH], Bennet and Tillery, eds., *Struggle for the Life*, 76.

6. Hovey's *OR* Report, 766; "Report of Brig. Gen. John M. Thayer," *OR* I, 17; I, 769–70.

7. Hovey's *OR* Report, 765–66.

8. Ritner [25 IA] to Emeline, Larimer, ed., *Love and Valor*, Jan. 13, 1863, 101.

9. W. R. Oake [26 IA], Allen, ed., *On the Skirmish Line*, 68.

10. "Nelson" [25 IA] to *Burlington Weekly Hawk-Eye,* Jan. 31, 1863.

11. Farwell [31 IA] to Brother, Jan. 13, 1863, Farwell Papers, SHSI Iowa City.

12. Farwell [31 IA] to Brother, Jan. 13, 1863.

13. Farwell [31 IA] to Brother, Jan. 13, 1863.

14. Ritner [25 IA] to Emeline, Jan. 13, 1863, Larimer, ed., *Love and Valor,* 101.

15. Miller [76 OH], Bennet and Tillery, eds., *Struggle for the Life,* 76.

16. W. R. Oake [26 IA], Allen, ed., *On the Skirmish Line,* 68–69.

17. Ballard, *Vicksburg,* 149–50; "Reports of Maj. Gen. John A. McClernand," Jan. 11, 1863, *OR* I, 17; I, 702.

18. "Report of Col. Giles A. Smith," Jan. 12, 1863, *OR* I, 17; I, 775–76. "THE VICTORY OF ARKANSAS POST," Correspondent to *Daily Missouri Republican,* Jan. 12, 1863, published Jan. 23, 1863.

19. "THE VICTORY OF ARKANSAS POST," Correspondent to *Daily Missouri Republican,* Jan. 12, 1863, published Jan. 23, 1863.

20. Hovey's *OR* Report, 766.

21. Cutrer, *Theater of a Separate War,* 162.

22. Ballard, *Vicksburg,* 151.

23. Griffith, *Battle Tactics of the Civil War,* 143; Nosworthy, *Bloody Crucible of Courage,* 599–601; Hess, *Rifle Musket.*

24. Nosworthy, *Bloody Crucible of Courage,* 277.

25. Keegan, *Face of Battle,* 128; Nosworthy, *Bloody Crucible of Courage,* 247.

26. WTS to Blair, Feb. 3, 1863, *OR* I, 17; II, 589.

27. John T. Buegel [3 MO] Diary, State Historical Society of Missouri–Columbia [SHSM Columbia], 23–24.

28. Miller [76 OH], Bennet and Tillery, eds., *Struggle for the Life,* 77.

29. "Report of Col. Charles R. Woods," Jan. 12, 1863, *OR* I, 17; I, 768. Miller [76 OH], Bennet and Tillery, eds., *Struggle for the Life,* 77.

30. Miller [76 OH], Bennet and Tillery, eds., *Struggle for the Life,* 77.

31. W. R. Oake [26 IA], Allen, ed., *On the Skirmish Line,* 69.

32. W. R. Oake [26 IA], Allen, ed., *On the Skirmish Line,* 69.

33. Thayer's *OR* Report, 769–70.

34. "Report of Lieut. Col. W. M. G. Torrence," Jan. 13, 1863, *OR* I, 17; I, 770–71.

35. Hovey's *OR* Report, 766–67; Schultz, *March to the River,* 216–17.

36. Ballard, *Grant at Vicksburg,* 70; Buegel [3 MO] Diary, SHSM Columbia, 5, 15, 18–19.

37. Stuart, *Iowa Colonels and Regiments,* 474; Farwell [31 IA] to Brother, Jan. 13, 1863, Farwell Papers, SHSI Iowa City.

38. Hovey's *OR* Report, 766–67.

39. Farwell [31 IA] to Brother, Jan. 13, 1863, Farwell Letters, SHSI Iowa City.

40. W. R. Oake [26 IA], Allen, ed., *On the Skirmish Line,* 69.

41. A. J. Withrow [25 IA] to Lib, Jan. 12, 1863, Withrow Papers, Southern Historical Collection, Wilson Library, University of North Carolina at Chapel Hill [SHC-UNC].

42. Elisha Coon [25 IA] to Family, Jan. 13, 1863, Coon Letters, SHSI Des Moines.

43. W. R. Oake [26 IA], Allen, ed., *On the Skirmish Line,* 69.

44. Hovey's *OR* Report, 766–67.

45. Hovey's *OR* Report, 766–67.

46. Wood's *OR* Report, 768.

47. Ritner [25 IA] to Emeline, Jan. 13, 1863, Larimer, ed., *Love and Valor*, 102.

48. Wood's *OR* Report, 768; Miller [76 OH], Bennet and Tillery, eds., *Struggle for the Life*, 77–78.

49. Wood's *OR* Report, 768; Miller [76 OH], Bennet and Tillery, eds., *Struggle for the Life*, 77–78.

50. Miller [76 OH], Bennet and Tillery, eds., *Struggle for the Life*, 77–78.

51. "Nelson" [25 IA] to *Burlington Weekly Hawk-Eye*, Jan. 31, 1863.

52. Miller [76 OH], Bennet and Tillery, eds., *Struggle for the Life*, 77–78. Although only 20 percent of the Rebels to Woods's front were armed with Enfield rifles, their commander later reported the rest as "armed with double-barreled shot-guns, [and] rifles of miscellaneous caliber." The manufacture and caliber were mostly immaterial to the increased range their rifling provided. "Report of Col. James Deshler," Mar. 25, 1863, *OR* I, 17; I, 791.

53. Miller [76 OH], Bennet and Tillery, eds., *Struggle for the Life*, 78; Woods's *OR* Report, 768–69.

54. Woods's *OR* Report, 768.

55. Woods's *OR* Report, 768.

56. Woods's *OR* Report, 768.

57. Woods's *OR* Report, 768; Miller [76 OH], Bennet and Tillery, eds., *Struggle for the Life*, 78.

58. Miller [76 OH], Bennet and Tillery, eds., *Struggle for the Life*, 78.

59. Withrow [25 IA] to Lib, Jan. 12, 1863, Withrow Papers, SHC-UNC.

60. Withrow [25 IA] to Lib, Jan. 12, 1863.

61. "Nelson" [25 IA] to *Burlington Weekly Hawk-Eye*, Jan. 31, 1863.

62. Miller [76 OH], Bennet and Tillery, eds., *Struggle for the Life*, 81.

63. "Nelson" [25 IA] to *Burlington Weekly Hawk-Eye*, Jan. 31, 1863.

64. "Nelson" [25 IA] to *Burlington Weekly Hawk-Eye*, Jan. 31, 1863.

65. Miller [76 OH], Bennet and Tillery, eds., *Struggle for the Life*, 78.

66. Woods's *OR* Report, 769.

67. Buegel [3 MO] Diary [Memoirs], SHSM Columbia, 23–24.

68. Farwell [31 IA] to Brother, Jan. 13, 1863, Farwell Papers, SHSI Iowa City.

69. Farwell [31 IA] to Brother, Jan. 13, 1863.

70. Farwell [31 IA] to Brother, Jan. 13, 1863.

71. E. Burke Wylie [31 IA] to Mother, Jan. 13, 1863, Wylie Letters, SHSI Iowa City.

72. Farwell [31 IA] to Brother, Jan. 13, 1863, Farwell Letters, SHSI Iowa City.

73. Farwell [31 IA] to Brother, Jan. 13, 1863.

74. Buegel [3 MO] Diary [Memoirs], SHSM Columbia, 23–24.

75. Hovey's *OR* Report, 766–67.

76. Buegel [3 MO] Diary [Memoirs], SHSM Columbia, 24.

77. Hovey's *OR* Report, 766–67.

78. Buegel [3 MO] Diary [Memoirs], SHSM Columbia, 24.

79. Farwell [31 IA] to Brother, Jan. 13, 1863, Farwell Papers, SHSI Iowa City.

80. Buegel [3 MO] Diary [Memoirs], SHSM Columbia, 24.

81. Farwell [31 IA] to Brother, Jan. 13, 1863, Farwell Letters, SHSI Iowa City.

82. Farwell [31 IA] to Brother, Jan. 13, 1863.

83. Wylie [31 IA] to Brother, Jan. 13, 1863, Wylie Letters, SHSI Iowa City.

84. Farwell [31 IA] to Brother, Jan. 13, 1863, Farwell Letters, SHSI Iowa City.

85. Farwell [31 IA] to Brother, Jan. 13, 1863.

86. "Return of Casualties in the Union forces engaged at Arkansas Post," Jan. 11, 1863, OR I, 17; I, 717–18.

87. W. R. Oake [26 IA], Allen, ed., On the Skirmish Line, 69.

88. Torrence [30 IA] OR Report, 770.

89. W. R. Oake [26 IA], Allen, ed., On the Skirmish Line, 69–70.

90. Torrence [30 IA] OR Report, 770.

91. Torrence [30 IA] OR Report, 770.

92. W. R. Oake [26 IA], Allen, ed., On the Skirmish Line, 70.

93. W. R. Oake [26 IA], Allen, ed., On the Skirmish Line, 70.

94. Torrence [30 IA] OR Report, 770.

95. W. R. Oake [26 IA], Allen, ed., On the Skirmish Line, 70.

96. "Report of Col. James Deshler, C.S. Army," Mar. 25, 1863, OR I, 17; I, 795.

97. W. R. Oake [26 IA], Allen, ed., On the Skirmish Line, 70.

98. W. R. Oake [26 IA], Allen, ed., On the Skirmish Line, 70–71.

99. W. R. Oake [26 IA], Allen, ed., On the Skirmish Line, 71.

100. "Report of Brig. Gen. David Stuart," Jan. 14, 1863, OR I, 17; I, 772.

101. Stuart's OR Report, 772.

102. Stuart's OR Report, 772.

103. "Report of Col. Giles A. Smith," Jan. 12, 1863, OR I, 17; I, 775.

104. T. Kilby Smith to Wife, Jan. 14, 1863, Smith, ed., Life and Letters, 260.

105. Bear [116 IL] to Family, Jan. 13, 1863, Temple, ed., Civil War Letters, 29.

106. G. A. Smith's OR Report; Bear [116 IL] to Family, Jan. 13, 1863. Smith judged the duration of the barrage at "about half an hour," and Private Henry Bear of the 116th IL had the same sense.

107. Stuart's OR Report, 772.

108. Stuart's OR Report, 772–73.

109. Bear [116 IL] to Family, Jan. 13, 1863, Temple, ed., Civil War Letters, 29.

110. Stuart's OR Report, 773.

111. Bear [116 IL] to Family, Jan. 13, 1863, Temple, ed., Civil War Letters, 29.

112. Stuart's OR Report, 773; G. A. Smith's OR Report, 776.

113. G. A. Smith's OR Report, 776; Crooker et al., Story of the Fifty-Fifth, 202.

114. Hovey's OR Report, 766–67.

115. "Letter from Young's Point," Daily Missouri Democrat, Mar. 16, 1863.

116. Stuart's OR Report., 773.

117. Bear [116 IL] to Family, Jan. 13, 1863, Temple, ed., Civil War Letters, 29; Stuart's OR Report, 773.

118. Crooker et al., Story of the Fifty-Fifth, 201–2.

119. G. A. Smith's OR Report, 776; Stuart's OR Report, 773; "The Victory of Arkansas Post," Correspondent to the Daily Missouri Republican, Jan. 23, 1863.

120. Bear [116 IL] to Family, Jan. 13, 1863, Temple, ed., Civil War Letters, 29.

121. "The Victory of Arkansas Post," Correspondent to Daily Missouri Republican, Jan. 23, 1863.

122. "The Victory of Arkansas Post," *Daily Missouri Republican,* Jan. 23, 1863.

123. Stuart's *OR* Report, 773; G. A. Smith's *OR* Report, 776.

124. Stuart's *OR* Report, 773.

125. Crooker et al., *Story of the Fifth-Fifth,* 202.

126. Hiram McClintock [127 IL] to Sarah North, Jan. 19, 1863, Hiram McClintock Letters, Flagg Creek Heritage Society.

127. "Return of Casualties in the Union forces engaged at Arkansas Post," Jan. 11, 1863, *OR* I, 17; I, 717–18.

128. Deshler [CSA] *OR* Report, 793.

129. "Report of Col. Robert R. Garland, Sixth Texas Infantry," *OR* I, 17; I, 785.

130. Bearss, *Campaign for Vicksburg* 1: 402–5.

131. Wylie [31 IA] to Tappan, Jan. 3, 1863, Wylie Letters, SHSI Iowa City.

132. Crooker et al., *Story of the Fifty-Fifth,* 196; Buegel [3 MO] Diary, 22, SHSM Columbia; Seaward [9 IA] Diary, Jan. 1, 1863, Seaward Papers, SHSI Des Moines.

133. Robert W. Henry [26 IA] to Wife, Feb. 1, 1863, Henry Letters, SHSI Iowa City.

134. Seay [32 MO], Jan. 1, 1863, Sigler and Sigler, eds., *Civil War Diary,* 17.

135. James Maxwell [127 IL] to Sister, Jan. 5, 1863, Maxwell Letters, Past Voices Digital Collection.

136. Steele's Division boasted 12,510 present for duty across four brigades on Dec. 21, whereas Smith's Division of only two brigades reported a mere 5,570 effectives on Dec. 16. *OR* I, 17; I, 602, 604, 614–15.

137. "Return of Casualties," *OR* I, 17; I, 625.

138. Capt. Lewis Dayton to Ellen Sherman, Jan. 14, 1863, Sherman Papers, LOC.

139. 116th Illinois Infantry Regimental Books, Consolidated Morning Report, RG 94, NARA.

140. 25th Iowa Infantry Consolidated Morning Report Book, RG 101, Iowa State Archives; 31st Iowa Infantry Consolidated Morning Report Book, RG 101, Iowa State Archives.

141. Miller [76 OH], Bennet and Tillery, eds., *Struggle for the Life,* 81.

142. Seaward [9 IA], Jan. 14, 1863, Seaward Papers, SHSI Des Moines, 23.

143. Alonzo Abernathy [9 IA] Diary, Jan. 14, 1863, Abernathy Papers, SHSI Des Moines.

144. Seaward [9 IA], Jan. 14, 1863, Seaward Papers, SHSI Des Moines, 23

145. Seaward [9 IA] Diary, Jan. 13, 1863, Seaward Papers, SHSI Des Moines, 22–23.

146. Farwell [31 IA] to Brother, Jan. 13, 1863, Farwell Papers, SHSI Iowa City.

147. Seaward [9 IA] Diary, Jan. 13, 1863, Seaward Papers, SHSI Des Moines, 22–23.

148. Ritner [25 IA] to Emeline, Jan. 15, 1863, Larimer, ed., *Love and Valor,* 103–4.

149. Ballard, *Vicksburg,* 154–55; Farwell [31 IA] to Brother, Jan. 13, 1863, Farwell Letters, SHSI Iowa City.

150. Wylie [31 IA] to Mother, Jan. 13, 1863, Wylie Letters, SHSI Iowa City.

151. Linderman, *Embattled Courage,* 21; Hess, *Union Soldier in Battle,* 1–4.

152. Farwell [31 IA] to Brother, Jan. 13, 1863, Farwell Letters, SHSI Iowa City; Ballard, *Vicksburg,* 152.

153. Wagner, *Organization and Tactics,* 68.

154. WTS to John Sherman, Apr. 23, 1863, *SCW,* 458.

155. Wylie [31 IA] to Mother, Jan. 13, 1863, Wylie Letters, SHSI Iowa City; Farwell [31 IA] to Brother, Jan. 13, 1863, Farwell Letters, SHSI Iowa City.

156. This shared belief and survival tactic is also described in Hess, *Storming Vicksburg*, 382.

157. Withrow [25 IA] to Lib, Jan. 22, 1863, Withrow Papers, SHC-UNC; Farwell [31 IA] to Brother, Jan. 13, 1863, Farwell Letters, SHSI Iowa City.

158. Dayton to EES, Jan. 14, 1863, Sherman Letters, LOC.

159. Dayton to EES, Jan. 14, 1863.

160. WTS to Ellen Sherman, Jan. 12, 1863, *SCW*, 353.

161. Bonura, *Under the Shadow of Napoleon*, 36–39; Hsieh, *West Pointers*, 5.

162. Bonura, *Under the Shadow of Napoleon*, 37.

163. J. H. Hammond Diary, Jan. 11, 1863, Hammond Papers, Filson Historical Society.

164. J. H. Hammond Diary, Jan. 11, 1863.

165. Hsieh, *West Pointers*, 9.

4. EXPERIENCE WHICH WOULD SERVE US

1. James Giuaque [30 IA] to Family, Jan. 23, 1863, Giauque Papers, University of Iowa.

2. Seay [32 MO], Jan. 20, 1863, Sigler and Sigler, eds., *Civil War Diary*, 18–19.

3. WTS to EES, Jan. 16, 1863, *SCW*, 358.

4. "Report of Col. Hugh Ewing," Sept. 14, 1862, *OR* I, 13; I, 469. "Report of Maj. George H. Hildt," Sept. 20, 1862, *OR* I, 14; I, 469.

5. Ballard, *Vicksburg*, 157–59.

6. WTS to McClernand, Jan. 24, 1863, *OR* I, 24; III, 10.

7. S.O. 12, HQ 2 DIV 15 AC, Jan. 31, 1863, 83 IN Regimental Order Book, RG 94, NARA.

8. These statistics are derived from a comprehensive tabulation of the professions provided by recruits upon enlistment and recorded upon the descriptive rolls of every volunteer regiment in Second Division. Most of these rolls are available within RG 94, NARA, though several were also accessed within state repositories. (See bibliography for full citations.)

9. S.O. 36, 15 AC, Feb. 8, 1863, *OR* I, 25; III, 40.

10. G.O. 7, HQ 15 AC, Jan. 26, 1863, *OR* I, 24; III, 16.

11. Oake [26 IA], Allen, ed., *On the Skirmish Line*, 94.

12. David Holmes [55 IL] to Parents, Feb. 14, 1863, Holmes Letters, ALPL.

13. Seay [32 MO], Feb. 1, 1863, Sigler and Sigler, eds., *Civil War Diary*, 22.

14. Thaddeus Capron [55 IL], Feb. 10, 1863, "War Diary," 358.

15. Edward P. Reicchelm [3 MO], "The Taking of Vicksburg," *Bayonne Herald*, Jan. 4, 1902, 3.

16. Crooker et al., *Story of the Fifty-Fifth*, 211.

17. Crooker et al., *Story of the Fifty-Fifth*, 211.

18. Henry [26 IA] to Wife, Mar. 13, 1863, Henry Letters, SHSI Iowa City.

19. Bear [116 IL] to Wife, Jan. 26, 1863, Temple, ed., *Civil War Letters*, 33.

20. Reicchelm [3 MO], "Taking of Vicksburg," *Bayonne Herald*, Jan. 4, 1902, 3.

21. Browning [54 OH] to Wife, Feb. 16, 1863, Browning Papers, Nau Civil War Collection.

22. Henry [26 IA] to Friends, Mar. 29, 1863, Henry Letters, SHSI Iowa City.

23. Browning [54 OH] to Wife, Feb. 16, 1863, Browning Papers, Nau Civil War Collection.

24. Seay [32 MO], Feb. 12, 1863, Sigler and Sigler, eds., *Civil War Diary*, 24.

25. Crooker et al., *Story of the Fifty-Fifth*, 212.

26. Henry [26 IA] to Wife, Feb. 18, 1863, Henry Letters, SHSI Iowa City.

27. Hammond Diary, Jan. 28, 1863, Hammond Papers, Filson Historical Society.

28. Hammond Diary, Jan. 28, 1863.

29. Bell, *Mosquito Soldiers*, 25; WTS to JS, Mar. 14, 1863, *SCW,* 419-20.

30. WTS to JS, Mar. 14, 1863, *SCW,* 420.

31. WTS to JS, Feb. 12, 1863, *SCW,* 397.

32. G.O. 19, HQ 25 IA, Jan. 23, 1863, 25th IA Regimental Order Book, RG 94, NARA.

33. G.O. 19 1/4, HQ 25 IA, Jan. 23, 1863, 25th IA Regimental Order Book.

34. Withrow [25 IA] to Lib, Feb. 2, 1863, Withrow Papers, SHC-UNC.

35. G.O. 19 1/4, HQ 25 IA, Jan. 23, 1863, 25th IA Regimental Order Book, RG 94, NARA.

36. G.O. 17, HQ 25 IA, Jan. 25, 1863, 25th IA Regimental Order Book.

37. G.O. 19, HQ 25 IA, Jan. 27, 1863, 25th IA Regimental Order Book.

38. TKS to Mother, Feb. 4, 1863, Smith, ed., *Life and Letters,* 270.

39. Bear [116 IL] to Wife, Feb. 14, 1863, Temple, ed., *Civil War Letters,* 35.

40. Edward P. Reichhelm [3 MO], "The Taking of Vicksburg," *Bayonne Herald,* Jan. 4, 1902, 4.

41. The figures in this paragraph and the next are derived from a tabulation of figures reported throughout a number of different sources. Many regiments submitted detailed monthly returns concerning numbers present and lost over a given period, and when available these have been consulted at their respective state archives in Ohio, Illinois, Iowa, or Missouri. The data on other regiments are only extant within their respective regimental records within RG 94, NARA. Others, by far the most painstaking, required hand tabulation of losses reported between January and April 1863 listed within each state's adjutant general's report compiled at the end of the war or immediately thereafter.

42. Ballard, *Vicksburg,* 167, 171, 174-83, 188-90.

43. Woodworth, *Nothing but Victory,* 308-9.

44. "Report of Maj. Gen. William T. Sherman," Mar. 21, 1863, *OR* I, 24; I, 432.

45. The 55th IL was at that time absent on detached foraging duty. "Report of Brig. Gen. David Stuart," Mar. 29, 1863, *OR* I, 24; I, 437.

46. Stuart's *OR* Report, Mar. 29, 1863, *OR* I, 24; I, 437.

47. "Galway," "Operations on the Mississippi," *New York Times,* Apr. 4, 1863.

48. Stuart's *OR* Report, Mar. 29, 1863, *OR* I, 24; I, 437.

49. Stuart's *OR* Report, Mar. 29, 1863, *OR* I, 24; I, 437. "Report of Brig. Gen. Hugh Ewing," Mar. 29, 1863, *OR* I, 24; I, 449-50.

50. "Report of Hugh Ewing," Mar. 29, 1863, *OR* I, 24; I, 449-50. Average water temperature likely hovered around 50 degrees Fahrenheit. Hirsch, "Mississippi River Water Temperatures at New Orleans," 415.

51. "The Recent Expedition of Gen. Sherman," *Chicago Tribune,* Apr. 4, 1863, 1.

52. "Galway," "Operations on the Mississippi," *New York Times,* Apr. 4, 1863.

53. Stuart's *OR* Report, Mar. 29, 1863, *OR* I, 24; I, 438.

54. Sherman's Report, Mar. 16, 1863, *OR* I, 24; I, 431.

55. Sherman's Report, Mar. 16, 1863, *OR* I, 24; I, 431.

56. "Report of Brig. Gen. Giles A. Smith," Mar. 28, 1863, *OR* I, 24; I, 439.

57. Sherman's Report, Mar. 21, 1863, *OR* I, 24; I, 433.

58. Giles Smith's *OR* Report, Mar. 28, 1863, *OR* I, 24; I; 439.

59. Smith's *OR* Report, Mar. 28, 1863, *OR* I, 24; I, 439.

60. Matthew Egan [6 MO], Widow's Pension File, RG 15, NARA.

61. Giles Smith's *OR* Report, Mar. 28, 1863, *OR* I, 24; I, 439.

62. W. H. Michael, "Mississippi Flotilla," *National Tribune*, June 28, 1888, 1.

63. Sherman's Report, Mar. 29, 1863, *OR* I, 24; I, 434–35.

64. WTS, *Memoirs*, 333.

65. "Report of Lt. Col. Cyrus Fisher" [54 OH], *OR* I, 24; I, 448.

66. Michael, "Mississippi Flotilla," *National Tribune*, June 28, 1888, 1.

67. Grecian, *History of the Eighty-Third*, 27–28.

68. "The Recent Expedition of Gen. Sherman," *Chicago Tribune*, Apr. 4, 1863, 1.

69. "Galway," "Operations on the Mississippi," *New York Times*, Apr. 4, 1863. Among the planters who unsuccessfully applied for compensation through the Southern Claims Commission after the war for losses to Stuart's division were Benjamin B. Fore, Lewis C. Watson, R. L. Wright, and Robert J. Turnbull. Issaquena County, Mississippi, Barred and Disallowed Case Files of the Southern Claims Commission, 1871–1880, M1407, NARA.

70. "Recent Expedition of Gen. Sherman," *Chicago Tribune*, Apr. 4, 1863, 1.

71. "Galway," "Operations on the Mississippi," *New York Times*, Apr. 6, 1863.

72. Issaquena County, Mississippi, 1860 US Federal Census Slave Schedule.

73. "Recent Expedition of Gen. Sherman," *Chicago Tribune*, Apr. 4, 1863, 1.

74. "Blasted Nigger," *Chicago Tribune*, Apr. 6, 1863, 2.

75. "Recent Expedition of Gen. Sherman," *Chicago Tribune*, Apr. 4, 1863, 1.

76. "Recent Expedition of Gen. Sherman," 1.

77. Jenney, "Personal Recollections of Vicksburg," *Military Essays and Recollections* 3: 256.

78. Porter, *Incidents and Anecdotes*, 171.

79. Ballard, *Vicksburg*, 198–203.

80. Grimsley, *Hard Hand of War*, 151–52.

81. WTS to Steele, Mar. 31, 1863, *OR* I, 24; III, 158.

82. Bearss, *Campaign for Vicksburg* 2: 108–10.

83. Seay [32 MO], Apr. 6, 1863, Sigler and Sigler, eds., *Civil War Diary*, 34.

84. Ritner [25 IA] to Emeline, April 12, 1863, Larimer, ed., *Love and Valor*, 151.

85. John Gay [25 IA] Diary, Apr. 6, 1863, SHSI Iowa City.

86. John Gay [25 IA] Diary, Apr. 9, 1863; Farwell [31 IA] to Brother, Apr. 17, 1863, Farwell Letters, SHSI Iowa City.

87. Farwell [31 IA] to Sister, Apr. 12, 1863, Farwell Letters, SHSI Iowa City.

88. Willis, *Forgotten Time*, 5–8; McCain and Capers, eds., *Memoirs of Henry Tillinghast Ireys*.

89. "Henry T. Irish," 1850 U.S. Federal Census Slave Schedule, Washington County, Mississippi, 92.

90. "Examination of Anderson Copeland, Feb. 11, 1874," Henry T. Irish File, Washington County, Mississippi, Barred and Disallowed Case Files of the Southern Claims Commission, 1871–1880, M1407, NARA.

91. Irish File, M1407.

92. Irish File, M1407.

93. Irish File, M1407.

94. Reichhelm [3 MO], "Taking of Vicksburg," *Bayonne Herald*, Jan. 4, 1902, 3.

95. Alonzo Abernathy [9 IA] Diary, Apr. 7, 1863, Abernathy Papers, SHSI Des Moines.

96. John Bell [25 IA], Apr. 9, 1863, Bearss, "Diary of Captain John N. Bell," 188.

97. Ritner [25 IA] to Emeline, Apr. 12, 1863, Larimer, ed., *Love and Valor*, 151.

98. Ritner [25 IA] to Emeline, Apr. 12, 1863, 150.

99. Oake [26 IA], Allen, ed., *On the Skirmish Line*, 99–101.

100. Committee of the Regiment, *Military History and Reminiscences of the Thirteenth Regiment*, 302.

101. Alonzo Abernathy [9 IA] Diary, Apr. 9, 1863, Abernathy Papers, SHSI Des Moines.

102. Abernathy [9 IA] Diary, Apr. 7, 1863.

103. Farwell [31 IA] to Wife, Apr. 12, 1863, Farwell Letters, SHSI Iowa City.

104. Bell [25 IA], Apr. 6, 1863, Bearss, "Diary of Captain John N. Bell," 186.

105. Seay [32 MO], Apr. 10, 1863, Sigler and Sigler, eds., *Civil War Diary*, 35.

106. Farwell [31 IA] to Wife, Apr. 12, 1863, Farwell Letters, SHSI Iowa City.

107. Alonzo Abernathy [9 IA] Diary, Apr. 9, 1863, Abernathy Papers, SHSI Des Moines.

108. Seay [32 MO], Apr. 9, 1863, Sigler and Sigler, eds., *Civil War Diary*, 35.

109. WTS to Steele, Apr. 19, 1863, *OR* I, 24; III, 209.

110. Farwell [31 IA] to Wife, Apr. 12, 1863, Farwell Letters, SHSI Iowa City.

111. Farwell [31 IA] to Sister, Apr. 12, 1863.

112. Farwell [31 IA] to Wife, Apr. 12, 1863.

113. Bell [25 IA], Apr. 16, 1863, Bearss, "Diary of Captain John N. Bell," 190–91; Ritner [25 IA] to Emeline, Apr. 17, 1863, Larimer, ed., *Love and Valor*, 154.

114. Ritner [25 IA] to Emeline, Apr. 17, 1863, 154.

115. Ritner [25 IA] to Emeline, Apr. 22, 1863, 157.

116. Ritner [25 IA] to Emeline, Apr. 17, 1863, 154.

117. Ritner [25 IA] to Emeline, Apr. 22, 1863, 157.

118. Teters, *Practical Liberators*, 76–77.

119. WTS to EES, Apr. 17, 1863, *SCW*, 451.

120. WTS to JS, Apr. 26, 1863, *SCW*, 461.

121. Ritner [25 IA] to Emeline, Apr. 29, 1863, Larimer, ed., *Love and Valor*, 159.

122. Alonzo Abernathy [9 IA] Diary, Apr. 23, 1863, Abernathy Papers, SHSI Des Moines.

123. Ritner [25 IA] to Emeline, Apr. 29, 1863, Larimer, ed., *Love and Valor*, 159; Bell [25 IA], Apr. 23, 1863, Bearss, "Diary of Captain John N. Bell," 193.

124. Joseph F. Orr [76 OH] to Parents, Apr. 24, 1863. Reluctant Yanks, www.orrbrosletters.wordpress.com.

125. Orr [76 OH] to Parents, Apr. 24, 1863.

126. Bell [25 IA], Apr. 18, 1863, Bearss, "Diary of Captain John N. Bell," 191; Ritner [25 IA] to Emeline, Apr. 22, 1863, Larimer, ed., *Love and Valor*, 157.

127. Ritner [25 IA] to Emeline, Apr. 22, 1863 157.

128. Farwell [31 IA] to Wife, Apr. 21, 1863, Farwell Letters, SHSI Iowa City; Farwell [31 IA] to Brother, Apr. 22, 1863, Farwell Letters, SHSI Iowa City; John Metzgar [76 OH] to Carrie, Apr. 23, 1863, John J. Metzgar Papers, SHC-UNC.

129. Metzgar [76 OH] to Carrie, Apr. 23, 1863.

130. Robert Stitt [4 IA] to Wife, Apr. 23, 1863, Robert Stitt Papers, SHSI Des Moines.

131. Ritner [25 IA] to Emeline, Apr. 22, 1863, Larimer, ed., *Love and Valor,* 157.

132. Farwell to Brother, Apr. 22, 1863, Farwell Letters, SHSI Iowa City.

133. Ritner [25 IA] to Emeline, Apr. 17, 1863, Larimer, ed., *Love and Valor,* 154.

134. "Letter from Young's Point," *Daily Missouri Democrat,* Mar. 6, 1863.

135. Lee, "Warfare and Culture," in Lee, ed., *Warfare and Culture,* 7.

136. WTS to JS, Apr. 3, 1863, *SCW,* 437.

137. WTS to JS, Apr. 3, 1863, *SCW,* 439.

5. THE MEN CANNOT BE MADE TO DO IT

1. G.O. 6, HQ 2 DIV 15 AC, Apr. 3, 1863, RG 393, NARA.

2. Dyer, *Compendium of the War of the Rebellion* 1: 500–501.

3. WTS Report, May 24, 1863, *OR* I, 24; I; 751–52.

4. WTS Report, May 24, 1863, *OR* I, 24; I, 752.

5. WTS Report, May 24, 1863, *OR* I, 24; I, 752.

6. G.O. 29, 15 AC, May 2, 1863, *OR* I, 24; III, 264. Farwell [31 IA] to Brother, May 6, 1863, Farwell Letters, SHSI Iowa City. Bell [25 IA], May 15, 1863, Bearss, "Diary of Captain John N. Bell," 203.

7. WTS Report, May 24, 1863, *OR* I, 24; I, 753. Charles Woods Report, May 25, 1863, *OR* I, 24; II, 250.

8. WTS Report, May 24, 1863, *OR* I, 24; I, 753.

9. Bell [25 IA], May 11, 1863, Bearss, "Diary of Captain John N. Bell"; Seay [32 MO], May 4, 1863, Sigler and Sigler, eds., *Civil War Diary,* 38–39; Bell [25 IA], May 13, 1863, Bearss, "Diary of Captain John N. Bell"; Seay [32 MO], Sigler and Sigler, eds., *Civil War Diary,* May 13, 1863, 43; Bell [25 IA], May 14, 1863, Bearss, "Diary of Captain John N. Bell"; Seay [32 MO], May 13, 1863, Sigler and Sigler, eds., *Civil War Diary,* 43; Reichhelm [3 MO], "Taking of Vicksburg," *Bayonne Herald,* Jan. 4, 1902.

10. WTS Report, *OR* I, 24; I, 753–54. Bearss, *Campaign for Vicksburg* 2: 535–42.

11. Farwell [31 IA] to Brother, May 15, 1863, Farwell Letters, SHSI Iowa City; Reichhelm [3 MO], "Taking of Vicksburg," *Bayonne Herald,* Jan. 4, 1902.

12. WTS Report, May 24, 1863, *OR* I, 24; I, 754. S.O. 105, HQ 15 AC, May 14, 1863, *OR* I, 24; III, 312.

13. WTS to Mower, May 15, 1863, *OR* I, 24; III, 315. S.O. 105, HQ 15 AC, May 14, 1863, *OR* I, 24; III, 312. Charles Woods [76 OH] Report, May 25, 1863, *OR* I, 24; II, 251. Bearss, *Campaign for Vicksburg* 2: 550. Charles Woods [76 OH] Report, May 25, 1863, *OR* I, 24; II, 251. Grabau, *Ninety-Eight Days,* 257. Willison [76 OH] *Reminiscences,* 53. "Report of Col. Charles R. Woods," May 25, 1863, *OR* I, 24; II, 251. Dossman, "Long March to Vicksburg," 81. "The Yankee Occupation of the City of Jackson—Terrible Destruction of Property," *Philadelphia Inquirer,* June 1, 1863, 4. Seay [32 MO], May 15, 1863, Sigler and Sigler, eds., *Civil War Diary,* 45. Alonzo Abernathy [9 IA] Diary, May 15, 1863, Abernathy Papers, SHSI Des Moines. Bearss, *Campaign for Vicksburg* 2: 550. WTS to Mower, May 15, 1863, *OR* I, 24; III, 314–15. Bell [25 IA], May 16, 1863, Bearss, "Diary of Captain John N. Bell," 205.

NOTES TO PAGES 155–165

14. Dossman, "Long March to Vicksburg," 88. WTS Report, May 24, 1863, *OR* I, 24; I, 754. Bearss, *Campaign for Vicksburg* 2: 551.

15. WTS to Mower, May 15, 1863, *OR* I, 24; III, 315. Alonzo Abernathy [9 IA] Diary, May 14, 1863, Abernathy Papers, SHSI Des Moines. Buegel [3 MO] Diary, SHSM Columbia, 28. "The Yankee Occupation of the City of Jackson—Terrible Destruction of Property," *Philadelphia Inquirer*, June 1, 1863. Dossman, "Long March to Vicksburg," 80. Wynne, *Mississippi's Civil War*, 111.

16. Hess, ed., *German in the Yankee Fatherland*, 97; Seay [32 MO], May 15, 1863, Sigler and Sigler, eds., *Civil War Diary*, 44–45; Willison [76 OH] *Reminiscences*, 54.

17. WTS Report, May 24, 1863, *OR* I, 24; I, 755. Willison [76 OH] *Reminiscences*, 54. Seay [32 MO], May 17, 1863, Sigler and Sigler, eds., *Civil War Diary*, 46.

18. "Report of Maj. Gen. William T. Sherman," May 24, 1863, *OR* I, 24; I, 755. "Report of Brig. Gen. Hugh Ewing," May 27, 1863, *OR* I, 24; II, 281.

19. "Report of Brig. Gen. Giles A. Smith," May 26, 1863, *OR* I, 24, 263.

20. "Report of Brig. Gen. Francis P. Blair, Jr.," May 24, 1863, *OR* I, 24; II, 254–56. Smith's *OR* Report, May 26, 1863, *OR* I, 24, 263. WTS, *OR* Report, May 24, 1863, *OR* I, 24; I, 755. Reicchelm [3 MO], "Taking of Vicksburg," *Bayonne Herald*, Jan. 11, 1902.

21. WTS Report, May 24, 1863, *OR* I, 24; I, 755.

22. Reichhelm [3 MO], "Taking of Vicksburg," *Bayonne Herald*, Jan. 11, 1902, 4; J. J. Kellogg [113 IL], *War Experiences*, 34; R.W. Burt [76 OH] Diary, May 17, 1863, 76th Ohio File, Vicksburg National Military Park; Reicchelm [3 MO], "The Taking of Vicksburg," *Bayonne Herald*, Jan. 4, 1902.

23. WTS Report, May 24, 1863, *OR* I, 24; I, 755.

24. Winschel, *Triumph & Defeat*, 118; Brinkerhoff, *History of the Thirtieth Regiment*, 68–69; Bearss, *Campaign for Vicksburg* 3: 761; Grabau, *Ninety-Eight Days*, 355–58; Smith, *Union Assaults*, 102–5.

25. "Report of Col. Thomas Kilby Smith," May 24, 1863, *OR* I, 24; II, 267.

26. Brinkerhoff, *History of the Thirtieth Regiment*, 68–69.

27. Blair's *OR* Report, May 24, 1863, *OR* I, 24; II, 257. T. K. Smith's *OR* Report, May 24, 1863, *OR* I, 24; II, 267.

28. Blair's *OR* Report, May 24, 1863, *OR* I, 24; II, 257. Smith's *OR* Report, May 26, 1863, *OR* I, 24; II, 264. Crooker et al., *Story of the Fifth-Fifth*, 235.

29. Winschel, *Triumph & Defeat*, 119; "On the Graveyard Road," *Tennessean*, Mar. 6, 1904; Smith, *Union Assaults*, 105–11.

30. T. K. Smith's *OR* Report, May 24, 1863, *OR* I, 24; II, 268. Committee of the Regiment, *Military History and Reminiscences of the Thirteenth Regiment*, 237. "Report of Col. H. N. Eldridge," May 28, 1863, *OR* I, 24; II, 274. T. K. Smith's *OR* Report, May 24, 1863, *OR* I, 24; II, 268.

31. T. K. Smith's *OR* Report, May 24, 1863, *OR* I, 24; II, 268.

32. Committee of the Regiment, *Military History and Reminiscences of the Thirteenth Regiment*, 237.

33. Committee of the Regiment, *Military History and Reminiscences*, 238; Bearss, *Campaign for Vicksburg* 3: 763.

34. T. K. Smith's *OR* Report, May 24, 1863, *OR* I, 24; II, 268.

35. T. K. Smith's *OR* Report, May 24, 1863, *OR* I, 24; II, 268.

36. "Report of Lt. Col. C. W. Fisher," May 24, 1863, *OR* I, 24; II, 276. T. K. Smith's *OR* Report, May 24, 1863, *OR* I, 24; II, 269.

37. Charles Hipp [37 OH] Report, May 23, 1863, *OR* I, 24; II, 283. Ewing's Report, May 27, 1863, *OR* I, 24; II, 281–82. James Dayton [4 WV] Report, May 25, 1863, Hugh Ewing Papers, Ohio History Center. Ewing's Report, May 27, 1863, *OR* I, 24; II, 282–83. Brinkerhoff, *History of the Thirtieth Regiment,* 70.

38. Grabau, *Ninety-Eight Days,* 361.

39. Blair's *OR* Report, May 24, 1863, *OR* I, 24; II, 257.

40. Grabau, *Ninety-Eight Days,* 361–62.

41. Seay [32 MO], May 20, 1863, Sigler and Sigler, eds., *Civil War Diary,* 47; Calvin Ainsworth [25 IA], May 19, 1863, Diary, Bentley Historical Library, University of Michigan (BHL); Alonzo Abernathy [9 IA] Diary, May 19, 1863, Alonzo Abernathy Papers, SHSI Des Moines; Bell [25 IA], May 19, 1863, Bearss, "Diary of Captain John N. Bell," 207; Ritner [25 IA] to Emeline, May 24, 1863, Larimer, ed., *Love and Valor,* 171.

42. Brinkerhoff, *History of the Thirtieth Regiment,* 70–71.

43. WTS, *Memoirs,* 351.

44. WTS, *Memoirs,* 351. G.O. 38, May 21, 1863, *OR* I, 24; III, 334–35.

45. G.O. 38, May 21, 1863, *OR* I, 24; III, 334–35.

46. Blair's *OR* Report, May 24, 1863, *OR* I, 24; II, 257. Crooker et al., *Story of the Fifty-Fifth,* 245.

47. Kilby Smith's *OR* Report, May 24, 1863, *OR* I, 24; II, 269. Blair's *OR* Report, May 24, 1863, *OR* I, 24; II, 257.

48. W. C. Porter [55 IL] Report, May 23, 1863, *OR* I, 24; II, 273–74. John O'Dea, "Vicksburg Again," *National Tribune,* May 26, 1892. Crooker et al., *Story of the Fifty-Fifth,* 245. W. C. Porter [55 IL] Report, May 23, 1863, *OR* I, 24; II, 273. John O'Dea, "Vicksburg Again," *National Tribune,* May 26, 1892. Crooker et al., *Story of the Fifty-Fifth,* 245.

49. Ewing's Report, May 27, 1863, *OR* I, 24; II, 281. Saunier, ed., *History of the Forty-seventh Regiment,* 144. Charles Hipp [37 OH] Report, May 23, 1863, *OR* I, 24; II, 273. Brinkerhoff, *History of the Thirtieth Regiment,* 72–73.

50. Brinkerhoff, *History of the Thirtieth Regiment,* 73–74.

51. Blair's *OR* Report, May 24, 1863, *OR* I, 24; II, 257–58.

52. Blair's *OR* Report, May 24, 1863, *OR* I, 24; II, 257. Ewing's *OR* Report, May 27, 1863, *OR* I, 24; II, 282. W. C. Porter [55 IL] May 23, 1863, *OR* I, 24; II, 273.

53. Blair's *OR* Report, May 24, 1863, *OR* I, 24; II, 257. Saunier, ed., *History of the Forty-seventh Regiment,* 148.

54. Ewing's *OR* Report, May 27, 1863, *OR* I, 24; II, 282. Saunier, ed., *History of the Forty-seventh Regiment,* 148, 153.

55. Blair's *OR* Report, May 24, 1863, *OR* I, 24; II, 257.

56. Crooker et al., *Story of the Fifty-Fifth,* 243. Blair's *OR* Report, May 24, 1863, *OR* I, 24; II, 257. Bearss, *Campaign for Vicksburg* 3: 817–18.

57. Smith's *OR* Report, May 26, 1863, *OR* I, 24; II, 264. Blair's *OR* Report, May 24, 1863, *OR* I, 24; II, 257.

58. WTS, *Memoirs,* 352.

59. Brinkerhoff, *History of the Thirtieth Regiment,* 75.

60. Bearss, *Campaign for Vicksburg* 3: 842.

61. Alonzo Abernathy [9 IA] Diary, May 22, 1863, Abernathy Papers, SHSI Des Moines.

62. Bell [25 IA], May 19, 1863, Bearss, "Diary of Captain John N. Bell," 207.

63. Ainsworth [25 IA], May 22, 1863, Diary, BHL.

64. Ainsworth [25 IA], May 22, 1863, Diary.

65. Ainsworth [25 IA], May 22, 1863, Diary.

66. Alonzo Abernathy [9 IA] Diary, May 22, 1863, Abernathy Papers, SHSI Des Moines.

67. Reichhelm, "Taking of Vicksburg," *Bayonne Herald,* Jan. 18, 1902; Bell [25 IA], May 22, 1863, Bearss, "Diary of Captain John N. Bell," 210.

68. Alonzo Abernathy [9 IA] Diary, May 22, 1863, Abernathy Papers, SHSI Des Moines; Henry Kircher [12 MO] to Mother, June 17, 1863, Hess, ed., *German in the Yankee Fatherland,* 108; Abernathy [9 IA] Diary, May 22, 1863, SHSI Des Moines; Ainsworth [25 IA] Diary, May 22, 1863, BHL.

69. Ewing's *OR* Report, *OR* I, 24; II, 283.

70. WTS, *Memoirs,* 353.

71. Farwell [31 IA] to Parents, June 2, 1863, Farwell Letters, SHSI Iowa City.

72. Crooker et al., *Story of the Fifty-Fifth,* 242; Charles Affeld [1 IL LA B] Diary, May 27, 1863, Charles Affeld Diary, Taylor's Battery Digital Collection; Ritner [25 IA] to Emeline, May 23, 1863, Larimer, ed., *Love and Valor,* 169; Ainsworth [25 IA] Diary, May 22, 1863, BHL; Buegel [3 MO] Diary, SHSM Columbia, 29; Farwell [31 IA] to Parents, May 24, 1863, Farwell Letters, SHSI Iowa City; Buegel [3 MO] Diary, SHSM Columbia, 29; Hess, *Storming Vicksburg,* 321.

73. Hess, *Storming Vicksburg,* 379.

74. Alonzo Abernathy [9 IA] Diary, May 22, 1863, Abernathy Papers, SHSI Des Moines; Henry Kircher [12 MO] to Mother, May 26, 1863, Hess, ed., *German in the Yankee Fatherland,* 101-2; Reichhelm [3 MO], "Taking of Vicksburg," *Bayonne Herald,* Jan. 4, 1902; Buegel [3 MO] Diary, 30 SHSM Columbia; Farwell [31 IA] to Brother, May 24, 1863, Farwell Letters, SHSI Iowa City; John Gay [25 IA] Diary, May 22, 1863, John Gay Diary, SHSI Iowa City.

75. Reichhelm, "Taking of Vicksburg," *Bayonne Herald,* Jan. 18, 1902.

76. Henry Kircher [12 MO] to Mother, May 24, 1863, Hess, ed., *German in the Yankee Fatherland,* 100.

77. Kircher [12 MO] Diary, May 22, 1863, Hess, ed., *German in the Yankee Fatherland,* 101.

78. Affeld [1 IL LA B] Diary, May 22, 1863, Taylor's Battery Digital Collection; Kircher [12 MO] to Mother, May 26, 1863, Hess, ed., *German in the Yankee Fatherland,* 102; Ritner [25 IA] to Emeline, May 23, 1863, Larimer, ed., *Love and Valor,* 169-70; Kircher [12 MO] to Mother, May 26, 1863, Hess, ed., *German in the Yankee Fatherland,* 102.

79. A recently more nuanced, if still critical, interpretation of Sherman's performance is Hess, *Storming Vicksburg,* 276, 379, 381.

80. Bearss, *Campaign for Vicksburg* 3: 844; Grabau, *Ninety-Eight Days,* 369-70.

81. WTS, *Memoirs,* 353; USG, *Personal Memoirs,* 277; Hess, *Storming Vicksburg,* 383.

82. "Siege of Vicksburg: News to Tuesday, May 26th," *Chicago Tribune,* June 2, 1863; "The Seige [*sic*] of Vicksburg," *New York Times,* June 2, 1863.

83. Farwell [31 IA] to Parents, May 24, 1863, Farwell Letters, SHSI Iowa City; Bell [25 IA], May 23, 1863, Bearss "Diary of Captain John N. Bell," 211; Bear [116 IL] to Wife, May 21, 1863, Temple, ed., *Civil War Letters,* 41; Seay [32 MO], May 22, 1863, Sigler and Sigler, eds., *Civil War Diary,* 48.

6. ONE OF THE BEST TRAINING SCHOOLS

1. WTS to Grant, May 22, 1863, *OR* I, 24; III, 341.

2. G.O. 39, HQ 15 AC, May 22, 1863, *OR* I, 24; III, 342.

3. G.O. 40, HQ 15 AC, May 24, 1863, *OR* I, 24; III, 344, 348.

4. Solonick, *Engineering Victory,* 4.

5. Sodergren, *Army of the Potomac,* 11; John D. Antwerp [26 IA] to Samuel Van Antwerp, June 5, 1863, Spared & Shared Digital Collection; Affeld [1 IL LA B] Diary, May 22, 1863, Taylor's Battery Digital Collection; Thomas B. Coffman [30 IA] to Jeannette, May 29, 1863, Thomas B. Coffman Letters, SHSI Iowa City.

6. G.O. 40, HQ, 15 AC, May 24, 1863, *OR* I, 24; III, 344.

7. G.O. 40, HQ, 15 AC, May 24, 1863, *OR* I, 24; III, 344. W. L. B. Jenney Report, Sept. 22, 1863, *OR* I, 24; II, 187. Seaward [9 IA] Diary, June 24, 1863, Seaward Papers, SHSI Des Moines.

8. Jenney Report, Sept. 22, 1863, *OR* I, 24; II, 188; Frederick Prime and Cyrus Comstock Report, *OR* I, 24; II, 171. Crooker et al., *Story of the Fifty-Fifth,* 249. Solonick, *Engineering Victory,* 63–64.

9. Crooker et al., *Story of the Fifty-Fifth,* 248.

10. Frederick Prime and Cyrus Comstock Report, *OR* I, 24; II, 172.

11. Bearss, *Campaign for Vicksburg* 3: 901–4.

12. Solonick, *Engineering Victory,* 93.

13. G.O. 44, 15 AC, June 9, 1863, *OR* I, 24; III, 394.

14. Willison [76 OH], *Reminiscences,* 56; Ritner [25 IA] to Emeline, May 30, 1863, Larimer, ed., *Love and Valor,* 174.

15. John Gay [25 IA], May 27, 1863, John Gay Diary, SHSI Iowa City.

16. Arch M. Brinkerhoff [4 IA], June 2, 1863, Edwin C. Bearss, ed., "Diary of Private Arch M. Brinkerhoff," 228.

17. Brinkerhoff [4 IA], June 4, 6, 1863, Bearss, "Diary of Private Arch M. Brinkerhoff," 228–29; Ritner [25 IA] to Emeline, June 5, 1863, Larimer, ed., *Love and Valor,* 179.

18. Crooker et al., *Story of the Fifty-Fifth,* 248; Willison [76 OH] *Reminiscences,* 57.

19. Ritner [25 IA] to Emeline, June 5, 1863, Larimer, ed., *Love and Valor,* 179.

20. Bearss, *Campaign for Vicksburg* 3: 897, 903.

21. Henry [26 IA] to Wife, June 20, 1863, Henry Letters, SHSI Iowa City.

22. Brinkerhoff [4 IA], June 8, 1863, Bearss, "Diary of Private Arch M. Brinkerhoff"; Bearss, *Campaign for Vicksburg* 3: 229.

23. Brinkerhoff [4 IA], June 17, 1863, Bearss, "Diary of Private Arch M. Brinkerhoff"; Bearss, *Campaign for Vicksburg* 3: 231.

24. Willison [76 OH], *Reminiscences,* 61.

25. Brinkheroff [4 IA], July 2, 1863, Bearss, "Diary of Private Arch M. Brinkerhoff," 235; Willison [76 OH], *Reminiscences,* 62; Bell [25 IA] Diary, June 1, 1863, Bearss, "Diary of Captain John N. Bell," 214.

26. John Mains [6 MO] to Father, July 26, 1863, John Mains Letters, SHSM Rolla; Brinkerhoff [4 IA], June 2, 8, 12, 13, 15, 16, 17, 18, 20, 1863, Bearss, "Diary of Private Arch M. Brinkerhoff"; Bearss, *Campaign for Vicksburg* 3: 228; Brinkerhoff, *History of the Thirtieth Regiment,* 30–31; Bell [25 IA] Diary, June 19, 1863, Bearss, "Diary of Captain John N. Bell," 220.

27. Brinkerhoff [4 IA], June 30, 1863, Bearss, "Diary of Private Arch M. Brinkerhoff," 234.

28. John D. Antwerp [26 IA] to Samuel Van Antwerp, June 5, 1863, Spared & Shared Digital Collection.

29. G.O. 26, HQ 26 IA, June 17, 1863; G.O. 27, HQ 26 IA, June 18, 1863, 26th IA Regimental Order Book, RG 94, NARA. Circular, HQ 30 IA, June 28, 1863, 30th IA Regimental Order Book, RG 94, NARA. G.O. 81, HQ 25 IA, June 8, 1863, Co. C, 25th IA Order Book, RG 94, NARA.

30. G.O. 44, 15 AC, June 9, 1863, *OR* I, 24; III, 395.

31. Farwell [31 IA] to Wife, June 28, 1863, Farwell Letters, SHSI Iowa City.

32. Farwell [31 IA] to Brother, July 1, 1863, Farwell Letters, SHSI Iowa City.

33. William Nugen [25 IA] to Mary, June 24, 1863, William Nugen Letters, David M. Rubenstein Rare Book and Manuscript Library, Duke University; "Abstract from Return," *OR* I, 24; III, 249, 453.

34. Willison [76 OH], *Reminiscences,* 60.

35. John Gay [25 IA], June 15, 1863, John Gay Diary, SHSI Iowa City.

36. David Holmes [55 IL] to Parents, June 2, 1863, Holmes Papers, ALPL.

37. Bell [25 IA], June 11, 1863, Bearss, "Diary of Captain John N. Bell," 218; Ritner [25 IA] to Emeline, June 15, 1863, Larimer, ed., *Love and Valor,* 185.

38. Crooker et al., *Story of the Fifth-Fifth,* 250.

39. Farwell [31 IA] to Sister, June 2, 1863, Farwell Letters, SHSI Iowa City; Crooker et al., *Story of the Fifth-Fifth,* 251.

40. Crooker et al., *Story of the Fifth-Fifth,* 253.

41. Ballard, *Vicksburg,* 394–95; Bearss, *Campaign for Vicksburg* 3: 969–1139.

42. Bearss, *Campaign for Vicksburg* 3: 901.

43. William Kossak Report, July 13, 1863, *OR* I, 24; II, 189–90. G.O. 48, 15 AC, June 19, 1863, *OR* I, 24; III, 419.

44. John Mains [6 MO] to Parents, June 24, 1863, Mains Letters, SHSM Rolla.

45. Farwell [31 IA] to Brother, June 14, 1863, Farwell Letters, SHSI Iowa City.

46. Farwell [31 IA] to Wife, June 7, 1863, Farwell Letters, SHSI Iowa City.

47. Capron [55 IL], June 29, 1863, "War Diary," 365.

48. Prime and Comstock Report, *OR* I, 24; II, 175. Kossak Report, *OR* I, 24; II, 190.

49. Prime and Comstock Report, *OR* I, 24; II, 170.

50. Kossak Report, *OR* I, 24; II, 190.

51. Wylie [31 IA] to Brother, July 4, 1863, Wylie Papers, SHSI Iowa City; Henry [26 IA] to Wife, July 4, 1863, Henry Letters, SHSI Iowa City.

52. Crooker et al., *Story of the Fifth-Fifth,* 255.

53. Seaward [9 IA] Diary, July 4, 1863, Seaward Papers, SHSI Des Moines.

54. Wylie [31 IA] to Brother, July 4, 1863, Wylie Papers, SHSI Iowa City.

55. Capron [55 IL], June 18, 1863, "War Diary," 364.

56. Capron [55 IL], July 4, 1863, "War Diary," 365.

57. Brinkerhoff, *History of the Thirtieth Regiment*, 31.

58. Miller [76 OH], Bennet and Tillery, eds., *Struggle for the Life*, 98, 105.

59. Miller [76 OH], Bennet and Tillery, eds., *Struggle for the Life*, 105.

60. Miller [76 OH], Bennet and Tillery, eds., *Struggle for the Life*, 98.

61. Solonick, *Engineering Victory*, 136-37, 155.

62. G. Froehlich Report [4 OH LA], July 29, 1863, Ewing Papers, Ohio History Center.

63. Froehlich Report [4 OH LA], July 29, 1863, Ewing Papers, Ohio History Center.

64. John W. Rumsey [1 IL LA A], August 11, 1863, Ewing Papers, Ohio History Center.

65. Affeld [1 IL LA B] Diary, May 22, 1863, Taylor's Battery Digital Collection.

66. Kimbell, *History of Battery "A,"* 64.

67. Coffman [30 IA] to Jeannette, May 29, 1863, Coffman Letters, SHSI Iowa City; Ewing Papers, Ohio History Center.

68. Affeld [1 IL LA B] Diary, May 22, 1863, Taylor's Battery Digital Collection.

69. Prime and Comstock Report, *OR* I, 24; II, 175.

70. Brinkerhoff [4 IA], May 28, 1863, Bearss, "Diary of Private Arch M. Brinkerhoff," 226.

71. Prime and Comstock Report, *OR* I, 24; II, 177.

72. Ritner [25 IA] to Emeline, June 5, 1863, Larimer, ed., *Love and Valor*, 179.

73. Crooker et al., *Story of the Fifth-Fifth*, 255.

74. Crooker et al., *Story of the Fifth-Fifth*, 257.

75. Henry [26 IA] to Wife, July 15, 1863, Henry Letters, SHSI Iowa City.

76. Crooker et al., *Story of the Fifty-Fifth*, 255-57; Kimbell, *History of Battery "A,"* 64; Farwell [31 IA], Undated Manuscript, Farwell Papers, SHSI Iowa City; Wylie [31 IA] to Brother, Aug. 9, 1863, Wylie Papers, SHSI Iowa City; *Thirteenth Regiment*, 333-34.

77. Crooker et al., *Story of the Fifty-Fifth*, 257.

78. Crooker et al., *Story of the Fifty-Fifth*, 258.

79. "Capture of Jackson," *New York Times*, Aug. 1, 1863.

80. WTS to Porter, July 19, 1863, *SCW*, 504.

81. Buegel [3 MO] Diary, SHSM Columbia, 30.

82. Crooker et al., *Story of the Fifth-Fifth*, 258.

83. Kimbell, *History of Battery "A,"* 64, 70-71.

84. Froehlich [4 OH LA] Report, July 29, 1863, Ewing Papers, Ohio History Center.

85. Crooker et al., *Story of the Fifth-Fifth*, 259.

86. Ballard, *Vicksburg*, 409-10.

87. USG to WTS, July 3, 1863, *OR* I, 24; III, 461. USG to WTS, July 4, 1863, *OR* I, 24; III, 473.

88. Grimsley, *Hard Hand of War*, 159.

89. WTS to USG, July 28, 1863, *OR* I, 24; II, 536.

90. WTS to Porter, July 19, 1863, *SCW*, 505.

91. WTS to USG, July 28, 1863, *OR* I, 24; II, 537.

92. "Capture of Jackson," *New York Times*, Aug. 1, 1863.

93. WTS to Grant, July 20, 1863, *OR* I, 24; II, 530.

94. WTS to USG, July 21, 1863, *OR* I, 24; II, 530. WTS to USG, July 22, 1863, *OR* I, 24; II, 531.

95. WTS to Grant, July 17, 1863, *OR* I, 24; II, 528. WTS to Grant, July 18, 1863, *OR* I, 24; II, 529. WTS to USG, July 20, 1863, *OR* I, 24; II, 530.

96. WTS to Philemon B. Ewing, July 28, 1863, *SCW,* 508; WTS to David Stuart, Aug. 1, 1863, *SCW,* 512.

97. Hart, *Sherman,* 202.

98. Farwell [31 IA] to Brother, July 22, 1863, Farwell Letters, SHSI Iowa City.

99. Willison [76 OH], *Reminiscences,* 66; G.O. 96, HQ 25 IA, Aug. 4, 1863, 25 IA Regimental Order Book, RG 94, NARA.

100. "Untitled Report," Ewing Papers, Ohio History Center; "Report of 76th Ohio," Ewing Papers.

7. JUST IN FROM THE MISSISSIPPI

1. Underwood, *Three Years' Service,* 177; Cozzens, *Shipwreck of Their Hopes;* Sword, *Mountains Touched with Fire.*

2. Sears, *Lincoln's Lieutenants,* 79–104; Rafuse, *McClellan's War,* 130–31; Glatthaar, *March to the Sea,* xii.

3. Underwood, *Three Years' Service,* 177; Henry [26 IA] to Wife, Dec. 9, 1863, Henry Letters, SHSI Iowa City.

4. Crooker et al., *Story of the Fifty-Fifth,* 280.

5. Ritner [25 IA] to Emeline, Nov. 20, 1863, Larimer, ed., *Love and Valor,* 244.

6. Crooker et al., *Story of the Fifty-Fifth,* 281.

7. Wiley, *Life of Billy Yank,* 321–24; Hess, *Civil War in the West,* 311–15.

8. Woodworth, *Nothing but Victory,* x.

9. G.O. 3, HQ 1 DIV 15 AC, Sept. 3, 1863, RG 393, NARA; G.O. 4, HQ 1 DIV 15 AC, Sept. 5, 1863, RG 393, NARA.

10. Cozzens, *Shipwreck of Their Hopes,* 108–10; Woodworth, *Nothing but Victory,* 460.

11. Farwell [31 IA] to Wife, Nov. 19, 1863, Farwell Letters, SHSI Iowa City.

12. Cozzens, *Shipwreck of Their Hopes,* 120–25.

13. Delos Van Deusen [6 MO] to Wife, Nov. 17, 1863, Van Deusen Papers, Huntington Library.

14. Ritner [25 IA] to Emeline, Nov. 17, 1863, Larimer, ed., *Love and Valor,* 238–39.

15. Crooker et al., *Story of the Fifty-Fifth,* 263.

16. "Abstract of Returns," Nov. 30, 1863, *OR* I, 31; III, 292.

17. Dyer, *Compendium of the War of the Rebellion* 1: 498.

18. Townsend, *Yankee Warhorse,* 120.

19. Buegel [3 MO] Diary, SHSM Columbia, 15.

20. Kircher [12 MO] to Mother, Sept. 26, 1863, Hess, ed., *German in the Yankee Fatherland,* 125.

21. Ainsworth [25 IA] Diary, BHL, 66.

22. Townsend, *Yankee Warhorse,* 118.

23. Townsend, *Yankee Warhorse,* 61.

24. Dyer, *Compendium of the War of the Rebellion* 1: 498.

25. Circular, Sept. 3, 1863, HQ 1 DIV 15 AC, RG 393, NARA.

26. S.O. 5, Sept. 5, 1863, HQ 1 DIV 15 AC, RG 393, NARA; Anderson, *Austro-Prussian War*, 18.

27. Dyer, *Compendium of the War of the Rebellion* 1: 499.

28. G.O. 1, Oct. 11, 1863, HQ 2 DIV 15 AC, RG 393, NARA.

29. Dyer, *Compendium of the War of the Rebellion* 1: 500–502.

30. Dyer, *Compendium of the War of the Rebellion* 1: 497.

31. Woodworth, *Nothing but Victory*, 462–63; Cozzens, *Shipwreck of Their Hopes*, 114–16.

32. USG to GHT, Nov. 18, 1863, in USG, *Memoirs*, 335.

33. WTS to JS, Dec. 29, 1863, *SCW*, 577.

34. Orders, 15 AC, Nov. 23, 1863, *OR* I, 31; II, 589–90.

35. Woodworth, *Nothing but Victory*, 465–66.

36. Sherman's Report, Dec. 19, 1863, *OR* I, 31; II, 572.

37. *History of the Thirty-Seventh Regiment*, 198; Crooker et al., *Story of the Fifth-Fifth*, 282; Saunier, ed., *History of the Forty-seventh Regiment*, 198.

38. Crooker et al., *Story of the Fifty-Fifth*, 283.

39. *History of the Thirty-Seventh Regiment*, 26.

40. Castel, *Tom Taylor's Civil War* [47 OH], 85.

41. Crooker et al., *Story of the Fifth-Fifth*, 283.

42. Castel, *Tom Taylor's Civil War*, 85–86.

43. Castel, *Tom Taylor's Civil War*, 86; Peterson, *Decisions at Chattanooga*, 44.

44. Sherman's Report, Dec. 19, 1863, *OR* I, 31; II, 573.

45. Woodworth, *Nothing but Victory*, 58; E. W. Muenscher [30 OH], "Missionary Ridge," *National Tribune*, Apr. 8, 1909, 7.

46. Muenscher [30 OH], "Missionary Ridge," 7; *Tom Taylor's Civil War*, 85.

47. Cozzens, *Shipwreck of Their Hopes*, 151–54. Report of Brig. Gen. Joseph Lightburn, Nov. 28, 1863, *OR* I, 31; II, 629.

48. Sherman's Report, Dec. 19, 1863, *OR* I, 31; II, 573. Woodworth, ed., *Chattanooga Campaign*, 59. Peterson, *Decisions at Chattanooga*, 62.

49. Sword, *Mountains Touched with Fire*, 198–99; N. M. Baker [116 IL], "Wounding of Gen. Giles A. Smith," *National Tribune*, July 24, 1902, 3.

50. USG to WTS, Nov. 24, 1863, *PUSG* 9: 441.

51. Woodworth, ed., *Chattanooga Campaign*, 67–68.

52. Sherman's Report, Dec. 19, 1863, *OR* I, 31; II, 574;

53. Cozzens, *Shipwreck of Their Hopes*, 206.

54. Lightburn's Report, *OR* I, 31; II, 629. Muenscher [30 OH], "Missionary Ridge," *National Tribune*, Apr. 8, 1909, 7.

55. Cozzens, *Shipwreck of Their Hopes*, 204–10.

56. Cozzens, *Shipwreck of Their Hopes*, 211–43. Woodworth, ed., *Chattanooga Campaign*, 61–65. Report of Brig. Gen. Hugh Ewing, Nov. 28, 1863, *OR* I, 31; II, 631–32. Report of Col. John M. Loomis, Dec. 6, 1863, *OR* I, 31; II, 633–35.

57. Cozzens, *Shipwreck of Their Hopes*, 235–39.

58. Thomas Taylor [47 OH] to Netta, Dec. 20, 1863, Thomas Taylor Papers, Ohio History Center [OHC].

59. Powell, *Impulse of Victory*, 181.

60. Cozzens, *Shipwreck of Their Hopes*, 241.

61. Peterson, *Decisions at Chattanooga*, 69.

62. Smith, "Historical Sketch," 210.

63. Cozzens, *Shipwreck of their Hopes*, 241-43.

64. Capron [55 IL] to Family, Nov. 29, 1863, "War Diary," 371.

65. Hart, *Sherman*, 221.

66. Kircher [12 MO] Diary, May 22, 1863, Hess, ed., *German in the Yankee Fatherland*, 101; Kircher [12 MO] to Mother, May 24, 1863, 100.

8. THE WAY IN WHICH THEY ATTEMPTED TO GO

1. Townsend, *Yankee Warhorse*, 124-25.

2. Cozzens, *Shipwreck of Their Hopes*, 159-63.

3. Townsend, *Yankee Warhorse*, 124.

4. Cozzens, *Shipwreck of Their Hopes*, 162.

5. "Report of Brig. Gen. Peter J. Osterhaus," Dec. 1863, *OR* I, 31; II, 598-600. "Report of Brig. Gen. Charles R. Woods," Nov. 28, 1863, *OR* I, 31; II, 606-7.

6. Ainsworth [25 IA] Diary, Nov. 24, 1863, BHL.

7. Wilhelm Osterhorn [31 MO] to Minna, Dec. 8, 1863, Osterhorn Papers, MHM.

8. Ainsworth [25 IA] Diary, Nov. 24, 1863, BHL; Seaward [9 IA] Diary, Nov. 25, 1863, Seaward Papers, SHSI Des Moines, 113.

9. W. R. Oake [26 IA], Allen, ed., *On the Skirmish Line*, 142.

10. Osterhaus's *OR* Report, 601-62; Woods's *OR* Report, 607; Townsend, *Yankee Warhorse*, 128.

11. Woods's *OR* Report, 607-9; Oake [26 IA], Allen, ed., *On the Skirmish Line*, 143-44.

12. Osterhaus's *OR* Report, 602. Buegel [3 MO] Diary, SHSM Columbia, 34. Townsend, *Yankee Warhorse*, 128-29. "Report of Col. James A. Williamson," Nov. 28, 1863, *OR* I, 31; II, 613-14.

13. Henry [26 IA] to Wife, Dec. 9, 1863, Henry Letters, SHSI Iowa City.

14. Henry [26 IA] to Wife, Dec. 9, 1863.

15. Woods's *OR* Report, 607; Williamson's *OR* Report, 614; Townsend, *Yankee Warhorse*, 128.

16. Buegel [3 MO] Diary, SHSM Columbia, 34.

17. Buegel [3 MO] Diary, 34.

18. *Thirteenth Regiment*, 375.

19. Wylie [31 IA] to Father, Dec. 2, 1863, Wylie Letters, SHSI Iowa City.

20. Cozzens, *Shipwreck of Their Hopes*, 197-98.

21. Buegel [3 MO] Diary, SHSM Columbia, 34.

22. Ainsworth [25 IA] Diary, Nov. 25, 1863, BHL; Townsend, *Yankee Warhorse*, 130.

23. Osterhaus's *OR* Report, 600. Townsend, *Yankee Warhorse*, 131. "Report of Col. Thomas Curly" [27 MO], Dec. 13, 1863, *OR* I, 31; II, 610-11.

24. Osterhaus's *OR* Report, 600-601; Woods's *OR* Report, 607; Williamson's *OR* Report, 614-15; Townsend, *Yankee Warhorse*, 131-32.

25. Seay [32 MO], Sigler and Sigler, eds., *Civil War Diary*, 63; Osterhaus's *OR* Report, 601-2; Williamson's *OR* Report, 615; Woods's *OR* Report, 607-9; Townsend, *Yankee Warhorse*, 131-33.

26. Willison [76 OH], *Reminiscences,* 77; Osterhorn [31 MO] to Minna, Dec. 8, 1863, Osterhorn Family Papers, MHM.

27. Townsend, *Yankee Warhorse,* 132-35; Osterhaus's *OR* Report, 601-2; Woods's *OR* Report, 607-8; Williamson's *OR* Report, 615-16.

28. Townsend, *Yankee Warhorse,* 134; Cozzens, *Shipwreck of Their Hopes,* 315-19.

29. Townsend, *Yankee Warhorse,* 135. The best operational treatments of the battle of Ringgold Gap can be found in Justin S. Solonick, "Saving the Army of Tennessee: The Confederate Rear Guard at Ringgold Gap," in Woodworth, ed., *Chattanooga Campaign,* 132-50; Cozzens, *Shipwreck of Their Hopes,* 370-84; and Sword, *Mountains Touched with Fire,* 334-46.

30. Osterhaus's *OR* Report, 603; Townsend, *Yankee Warhorse,* 135-36.

31. Osterhaus's *OR* Report, 604; Townsend, *Yankee Warhorse,* 136-37.

32. Buegel [3 MO] Diary, SHSM Columbia, 35.

33. Osterhaus's *OR* Report, 604; Townsend, *Yankee Warhorse,* 138.

34. Osterhaus's *OR* Report, 604; Woods's *OR* Report, 608.

35. *Thirteenth Regiment,* 384; Woods's *OR* Report, 608.

36. Osterhaus's *OR* Report, 604; Solonick, "Saving the Army of Tennessee," in Woodworth, ed., *Chattanooga Campaign,* 138.

37. Williamson's *OR* Report, 616-17.

38. Ainsworth [25 IA] Diary, Nov. 27, 1863, BHL.

39. Ainsworth [25 IA] Diary, Nov. 27, 1863.

40. W. R. Oake [26 IA], Allen, ed., *On the Skirmish Line,* 148.

41. Williamson's *OR* Report, 616-17.

42. Osterhaus's *OR* Report, 604; Osterhorn [31 MO] to Minna, Dec. 8, 1863, MHM; Woods's *OR* Report, 608.

43. "Report of Col. Thomas J. Ahl" [28 PA], *OR* I, 31; II, 413-14.

44. "Report of Capt. E. J. Krieger" [7 OH], *OR* I, 31; II, 417-19.

45. Cozzens, *Shipwreck of Their Hopes,* 381.

46. Williamson's *OR* Report, 616-17. "Report of Col. George Stone," Nov. 28, 1863, *OR* I, 31; II, 623. Ainsworth [25 IA] Diary, Nov. 27, 1863, BHL.

47. Krieger [7 OH] Report, Dec. 3, 1863, *OR* I, 31; II, 418.

48. Skinner, *Pennsylvania at Chickamauga and Chattanooga,* 84.

49. Skinner, *Pennsylvania at Chickamauga and Chattanooga,* 84.

50. E. J. Krieger [7 OH] Report, Dec. 3, 1863, *OR* I, 31; II, 418.

51. Cozzens, *Shipwreck of Their Hopes,* 382; Skinner, *Pennsylvania at Chickamauga and Chattanooga,* 84.

52. Ainsworth [25 IA] Diary, Nov. 27, 1863, BHL.

53. Ainsworth [25 IA] Diary, Nov. 27, 1863.

54. Williamson's *OR* Report, 617. "Report of Maj. Willard Warner" [76 OH], Nov. 28, 1863, *OR* I, 31; II, 611-12.

55. Williamson's *OR* Report, 616-17.

56. Dyer, *Compendium of the War of the Rebellion* 2: 1499, 1527-28, 1586; Wilson, *Itinerary of the Seventh Ohio;* Wood, *Seventh Regiment.*

57. Wilson, *Itinerary of the Seventh Ohio,* 134-43; Wood, *Seventh Regiment,* 94-103.

58. Wood, *Seventh Regiment*, 101, 126-27; Wilson, *Itinerary of the Seventh Ohio*, 166-70, 183-93.

59. Lynn, "The Battle Culture of Forbearance, 1660-1789," in Lee, ed., *Warfare and Culture*, 89-113.

60. Wood, *Seventh Regiment*, 137-51; Wilson, *Itinerary of the Seventh Ohio*, 202-14.

61. Van Deusen [6 MO] to Wife, Nov. 27, 1863, Van Deusen Papers, Huntington Library.

62. *37th Regiment*, 27.

63. Capron [55 IL], Nov. 29, 1863, "War Diary," 370-72.

64. George Hildt [30 OH] to Parents, Jan. 2, 1864, Hildt Papers, OHC; Muenscher [30 OH], "Missionary Ridge," *National Tribune*, Apr. 8, 1909, 7.

65. Ainsworth [25 IA] Diary, Nov. 27, 1863, BHL.

66. Withrow [25 IA] to Lib, Dec. 2, 1863, Withrow Papers, SHC-UNC.

67. Van Deusen [6 MO] to Wife, Nov. 27, 1863, Van Deusen Papers, Huntington Library.

68. Van Deusen [6 MO] to Wife, Nov. 28, 1863.

69. Ritner [25 IA] to Emeline, Nov. 29, 1863, Larimer, ed., *Love and Valor*, 257.

CONCLUSION

1. "Consolidated Monthly Return," 1 DIV, 15 AC, April 1864, RG 393, NARA.

2. Dyer, *Compendium of the War of the Rebellion* 1: 497-98.

3. S.O. 55, HQ 1 DIV, 15 AC, Feb. 24, 1864, RG 393, NARA.

4. S.O. 92, HQ 1 DIV, 15 AC, Apr. 1, 1864, RG 393, NARA. By contrast, all Rebel commands had been ordered by the Confederate government in Richmond to form their own dedicated "sharpshooter battalions" as early as May 1862. Haughton, *Training, Tactics, and Leadership*, 84-85.

5. S.O. 65, HQ 1 DIV, 15 AC, Mar. 5, 1864, RG 393, NARA.

6. 1870 US Federal Census.

7. Hess, *Fighting for Atlanta*, 4.

8. Jones, *Blackjack*, 195; WTS to JS, June 9, 1864, *SCW*, 645; Hess, *Fighting for Atlanta*, 4.

9. Hess, *Rifle Musket*, 156-57.

10. Hess, *Civil War Infantry Tactics*, 101.

11. Haughton, *Training, Tactics, and Leadership*.

12. "Report of Brig. Gen. Giles A. Smith," May 22, 1864, *OR* I, 38; III, 191. Hess, *Fighting for Atlanta*, 47.

13. "Report of Brig. Gen. Joseph A. J. Lightburn," June 28, 1864, *OR* I, 38; III, 222.

14. Baumgartner and Strayer, *Kennesaw Mountain*, 114-20.

15. WTS to Thomas, June 27, 1864, *OR* I, 38; IV, 611. Thomas to WTS, June 27, 1864, *OR* I, 38; IV, 610.

16. WTS to Ellen Sherman, June 30, 1864, *SCW*, 660.

17. WTS to Ellen Sherman, July 9, 1864, *SCW*, 663.

18. Woodworth, *Nothing but Victory*, 507-19.

19. The most comprehensive treatments of the battle of Atlanta remain Ecelbarger, *The Day Dixie Died*, and Bonds, *War Like a Thunderbolt*. Castel, *Decision in the West*, 408.

20. The most comprehensive modern treatments of the battle of Ezra Church are Ecelbarger, *Slaughter at the Chapel,* and Hess, *The Battle of Ezra Church and the Struggle for Atlanta.* Ecelbarger, *Slaughter at the Chapel,* 88.

21. WTS, *Memoirs,* 885.

22. Hess, *Rifle Musket,* 173-74.

23. "Army Circles Astonished," *New York Times,* Mar. 17, 1881, 5; Clark, *Preparing for War,* 93.

24. 1870 US Federal Census; Nosworthy, *Bloody Crucible of Courage,* 313.

25. Muir, *Tactics and the Experience of Battle,* 16.

26. Burns, "How did the British Army adapt to North America in the French and Indian War."

27. Rothenberg, *Art of Warfare,* 21.

28. Spring, *With Zeal and With Bayonets Only.*

29. Watson, *Jackson's Sword,* 14; Bonura, *Under the Shadow of Napoleon;* Hsieh, *West Pointers.*

30. Hess, *Union Soldier in Battle,* 47.

31. Nosworthy, *Bloody Crucible of Courage,* 22-60; Hess, *Rifled Musket,* 9-34.

32. Hsieh, *West Pointers,* 8.

33. Glatthaar, *March to the Sea,* 38; Gibbons, *Destroying Angel.*

34. Muir, *Tactics and the Experience of Battle,* 67.

35. Mahan, *Elementary Treatise,* 42; Craighill, *1862 Army Officer's Pocket Companion,* 176-78.

36. Mahan, *Elementary Treatise,* 51.

37. Mahan, *Elementary Treatise,* 50.

38. Mahan, *Elementary Treatise,* 41.

39. Mahan, *Elementary Treatise,* 41.

40. Mahan, *Elementary Treatise,* 41-42.

41. Mahan, *Elementary Treatise,* 41.

42. Sodergren, *Army of the Potomac.*

43. De Peyster, "American Infantry Tactics," *Army and Navy Journal,* Oct. 28, 1865, 149-50.

44. De Peyster, "Our Infantry Tactics," *Army and Navy Journal,* Nov. 4, 1865, 164-65.

45. De Peyster, "Our Infantry Tactics," 164-65.

46. Wagner, *Organization and Tactics,* 96.

47. Wagner, *Organization and Tactics,* 119.

48. Wagner, *Organization and Tactics,* 101-2.

49. Wagner, *Organization and Tactics,* 102.

50. Wagner, *Organization and Tactics,* 105.

51. Jamieson, *Crossing the Deadly Ground,* 93.

52. Jamieson, *Crossing the Deadly Ground,* 93, 101-3.

53. US Army, *Infantry Drill Regulations,* adopted October 3, 1891.

54. Earl Hess has observed how the coordinative challenges of large-unit frontal assaults tended to hamper the offensive operations of the Army of the Tennessee more than other Civil War field armies. This work has provided an answer for why this was the case for at least one of the army's three primary corps. Hess, *Storming Vicksburg,* 379-80.

55. For a more comprehensive discussion of the evolution of US Army infantry assault tactics during the period, see Jamieson, *Crossing the Deadly Ground.* The still surviving obses-

sion with the power of the bayonet even as late as 1918 is evident in Grotelueschen, *The AEF Way of War,* 1-58. Also see Bonura, *Under the Shadow of Napoleon.*

56. By far the best work concerning the influence of the Peninsula Campaign on the Lincoln administration's embrace of emancipation is Brasher, *The Peninsula Campaign & the Necessity of Emancipation.*

57. Grimsley, *Hard Hand of War,* 3-4, 104.

58. Teters, *Practical Liberators.*

BIBLIOGRAPHY

MANUSCRIPTS

Abraham Lincoln Presidential Library [ALPL]
  David Holmes Papers

Bentley Historical Library, University of Michigan [BHL]
  Calvin Ainsworth Diary

David M. Rubenstein Rare Book and Manuscript Library, Duke University
  Robert Bruce Hoadley Papers
  9th Iowa Letters
  William H. Nugen Papers
  Snow Family Papers

Filson Historical Society
  J. H. Hammond Papers and Diaries

Flagg Creek Heritage Society
  Hiram McClintock Letters

Huntington Library
  Delos Van Deusen Papers

Iowa State Archives, Des Moines
  Adjutant General Records
    Civil War Regimental Morning Reports
      4th Iowa Infantry
      9th Iowa Infantry
      25th Iowa Infantry
      30th Iowa Infantry
      31st Iowa Infantry

John L. Nau Civil War Collection
    George W. Browning Papers

Library of Congress
    William T. Sherman Papers

Missouri History Museum [MHM]
    David Allan Jr. Letters
    William Augustus Letters
    John T. Clarke Letters
    Howard A. Cooper Papers
    John Downey Papers
    Hiffman Family Papers
    Leonard A. Horn Papers
    David Monlux Letters
    Johann Wilhelm Osterhorn Papers
    William Charlds Pfeffer Diary
    John Schenk Quartermaster Record Books
    Henry Voelkner Letters
    Alpheus C. Williams Diary

Missouri State Archives, Springfield
    Adjutant General's Records
        Regimental Muster Rolls and Morning Reports
            6th Missouri Infantry
            8th Missouri Infantry
            12th Missouri Infantry
            17th Missouri Infantry
            29th Missouri Infantry
            30th Missouri Infantry
            31st Missouri Infantry
            32nd Missouri Infantry

        Record Group 133: Unbound Regimental Records
            8th Missouri Infantry

National Archives and Records Administration [NARA]
    M619: Letters Received by the Adjutant General, 1861–1870
        Morgan L. Smith

M1407: Barred and Disallowed Case Files of the Southern Claims Commission, 1871–1880
  Issaquena County, Mississippi
  Washington County, Mississippi

Record Group 15: Department of Veterans Affairs
  Matthew Egan Widow's Pension Application
  John A. Miller Widow's Pension Application

Record Group 94: Records of the Adjutant General's Office, 1775–1928
  Register of Enlistments in the U.S. Army, 1798–1914

Record Group 94.2.4: Records Relating to Volunteers and Volunteer Organizations
    1st Illinois Light Artillery
    13th Illinois Infantry
    55th Illinois Infantry
    111th Illinois Infantry
    116th Illinois Infantry
    127th Illinois Infantry
    83rd Indiana Infantry
    1st Iowa Light Artillery
    4th Iowa Infantry
    9th Iowa Infantry
    25th Iowa Infantry
    30th Iowa Infantry
    31st Iowa Infantry
    28th/29th Louisiana Infantry
    3rd Missouri Infantry
    6th Missouri Infantry
    8th Missouri Infantry
    12th Missouri Infantry
    17th Missouri Infantry
    29th Missouri Infantry
    30th Missouri Infantry
    31st Missouri Infantry
    32nd Missouri Infantry
    4th Ohio Light Artillery
    30th Ohio Infantry

37th Ohio Infantry
47th Ohio Infantry
54th Ohio Infantry
57th Ohio Infantry
76th Ohio Infantry
Colonel Joseph Octave Landry, C.S., Combined Service Record
Colonel Allen Thomas, C.S., Combined Service Record

Record Group 393: Records of United States Army Continental Commands, 1821—1920
   Headquarters, 15th Army Corps
   1st Division, 15th Army Corps
   2nd Division, 15th Army Corps

Northern Illinois University—Digital Library, digital.lib.niu.edu
   The Civil War Journals of Wilson E. Chapel

Ohio History Center [OHC]
   Stephen P. Bonner Papers
   Hugh Boyle Ewing Papers
   George Hildt Papers
   Harrison H. Kerr Papers
   James M. Merryman Diary
   Thomas Taylor Papers

Past Voices Digital Collection, www.pastvoices.com
   James Maxwell Letters

Peoria Historical Society
   Philip Smith Diary

Southern Historical Collection, Wilson Library, University of North Carolina at Chapel Hill [SHC-UNC]
   D. Garver Letters
   John J. Metzgar Papers
   Henry Clay Warmouth Papers
   Adoniram J. Withrow Papers

Spared & Shared Digital Collection, www.sparedshared13.wordpress.com
   John D. Antwerp Letter

State Historical Society of Iowa–Des Moines [SHSI Des Moines]
    Alonzo Abernathy Papers
    Henry Giese Ankeny Papers
    Nathaniel M. Baughman Diary and Papers
    Joshua F. Bishop Memoir
    Edmund Cook Little Papers
    Elisha Coon Letters
    David M. Cooper Letter
    Samuel F. Cooper Papers
    Robert Davis Letter
    Moses DeMarce Diary
    Joseph H. Evans Papers
    Alfred Ames Gates War Recollections
    Henry W. Lane Papers
    Francis Rowen Papers
    William T. Seaward Papers
    Charles Spragg Letters
    Robert A. Stitt Papers

State Historical Society of Iowa–Iowa City [SHSI Iowa City]
    Anonymous 9th Iowa Diary
    Jennett Bowles Collection
    Thomas Coffman Letters
    Robert Davis Papers
    Jeremiah E. and Mollie Elson Papers
    Henry M. Farr Diary
    Sewall S. Farwell Letters
    John Gay Diary
    Robert W. Henry Letters
    Thomas D. Pollock Letter
    Shedd Family Civil War Collection
    Harry J. Simpson Letters
    Enos H. Whitacre Letters
    E. Burke Wylie Letters

State Historical Society of Missouri–Columbia [SHSM Columbia]
    John T. Buegel Civil War Diary
    William H. Lynch Diaries
    6th Missouri Infantry, Co. D Records

8th Missouri Infantry, "The Zouave Register"
A. W. Reese Papers

State Historical Society of Missouri–Rolla [SHSM Rolla].
Elizabeth Coleman Family Correspondence.
Beverly A. Davis Letters.
William Henry Lynch Papers.
John B. Mains Letters.
John Wesley Matthews Letters.
Philip A. Reilly Letters.
Jesse N. Self Letters.
James S. Spencer Diary.

Stuart A. Rose Manuscript, Archives, and Rare Book Library, Emory University.
Anthony Baurdick Papers.

Taylor's Battery Digital Collection, taylors-battery.com.
Charles Affeld Diary.
Schuyler Coe Letters.

Trempealeau County Historical Society.
Walter Hunter Letter.

University of Iowa–Special Collections.
Giauque Family Papers.

Vicksburg National Military Park.
R. W. Burt Diary.

NEWSPAPERS

Army and Navy Journal
Bayonne Herald
Burlington Weekly Hawk-Eye
Cedar Falls Gazette
Chicago Times
Chicago Tribune
Cincinnati Enquirer
Cleveland Daily Leader

Daily Missouri Democrat
Daily Missouri Republican
Harper's Weekly
Inter Ocean
National Tribune
New York Herald
New York Times
Philadelphia Inquirer
Soldier's Casket
Tennessean
Wauwatosa News
Western Reserve Chronicle

PRINTED AND WEB RESOURCES

Allen, Stacy Dale, ed. *On the Skirmish Line Behind a Friendly Tree: The Civil War Memoirs of William Royal Oake.* Helena, AR: Carcountry Press, 2006.

Ambrose, Stephen. *Halleck: Lincoln's Chief of Staff.* Baton Rouge: Louisiana State University Press, 1962.

Anderson, J. H. *The Austro-Prussian War in Bohemia, 1866.* London: Hugh Rees, Ltd., 1908.

Army, Thomas F., Jr. *Engineering Victory: How Technology Won the Civil War.* Baltimore: Johns Hopkins University Press, 2016.

Atack, Jeremy, and Fred Bateman. *To Their Own Soil: Agriculture in the Antebellum North.* Ames: Iowa State University Press, 1987.

Baker, Thomas R. *The Sacred Cause of Union: Iowa in the Civil War.* Iowa City: University of Iowa Press, 2016.

Ballard, Michael. *Vicksburg: The Campaign That Opened the Mississippi.* Chapel Hill: University of North Carolina Press, 2004.

———. *Grant at Vicksburg: The General and the Siege.* Carbondale: Southern Illinois University Press, 2013.

Bastian, David F. *Grant's Canal: The Union's Attempt to Bypass Vicksburg.* Shippensburg, PA: Burd Street Press, 1995.

Baumgartner, Richard A., and Larry M. Strayer. *Kennesaw Mountain: June 1864.* Huntington, WV: Blue Acorn Press, 1998.

Bearss, Edwin Cole. "Diary of Captain John N. Bell of Co. E, 25th Iowa Infantry, at Vicksburg." *Iowa Journal of History* 59, no. 2 (Apr. 1961): 181–221.

———. "Diary of Private Arch M. Brinkerhoff, Co. H, 4th Iowa Infantry, at Vicksburg." *Iowa Journal of History* 59, no. 2 (Apr. 1961): 267–96.

———. *The Campaign for Vicksburg.* 3 vols. Dayton, OH: Morningside Press, 1985.

Beilein, Joseph M., Jr. *Bushwhackers: Guerrilla Warfare, Manhood, and the Household in Civil War Missouri.* Kent, OH: Kent State University Press, 2016.

Bell, Andrew McIlwaine. *Mosquito Soldiers: Malaria, Yellow Fever, and the Course of the American Civil War.* Baton Rouge: Louisiana State University Press, 2010.

Bennet, Stewart, and Barbara Tillery, eds. *The Struggle for the Life of the Republic.* Kent, OH: Kent State University Press, 2004.

Bergeron, Paul H., ed. *The Papers of Andrew Johnson. Vol. 10: February–July 1866.* Knoxville: University of Tennessee Press, 1992.

Biddle, Stephen. *Military Power: Explaining Victory and Defeat in Modern Battle.* Princeton, NJ: Princeton University Press, 2004.

Black, Robert C., III. *The Railroads of the Confederacy.* Chapel Hill: University of North Carolina Press, 1998.

Bogue, Allan G. *From Prairie to Corn Belt: Farming on the Illinois and Iowa Prairies in the Nineteenth Century.* Lanham, MD: Ivan R. Dee, 2011.

Bonds, Russell S. *War Like a Thunderbolt: The Battle and Burning of Atlanta.* Yardley, PA: Westholme, 2009.

Bonura, Michael A. *Under the Shadow of Napoleon: French Influence on the American Way of Warfare from the War of 1812 to the Outbreak of WWII.* New York: New York University Press, 2012.

Borit, Gabor S., ed. *Why the Confederacy Lost.* New York: Oxford University Press, 1992.

Brasher, Glenn David. *The Peninsula Campaign & the Necessity of Emancipation: African Americans & the Fight for Freedom.* Chapel Hill: University of North Carolina Press, 2012.

Brinkerhoff, Henry R. *History of the Thirtieth Regiment Ohio Infantry.* Columbus, OH: James W. Osgood, 1863.

Burns, Alex. "How did the British Army adapt to North America in the French and Indian War." *Kabinettskriege,* June 20, 2017. kabinettskriege.blogspot.com/2017/06/how-did-british-army-adapt-to-north.html.

Capron, Thaddeus H., "War Diary of Thaddeus H. Capron, 1861–1865." *Journal of the Illinois State Historical Society* 12, no. 3 (Oct. 1919): 330–406.

Casey, Silas. *Infantry Tactics,* Vol. 2. New York: D. Van Nostrand, 1862.

Castel, Albert. *Decision in the West: The Atlanta Campaign of 1864.* Lawrence: University Press of Kansas, 1992.

———. *Tom Taylor's Civil War.* Lawrence: University Press of Kansas, 2000.

Catton, Bruce. *Grant Moves South.* Boston: Little, Brown, 1960.

Caudill, Edward, and Paul Ashdown. *Sherman's March in Myth and Memory.* Lanham, MD: Rowman & Littlefield, 2008.

Cayton, Drew, and Peter Onuf. *The Midwest and the Nation: Rethinking the History of an American Region.* Bloomington: Indiana University Press, 1990.

Chapel, Wilson E. *Civil War Journals*. Northern Illinois University Digital Library, digital.lib.niu.edu.

Citino, Robert M. "Review Essay: Military Histories Old and New: A Reintroduction." *American Historical Review* 112 (Oct. 2007): 1070–90.

Clark, J. P. *Preparing for War: The Emergence of the Modern U.S. Army, 1815–1917*. Cambridge, MA: Harvard University Press, 2017.

Committee of the Regiment. *Military History and Reminiscences of the Thirteenth Regiment of Illinois Volunteer Infantry in the Civil War in the United States 1861–1865*. Chicago: Women's Temperance Publishing Association, 1892.

———. *History of the Thirty-seventh Regiment, Ohio Veteran Volunteer Infantry and Proceedings of the Ninth Reunion, 1889*. Columbus: Ohio Historical Society, 1988.

Cozzens, Peter. *The Shipwreck of Their Hopes: The Battles for Chattanooga*. Urbana: University of Illinois Press, 1994.

Craighill, William P. *The 1862 Army Officer's Pocket Companion*. Mechanicsburg. PA: Stackpole Books, 2002.

Crane, Stephen. *The Little Regiment, and Other Episodes of the American Civil War*. New York: Appleton, 1896.

Crooker, Lucien B., Henry S. Nourse, and John G. Brown. *The Story of the Fifty-Fifth Regiment Illinois Volunteer Infantry in the Civil War, 1861–1865*. Clinton, MA: W. J. Coulter, 1887.

Cutrer, Thomas W. *Theater of a Separate War: The Civil War West of the Mississippi River 1861–1865*. Chapel Hill: University of North Carolina Press, 2017.

Daniel, Larry J. *Conquered: Why the Army of the Tennessee Failed*. Chapel Hill: University of North Carolina Press, 2019.

Dossman, Stephen Nathaniel. "The Long March to Vicksburg: Soldier and Civilian Interaction in the Vicksburg Campaign." PhD diss., Texas Christian University, 2006.

Dyer, Frederick H. *A Compendium of the War of the Rebellion*. Des Moines, IA: Dyer Publishing Co., 1908.

Ecelbarger, Gary. *The Day Dixie Died: The Battle of Atlanta*. New York: St. Martin's Press, 2010.

———. *Slaughter at the Chapel: The Battle of Ezra Church 1864*. Norman: University of Oklahoma Press, 2016.

Flood, Charles. *Grant and Sherman: The Friendship That Won the Civil War*. New York: Farrar, Straus and Giroux, 2005.

Forsyth, Michael J. *The Camden Expedition of 1864 and the Opportunity Lost by the Confederacy to Change the Civil War*. Jefferson, NC: McFarland & Co., 2003.

Frank, Joseph Allen, and George A. Reaves. *"Seeing the Elephant": Raw Recruits at the Battle of Shiloh*. New York: Greenwood Press, 1989.

Freidel, Frank. *Union Pamphlets of the Civil War, 1861–1865*. Cambridge, MA: Harvard University Press, 1967.

Gibbons, Brett. *The Destroying Angel: The Rifle Musket as the First Modern Infantry Weapon.* N.p.: Brett A. Gibbons, 2018.

Gilham, William. *Manual of Instruction for the Volunteers and Militia of the United States.* Philadelphia: Charles Desilver, 1861.

Glatthaar, Joseph T. *The March to the Sea and Beyond: Sherman's Troops in the Savannah and Carolinas Campaigns.* Baton Rouge: Louisiana State University Press, 1985.

———. *Partners in Command: The Relationships Between Leaders in the Civil War.* New York: Free Press, 1994.

———. "A Tale of Two Armies: The Confederate Army of Northern Virginia and the Union Army of the Potomac and Their Cultures." *Journal of the Civil War Era* 6 (Sept. 2016): 315–46.

Grabau, Warren E. *Ninety-Eight Days: A Geographer's View of the Vicksburg Campaign.* Knoxville: University of Tennessee Press, 2000.

Grant, Ulysses S. [USG.] *Personal Memoirs of U.S. Grant.* New York: World Publishing Co., 1952.

——— and E. B. Long, ed. *Personal Memoirs of U.S. Grant.* New York: Da Capo Press, 1982.

Grecian, J. *History of the Eighty-Third Regiment, Indiana Volunteer Infantry.* Cincinnati: John F. Uhlhorn, 1865.

Grotelueschen, Mark E. *The AEF Way of War: The American Army and Combat in World War I.* Cambridge, UK: Cambridge University Press, 2006.

Griffith, Paddy. *Battle Tactics of the Civil War.* New Haven, CT: Yale University Press, 1987.

Grimsley, Mark. *The Hard Hand of War: Union Military Policy Toward Southern Civilians, 1861–1865.* New York: Cambridge University Press, 1995.

Hagerman, Edward. *The American Civil War and the Origins of Modern Warfare: Ideas, Organization, and Field Command.* Bloomington: Indiana University Press, 1988.

Hall, Winchester. *The Story of the 26th Louisiana Infantry, in the Service of the Confederate States.* 1890. Rpt. Scholar's Choice, 2015.

Hardee, W. J. *Rifle and Light Infantry Tactics.* Philadelphia: J. B. Lippincott & Co., 1861.

Hart, B. H. Liddell. *Sherman: Soldier, Realist, American.* New York: Dodd, Mead & Co., 1929.

Haughton, Andrew. *Training, Tactics, and Leadership in the Confederate Army of Tennessee: Seeds of Failure.* London: Frank Cass, 2000.

Heineman, Kenneth J. *Civil War Dynasty: The Ewing Family of Ohio.* New York: New York University Press, 2013.

Heitman, Francis B. *Historical Register and Dictionary of the United States Army, From its Organization, September 29, 1789, to March 2, 1903.* Washington, DC: Government Printing Office, 1903.

Hess, Earl J. "Confiscation and the Northern War Effort: The Army of the Southwest at Helena." *Arkansas Historical Quarterly* 44, no. 1 (Spring 1985): 56–75.

———. *The Union Soldier in Battle: Enduring the Ordeal of Combat.* Lawrence: University Press of Kansas, 1997.

———. *The Rifle Musket in Civil War Combat: Reality and Myth.* Lawrence: University Press of Kansas, 2008.

———. *The Civil War in the West: Victory and Defeat from the Appalachians to the Mississippi.* Chapel Hill: University of North Carolina Press, 2012.

———. *Kennesaw Mountain: Sherman, Johnston, and the Atlanta Campaign.* Chapel Hill: University of North Carolina Press, 2013.

———. *Civil War Infantry Tactics: Training, Combat, and Small-Unit Effectiveness.* Baton Rouge: Louisiana State University Press, 2015.

———. *The Battle of Ezra Church and the Struggle for Atlanta.* Chapel Hill: University of North Carolina Press, 2015.

———. *Fighting for Atlanta: Tactics, Terrain, and Trenches in the Civil War.* Chapel Hill: University of North Carolina Press, 2018.

———. *Storming Vicksburg: Grant, Pemberton, and the Battles of May 19–22, 1863.* Chapel Hill: University of North Carolina Press, 2020.

———, ed. *A German in the Yankee Fatherland: The Civil War Letters of Henry A. Kircher.* Kent, OH: Kent State University Press, 1983.

——— and William Shea. *Pea Ridge: Civil War Campaign in the West.* Chapel Hill: University of North Carolina Press, 1997.

Hirsch, A. A. "Mississippi River Water Temperature at New Orleans." *Monthly Weather Review* 67, no. 11 (1939): 415.

History of the Thirty-Seventh Regiment, O.V.V.I. Toledo, OH: Montgomery & Vrooman, 1889.

Hsieh, Wayne Wei-Siang. *West Pointers and the Civil War: The Old Army in War and Peace.* Chapel Hill: University of North Carolina Press, 2009.

Hull, Isabel V. *Absolute Destruction: Military Culture and the Practices of War in Imperial Germany.* Ithaca, NY: Cornell University Press, 2005.

Hyde, William, and Howard Louis Conard, eds. *Encyclopedia of the History of St. Louis: A Compendium of History and Biography for Ready Reference. Vol. 3.* New York: Southern History Companion, 1899.

Ingesson, Tony. *"The Politics of Combat: The Political and Strategic Impact of Tactical-Level Subcultures, 1939–1995."* Diss., Lund University, 2016.

Iowa, Adjutant General. *Report of the Adjutant General of the State of Iowa to the Governor, for the Year Ending December 31, 1861.* Des Moines: F. W. Palmer, 1861.

Iowa, General Assembly. *Roster and Record of Iowa Soldiers in the War of the Rebellion. Vol. 1.* Des Moines, OH: Emory H. English, 1908.

Jamieson, Perry D. *Crossing the Deadly Ground: United States Army Tactics, 1865–1899.* Tuscaloosa: University of Alabama Press, 1994.

Jenney, William L. B. "Personal Recollections of Vicksburg." In *Military Essays and Recollections: Papers Read Before the Commandery of the State of Illinois, Military Order of the Loyal Legion of the United States. Vol. 3.* Chicago: Dial Press, 1899.

Jomini, Baron De. *The Art of War.* Trans. Capt. G. H. Mendell and Lieut. W. P. Craighill. Philadelphia: J. B. Lippincott & Co., 1862.

Jones, James Pickett. *Blackjack: John A. Logan and Southern Illinois in the Civil War Era.* Carbondale: Southern Illinois University Press, 1967.

Keegan, John. *The Face of Battle: A Study of Agincourt, Waterloo, and the Somme.* New York: Viking Press, 1976.

Kellogg, J. J. *War Experiences and the Story of the Vicksburg Campaign from 'Milliken's Bend' to July 4, 1863.* Washington, IA: J. J. Kellogg, 1913.

Kerr, Richard E. "Wall of Fire: The Rifle and Civil War Infantry Tactics." Thesis. US Army Command and General Staff College, Fort Leavenworth, 1990.

Kimbell, Charles B. *History of Battery "A," First Illinois Light Artillery Volunteers.* Chicago: Cushing Printing Co., 1899.

Kohl, Rhonda M. "'This Godforsaken Town': Death and Disease at Helena, Arkansas, 1862–63." *Civil War History* 50, no. 2 (June 2004): 109–44.

Konijnendijk, Roel. *Classical Greek Tactics: A Cultural History.* Leiden: Brill NV, 2018.

Kreiser, Lawrence, Jr. *Defeating Lee: A History of the Second Corps, Army of the Potomac.* Bloomington: Indiana University Press, 2011.

Lacey, John F. "Major-General Frederick Steele." *Annals of Iowa: A Historical Quarterly* 3, no. 1 (Apr. 1897): 424–38.

Larimer, Charles, ed. *Love and Valor: Intimate Civil War Letters Between Captain Jacob and Emeline Ritner.* Western Springs, IL: Sigourney Press, 2000.

Lee, Wayne. "Mind and Matter—Cultural Analysis in American Military History." *Journal of American History* 93 (Mar. 2007): 1116–42.

———, ed. *Warfare and Culture in World History.* New York: New York University Press, 2011.

Linderman, Gerald F. *Embattled Courage: The Experience of Combat in the American Civil War.* New York: Free Press, 1987.

Logan, Guy E. *Roster and Record of Iowa Troops in the Rebellion. Vol. 1.* Des Moines: E. H. English, 1908.

Lucas, Marion B. *Sherman and the Burning of Columbia.* Columbia: University of South Carolina Press, 2000.

Lynn, John A. *Battle: A History of Combat and Culture.* Philadelphia: Basic Books, 2008.

Mahan, D. H. *An Elementary Treatise on Advanced-Guard, Out-Post, and Detachment Service of Troops, and the Manner of Posting and Handling Them in Presence of an Enemy.* New York: John Wiley, 1862.

Mahon, John K. "Civil War Infantry Assault Tactics." *Military Affairs* 25, no. 2 (Aug. 1961): 63–64.

March, James G. *The Ambiguities of Experience*. Ithaca, NY: Cornell University Press, 2010.

Marszalek, John F. *Sherman: A Soldier's Passion for Order*. New York: Free Press, 1993.

McCain, William, and Charlotte Capers, eds. *Memoirs of Henry Tillinghast Ireys: Papers of the Washington County Historical Society, 1910–1915*. Jackson: Mississippi Department of Archives and History and Mississippi Historical Society, 1954.

McKnight, Brian D., and Barton Myers, eds. *The Guerrilla Hunters: Irregular Conflicts during the Civil War*. Baton Rouge: Louisiana State University Press, 2017.

Meinig, D. W. *The Shaping of America: A Geographical Perspective on 500 Years of History. Vol. 2: Continental America, 1800–1867*. New Haven, CT: Yale University Press, 1988.

Meyers, Christopher C. *Union General John A. McClernand and the Politics of Command*. Jefferson, NC: McFarland & Co., 2010.

Miers, Earl Schenk, ed. *When the World Ended: The Diary of Emma LeConte*. Lincoln: University of Nebraska Press, 1957.

Miller, Donald L. *Vicksburg: Grant's Campaign That Broke the Confederacy*. New York: Simon & Schuster, 2019.

Muir, Rory. *Tactics and the Experience of Battle in the Age of Napoleon*. New Haven, CT: Yale University Press, 1998.

Nosworthy, Brent. *The Bloody Crucible of Courage: Fighting Methods and Combat Experience of the Civil War*. New York: Carroll and Graf, 2003.

Parrish, William E. *Frank Blair: Lincoln's Conservative*. Columbia: University of Missouri Press, 1998.

Patrick, Jeffrey L., ed. *Three Years With Wallace's Zouaves: The Civil War Memoirs of Thomas Wise Durham*. Macon, GA: Mercer University Press, 2003.

Peterson, Larry. *Decisions at Chattanooga*. Knoxville: University of Tennessee Press, 2018.

Phillips, Jason. "Battling Stereotypes: A Taxonomy of Common Soldiers in Civil War History." *History Compass* 6 (Nov. 2008): 1407–25.

Piston, William Garrett, and Richard W. Hatcher III. *Wilson's Creek: The Second Battle of the Civil War and the Men Who Fought It*. Chapel Hill: University of North Carolina Press, 2000.

Porter, David D. *Incidents and Anecdotes of the Civil War*. New York: D. Appleton and Co., 1886.

Powell, David Alan. *The Impulse of Victory: Ulysses S. Grant at Chattanooga*. Carbondale: Southern Illinois University Press, 2020.

Powell, James S. *Learning Under Fire: The 112th Cavalry Regiment in World War II*. College Station: Texas A&M University Press, 2010.

Proceedings of Crocker's Iowa Brigade at the Ninth Biennial Reunion. Cedar Rapids: Record Printing Co., 1902.

Rafuse, Ethan S. *McClellan's War*. Bloomington: Indiana University Press, 2005.

——, ed. *Corps Commanders in Blue: Union Major Generals in the Civil War*. Baton Rouge: Louisiana State University Press, 2014.

Renatus, Flavius Vegetius. *De re militari*. Leonaur, 2012.

Rothenberg, Gunther E. *The Art of Warfare in the Age of Napoleon*. Bloomington: Indiana University Press, 1980.

Saunier, Joseph A., ed. *A History of the Forty-seventh Regiment Ohio Volunteer Infantry*. Hillsboro, OH: Lyle Printing Co., 1903.

Saxe, Maurice, Count de. *Reveries, or, memoirs concerning the art of war*. Edinburgh: Sands, Donaldson, Murray, and Cochran, 1759.

Schein, Edgar H. *Organizational Culture and Leadership*. San Francisco: Jossey-Bass, 1992.

Schob, David E. *Hired Hands and Plowboys: Farm Labor in the Midwest, 1815–60*. Urbana: University of Illinois Press, 1975.

Schultz, Robert G. *The March to the River: From the Battle of Pea Ridge to Helena, Spring 1862*. Iowa City: Camp Pope Publishing, 2014.

Sears, Stephen. *Lincoln's Lieutenants: The High Command of the Army of the Potomac*. Boston: Houghton Mifflin Harcourt, 2017.

Shea, William L., and Terrence J. Winschel. *Vicksburg Is the Key: The Struggle for the Mississippi River*. Lincoln: University of Nebraska Press, 2003.

Sherman, William T. [WTS.] *Memoirs of General William T. Sherman*. 2 vols. New York: Library of America, 1990.

Showalter, Dennis. "A Modest Plea for Drums and Trumpets." *Military Affairs* 39 (1975): 72.

Sigler, Virginia, and A. J. Sigler, eds. *The Civil War Diary of A. J. Seay*. N.p.: Virginia A. Sigler and A. J. Sigler, 1968.

Simon, John Y., ed. *Army Life of an Illinois Soldier*. Carbondale: Southern Illinois University Press, 1996.

——, ed. *The Papers of Ulysses S. Grant. [PUSG.]* Carbondale: Southern Illinois University Press, 1967–2009.

Simpson, Brooks D., and Jean V. Berlin, eds. *Sherman's Civil War: Selected Correspondence of William T. Sherman, 1860–1865. [SCW.]* Chapel Hill: University of North Carolina Press, 1999.

Skinner, George. *Pennsylvania at Chickamauga and Chattanooga*. W. M. Stanley Bay, 1900.

Smith, Timothy B. *Corinth 1862: Siege, Battle, Occupation*. Lawrence: University Press of Kansas, 2012.

——. *The Decision Was Always My Own: Ulysses S. Grant and the Vicksburg Campaign*. Carbondale: Southern Illinois University Press, 2018.

———. *The Union Assaults at Vicksburg: Grant Attacks Pemberton, May 17–22, 1863.* Lawrence: University Press of Kansas, 2020.

———. *The Siege of Vicksburg: Climax of the Campaign to Open the Mississippi River, May 23–July 4, 1863.* Lawrence: University Press of Kansas, 2021.

Smith, Walter G., ed. *Life and Letters of Thomas Kilby Smith, Brevet Major-General, United States Volunteers, 1820–1887.* New York: G. P. Putnam's Sons, 1898.

Smith, William F. "An Historical Sketch of the Military Operations Around Chattanooga, Tennessee, September 22 to November 27, 1863." In *Papers of the Military Historical Society of Massachusetts,* vol. 3: 149–247. Boston: Military Historical Society of Massachusetts, 1910.

Sodergren, Steven E. *The Army of the Potomac in the Overland & Petersburg Campaigns: Union Soldiers and Trench Warfare, 1864–1865.* Baton Rouge: Louisiana State University Press, 2017.

Solonick, Justin S. *Engineering Victory: The Union Siege of Vicksburg.* Carbondale: Southern Illinois University Press, 2015.

Spring, Matthew H. *With Zeal and With Bayonets Only: The British Army on Campaign in North America, 1775–1783.* Norman: University of Oklahoma Press, 2008.

Stephens, Gail. *Shadow of Shiloh: Major General Lew Wallace in the Civil War.* Indianapolis: Indiana Historical Society, 2010.

Sternhell, Yael. "The Afterlives of a Confederate Archive: Civil War Documents and the Making of Sectional Reconciliation." *Journal of American History* 102, no. 4 (Mar. 2016): 1025–50.

Stuart, Addison A. *Iowa Colonels and Regiments: Being a History of Iowa Regiments in the War of the Rebellion.* Des Moines: Mill & Co., 1865.

Swidler, Anne. "Culture in Action: Symbols and Strategies." *American Sociological Review* 51, no. 2: 273–86.

Sword, Wiley. *Mountains Touched with Fire: Chattanooga Besieged, 1863.* New York: St. Martin's Press, 1995.

Temple, Wayne C., ed. *The Civil War Letters of Henry C. Bear.* Harrogate, TN: Lincoln Memorial University Press, 1961.

Tenkotte, Paul A., and James C. Claypool, eds. *The Encyclopedia of Northern Kentucky.* Lexington: University Press of Kentucky, 2009.

Teters, Kristopher A. *Practical Liberators: Union Officers in the Western Theater During the Civil War.* Chapel Hill: University of North Carolina Press, 2018.

Townsend, Mary Bobbitt. *Yankee Warhorse: A Biography of Major General Peter Osterhaus.* Columbia: University of Missouri Press, 2010.

Underwood, Adin Ballou. *Three Years' Service of the Thirty-third Mass. Infantry Regiment, 1862–1865.* Boston: A. Williams & Co., 1881.

United States. *Reports of Experiments with Small Arms for Military Services, by Officers of the Ordnance, U.S. Army.* Washington, DC: A. O. P. Nicholson, 1856.

———. 1860 US Federal Census Schedule.

———. 1860 US Federal Census, Slave Schedule.

———. *Revised United States Army Regulations of 1861.* Washington, DC: Government Printing Office, 1863.

———. 1870 US Federal Census.

———. *Who Burnt Columbia? Official Depositions of Wm. Tecumseh Sherman, 'General of the Army of the United States,' and Gen. O. O. Howard, U.S.A., For the Defence.* Charleston, SC: Walker, Evans & Cogswell, 1873.

US Army. *Infantry Drill Regulations, United States Army.* New York: Army and Navy Journal, 1891.

Wagner, Arthur L. *Organization and Tactics.* Kansas City, MO: Hudson-Kimberly Publishing Co., 1906.

Wallace, Lew, and Jim Leeke, eds. *Smoke, Sound & Fury: The Civil War Memoirs of Major-General Lew Wallace, U.S. Volunteers.* Portland, OR: Strawberry Hill Press, 1998.

Warmoth, Henry Clay. *War, Politics, and Reconstruction: Stormy Days in Louisiana.* Columbia: University of South Carolina Press, 2006.

Warner, Ezra J. *Generals in Blue: Lives of the Union Commanders.* Baton Rouge: Louisiana State University Press, 1964.

The War of the Rebellion: A Compilation of the Official Records of the Union and Confederate Armies [OR]. 128 vols. Washington, DC: US Government Printing Office, 1880–1901.

Watson, Samuel. *Jackson's Sword: The Army Officer Corps on the American Frontier, 1810–1821.* Lawrence: University Press of Kansas, 2012.

Wiley, Bell Irvin. *The Life of Billy Yank: The Common Soldier of the Union.* Indianapolis: Bobbs-Merrill, 1952.

Williams, Kenneth P. *Grant Rises in the West: The First Year, 1861–1862.* Lincoln: University of Nebraska Press, 1997.

Willis, John C. *Forgotten Time: The Yazoo-Mississippi Delta After the Civil War.* Charlottesville: University Press of Virginia, 2000.

Willison, Charles. *Reminiscences of a boy's service with the 76th Ohio, in the Fifteenth Army Corps.* Menasha, WI: George Banta Publishing Co., 1908.

Wilson, Lawrence. *Itinerary of the Seventh Ohio Volunteer Infantry, 1861–1864, with Roster, Portraits, and Biographies.* New York: Neale Publishing Co., 1907.

Winschel, Terrence J. *Triumph & Defeat: The Vicksburg Campaign.* Mason City, IA: Savas Publishing Co., 1999.

Wipperman, Darin. *First for the Union: Life and Death in a Civil War Army Corps from Antietam to Gettysburg.* Lanham, MD: Stackpole Books, 2020.

Wood, George L. *Seventh Regiment: A Record.* New York: James Miller, 1865.

Woodworth, Steven E. *Nothing but Victory: The Army of the Tennessee, 1861–1865*. New York: Alfred A. Knopf, 2005.

——. ed. *Grant's Lieutenants: From Cairo to Vicksburg*. Lawrence: University Press of Kansas, 2001.

——, ed. *The Chattanooga Campaign*. Carbondale: Southern Illinois University Press, 2012.

Work, David. *Lincoln's Political Generals*. Urbana: University of Illinois Press, 2009.

Wynne, Ben. *Mississippi's Civil War*. Macon, GA: Mercer University Press, 2006.

INDEX

CPSIA information can be obtained
at www.ICGtesting.com
Printed in the USA
LVHW111635181022
730975LV00020B/537/J